D1737113

The Tomb of Beowulf

To
Eric W. Robinson
scholar, friend, son

The Tomb of Beowulf

and other essays on Old English

Fred C. Robinson

BLACKWELL
Oxford UK & Cambridge USA

Copyright © Fred C. Robinson, 1993

(Full copyright details for previously published essays can be found in the Acknowledgments and on the first page of the relevant chapter.)

The right of Fred C. Robinson to be identified as author of this work has been asserted in accordance with the Copyright, Designs and Patents Act 1988.

First published 1993

Blackwell Publishers
2138 Main Street, Suite 501
Cambridge, Massachusetts 02142
USA

108 Cowley Road
Oxford OX4 1JF
UK

All rights reserved. Except for the quotation of short passages for the purposes of criticism and review, no part of this publication may be reproduced, stored in a retrieval system, or transmitted, in any form or by any means, electronic, mechanical, photocopying, recording or otherwise, without the prior permission of the publisher.

Except in the United States of America, this book is sold subject to the condition that it shall not, by way of trade or otherwise, be lent, resold, hired out, or otherwise circulated without the publisher's prior consent in any form of binding or cover other than that in which it is published and without a similar condition including this condition being imposed on the subsequent purchaser.

Library of Congress Cataloging-in-Publication Data

Robinson, Fred C.
  The tomb of Beowulf and other essays on Old English / Fred C. Robinson.
    p.   cm.
  Includes bibliographical references and index.
  ISBN 0-631-17328-5 (alk. paper)
    1. English literature – Old English, ca. 450–1100 – History and criticism. 2. English philology – Old English, ca. 450–1100 – Study and teaching – History – 20th century. 3. Epic poetry, English (Old) – History and criticism. 4. Women and literature – England – History. 5. Names, English (Old), in literature. 6. Beowulf. I. Title.
PR181.R63   1993
829'.09 – dc20   92-27331
                                                                                      CIP

British Library Cataloguing in Publication Data

A CIP catalogue record for this book is available from the British Library.

Typeset in 10 on 12 pt. Ehrhardt
by Joshua Associates Limited, Oxford
Printed in Great Britain by
T. J. Press Ltd, Padstow, Cornwall

This book is printed on acid-free paper

Contents

Foreword	vii
Acknowledgments	viii
Abbreviations	x

Part I Literary Interpretation: *Beowulf* — 1

1	The Tomb of Beowulf	3
2	Elements of the Marvelous in the Characterization of Beowulf: A Reconsideration of the Textual Evidence	20
3	History, Religion, Culture: The Background Necessary for Teaching *Beowulf*	36
4	An Introduction to *Beowulf*	52

Part II Literary Interpretation: Several Poems — 69

5	Two Aspects of Variation in Old English Poetry	71
6	Understanding an Old English Wisdom Verse: *Maxims II*, lines 10ff	87
7	Artful Ambiguities in the Old English "Book-Moth" Riddle	98
8	God, Death, and Loyalty in *The Battle of Maldon*	105
9	Some Aspects of the *Maldon* Poet's Artistry	122
10	Literary Dialect in *Maldon* and the Casley Transcript	138
11	Lexicography and Literary Criticism: A Caveat	140

Part III Women in Old English Literature — 153

12	The Prescient Woman in Old English Literature	155
13	Old English Poetry: The Question of Authorship	164
14	A Metronymic in *The Battle of Maldon*?	170
15	European Clothing Names and the Etymology of *Girl*	175

Part IV Names in Old English Literature — 183

16	The Significance of Names in Old English Literature	185
17	Personal Names in Medieval Narrative and the Name of Unferth in *Beowulf*	219

18 Anglo-Saxon Onomastics in the Old English *Andreas*	224
19 Some Uses of Name-Meanings in Old English Poetry	228

Part V   Old English in the Twentieth Century — 237

20 "The Might of the North": Pound's Anglo-Saxon Studies and *The Seafarer*   239
21 Ezra Pound and the Old English Translational Tradition   259
22 The Afterlife of Old English: A Brief History of Composition in Old English after the Close of the Anglo-Saxon Period   275
23 *Medieval*, the *Middle Ages*   304

List of Essays and Notes by Fred C. Robinson Not Included in this Volume   316

Index   320

Foreword

In addition to the three essays published in this volume for the first time (items 1, 21, and 22), I am reprinting here a number of previously published essays which I think might still be of interest to students of Old English. (On pp. 316–19 I supply a list of essays and notes which I am omitting from this volume, some because they deal with later English, some because I believe they may be dated now and hence no longer of interest, and some because they deal with textual problems, and I am planning to reprint these in a separate volume devoted exclusively to Old English texts and their manuscript contexts.) Reviews of books are neither reprinted here nor listed at the end of the volume. The sections into which the essays have been divided represent fairly accurately aspects of Old English which have claimed my attention over the years, with the exception of textual criticism. It will be obvious to any reader, however, that some of the essays combine more than one interest and could with equal appropriateness be included under two or more groupings.

I have taken the opportunity which this volume offers to correct or supplement some of the essays reprinted here, although I make no claim to a systematic revision of them. Misprints and minor slips which I have noticed have been silently corrected, and occasionally footnotes updated. I have in one or two cases added an "Afterword 1992" and elsewhere an occasional footnote to comment on subsequent publications which have engaged the subject treated in the immediately foregoing essay, and I have to some extent given the essays a more common format than they originally had. But I have not attempted a thorough normalization of them. For example, quotations from early languages or modern foreign languages are supplied with translations where the editor of the original publication required them but not in other cases.

Fred C. Robinson
Berkeley College
Yale University
October 1992

Acknowledgments

The essays in this volume were written over a span of twenty-five years, and in the process of time I have incurred more debts than I can possibly acknowledge here. But some must be mentioned.

I am grateful to Marijane Osborn and Nicholas P. Howe for originally (and independently) suggesting that I should prepare a collection of my essays and to John Davey, a publisher whom I have admired and appreciated more and more during our ten years of collaboration, for proposing that Blackwell should publish it. I am also indebted to him for the great favor of recommending Peter Solomon as an editor to help me prepare these essays for (re)publication. The volume has been much improved by Solomon's wise scrutiny and tactful suggestions.

I owe warm thanks to Yale University's superb libraries and dedicated librarians and to the enlightened administration of Yale, which makes available to both its junior and senior faculty ample research time so that they may make use of these libraries.

To the American Philosophical Society, the John Simon Guggenheim Foundation, the American Council of Learned Societies, the National Endowment for the Humanities, and to the Institute of Social and Economic Research of Rhodes University (Republic of South Africa) I am indebted for material support, as I am to the Japan Society for the Promotion of Science, which awarded me a Research Fellowship at the time I was completing this volume; my delightful visit to Japan enabled me to hold stimulating discussions with Yoshio Terasawa, Tadao Kubouchi, Michiko Ogura, Yoshihiro Yoshino, Akio Oizumi, and many other scholars in the lively community of medieval English scholars in Japan today.

To the late Norman E. Eliason, who set me on the course which is now marked by these essays, I owe deep thanks for his guidance, support, and example. I am similarly grateful to the late Herbert Dean Meritt, whose delightful company and treasured friendship filled with warmth and pleasure one of the great learning experiences of my life during the years when we were colleagues at Stanford University. For his friendship, trust, and inspiration over twenty-five years I am indebted to Bruce Mitchell, with whom I have had the honor of collaborating on more than one Old English project. *Hē is bōcera betsta, frēonda trēowesta*. The comradeship of Marie Borroff, John Pope, and Eric Stanley, all of whom have labored in the same pleasant vineyard as I, has meant much to me, as has that of Robert E. Kaske, Larry Benson, Carl Berkhout, Helmut Gneuss, Alfred Bammesberger, Antonette diPaolo Healey, Paul Beekman Taylor, Roberta Frank, J. R. Hall, Paul Szarmach, Kevin Kiernan, the Boys Friendly, and the Persons from Porlock. Such colleagues deserve more and better scholarship from me than I have to show at this point, but I am consoled for my inadequacies by the reflected glory which I enjoy – however undeservedly – from the work done by the students whom I have been privileged to direct in their doctoral programs, all of whom I admire deeply and who count among my dearest friends.

For permission to reprint these essays I am grateful to the University of Toronto Press (for item 2), the Modern Languages Association of America (for item 3), the University of California Press (for items 4 and 5), Medieval Institute Publications of Western Michigan University (for item 6), University of Notre Dame Press (for item 7), Cornell University Press (item 8), University of Illinois Press (for item 9), University of Kentucky Press (for items 10 and 13), Mouton de Gruyter, A Division of Walter de Gruyter and Co. (for item 11), Kenkyusha Publishers (for item 12), The University of the South (for item 14), Max Niemeyer Verlag (for item 16), Birmingham-Southern College (item 17), The American Name Society (item 18), La Société Néophilologique de Helsinki (for item 19), *The Yale Review* (item 20), *Speculum: A Journal of Medieval Studies* (item 23).

For preparing the index and identifying several typographical errors I am indebted to Anne E. Borelli.

Abbreviations

ASPR	The Anglo-Saxon Poetic Records, ed. G. P. Krapp and E. V. K. Dobbie (New York, 1931–53)
BasPr.	Bibliothek der angelsächsischen Prosa, ed. C. W. M. Grein, R. P. Wülker, and Hans Hecht (Cassel, 1872–1933)
BTD	An Anglo-Saxon Dictionary, based on the manuscript collections of the late Joseph Bosworth, ed. and enlarged T. Toller (Oxford, 1882–98)
BTS	An Anglo-Saxon Dictionary, Supplement, by T. Toller (Oxford, 1908–21)
CCCC	Corpus Christi College, Cambridge
CCL	Corpus Christianorum, Series Latina
CHM	A Concise Anglo-Saxon Dictionary, 4th edn with a supplement by H. D. Meritt (Cambridge, 1960)
EETS	Early English Text Society
ELN	English Language Notes
ES	English Studies
JEGP	Journal of English and Germanic Philology
MÆ	Medium Ævum
MGH	Monumenta Germaniæ Historica, cited by subseries and volume
MLN	Modern Language Notes
MLR	Modern Language Review
MP	Modern Philology
NM	Neuphilologische Mitteilungen
NQ	Notes and Queries
n.s.	new series
o.s.	old series [after *NQ*], original series [after EETS]
PL	Patrologia Latina, ed. J. Migne (Paris, 1844–1903)
PMLA	Publications of the Modern Language Association
PQ	Philological Quarterly
RES	Review of English Studies
SP	Studies in Philology
s.s.	supplementary series
UTQ	University of Toronto Quarterly

Part I

Literary Interpretation: *Beowulf*

I
The Tomb of Beowulf

The Old English poem to which we have assigned the name *Beowulf* was composed, apparently, by a Christian poet – some say a monk or a priest – who was concerned to extol the virtues of ancient Germanic heroes while acknowledging regretfully (for example, in lines 175–88) that they were deprived of the Christian revelation enjoyed in his own era. This poignant intermingling of veneration and regret, of pride in the Anglo-Saxons' Germanic ancestors shadowed by sadness over the perilous state of their souls, permeates, I believe, the poem's tone and lends it intellectual sophistication and complexity which exceed mere admiration of a heroic past.[1] Young Beowulf's achievements in the first part of the poem – his deliverance of the Danes from the incursions of the Grendelkin, his farsighted diplomacy in committing his nation to an alliance with the Danish royal family, and his discerning report to his own king Hygelac on the state of the nation which he has just visited – are all circumscribed by discreet reminders of the heathen status of the heroic participants; and the displays of wisdom, such as the speeches of Hrothgar, leave us simultaneously impressed by their loftiness of thought and saddened by their always falling short of ultimate truth, which, to a medieval English audience, would have been Christian truth. In the last half of the poem we see the hero devoting his strength, courage, and wisdom to the protection of his nation until, at the end of his fifty-year reign as king, he protects them against the attacks of the dragon, which he slays at the cost of his own life. At his death he leaves to his people as a legacy a vast hoard of treasure, which he seems to think might ensure their survival in the militant and hostile world surrounding them:

> Nū ic on māðma hord   mīne bebohte
> frōde feorhlege,   fremmað gēna
> lēoda þearfe;   ne mæg ic hēr leng wesan.[2]
>
> (2799–801)

[1] I have discussed this feature of the poem *in extenso* in *Beowulf and the Appositive Style* (Knoxville, TN, 1985).

[2] *Beowulf and the Fight at Finnsburg*, ed. Fr. Klaeber, 3rd edn with 1st and 2nd supplements (Boston, 1950). All quotations from the poem are from this edition. Quotations from other Old English poems will be from *ASPR*.

"Now that I have exchanged my old life for this hoard of treasures, they will now meet the needs of the people; I can be here no longer."[3] But, in a gesture which seems to express that sense of despair which darkens all the triumphs and hazards in the poem, the Geatas bury the treasure with the ashes of their king – a pagan ritual following upon the pagan rite of cremation – and the last words of the poem are the warriors' solemn encomia as they pace their horses around his splendid tomb.

The tomb of Beowulf and the rites enacted there make up a scene of strange and somber majesty which readers have often found reverberant with dark implications beyond the merely scenic. The hero's obsequies have also been regarded as problematic by scholars of the poem, who are troubled by the fact that Beowulf's funeral rites are not merely grander than the funerals of other characters described in the poem, but peculiarly complex in a way that makes them unique. The hero's obsequies begin with these verses:

> Him ðā gegiredan   Gēata lēode
> ād on eorðan   unwāclīcne,
> helm[um] behongen,   hildebordum,
> beorhtum byrnum,   swā hē bēna wæs;
> ālegdon ðā tōmiddes   mærne þēoden
> hæleð hīofende,   hlāford lēofne.
>
> (3137–42)

"The people of the Geatas erected then on the ground a splendid pyre hung about with helmets, with battle-shields, and with shining mail-coats, as he had asked; then the lamenting warriors laid in the midst the renowned king, their beloved lord." The poet then tells us that the roaring flames and dark smoke rise into the sky, intertwined with the lamentations of the mourners. "With grief-stricken hearts they bemoaned their sorrow, the death of their king" (3148–9), he says, and following this a mysterious old woman steps forward and prophesies the doom of the nation now that their king and protector has fallen. The scene closes with the evocative detail *Heofon rēce swealg* ("Heaven swallowed up the smoke.")[4]

---

[3] Charles Donahue, "Potlatch and charity: notes on the heroic in *Beowulf*," in *Anglo-Saxon Poetry: essays in appreciation: for John C. McGalliard*, ed. Lewis E. Nicholson and Dolores Warwick Frese (Notre Dame, 1975), p. 32, reminds us that the plural *fremmað* cannot be an imperative singular addressed to Wiglaf, as some have thought.

[4] The prophesying woman and the rising smoke are among the details that scholars have found suggestive of some special significance. Several people have noted that the smoke from the cremation fire passing directly up to the heavens is a Germanic pagan motif documented in the *Ynglinga saga*; see for example Paul Beekman Taylor, "*Heofon riece swealg*: a sign of Beowulf's state of grace," *Philological Quarterly*, 42 (1963), 257–9. On the funeral in general see both text and bibliographical footnotes in Ute Schwab, *Servire il Signore Morto: Funzione e trasformazione di riti funebri germanici nell'epica medievale inglese e tedesca*, Università Catania: Collana di studi di filologia moderna 5 (Catania, 1990), pp. 22–5, 64–5.

This impressive tableau with grieving comrades, a lamenting woman, and flames consuming the corpse and battle-gear is much the same as the ritual cremation which followed the fight at Finnsburg earlier in the poem. The peculiarity of Beowulf's last rites is that ten days after the very formal closure of the scene we have just examined, Beowulf's subjects initiate a whole new series of ceremonies. Having erected a magnificent *beorh* or tumulus, which they fill with sumptuous treasure together with their king's ashes, they surround it with a splendid wall devised by *foresnotere men* "exceedingly wise people," and then twelve mounted, chanting warriors circle the wall:

> þā ymbe hlǣw riodan   hildedēore,
> æþelinga bearn,   ealra twelfe,
> woldon (care) cwīðan,   [ond] kyning mǣnan,
> wordgyd wrecan,   ond ymb w(er) sprecan;
> eahtodan eorlscipe   ond his ellenweorc
> duguðum dēmdon, –   swā hit gedē(fe) bið,
> þæt mon his winedryhten   wordum herge,
> ferhðum frēoge,   þonne hē forð scile
> of līchaman   (lǣded) weorðan.
> Swā begnornodon   Gēata lēode
> hlāfordes (hry)re,   heorðgenēatas;
> cwǣdon þæt hē wǣre   wyruldcyning[a]
> manna mildust   ond mon(ðw)ǣrust,
> lēodum līðost   ond lofgeornost.
>
> (3169–82)

"Then around the barrow rode twelve sons of noblemen, valiant in battle. They wanted to declare their sorrow and speak of their king, to utter a chant and speak of the man. They praised his nobility and his deeds of valor, proclaimed them majestically, as it is fitting that one should do – to extol with words and cherish in the heart one's lord and friend when he must be led forth from his garment of flesh. Thus the people of the Geats, the companions of his hearth, bewailed the fall of their lord. They said that he was of all the kings of the world the kindest and most mildhearted of men, the most gracious to his people, and the most eager for praise." The sentiment in this passage is so noble, the style so consciously sublime, that an early translator of *Beowulf* and the only prominent poet ever to edit the poem – N. S. V. Grundtvig – believed that the closing scene is central to the meaning of *Beowulf* and therefore he named the poem *Beowulfes Beorh* "the tomb of Beowulf" (cf. line 2807). Grundtvig even composed a poem of his own in Old English and in Danish in which he justifies this title, suggesting that the *beorh* of Beowulf is analogous to the poem itself, both being monuments which preserve the hero's name and fame in succeeding ages. (A modern English translation of Grundtvig's poem is supplied in the twenty-second essay in this volume.)

But however much we might agree with Grundtvig that the memorable closing of *Beowulf* distills and reifies the sense of the whole narrative, we cannot deny that it is also problematic. "It is the peculiarity of the *Beowulf* account," says Klaeber, "that two distinct and, as it were, parallel funeral ceremonies are related in detail, ... and that the greater emphasis is placed on the closing stage, which is made the occasion of rehearsing solemn and inspiring songs."[5] The archeologist Knut Stjerna found the two ceremonies such an extraordinary departure from actual practice in pagan days that he concluded the poet must have had two separate sources treating Beowulf's funeral, one in which he was cremated and one in which he was buried with treasure, and that he somewhat ineptly conflated them in his poem; but R. W. Chambers disagrees, saying that the double ceremony simply shows the Christian poet's ignorance of pagan practice.[6] He would agree no doubt with a recent scholar's judgment that "there must be some confusion of tradition."[7] No one has ever doubted, so far as I am aware, that the ceremony around the walled monument is simply a second funeral for Beowulf, a curious redundancy which, however impressive, means nothing more than that the poet was confused about pagan burial customs.[8]

My purpose in this essay is to suggest that the second rite described at the end of *Beowulf* may have had a significance beyond confused redundancy. I shall supply evidence to suggest that at least some in the poet's audience would have seen in the final ceremony of the poem suggestions of an apotheosis. King Beowulf's bereaved subjects, I will suggest, are so overawed by their fallen leader's accomplishments and so unwilling to accept the finality of his death that they turn desperately to the pagan resources available to them to accord him ultimate veneration and, perhaps, recruit his protective force beyond the grave. Such an act would be a closing parallel with the act of the Danes at the beginning of the poem in lines 175–88, where in a time of crisis they turn to their heathen gods with propitiatory sacrifices.

My procedure will be to survey the cultural background of the Anglo-Saxons to determine how familiar they would have been with the concept of deifying a deceased hero and to see whether manifestations of apotheosis in their culture

---

[5] Klaeber, *Beowulf and the Fight at Finnsburg*, p. 229.

[6] Chambers, *Beowulf: an introduction to the study of the poem*, 3rd edn with a supplement by C. L. Wrenn (Cambridge, 1959), p. 124.

[7] Paula Loikala, "Funeral rites in *Beowulf*," *Quaderni di Filologia Germanica della Facoltà di Lettere e Filosofia dell'Università di Bologna*, 2 (1982), 287.

[8] That the Geatas should erect a monument on the cliff as Beowulf wished (2802–8) is of course to be expected. But the consignment of a vast treasure to the *beorh* and (especially) the ceremony of chants and marching seem to be a puzzling repetition and expansion of what went on at the cremation ten days before.

bear any resemblance to the events described at the end of *Beowulf*. And finally I shall consider what the attitude of at least a portion of a Christian Anglo-Saxon audience might have been toward a poem that implies that their ancestors may have ascribed divine status to a slain hero.[9]

Herotheism is attested fairly widely in the early stages of the western European culture of which Anglo-Saxon England forms a part. We might begin with a glance at the classical world.[10] Hector, whose funeral ceremony in the *Iliad* has so often been compared with that of Beowulf, was worshipped in the Troad and also at Tanagra, east of Thebes, and later poetry speaks of him as a god. Theseus was worshipped in Athens, and there were cults of Oedipus, while the Argive hero Adrastus of Sicyon was venerated at a *heroön* (a shrine to a hero, which is usually located at or identical with his tomb) in the marketplace of that city, with tragic choruses recounting his sad fate being sung in his honor. Turning to the Romans, an Anglo-Saxon who read Virgil would have seen that in book VI of the *Aeneid* Palinurus is assured that he will be deified and worshipped at his tomb, and Dardanus in book VII is similarly deified and worshipped. In book XII Juno says that Aeneas has his niche as a god in heaven. Pliny discusses the *heroön*, using the Latinized name *heroum*. These instances are all from the realm of classical legend or literature, but, as is well known, the deification of mortals was also a part of ancient history. Alexander the Great, after he was hailed as the son of Amon-Zeus by the oracle of Amon in 332 BC, became increasingly convinced that he was a god and as such began

---

[9] The verb "implies" is carefully chosen here. I am also careful to say that the implication would have been understood by "at least a portion of" the poet's audience. I am mindful of Bruce Mitchell's well-directed impatience with some scholars' "assumption that the audience of *Beowulf* was homogeneous; that all its members reacted in the same way, had all heard – or not heard – the story before hearing the poem, had all heard – or not heard – the poem before; were all equally intelligent and equally knowledgeable about theology or the Church Fathers or scriptural exegesis or whatever; were all equally sensitive and capable – or insensitive and incapable – of making such connexions." (See "1987: postscript on *Beowulf*," in *On Old English* (Oxford, 1988), pp. 41–2.) On the other hand, I would not think that the point of this essay were worth making if I did not believe that the implication was likely to be a conscious element in the poet's design, available to that part of his audience which was knowledgeable and attentive enough to perceive it. As I have suggested elsewhere (see footnote 1), a medieval Christian who addresses a Christian audience about their pagan ancestors will necessarily work more by implication than by overt declaration.

[10] The ensuing examples (and many others) are cited in *Paulys Realencyclopädie der classischen Altertumswissenschaft*, neue Bearbeitung begonnen von Georg Wissowa, vol. 14 (Stuttgart, 1912), pp. 2814–15, s.v. *Heros*, and vol. 15, pp. 1119–27, s.v. *Heros... Der Kultus*; also *The Oxford Classical Dictionary*, ed. N. G. L. Hammond and H. H. Scullard, 2nd edn (Oxford, 1970), p. 491, s.v. *Hector*, and p. 506, s.v. *Hero-cult*. In Greek, it should be mentioned, a hero was less powerful than the primary gods but had divine status, and cult was paid to him, usually at his tomb or *heroön*. Conceived of as mortals who had died and were apotheosized, heroes in this sense were not the same as the heroes of Homer – Ajax, Odysseus, etc. – although some (e.g. Hector) were in both groups. In the case of Hercules the distinction between god and hero was uncertain, as it was in some others.

demanding veneration from his subjects. The Spartans' cynical response to this demand ("If Alexander wants to be a god, let him be a god") finds an echo in the Old English *Orosius*, where Alexander's claims to divinity are similarly scorned. But the example of Alexander was not lost on the Roman emperors, who came to make similar pretensions. Later we shall return to these historical examples as they impinged on the Anglo-Saxon consciousness.

In the Germanic world texts both early and late attest to deification of heroes.[11] Jordanes tells us that during the reign of Domitian (one of the self-deified Roman emperors) the Goths so venerated the generals who had led them to victory that they elevated them to the status of demigods. The Latin word Jordanes uses is *semideos*, which he translates for his Gothic audience, "id est *ansis*."[12] *Ansis* is the Gothic word for "gods," cognate with Old Icelandic *Æsir* (and Old English *ōs*, preserved in personal names and the rune-name). The Gothic royal family known as the Amali always claimed to be the descendants of the *ansis*. More deifications of kings occur in Scandinavia. The eleventh-century historian Adam of Bremen reports that the Swedes made gods out of men who had accomplished extraordinary deeds, and he cites the example of a King Eric, who, according to the *Vita Anskarii* of Rimbert, was deified by his people after his death and worshipped by them with prayers and sacrifices at his *heroön*.[13] Another king who was deified and served with sacrifices after his death was King Olaf, brother of Halfdan, who according to the Icelandic *Flateyarbók* is laid in a mound with a certain amount of silver coin and venerated there as *geirstaðaálfr* by his subjects.[14] Icelandic sagas tell us that King Guðmundr was proclaimed a god and worshipped after his death, as was another Icelander named Barðr.[15] In the *Skáldskaparmál* Snorri Sturlusson says, "That king who is called Helgi, after whom Halogaland is named, was the father of Þorgerðr Hölgabrúðr; they were both worshipped with sacrifice, and a mound was reared for Helgi, one layer being of gold and silver – that was the sacrificial wealth – and the other of earth and stones."[16]

[11] Among the works of reference I have drawn on are Richard M. Meyer, *Altgermanische Religionsgeschichte* (Leipzig, 1910), esp. pp. 90–2, Wolfgang Golther, *Handbuch der germanischen Mythologie* (Leipzig, 1895), esp. pp. 92–5, and Hilda Roderick Ellis, *The Road to Hel: a study of the conception of the dead in Old Norse literature* (Cambridge, 1943), esp. pp. 99–111.

[12] Jordanes, *Getica*, XIII, 78: "iam proceres suos, quorum quasi fortuna vincebant, non puros homines, sed semideos, id est ansis, vocaverunt." Herwig Wolfram, *History of the Goths*, tr. Thomas Dunlap (Berkeley, CA, 1987), p. 324, points out that Theodoric continued to encourage the belief in the divinity of the Amali rulers. See also Walter Goffart's comments on barbarian *memoria* in *Barbarians and Romans: techniques of accommodation* (Princeton, 1980), esp. pp. 21–4.

[13] Golther, *Handbuch*, pp. 93–4, supplies full Latin text with translation.

[14] Golther, *Handbuch*, pp. 94–5, and Ellis, *The Road to Hel*, pp. 100–2, who draws attention also to the sacrifices offered after the death of Halfdan the Black at the burial mounds containing his remains.

[15] Ellis, *The Road to Hel*, p. 102.

[16] Quoted in Ellis, *The Road to Hel*, p. 105.

"Die Apotheose bleibt in der Regel auf Könige beschränkt," observes Richard Meyer, but he notes that others too are deified from time to time.[17] The *Landnámabók* tells of a Norwegian chieftain named Grimr who was so popular among his people that after his death he was worshipped with sacrifices.[18] We have already seen that Þorgerðr Hölgabrúðr was worshipped as a goddess along with her father, King Helgi. Another woman who was regarded by the common people as a kind of goddess is a prophetess mentioned by Gregory of Tours in the *Historia Francorum*.[19]

The Frankish prophetess was apparently venerated during her lifetime, but worship of mortals among the Germanic peoples was normally accorded only to select persons among the dead, a practice which is documented from the early eighth century on, primarily in ecclesiastical prohibitions. In his letter to the people of Hesse and Thuringia Pope Gregory III lists sacrifices to the dead among the pagan Germanic customs which they must reject absolutely, and in his letter to the bishops in Bavaria and Alemania he tells the missionary bishops that they must make the people stop sacrificing to the dead.[20] In his publication of the decrees of the synod of 742, Karlmann, palace mayor of the Eastern Franks, says that every bishop within his own diocese must root out all the filth of the heathen, such as sacrifices to the dead.[21] The *Indiculus superstitionum et Paganiarum* (AD 743) has prohibitions "de sacrilegio ad sepulchra mortuorum" and "de sacrilegio super defunctos, id est, dadsisas" – thus supplying the native Germanic word for veneration of the dead.[22] The phrase *ad sepulchrum* is noteworthy, for it reminds us that worship of the dead was normally conducted at the tomb (or *heroön*) of the apotheosized mortal.[23]

Conforming with the widespread reports of deified kings and heroes in early Germanic times was the euhemeristic explanation of the origin of pagan gods, a theory that became increasingly popular as Christianity took root in Germanic lands. Euhemerus was a Sicilian mythographer who, in the third century BC, advanced the theory that the Greek gods had all been human kings or heroes who were deified after their deaths by the people they had ruled over or benefited. Early Christians seized eagerly on the euhemeristic rationale since it

---

[17] Meyer, *Altgermanische Religionsgeschichte*, p. 91.

[18] Golther, *Handbuch*, p. 94.

[19] *Gregoire de Tours: Histoire des Francs*, ed. Henri Omont and Gaston Collon, 2 vols (Paris, 1886–93), VII, 44.

[20] *Die Briefe des heiligen Bonifatius und Lullus*, ed. Michael Tangl (Berlin, 1916), XXXIII, 43, and XXXIV, 44.

[21] Ibid., XLIV, 56.

[22] Quoted from Francis B. Gummere, *Founders of England*, with a supplementary note by Francis B. Magoun, Jr (New York, 1930), p. 349. Gummere's entire chapter on "The worship of the dead," pp. 337–65, supplies a wealth of evidence for Germanic practices.

[23] Ellis, *The Road to Hel*, pp. 100–5 provides a detailed survey of the evidence for worship at the grave-mound.

provided a simple explanation for how so many different pagan gods could have come into existence among so many different peoples. The Icelander Snorri Sturlusson provides euhemeristic origins for Odin and Frey, and the manner in which their deification took place has some remarkable similarities to Beowulf's death and funeral.[24] In the *Ynglinga Saga*, chapter 10, we are told that Odin was a king, and when he died after a long and prosperous reign, his subjects prepared a sumptuously provided pyre for him and cremated his remains. After the cremation they believed he was a god in Asgaard and prayed to him. Snorri explains that the smoke of the funeral pyre rising into the air was a sign to the people that Odin was being exalted. In chapters 12 and 13 we learn that Frey became king in later days, and after a successful reign he died and was placed in a great mound with a lavish hoard of gold, silver, and copper. His Swedish subjects proclaimed him a god and made sacrifices to him. Saxo Grammaticus's *Gesta Danorum* explains the origin of Norse gods euhemeristically too, as do the *Historia Norvegiæ*, the *Íslendingabók*, and other Scandinavian writings. Outside of Scandinavia, Gregory's *History of the Franks*, II, 29, tells how Queen Clotild the Christian explains to her husband Clovis that his pagan gods are merely mortal men who came to be worshipped by the Germanic heathens. The euhemeristic explanation was codified in the broadly influential *Etymologiae* of Isidore of Seville and in the "De diis gentium" section of Rabanus Maurus's *De universo*, where he emphasizes that powerful men and founders of cities were especially venerated by pagan communities. The pervasive use by Christians of the euhemeristic account of the origin of pagan gods must have served as a constant reminder to Germanic Christians that their ancestors had been accustomed to deifying kings and heroes.

The evidence supplied thus far for Germanic apotheosis comes from a wide range of sources both Latin and vernacular, but we have not yet investigated the most important Germanic culture for our purposes – the Anglo-Saxon – except for our glances at certain passages in the eighth-century correspondence of Boniface. In fact, allusions to deification of heroes, to worship of the dead, and to the Germanic pantheon being mere deified rulers are prominent in Old English and Anglo-Latin writings right up to the end of the Anglo-Saxon period. In his *De falsis Deis*, Wulfstan tells how pagan men were not satisfied with the gods they had but took to worshipping "strenuous worldly men who had become mighty in worldly powers and were awesome when they were alive" – a formulation which would fit Beowulf admirably.[25] In his source-text, Ælfric's *De falsis Diis*, we are told that the pagans took for their gods powerful men and giants.[26] This view of pagan worship would no doubt have

---

[24] For a skillful survey and synopsis of euhemerism in the Germanic lands see Anthony Faulkes, "Descent from the gods," *Mediaeval Scandinavia*, 11 (1978–9), 92–125.

[25] *The Homilies of Wulfstan*, ed. Dorothy Bethurum (Oxford, 1957), p. 222.

[26] *Homilies of Ælfric: a supplementary collection*, ed. John C. Pope, EETS o.s. 260 (London, 1968), pp. 681–2.

seemed to Ælfric and Wulfstan to be confirmed by Romans 1: 18–25. In his *Canons of Edgar* Wulfstan urges the priests to tell their congregations that the worship of human beings (*manweorðunga*) is expressly forbidden.[27] Clerics like Ælfric and Wulfstan become especially anxious about lapses into *manweorðung* when they discuss funerals; they evidently thought that it is when saying farewell to the deceased that an Anglo-Saxon is most likely to begin worshipping a mortal. Ælfric tells priests that if they are invited to ceremonies for the dead they must forbid heathen chants by the layfolk and must not participate in drinking and eating in the presence of the corpse.[28] A letter of Pope Zacharius to the Anglo-Saxon Boniface in the early eighth century shows what lies behind these prohibitions: the pope speaks of sacrilegious priests who lapsed into the heathen practice of eating the offerings to the dead.[29] Wulfstan admonishes that when someone dies the people must avoid any vain practices *æt þam lice*, and confessionals and penitentials both early and late forbid the burning of grain to the dead in order to heal living people who are sick.[30] The Old English translator of the *Dicts of Cato* gives biblical authority to warnings against illicit commerce with the deceased by incorporating in his text the Old Testament prohibition against seeking truth from the dead (Deuteronomy 18: 12).[31] The assumption of preternatural powers of healing and omniscience on the part of the dead is like the Scandinavians' belief that their deified kings could provide abundant crops.[32]

As we shall see later on, all these practices and prohibitions which we have been examining could have a bearing on the obsequies of Beowulf. For the moment it may be sufficient to observe that while we have long recognized that the cremation of Beowulf and the burial of him with lavish grave goods were flagrant violations of the church's teachings in the poet's day, it seems possible that the chants and processions of the warriors before the hero's grave-mound would have been seen as no less flagrant an infraction of Christian observance.

Deification of their rulers by the ancients in the classical world was known to the Anglo-Saxons both through King Alfred the Great and through the anonymous translator of the Orosius.[33] In one of his original insertions into the text of his translation of Boethius's *De consolatione philosophiae*, Alfred explains to his subjects that Apollo, Jupiter, and Saturn were simply mortals who were members of the royal family and whose foolish subjects (*dysige folc*) believed

---

[27] *Wulfstan's Canons of Edgar*, ed. Roger Fowler, EETS o.s. 266 (London, 1972), p. 4.
[28] *Die Hirtenbriefe Ælfrics*, ed. Bernhard Fehr, reprinted with a supplement to the introduction by Peter Clemoes (Darmstadt, 1966), p. 25.
[29] *Die Briefe des heiligen Bonifatius*, LXIV, 80.
[30] *Wulfstan's Canons*, p. 17.
[31] R. S. Cox, "The Old English Dicts of Cato," *Anglia*, 90 (1972), 16.
[32] Ellis, *The Road to Hel*, pp. 100–1.
[33] *King Alfred's Old English Version of Boethius*, ed. Walter John Sedgefield (Oxford, 1899), pp. 115–16, and *The Old English Orosius*, ed. Janet Bately, EETS s.s. 6 (London, 1980), p. 139.

them when they claimed to be gods. The Orosius translator mentions both Alexander the Great's pretensions to divinity and the deification of the Roman emperor Domitian, who demanded that his people bow to him as to a god. The Anglo-Saxons' added comments about the arrogance of the rulers and the folly of the people may be the result not only of Christian piety but also of the fact that when their own pagan ancestors practiced deification it was almost always a rite performed after the death of the mortal who was to be deified and not a status rulers would assume during their lifetimes. The later Roman practice of deifying emperors posthumously by senatorial decrees would perhaps have seemed less absurd – though not less wicked – to Alfred and his contemporaries.

Euhemeristic explanations of the pagan gods were widespread among the Christian Anglo-Saxons both early and late. Daniel, bishop of Winchester from 705 to 744, writes a letter to Boniface advising him to inform the heathen Germanic tribes on the continent that their gods were actually mortals, not gods.[34] In their treatises on false gods, which are the fullest euhemeristic analyses in a Germanic language, Ælfric and Wulfstan give detailed accounts of how each pagan god was originally a powerful or distinguished man who was declared a god after his death and venerated. Ælfric treats euhemerism further in *De initio creaturae*[35] and in his *Passion of St Sebastian, Martyr*.[36] In his life of King Alfred, Asser says that the king's ancestors Ingild and Ine were descendants of Geat, "whom the pagans worshipped for a long time as a god."[37] (Nennius says people called Geat the son of a god.)[38] The life of St Kentigern says, "Woden, whom the Angles worship as chief god, and from whom they derive their origin, was a mortal man, and king of the Saxons, and father of many races."[39]

Anglo-Saxon euhemerism, or, more specifically, the concept of pagan Germanic kings being deified, was woven into the fabric of the culture in yet another important way. The numerous surviving Anglo-Saxon royal genealogies, drawn up to establish the kings' ancestral right to rule, always include

---

[34] *Die Briefe des heiligen Bonifatius*, XV, 23.

[35] *Homilies of the Anglo-Saxon Church*, ed. Benjamin Thorpe, vol. 1 (London, 1843), p. 82. Ælfric's euhemeristic account is widely adopted by later homilists: e.g. a sermon from a twelfth-century manuscript draws heavily on Ælfric's *De falsis diis*: see Rubie D. N. Warner, *Early English Homilies from the Twelfth Century MS. Vesp. D.XIV*, EETS o.s. 152 (London, 1910), pp. 34–41.

[36] *Ælfric's Lives of Saints*, ed. W. W. Skeat, EETS o.s. 76 (1881), pp. 126–8.

[37] This translation is from *Alfred the Great: Asser's Life of King Alfred and other contemporary sources*, tr. with an introduction and notes Simon Keynes and Michael Lapidge (Harmondsworth, Middlesex, 1983), p. 67. For the Latin text see Klaeber, *Beowulf and the Fight at Finnsburg*, p. 254.

[38] "Geta, qui fuit, ut aiunt, filius dei:" John Morris, in his edition and translation, *Nennius: British history and the Welsh annals* (London, 1980), p. 26, mistakenly capitalizes *Dei* and *God* and mistranslates the passage: "Geta, who said they were son of God."

[39] Gummere, *Founders of England*, p. 421.

among the names of ancestors listed the names of pagan Germanic gods. Thus Woden (or Seaxnet) appears in the genealogies as an ancestor in the royal houses of Kent, Essex, Wessex, Deira, Bernicia, East Anglia, Mercia, and Lindsey.[40] Woden's ancestor Geata is also listed, and an annotation in one manuscript (Textus Roffensis) gives us an idea of how the Anglo-Saxons understood this curious incorporation of pagan gods in the lineage of their Christian kings: *Geata, ðene ða hæpena wurþedon for god* ("Geata, whom the heathens worshipped as a god").[41] Æthelweard too attests to the Christian Anglo-Saxons' assumptions about the Germanic god Woden's appearance in the genealogies: he was actually a king of barbarian hordes whose followers ignorantly deified him.[42] Anthony Faulkes is right, then, when he says that "always when such genealogies are recorded by Christian writers (e.g. Bede, *Historia Ecclesiastica* I 15), the gods that appear in them will have been interpreted euhemeristically, i.e. as great kings or heroes who came to be worshipped as gods after their deaths."[43] And, we might add, the same interpretation would presumably have been made by those who read or heard the genealogies, including the kings themselves.[44] It seems likely, moreover, that Alistair Campbell was right in assuming that the *Beowulf* poet had first-hand acquaintance with one or more of the many genealogies in circulation, for they also contained the names of several important characters in his poem – Scyld Scefing, Heremod, Beaw, Offa, and perhaps Wermund and Eomær. Campbell argues in particular that the account of Scyld Scefing at the beginning of the poem is based on an annotation to a royal genealogy.[45]

This selective interrogation of the surviving records has yielded more copious evidence than we might have expected that posthumous deification of Germanic heroes in pre-Christian days was a subject familiar to the Anglo-Saxons in later, Christian times. An Anglo-Saxon audience contemplating the final scene of *Beowulf* could possibly have had the euhemeristic accounts of deified heathens preached at them in sermons, explained to them by their scholars, and evoked in the genealogies of their kings. They were probably aware that their missionaries tried to convert Germanic heathens (whether

---

[40] Kenneth Sisam, "Anglo-Saxon royal genealogies," *Proceedings of the British Academy*, 39 (1953), 32. Cf. J. S. Ryan, "Othin in England," *Folklore*, 74 (1963), 462.

[41] Chambers, *Beowulf: an introduction*, p. 202 (with *wuþedon* misprinted for *wurþedon*). The source of the comment in both Textus Roffensis and in Asser (n. 5 above) is presumably Nennius's *Historia Brittonum*; see Sisam, "Anglo-Saxon royal genealogies," pp. 313–14.

[42] Chambers, *Beowulf: an introduction*, p. 320, n. 1.

[43] Faulkes, "Descent from the gods," p. 93.

[44] For a convenient assemblage of the relevant genealogical texts, see Chambers, *Beowulf: an introduction*, pp. 195, 197–203, 311–12.

[45] Alistair Campbell, "The use in *Beowulf* of earlier heroic verse," *England before the Conquest: studies in primary sources presented to Dorothy Whitelock*, ed. Peter Clemoes and Kathleen Hughes (Cambridge, 1971), p. 290.

Scandinavians in England or their Germanic cousins on the continent) by explaining to them that their pagan deities were mere mortals whom the misguided ancestors had proclaimed gods at their deaths. The Anglo-Saxon audience had available the word *mannweorðung* "worship of human beings" and knew that this was something condemned in both canon and sermon. The sermons also ring with warnings that funerals are flashpoints for outbreaks of heathen practices among Germanic people, whether Anglo-Saxon, Danish, or others. Is it not likely that an Anglo-Saxon contemplating Beowulf's last rites – the pagan cremation followed by the pagan interment of his ashes with lavish treasures as the warriors circle his *bēcn* chanting of his fame – might be reminded of the men of old deifying their kings? The *praecognita* to an understanding of the closing ritual as a dark Germanic apotheosis were to be found, as we have seen, not only in sermons but also in Asser's biography of Alfred, in Nennius, in saints' lives, and in annotations to royal genealogies.

Let us turn again to the actual words spoken by the twelve noblemen who march their horses around the *bēcn*:

> þā ymbe hlǣw riodan   hildedēore,
> æþelinga bearn,   ealra twelfe,
> woldon (care) cwīðan,   [ond] kyning mǣnan,
> wordgyd wrecan,   ond ymb w(er) sprecan;
>
> (3169–72)

Their utterance is described as a *wordgyd*. This is a nonce-word which Klaeber says means "elegy" and Clark Hall "dirge," but it means nothing so specific as that.[46] Their chant is as much an encomium as a lament and could just as well refer to *dadsisas*, the heathen litany which the *Indiculus... paganiarum* forbids the eighth-century Saxons to say in the presence of the dead. The noblemen's chant continues:

> eahtodan eorlscipe   ond his ellenweorc
> duguðum dēmdon, –   swā hit gedē(fe) bið,
> þæt mon his winedryhten   wordum herge,
> ferhðum frēoge,   þonne hē forð scile
> of līchaman   (lǣded) weorðan.
>
> (3173–7)

"They praised his nobility and his deeds of valor, praised them fittingly, as it is proper that one should do – to extol with words and cherish in the heart one's friend and lord when he must be led forth from the fleshly garment." Klaeber

---

[46] Klaeber, *Beowulf and the Fight at Finnsburg*, p. 428; John R. Clark Hall, *A Concise Anglo-Saxon Dictionary*, 4th edn with a supplement by Herbert D. Meritt (Cambridge, 1960), s.v. *wordgydd*.

says of this passage, "The lines setting forth the praise of Beowulf by his faithful thanes sound like an echo of divine service, and closely resemble *Gen[esis]* 1ff, 15ff" (p. 230). The verses in *Genesis A* to which he refers are the poem's opening, which is based upon the Common Preface to the Mass –

> Us is riht micel ðæt we rodera weard,
> wereda wuldorcining, wordum herigen,
> modum lufien!

"It is right that we praise the Lord of heaven, the glorious King of hosts, cherish him in our hearts" – and the angels' praise of God:

> þegnas þrymfæste þeoden heredon,
> sægdon lustum lof, heora liffrean
> demdon drihtenes,
>
> (15–17)

which one translator has rendered, "Servants in glory worshipped the Prince, gladly uttered praise of their Lord of life, glorified God."[47] If we transfer these lexical renderings of *herian* and *deman* to the *Beowulf* passage, the import of the lines will be unambiguously devotional. In any case, the similarities are striking. The prayer-like quality of the *Beowulf* passage is also suggested by Klaeber's further observation that the phrase *manna mildust* in 3181 occurs in the Old High German *Wessobrun Prayer* with reference to God: *almahtico Cot, / manno miltisto*. Klaeber offers no surmise as to why the poet has the warriors' chant echo these prayers, but some modern scholars have suggested that these phrases impart a Christian tone to the passage and imply a Christian Beowulf. It is difficult to see what sense can be made of supposed Christian allusions in a speech made about a pagan hero by his pagan comrades at his emphatically pagan obsequies. But in making the chant prayer-like, the poet is not necessarily making it Christian. (The supplication *kyrie, eleison* was addressed by pagan Greeks to their pagan rulers long before it was transformed into a prayer to Christ, and it implies reverent entreaty in either context.) The chant is not Christian, but it does have a worshipful quality, and perhaps this is what has led more than one modern scholar to see godlike qualities in the hero.[48] And as

---

[47] R. K. Gordon, *Anglo-Saxon Poetry Selected and Translated* (London, 1926), pp. 95–6. Gordon's punctuation is used in both translation and original.

[48] Robert P. Creed observes, "The *Beowulf*-poet even seems to have sensed, with disapproval, that Beowulf had been regarded as some sort of god. Now the Christian poet was not about to violate the First Commandment. If earlier people had regarded Beowulf as a god, they had simply been mistaken.... Beowulf the god seems always to have come from afar, probably at the request of suppliants": "The remaking of *Beowulf*," in *Oral Tradition in Literature: interpretation in context*, ed. John Miles Foley (Columbia, MS, 1986), pp. 144–5. Earlier, Edward B. Irving suggested much more tentatively that "a mysterious and half-mythic atmosphere surrounds the funeral rites [for Beowulf], perhaps largely because we half recognize the striking of those same notes of feeling we

for the phrase *manna mildust*, its closest analogue in Old English writings is a comment inserted by the Anglo-Saxon translator of *Orosius* into his text: *He wæs eallra monna mildheortast on þæm dagum* "He was the most mild-hearted of all men in those days" – a comment referring to a heathen ruler who was deified.[49]

Lines 3174–7, as they are usually read, are puzzling:

> swā hit gedē(fe) bið,
> þæt mon his winedryhten   wordum herge,
> ferhðum frēoge,   þonne hē forð scile
> of līchaman   (læded) weorðan.

They seem to imply that ten days after his cremation Beowulf's soul is still in his body, and only now, as the warriors chant Beowulf's praises, is his spirit departing. But a closer look at the text makes clear that this clause does not say "when his soul leaves his body" but rather "when *he* is transported from his physical covering."[50] Perhaps this vaguer statement – "when *he* must go on to another state" – gives latitude for a broader range of meanings so that we are not obliged to assume that the poet has carelessly forgotten that Beowulf's soul parted from his body more than ten days before; he could be referring, rather, to the hero's translation to a higher state.

Finally, let us turn to the actual tomb of Beowulf, the *beorh* on Hronesnæs. When Beowulf conceives of a monument for himself in lines 2802–8 –

> Hātað heaðomǣre   hlǣw gewyrcean
> beorhtne æfter bǣle   æt brimes nosan;
> sē scel tō gemyndum   mīnum lēodum
> hēah hlīfian   on Hronesnæsse,
> þæt hit sǣlīðend   syððan hātan

---

heard in the description of Scyld's funeral.... The similarity does not imply that Beowulf is a god, but it lays stress on the hero's role as a rescuer, protector, shield of his people, ... and hints at some possible unknown order beyond the known seas of men": *Introduction to Beowulf* (Englewood Cliffs, NJ, 1969), p. 99. As for Scyld's funeral, Adrien Bonjour, *The Digressions in Beowulf* (Oxford, 1950), p. 9, says it "is almost an apotheosis."

[49] *The Old English Orosius*, p. 128. The reference is to Julius Caesar.

[50] *Beowulf*, 3176–7, is frequently compared with *Soul and Body II*, 20–1, "*to won þinre sawle sið   siþþan wurde, / siþþan heo of lichoman   læded wære*," which is, in fact, the basis for editors' supplying *læded* for the manuscript lacuna in *Beowulf*, 3177. Kemp Malone, "Some *Beowulf* readings," *Franciplegius: medieval and linguistic studies in honor of Francis Peabody Magoun, Jr.*, ed. Jess B. Bessinger Jr, and Robert P. Creed (New York, 1965), pp. 122–3, rejects the reconstruction *læded* because, he says, the word is too long for the space available in the manuscript. But if this is so, we can simply assume that the scribe (who is everywhere economizing on space as he brings the poem to a close) used the reduced form (by syncopation and simplification of final double consonants) *læd*. In any case, it is significant that while the two passages are otherwise parallel, *heo* (the soul) is the subject of the subordinate clause in *Soul and Body II* while *he* (Beowulf) is the subject in *Beowulf*.

> Bīowulfes biorh, ðā ðe brentingas
> ofer flōda genipu feorran drīfað,

his concern is that he be remembered after his death. He wants a monument *to gemyndum minum leodum* "as a remembrance among my people," and he wishes to have it located so that seafarers will see it and, hearing that it is *Beowulfes beorh*, will carry his name to distant lands. This desire that a physical memorial keep his name alive in people's memory after his death is typical of early Germanic folk throughout their era. The great Rök column in Sweden, the Istaby memorial stone in Blekinge, Denmark, the Norse *bautasteinar* in general, and the many Anglo-Saxon memorial stones such as those at Hackness, Thorhill, Great Urswick, Yarm, and Overchurch bear witness to this concern. But the monument and ceremony that Beowulf's survivors provide go far beyond anything he requests in his dying speech. He says nothing about having a splendid wall built around his *becn* and enshrining his ashes within it; he says nothing about filling the structure with treasure and certainly nothing about ritual chants and processions. These elements are all conceived by his bereaved subjects, and it is these elements that make the structure seem like something more than a monument and the occasion something more than a second funeral.

The words *hlǣw* and *beorh* used to designate the monument are quite general. By far the largest number of their documented occurrences are in charters or placenames, where they seem to mean "mountain, hill, mound" and refer to landmarks. They can also mean a hollow mound such as a dragon might occupy or such as men might use for a tomb. Placenames like *Wodnes beorh* "Woden's barrow," which occurs in the *Chronicle* (for 592 and 715) and in charters, and *þunores hlǣw* "Thor's barrow," which occurs in the life of St Mildred, suggest that these nouns could also refer to a place for worshipping pagan gods – a shrine or *heroön*.[51] The noun *bēcn* used of the monument in line 3160 lends it a numinous quality, since *bēcn* means "sign, portent, idol," and it is used in Christian times to refer to the Cross and to

---

[51] "Association with a mound or tumulus occurs three times in the case of Woden, twice in the case of Thunor," according to Margaret Gelling, "Place-names and Anglo-Saxon paganism," *University of Birmingham Historical Journal*, 3 (1961), 15. Conjuncture of tomb and temple is not unusual. Clement of Alexandria in his *Exhortation to the Heathen*, chapter 3, states contemptuously that pagan temples are simply tombs at which the heathen began worshipping, and he provides a catalogue of people who had died and whose tombs became places of worship. (In chapter 2 he says that the native countries, the biographies, and especially the sepulchers of the heathen gods prove that they were nothing but human beings.) We have seen earlier that Snorri Sturlusson describes Germanic people worshipping at the tombs of their gods. Even in Christian times the tomb can serve as a shrine. In Spain there is a tradition that a tomb cult developed at the grave of the Cid; see W. J. Entwistle, "La Estoria del noble varón el Cid Ruiz Díaz," *Hispanic Review*, 15 (1947), 206–11, and P. E. Russell, "San Pedro de Cardeña and the heroic history of the Cid," *Medium Ævum*, 27 (1958), 57–79.

Christ's miracles.[52] It can designate memorial stones (especially in the inscriptions written on such stones) but never refers to a tomb in Old English. The *beorh* which the Geatas prepared for Beowulf is twice described as *heah* "high" (2805 and 3157), and of course it was, both because it stood on a lofty promontory and because the structure itself was built *hēah ond brād* (3157). High *beorgas* are mentioned also in Ælfric's *De falsis diis*, where it says of Woden, *þone macodan ða hæðenan him to mæran gode, . . . and to heagum beorgum him brohton onsæg[ed]nysse* "the heathens made that one [that is, Woden] their famous god . . . and brought sacrifices to him on high *beorgas*."[53] Wulfstan's account of the deification of Woden is much the same, noting that the heathens *to heagum beorgum him brohton oft mistlice loflac* "often brought manifold offerings to him on high *beorgas*."[54] Pope and Bethurum offer abundant evidence from other sources confirming that cult was paid to pagan Germanic gods at high mounds,[55] and the placename *Wodnes beorh* itself would seem to offer some corroboration. These data in aggregate suggest, I believe, that the monument that the Geatas prepare for Beowulf is patient of an interpretation which would view it as a shrine or *heroön*.

This essay proposes, then, a possible rationale for the funeral rites' "mysterious and half-mythic atmosphere" which "hints at some possible unknown order beyond the known seas of men."[56] It suggests that some in the poet's audience might have sensed a darker purpose in the Geatas' ceremonies than that of having a redundant second funeral, a purpose which the poet intimates through muted hints, as is his wont in alluding to his characters' paganism. An overt statement that the Geatas proclaimed dead Beowulf a god would have alienated a Christian Anglo-Saxon audience,[57] but by appealing subtly to the knowledge he knew they shared about Germanic apotheosis, he could arouse suspicions that the somber majesty of the ceremonies was an expression of something more precise than the "mysterious and half-mythic," of something more disquieting than mere grief. For those in the audience who thought of pagan deification, the closing rites would have been a powerful culmination of the pervasive tension throughout the poem between inspiring heroism and the sad shame of heathenism. The poet reveres the exemplary

---

[52] See *Dictionary of Old English: B*, ed. Antonette diPaolo Healey (Toronto, 1991), s.v. *bēacen*. See also Elisabeth Okasha, "'Beacen' in Old English poetry," *Notes and Queries*, 221 (1976), 200–8. Among the senses established by Okasha are "idolatrous monument" (p. 205).

[53] *Homilies of Ælfric: a supplementary collection*, p. 684.

[54] *The Homilies of Wulfstan*, p. 223.

[55] See the notes to these passages in the editions of Pope and Bethurum; cf. Ursula Dronke's note to *at Sigtýs bergi* on p. 64 of *The Poetic Edda*, vol. 1: *Heroic Poems* (Oxford, 1969).

[56] See above, n. 48.

[57] Howell D. Chickering, Jr, *Beowulf Translated with an Introduction and Commentary* (Garden City, NY, 1977), p. 377, rightly observes that the pagan element "is strong without being explicitly cultic." Allusions to heathenism are common in the poem, but they are always restrained.

conduct of Beowulf and his people while deploring the pagan darkness which leaves that whole world in danger of perdition. His moving depiction of the solemn ritual around Beowulf's *beorh* is his last, melancholy, admiring gaze back on a man so great that people would think him a god; on a people so benighted that they thought a man might become a god.[58]

[58] I wish to thank Robert E. Bjork of Arizona State University for some helpful suggestions he made after hearing this essay read as a lecture.

2

Elements of the Marvelous in the Characterization of Beowulf: A Reconsideration of the Textual Evidence

Elements of the marvelous are not uncommon in *Beowulf*. A fire-breathing dragon, sea monsters, and magically protected ogres from the race of Cain are but some of the fabulous wonders that the poet has admitted to his story. But in general the wonders are carefully restricted to the devil's party. Against these superhuman (as well as many human) adversaries the hero Beowulf can pit only his man's strength and his man's courage.[1] True, he is not an average man – *se þe manna wæs   mægene strengest / on þæm dæge   þysses lifes* (789–90)[2] – but he is *only* a strong man, and the poem thus reveals how the best of human beings might comport themselves in their struggle against the hopeless odds of the Enemy. If the poet had been indiscriminate in his use of the supernatural, if he had lavished fabulous powers on ogre and champion alike, then the hero would have become a kind of monster himself, and *Beowulf*, instead of being a heroic poem, would have been a romantic fable describing the conflict between good monsters and bad monsters.

The poet's concern to portray Beowulf as a man rather than as superhuman is revealed in his repeated allusions to the hero's physical limitations and vulnerability. Most memorable, perhaps, is the account of Beowulf's suffering and death in the last part of the poem, a subject which is discussed with characteristic eloquence in John C. Pope's essay for the Meritt *Festschrift*.[3] But

Reprinted from *Old English Studies in Honour of John C. Pope*, ed. Robert B. Burlin and Edward B. Irving, Jr (Toronto, 1974), pp. 119–37.

[1] Of course this does not mean that he was ineligible for divine favor. Just as Achilles enjoys the patronage of Athene and Hera, Beowulf occasionally receives the support of a God whom he but little knows or understands. In a Christian view such favor would not set him apart from other men.

[2] All quotations from *Beowulf* are from Klaeber's edition, *Beowulf and the Fight at Finnsburg*, 3rd edn (Boston, 1950), except that I have dispensed with Klaeber's macrons and other diacritics. Quotations from other Old English poems are taken from *ASPR*.

[3] Pope, "Beowulf's old age," in *Philological Essays: studies in Old and Middle English language and literature in honour of Herbert Dean Meritt*, ed. J. L. Rosier (The Hague, 1970), pp. 55–64.

there are earlier reminders of his human fallibility. In lines 739 and following we see that Beowulf is incapable of preventing Grendel from killing and devouring the Geatish warrior Hondscioh, and later he confesses to Hrothgar (960–2, 967–70) that he lacked the strength to hold the monster in the hall and kill him there, as he wanted to do. The poet tells us that Beowulf all but died in his struggle with the hag (1550ff), a fact which the hero himself acknowledges in his reports to Hrothgar (1655–7) and to Hygelac (2140ff). In the dragon fight, only Wiglaf's intervention saves Beowulf from an instant and ignominious death.[4] The inadequacy thus demonstrated was sensed by the hero earlier when he apologized for having to use a sword and armor in his last adventure (2518ff). Here as elsewhere in his closing speeches, "the sense of his own vulnerability seems to draw him closer to the period of boyhood dependency,"[5] and we are reminded that throughout the poem he has been portrayed as a man, not a demigod.

But is it really true that in characterizing Beowulf the poet systematically eschews elements of the marvelous? Doesn't he in fact sometimes allow the hero's physical powers to grow embarrassingly far beyond human dimensions? Beowulf remains underwater for hours – or perhaps for an entire day – as he descends to the bottom of Grendel's mere. Alone, he carries thirty suits of armor from the battlefield in Frisia and swims with them through the North Sea and the Skagerrak to Geatland, a distance of some five hundred miles. In early life he swam for five to seven days with his companion Breca, slaying sea-monsters by night. At these points in the narrative it would seem that the distinction between the powers of man and the powers of his supernatural adversaries becomes quite indistinct.

At least two critics of the poem have perceived just how important these lapses are for our understanding of the nature and meaning of *Beowulf*. Citing the three episodes just mentioned, Rodney Delasanta and James Slevin point out that such feats temporarily remove Beowulf from the category of "high mimetic hero" and mark him instead as a "romance hero," one who is superior not only to other men but also to his environment.[6] By applying Northrop

---

[4] Wiglaf's speech in 2663–8 is a fitting emblem of the poet's tactful merging of Beowulf's preeminence with his human limitations: *Leofa Biowulf, læst eall tela, / swa ðu on geoguðfeore geara gecwæde, / þæt ðu ne alæte be ðe lifigendum / dom gedreosan; sceall nu dædum rof, / æðeling anhydig, ealle mægene / feorh ealgian; ic ðe fullæstu.* Invoking the king's youthful boasts as a means of urging him on to a last desperate effort is fine, but best is the lexical play by which Wiglaf emphasizes that even in his own youth he is inferior to the mighty king: only Beowulf can "perform;" Wiglaf can but "supplement the performance" (*læst eall tela . . . ic ðe fullæstu*). Klaeber's note here that "there is a singular lack of propriety in making young Wiglaf administer fatherly advice to Beowulf" seems to me to overlook the studiously respectful tone of the speech.

[5] Pope, "Beowulf's old age," 60.

[6] Delasanta and Slevin, "*Beowulf* and the hypostatic union," *Neophilologus*, 52 (1968), 409–16. I disregard a fourth element of the "marvelous" which the authors mention ("his voyage from

Frye's terms to *Beowulf*, Delasanta and Slevin bring into clear focus the tensions between epic and romance qualities which seemed to trouble W. P. Ker: "There was a danger that Beowulf should be transformed into a sort of Amadis," he muses, and concludes uncertainly, "this danger is avoided, at least in part."[7]

It is my purpose in the present essay to argue that if we return to the text of *Beowulf* and examine each of the three occasions where Beowulf seems to be temporarily endowed with supernatural powers, we will discover a strange insubstantiality in the evidence for such endowments. In fact, I am convinced that the supposed evidence for a superhuman Beowulf is largely a fiction of editorial interpretation and comment and that Beowulf throughout is conceived of as a heroic man and not as a romance hero. The reason for the supernaturalizing misinterpretations, I shall further suggest, is that in reading the poem scholars may have been excessively influenced by its folktale analogues and so have sometimes read back into the sophisticated text of the poet a wild extravagance which he had carefully purged from the material he adopted.

The Descent into Grendel's Mere

In his account of Beowulf's fight with the ogress the poet is at some pains to explain that the conflict does not take place under water but rather in a dry chamber where no water could reach the combatants:

> Ða se eorl ongeat
> þæt he [in] niðsele   nathwylcum wæs,
> þær him nænig wæter   wihte ne sceþede,
> ne him for hrofsele   hrinan ne mehte
> færgripe flodes.
>
> (1512–16)[8]

Thus localized, Beowulf's exploit is one which we could imagine a human being performing, and as the fight progresses and he begins to lose ground, we are prepared to believe that the hero is indeed fighting desperately for his life.

Geatland to Denmark, although not miraculous, is surrounded by an aura of wonder and majesty") since this is a matter of interpretation. I also disregard here the main concern of the article, which tends toward theological explication. What I have found valuable is the authors' perceptive formulation of the apparently mixed quality of the characterization in the narrative.

[7] Ker, *Epic and Romance*, 2nd edn (London, 1908), p. 175. Cf. Frank Beaumont, "*Beowulf*," *Proceedings of the Royal Philosophical Society of Glasgow*, 38 (1906–7), 201–33, esp. 210–17.

[8] Comparable settings are indicated in Norse analogues, of course; cf. R. W. Chambers, *Beowulf: an introduction to the study of the poem*, 3rd edn with a supplement by C. L. Wrenn (Cambridge, 1959), pp. 52–3 and 451–85.

This careful circumscription of the hero's power is completely undercut, however, by the standard interpretation of the lines describing Beowulf's descent through the water:

> brimwylm onfeng
> hilderince.   Ða wæs hwil dæges,
> ær he þone grundwong   ongytan mehte.
>
> (1494-6)

"The surging water closed over the warrior. Then it was *the space of a day* before he could see the bottom of the mere." This is the sense supplied by early editors and translators. Later editors, apparently embarrassed by the hero's holding his breath and swimming downward for an entire day, endeavor to reduce the time spent sinking to the bottom: *hwil dæges*, says Klaeber (186), means "'a good part of the day,' not 'the space of a day,'" and most modern scholars have agreed.

But it is strange that there is no mention elsewhere of the hero's fantastic ability to travel underwater for hours on end, and stranger still that the poet proceeds immediately to contradict himself by depicting the distance from the surface of the mere to the bottom not as a day's journey but as a very short space. For in lines 1588 and following, when Beowulf beheads the monster, spilling his blood into the water, we are told that men standing above the mere immediately (*sona*) see the gore churn up to the top:

>   Hra wide sprong,
> syþðan he . . .
>   hine þa heafde becearf.
> Sona þæt gesawon   snottre ceorlas,
> þa ðe mid Hroðgare   on holm wliton,
> þæt wæs yðgeblond   eal gemenged,
> brim blode fah.
>
> (1588-94)

And the hero's own ascent to the shore seems a matter of moments (1618-24) rather than a day's journey. Such apparent inconsistencies certainly justify R. W. Chambers' exasperation: "We may render this phrase [i.e., *hwil dæges*] either 'a large part of the day' or 'the space of a day,' as we will; . . . unreason like this is possible in *Beowulf*, though one wonders how so farfetched an idea ever occurred to anybody."[9]

But is the farfetched idea really in the text, or is it only in the minds of the commentators? *Hwil dæges*, I believe, does not mean either "the space of a day" or "the large part of a day" but simply "daytime," and all the poet is saying is

[9] Chambers, *Beowulf: an introduction*, p. 465.

that by the time Beowulf reached the bottom of the mere it was already daylight. S. O. Andrew suggested this interpretation briefly in his *Postscript on Beowulf*, but E. V. K. Dobbie dismissed the idea without argument,[10] and so far as I am aware it has never been advocated since. An examination of the phrase *dæges hwil* in its occurrences throughout Old English poetry, however, suggests that Andrew was almost certainly correct:

> þa wæs on þam ofne, þær se engel becwom,
> windig and wynsum, wedere gelicost
> þonne hit on sumeres tid sended weorðeð
> dropena drearung on dæges hwile,
> wearmlic wolcna scur.
>
> (*Daniel*, 345–9)

"Then, when the angel came, it was airy and pleasant in the furnace, most like the weather in summer, when the dropping of rain, the warm shower from the clouds, is sent in the daytime."

> þonne on sumeres tid sended weorðe
> dropena dreorung mid dæges hwile.
>
> (*Azarias*, 63–4)

(From the same context as *Daniel*, 345–9) "when the dropping of the rain is sent during the daytime."

> hord eft gesceat,
> dryhtsele dyrnne ær dæges hwile.
>
> (*Beowulf*, 2319–20)

"He [i.e., the dragon, who flies only at night] returned to his hoard, his secret dwelling, before daylight."[11] A parallel phrase is used in the poet's statement indicating that the dragon flies by night:

> lyftwynne heold
> nihtes hwilum
>
> (*Beowulf*, 3043–4)

"he held sway in the joyous air by night."

---

[10] Andrew, *Postscript on Beowulf* (Cambridge, 1948), p. 99; *ASPR*, IV, p. 196.

[11] Dobbie's suggested translation of *dæges hwile* as "a [good] part of the day [had passed]" (p. 196) must have been arrived at without reference to the passages here cited from *Daniel* and *Azarias* and in the hope of offering some support for the traditional interpretation of 1495b in *Beowulf*. All the translations I have consulted agree in rendering *Beowulf* 2320b "before daytime / the time of day / daybreak / daylight / dawn" rather than "before a [good] part of the day [had passed]."

The manifest meaning of the phrase *dæges hwil* (and *nihtes hwil*) in these passages would seem to indicate that the only reasonable interpretation of *Beowulf*, 1495–6, is "Then it was daytime before he could get to the bottom." This reading not only preserves the human dimensions of the hero but also conforms with the poet's carefully marked time-sequence throughout the episode. Grendel's mother raids the hall at night, and Hrothgar is notified immediately (1279–1309). Beowulf is summoned, and he reaches Hrothgar's chamber *samod ærdæge* (1311) – that is, in the early hours of the morning before daybreak.[12] It is growing light as the warriors proceed toward the mere, for they are able to see the bloody track of the ogress over the moor (1402–4). In 1495 the poet says it was broad daylight (*hwil dæges*) when Beowulf plunged to the bottom of the lake. The struggle is arduous, and the Danes seem to wait a long time before giving up their watch at *non dæges*, that is, at mid-afternoon (1600). It is just then, however, that Beowulf overcomes the hag and beheads Grendel. He swims quickly to the top of the mere, rejoins his comrades, and they repair to the Danish hall, where Beowulf's triumph is celebrated until night falls and the banquet ends (1789–90). The poet's marking of the passage of time is exceptionally clear –

1311–12	Samod ærdæge / eode eorla sum . . .
1495	Ða wæs hwil dæges . . .
1600	Ða cwom non dæges . . .
1789–90	Nihthelm geswearc / deorc ofer dryhtgumum . . .

– provided we understand *hwil dæges* to mean "daytime" and not "the space of a day" or "the large part of a day."

The contextual relevance of the statement that it is daylight when Beowulf reaches the bottom of the mere is made clear by the ensuing clause in 1497–1500. Indeed, if we assign to *þa* in 1495b the sense "as" (which it seems to have in *Beowulf*, 201, 723, 967, 1103, 1621, 2550, 2676, etc.), we may read the two clauses as one long sentence: "As it was daytime before he [Beowulf] could get to the bottom, the grim and ravenous one who, furiously greedy, had guarded the watery region for fifty years immediately perceived that some man was exploring the alien creatures' domain from above." The fact that it was now daytime explains why the ogress detected Beowulf's presence so quickly.[13]

Once these factors are all taken into account, the meaning "daytime" rather

---

[12] *Ærdæg* appears to be equivalent to *uhta* (*Beowulf*, 126: *on uhtan mid ærdæge*; cf. *Andreas* 235, 1388; *Elene*, 105) and both words are used to translate Latin "matutinus." In the Cleopatra Glossary appears the explanation "Matutinum, uhttid, siue beforan dæge" (Thomas Wright, *Anglo-Saxon and Old English Vocabularies*, 2nd edn by Richard Paul Wülcker (London, 1884), p. 450: 3). Cf. F. Tupper, *Anglo-Saxon Dæg-mæl* (Baltimore, 1895), p. 37. The phrase *somod ærdæge* occurs again at *Beowulf*, 2942, referring, presumably, to the pre-dawn hour at which Hygelac's troops arrived and saved the Geatish raiding party from being destroyed by the Swedes *on mergenne* (2929).

[13] Andrew, *Postscript*, 11–12, and Bruce Mitchell, *Old English Syntax* (Oxford, 1985), vol. 2, p. 255.

than "space of a day" seems so inevitable that one wonders what could have given rise and longevity to the erroneous interpretation. The answer, I suspect, is implied in the comment with which Klaeber annotates the passage:

> 1495. hwil dæges, "a good part of the day," . . . A long time is required for the same purpose in several corresponding folk-tales, see Panzer 119.

Panzer does indeed provide examples of such descents requiring twenty-one days, a year, and even three years.[14] But neither here nor in other parts of *Beowulf*, so far as I am aware, does the poet show himself to be such a slave to folktale sources that he cannot alter an inappropriate detail when he wishes. I suspect that it is not so much his judgment as the judgment of modern scholars which has been overmastered by the folktale sources.

The Return from Frisia

Lines 2359b–68 of *Beowulf* are generally supposed to tell the story of an astounding *geste* performed by the hero after Hygelac's defeat in Frisia:

> þonan Biowulf com
> sylfes cræfte,   sundnytte dreah;
> hæfde him on earme   (ana) þritig
> hildegeatwa,   þa he to holme (st)ag . . .
> Oferswam ða sioleða bigong   sunu Ecgðeowes,
> earm anhaga   eft to leodum.

R. K. Gordon, who fairly represents all the translations of this passage which I have seen, renders the lines, "Beowulf came thence by his own strength; swam over the sea. Alone he held on his arm thirty suits of armour when he set out on the sea . . . The son of Ecgtheow swam over the stretch of the gulfs, the hapless solitary man back to his people."[15]

Some years ago I published a study of this passage in which I argued that the actual words of the manuscript (before editorial intercession) say less than has been generally assumed. In particular I was concerned to show that there is no clear statement that Beowulf held thirty suits of armor on his arm when he set out or that he leapt into the sea with whatever it is that he *was* holding in his arm. The most that can be gathered from the transmitted text, I suggested, is that he was in possession of an unspecified amount of war-gear when he left the field of battle.[16] Karl P. Wentersdorf has carried this analysis further, arguing that not only is there no basis for assuming that Beowulf swam to Geatland

[14] Friedrich Panzer, *Studien zur germanischen Sagengeschichte*, 1, *Beowulf* (Munich, 1910).
[15] *Anglo-Saxon Poetry*, selected and tr. R. K. Gordon (London, 1954), p. 47.
[16] "Beowulf's retreat from Frisia: some textual problems in Ll. 2361–2362," *SP*, 62 (1965), 1–16.

Elements of the Marvelous 27

with thirty suits of armor; indeed, there is no evidence that he swam anywhere at this time.[17] The unique phrase *sundnytte dreah*, he points out, can be pressed into no more specific meaning than "he made the sea trip,"[18] and the verb *oferswimman* clearly did not have the meaning "swim over," as a speaker of Modern English would expect, but meant to pass over the water by any one of various possible means of locomotion. This broad semantic range of Old English *swimman* is recognized in the standard dictionaries and is amply illustrated in *BTD*. Among documentations of the verb referring to a ship's movement through the water, a particularly clear specimen is that in Vercelli Homily XIX, which is not represented in the dictionaries: *þa sona swa þa menn þe on þam scipe wæron ut on þære sæs dypan gesegled hæfdon, þa onsende God mycelne ren 7 strangne wind 7 grimme yste on þa sæ, swa þæt þæt scip ne mihte naþer ne forð swymman ne underbæc*.[19]

A conflation of Wentersdorf's conclusions with my own would yield this interpretation of the verses quoted above: "From there [that is, from the battle] came Beowulf by means of his own physical strength – undertook a journey on the sea. He had held battle-gear[20] on his arm when he moved toward the sea . . . Then, alone and wretched, the son of Ecgtheow crossed the expanse of ocean, returning to his own people." This cautious translation is better founded, I believe, than previous ones based on the old editorial reconstructions and ad hoc interpretations of word-meanings. There is nothing in this translation about fantastic swimming feats, it will be noted, although there is no dearth of them in Panzer's collection of parallels (pp. 269–70).[21]

---

[17] Wentersdorf, "Beowulf's withdrawal from Frisia: a reconsideration," *SP*, 68 (1971), 395–415.

[18] Wentersdorf, "Beowulf's withdrawal," pp. 402–3. That *sund-* in *sundnytt* means "sea" rather than "swimming" seems to me particularly likely when we note that in every other nominal compound with *sund-* attested in the poetic corpus (*sundbuend, sundgebland, sundhelm, sundhengest, sundplega, sundreced, sundwudu*) the first element means "sea" and not "swimming." Further, in the other two Old English nominal compounds with *nytt*, the first element is in both cases a noun denoting the location of the act, not an abstract noun of means: *cyricnytt, weoroldnytt*. *Sundnytt*, then, would appear to mean "use of the sea" and the poetic phrase *sundnytte dreah* "he made use of the sea" or, as Wentersdorf suggests, "he made the sea trip."

[19] Paul E. Szarmach, "Three versions of the Jonah story: an investigation of narrative technique in Old English homilies," *Anglo-Saxon England*, 1 (1972), 186. The use of "swim" to refer to the progress of a boat over the water continues in Middle and early Modern English. (See Wentersdorf, "Beowulf's withdrawal," pp. 403–7.) Shakespeare uses the word in this sense in *Julius Caesar*, V.i.67, and in *As You Like It*, IV.i.40 ("you have swam in a gondola").

[20] As I point out in "Beowulf's retreat from Frisia," the customary translation of *hildegeatwe* as "suits of armor" and the emendation *ana* are incorrect, and the numeral XXX is not to be trusted. See especially pp. 2–7.

[21] Wentersdorf's linguistic critique, to which I have referred here, is but a part of his argument. His article subsequently explores analogues in Old English and cognate literatures which suggest that the *Beowulf* poet probably conceived of his hero as making his way from Frisia through the Skagerrak by ship.

The Swimming Feat with Breca

The story of Beowulf's exploit with Breca differs in kind from the two events discussed above. It does not take place in the poem's present time but is reported as something which occurred years earlier. This temporal distance gives the adventure a slightly different valence from that of the central narrative actions, one linking it as much with the remembered deeds of Hrethel, Heremod, and Scyld Scefing as with those of the mature Beowulf.[22] In another sense too the Breca episode is different: it never comes to us with the direct authority of the poet's own voice but is reported in two contrasting versions by characters within the poem – first by Unferth after he had drunk deep of the beer and wine (531, 1467) and then by the indignant Beowulf. Either the hostile circumstances of the telling or the temporal remoteness of the events described leads to a curious inconsistency and vagueness in the reports. Beowulf's counter-version plays down certain aspects of Unferth's initial account. He and Breca were together on the sea for five, not seven nights; they wore protective arms, and although the winds were cold, Beowulf does not say it was winter. Also, whereas Unferth makes it appear that the two contestants set out swimming (*eagorstream   earmum þehton... mundum brugdon*), Beowulf uses the verbs *rowan* ("to go by water, row, sail"),[23] and *fleotan* ("to float, drift, flow, sail").[24] (The only other occurrence of *fleotan* in the poem clearly has the meaning "sail": *fleat famigheals   forð ofer yðe*, 1909). It is only during the last night of the Breca episode that Beowulf describes himself as actually being in the water (553ff), and that is when he grapples with the *merefixas*. But even here the possibility of a raft or boat being present cannot be completely ruled out, although I consider this unlikely.[25] The setting is also somewhat unclear in

---

[22] This may seem a shadowy distinction, but I believe it is a real one. Many readers would have been troubled, for example, if the author had introduced giants and the fabulous Weland as royal smiths at Hygelac's court, but it does not seem unfitting that Beowulf's heirloom armor is *Hrædlan laf, Welandes geweorc*, or that he wields an ancient sword called "the work of giants" (1558, 1562, 1690, etc.; cf. 2616, 2979). So long as they do not intrude into the poem's present time such fabulous elements seem to leave undispelled our sense that the characters are human beings.

[23] C. L. Wrenn, in his edition of *Beowulf with the Finnesburg Fragment*, 2nd edn, revised and enlarged (London, 1958), p. 195, says "*Rowan* 'swim' does not occur *in that sense* in poetry outside *Beowulf*." In his glossary he defines the word "*row*, hence *swim*."

[24] BTD records two prose occurrences of *fleotend* used specifically to modify *fisc* in the formula *fleotende fixas* and *fleogende fugelas*, but there are no instances of the word being used to describe men swimming.

[25] The earliest editor of the poem conceived that a vessel was present in the adventure – not through one of his many misunderstandings of the text but through retention of the manuscript reading *wudu weallendu* in 581, which he translates "*lignis spumantibus*." See G. J. Thorkelin, *De Danorum rebus gestis...* (Havni, 1815), p. 46. Zupitza's note to 581 in *Beowulf Reproduced in Facsimile ... with a Transliteration and Notes*, EETS o.s. (London, 1882), p. 26, says "*wudu* not *wadu* without

Beowulf's account. Usually he agrees with Unferth in locating the action on the open sea, but in line 568 he indicates that the monsters he fought were denizens of the fords.[26] Perhaps there is a rationale for these variations: Unferth exaggerates the dimensions of the episode in order to emphasize Beowulf's foolhardiness in undertaking it, and so Beowulf, in rebuttal, represents it as a somewhat less prodigious undertaking. But whatever the reason, Beowulf's version, which, I presume, we are expected to credit more seriously than we are Unferth's, presents the events of the swimming feat in terms less imposing and more non-committal than is the case with Unferth's jeering account.[27]

However problematical these details may be, such local probings ignore the great overriding uncertainty of the Breca episode – the mystery as to who Unferth is and what is the nature of the entire exchange between Beowulf and the *þyle*. It is this enigmatic quality of the "Unferth Intermezzo" that leaves scholars undecided as to whether the tale of Beowulf and Breca should be interpreted as sober history, a boisterous flyting, or "whopping lies."[28] Therefore, in the remaining pages of this essay I shall turn to the problem of Unferth, trying to determine afresh what we know and do not know about his character and how we are to interpret the story which his report introduces into the poem.

Although interpretations of Unferth's character have been richly diverse, in general they fall into two broad categories, those which conceive of the *þyle* as a

---

the least doubt; an *a* open at the top does not occur so late in English MSS." Subsequent editors uniformly emend to *wadu weallendu* in order to bring the line into conformity with 546a, although the formula occurs nowhere else. Syntactical considerations and the similarity of phrases like *brim weallendu* (*Beowulf*, 847) seems to me to argue strongly for the traditional emendation *wadu*. But it should not be forgotten that it is an emendation.

[26] Alistair Campbell, "The use in *Beowulf* of earlier heroic verse," in *England before the Conquest: studies in primary sources presented to Dorothy Whitelock*, ed. Peter Clemoes and Kathleen Hughes (Cambridge, 1971), p. 284, calls attention to the odd appearance of *ford* in this context and questions whether it should be emended to *flod*. Campbell also remarks the odd application of *rowan* ("row") to swimmers. Unferth (512) as well as Beowulf uses *rowan* in describing the feat.

[27] Beowulf's only heightening of the details of the episode would seem to be his introduction of the sea-monsters, and such prodigies, as we have seen, are a given in the poet's portrayal of the hero's adversaries. A further departure from Unferth's account, one which I have not mentioned above, is Beowulf's statement in 541–3 that he would not swim far from Breca, nor could Breca swim far from him. Prevailing opinion has it that this is an explicit contradiction of Unferth's statement that the adventure began as a race. Possibly, but there is a simpler explanation: perhaps the gallant hero intended to remain close to the weaker Breca until they were near their goal, at which time he would outstrip him and win the race without ever being beyond call if his companion should need help. Here, once again, the cryptic mode of the narrative does not permit certainties.

[28] The last phrase is that of Norman E. Eliason, "The þyle and scop in *Beowulf*," *Speculum*, 38 (1963), 272. This article is a valuable and provocative re-examination of the entire question of Unferth's character.

serious and powerful figure and those which see him as essentially a source of diversion or an object of ridicule in the Danish court.²⁹ Critics who view him as serious or sinister usually assume that the contest with Breca is to be taken more or less at face value. Those who view him as playing a lighter role often interpret the tale of the Breca swim as an exaggeration or a joke. Neither view has been firmly established or is likely to be. Quite possibly the *þyle* represented for the audience of the poem some social role involving a combination of grave and playful elements which is now beyond our ken, the institution itself having eluded precise record. Recently, however, it seems to me that increasing evidence has come to light which gives support to the less serious interpretations of Unferth and weakens the case for the somber readings. I shall review and supplement that evidence here.

Most critics have assumed that the designation *þyle* marks Unferth as holder of the solemn office of king's spokesman or counsellor, but the entry for *þyle* in *BTD* points out that the gloss *ðelum* to *scurris* suggests rather that "his [Unferth's] function was something like that of the later court jester, and the style of his attack on Beowulf hardly contradicts the supposition."³⁰ Subsequent studies have added force to this suggestion.³¹ Another fundamental datum for the advocates of a serious Unferth is his sinister name, for if we assume a certain amount of distortion in the letters and sounds, it can be construed as *Unfrið*, "discord, un-peace."³² But, as I have suggested elsewhere,³³ the meaning of the name in its attested form without distortion has at least as much to recommend it: *un-ferð* to the unbiased eye would seem to mean "unintelligence" or "folly" rather than "discord." (Cf. *leas-ferhð(nes)* ["levity, folly"], *ungemynd* ["distraction or confusion of mind"], *ungewitt* ["folly"], *ungeræd* ["folly"], *unræd* ["folly"].) Unferth's name and his official title point at least as much in the direction of a jeering, risible performer as they do of a serious one.

But is such a role consonant with the motivation which the poet gives for Unferth's railing attack?

---

[29] It is generally agreed, of course, that Unferth serves an important purpose within the economy of the poem in that he tests the hero at a crucial point in the narrative. This function is served whether he is a statesman or a poltroon.

[30] The gloss occurs in the Cleopatra Glossary as *de scurris · hof ðelum* (Wright-Wülcker, *Anglo-Saxon Vocabularies*, p. 385: 3). I agree with *BTD* that *hof* represents "of" (with inorganic "h-") rendering Latin "de." The associations of *scurra* and *þyle* in Old English are expertly treated in James L. Rosier, "Design for treachery: the Unferth intrigue," *PMLA*, 77 (1962), 1–3.

[31] See especially the articles by Rosier and Eliason.

[32] The most persuasive and influential statement of this view is that of Morton W. Bloomfield, "*Beowulf* and Christian allegory: an interpretation of Unferth," *Traditio*, 7 (1949–51), 410–15.

[33] "Personal names in medieval narrative and the name of Unferth in *Beowulf*," in *Essays in Honor of Richebourg Gaillard McWilliams*, ed. Howard Creed (Birmingham, AL, 1970), pp. 43–8.

>   wæs him Beowulfes sið,
> modges merefaran,   micel æfþunca,
> forþon þe he ne uþe,   þæt ænig oðer man
> æfre mærða þon ma   middangeardes
> gehede under heofenum   þonne he sylfa.
>
> (501–5)

Surely this clear statement justifies Bonjour's inference that Unferth is "jealous of his own glory" and that only a man "of his prominent position," "a distinguished and glorious thane," would harbor such concern for his martial reputation?[34] So it would seem, but the cited passage will bear scrutiny before the point is granted. As quoted, the passage says that Unferth was unwilling to admit that "any other man on earth should perform glorious deeds." But this meaning is achieved only by means of an emendation of the verb *gehedde* to *gehede*, which is then interpreted as preterite subjunctive of *gehegan* and assigned the unique meaning "to perform (deeds)." Elsewhere in Old English the verb always occurs with *þing*, *seonoð*, *spræc*, or *mæðel* as its direct object and means "to hold (a meeting)." Left in its original manuscript form, *gehedde* would be preterite of *gehedan* ("heed, care for") (see Klaeber's glossary, s.v. *hēdan*). If the sentence is read this way, then Unferth emerges as a character with a rather unheroic, Falstaffian attitude toward heroic deeds: he did not want to grant that other men cared for glory or for deeds of glory (*mærða*) any more than he himself did. This is not an inappropriate sentiment for a man who, the poet later tells us, willingly *forleas ellenmærðum* (1470–1). Perhaps there is more than a little of the swaggering coward in Unferth, and the speech reminding Beowulf of a past failure is motivated by a desire to scare the hero out of his commitment to face Grendel. If the speech is successful, then Unferth will have shown the Danes that he is not alone in his distaste for derring-do. Thus Unferth may very well be what Klaeber long ago said he was: "that singular personality of the 'Thersites' order."[35]

The accusation of fratricide (587ff, 1167ff) has widely, though not universally, been taken as a charge of cowardice against Unferth, and it is this interpretation that consorts best with the reading *gehedde* just advocated. Unferth was such a craven that he would not even fulfill the thane's duty to fight alongside his closest kin when they were in desperate straits. But if this is so, how are we to justify the vehemence and gravity of Beowulf's statement, *þæs þu in helle scealt / werhðo dreogan*? More than one critic has been troubled by the apparent excessiveness of this dark curse. Chambers suggested that Beowulf's taunt may be merely a "countercheck quarrelsome" to the abusive

---

[34] Adrien Bonjour, *The Digressions in Beowulf* (Oxford, 1950), pp. 17–22. See further the important modifications of Bonjour's analysis in his *Twelve Beowulf Papers* (Neuchatel, 1962), pp. 129–33.
[35] Klaeber, *Beowulf and the Fight at Finnsburg*, p. lxii.

þyle.³⁶ Charles Donahue says, "It is unlikely that Beowulf is referring here to a Christian *infernum*" since the hero who is elsewhere characterized as a pious pagan could hardly have knowledge of damnation in Christian terms.³⁷ He translates *helle* as "in the [pagan Germanic] realm of the dead." Donahue's point is well taken, and his translation, which mollifies Beowulf's taunt considerably, may be right.

Before interpreting the text, however, it is instructive once again to look at the words as they appear, or do not appear, in the manuscript. An examination of the facsimiles of Cotton Vitellius A.XV will show no trace of a word *helle* in the manuscript, and the commentaries of Zupitza and Malone confirm that the only vestige of a word at this point is a final "-e," which is now covered by the leaf binding. Modern editors have inserted the word *helle* solely on the authority of the Thorkelin transcripts, and these too merit scrutiny. Looking at Thorkelin's own copy (Thorkelin B), we find that the word *helle* has been inserted "on an original blank in another ink."³⁸ Evidently Thorkelin was unable to make out anything in the manuscript at this point and so left the space blank; later, he must have copied the word from Transcript A into his own transcription. It is likely, then, that Thorkelin A constitutes the sole authority for this reading.

The testimony of Thorkelin's copyist is not to be treated lightly, of course, and yet this is a peculiarly delicate case. Except for the covered "-e," there is no sign of a word *helle* in the manuscript today, and when Thorkelin examined the manuscript there was not enough there for him to make anything out. Surely the copyist, whose transcript preceded Thorkelin's "by a few months or weeks only,"³⁹ must have based his reading *helle* on manuscript evidence which was already quite deteriorated. Considering how much difficulty the copyist had in transcribing accurately even those words which are perfectly clear in the manuscript today (especially in the first part of the poem where he was struggling with an unfamiliar script), we might reasonably think of his *helle* as little more than a game try at reconstructing lost characters from the vestiges which he descried at the crumbling edge of the folio leaf.

One of the chronic errors in A's transcription is the adding or omitting of letters in a diphthong. Only four words after the moot *helle* he writes *þeaeh* for the manuscript reading *þeah*. Conversely, he writes *halle* for *healle* in line 89 and *hald* for *heald* in line 2247. He sometimes miswrites the *ea* diphthong as *e*,

---

[36] Chambers, *Beowulf: an introduction*, p. 28.
[37] Donahue, "*Beowulf* and Christian tradition: a reconsideration from a Celtic stance," *Traditio*, 21 (1965), 92.
[38] Zupitza, *Beowulf Reproduced in Facsimile*, p. 29.
[39] *The Thorkelin Transcripts of Beowulf in Facsimile*, ed. Kemp Malone, Early English Manuscripts in Facsimile, I (Copenhagen, 1951), p. 4. But see now Kevin S. Kiernan, *The Thorkelin Transcripts of "Beowulf"*, Anglistica, 25 (Copenhagen, 1986), esp. pp. 29–30.

as in *bedwa* for *beadwa* (709) and *begas* for *beagas* (3105), and he starts to write *pelhpeon* for *wealhpeon* (629) but "corrects" this to *pealhpeon*. In the light of this latter tendency and of his earlier misreading of the diphthong in *healle*, I conceive the disturbing possibility that the original word was *healle* rather than *helle* in line 588, in which case the passage would read *þæs þu in healle sceallt / werhðo dreogan*: "for that you must endure condemnation in the hall." It is not my concern here to promote this reading, although some might find it preferable on several counts to the *helle* of the transcripts. I want only to illustrate the tenuity of the hitherto unquestioned *helle*, which has been thought to introduce such seriousness into Beowulf's retort to Unferth.[40]

How then are we to interpret Unferth's character? If pressed insistently for an opinion, I would say that he seems to be a blustering, mean-spirited coward who does not enjoy the respect of his comrades[41] and who seeks to bolster his self-esteem by decrying Beowulf's past performance and present qualifications. Beowulf imperturbably answers his hostile jibes, first by giving a more modest and convincing version of the boyhood experience which Unferth recounted and then by alluding pointedly to the cowardice of the *þyle* and to his deficient *wit*, *hige*, and *sefa* (589–94). The Danes are amused and impressed by the hero's perceptiveness in seeing Unferth for what he is, and they rejoice that such a resourceful champion is prepared to assist them (607–11: *Da wæs on salum sinces brytta ... Ðær wæs hæleþa hleahtor*). Unferth resumes his accustomed state of disesteem in Heorot. But as the narrative progresses, Beowulf gradually regenerates the worthless Unferth into a man of some dignity and value in the court (an act of generosity which has been remarked by more than one student of the poem). By allowing Unferth to supply the sword needed for his second fight, the hero imparts a measure of reflected glory to the lesser man, whose pusillanimity nonetheless stands in effective contrast with the valor of Beowulf. Later, when he refuses to blame Hrunting for its failure and returns it to Unferth ceremoniously and with high praise (1659–60, 1807–12), Beowulf confers the most dignity he can upon the *þyle*, who is no longer called "Unferth," but only *sunu Ecglafes*.[42]

---

[40] A. G. Brodeur, *The Art of Beowulf* (Berkeley, CA, 1959), p. 155, speaks for many when he observes that "no one can ... ignore the weight of Beowulf's assertion that the penalty Unferth must pay for his brother's death is damnation in hell."

[41] The statement in 1165–6 that the men in the hall trusted in Unferth's *ferhþ* (probably a pun on his name) and *mod* means, I take it, that in the joyous atmosphere of the victory celebration good will was extended to even the meanest of the company. The statement is preceded by the allusion to the temporary good will between Hrothulf and Hrothgar and followed by the reminder that Unferth had failed his brothers *æt ecga gelacum*.

[42] Whether it was the Danish courtiers who conferred the demeaning name "Unferth" on the *þyle* or whether he acquired it elsewhere cannot be determined from the text. It is to be noted that Beowulf's sympathetic concern for rehabilitating Unferth takes on special poignancy when we recall that the hero himself was once held in low esteem by his fellow men (2183ff).

This hypothesis as to what Unferth's character and his relation to Beowulf may be would accord with my reading of the Breca-tale as a semi-serious affair and also has a certain inner consistency. Moreover, the relation I suggest here between hero and poltroon is much like that described in another narrative of the Danish court in Hrothgar's time – the *Hrolfs saga kraka*, chapter 23. There we are told that the royal house at Leire is plagued by a nocturnal monster, and when the bear-like hero Boðvarr Bjarki arrives on the scene prior to doing battle with the monster, he encounters the despised coward Hottr. Boðvarr treats Hottr roughly, but eventually, in the course of purging the Danish court of the monster, he regenerates the coward, just as Beowulf regenerated Unferth. In an incident involving the lending of a sword called *Gullinhjalti* (which scholars have noted is cognate with the *gylden hilt* of *Beowulf*, 1677), Boðvarr contrives to gain some esteem for Hottr from the monster-slaying, and the erstwhile buffoon gains a new reputation and a new name. Conceivably we have here a remote echo of the interplay between Beowulf and Unferth.

The characterization of Hottr in the saga demonstrates that a Germanic author could conceive of a relation such as I have suggested for Beowulf and Unferth, but it should be apparent from the skeptical treatment which I have given to analogues in the first part of this paper that I would be unwilling to regard the parallel as probative evidence of the Old English poet's intentions. Indeed, as I have said before, I find the data insufficient to warrant any definitive interpretation of Unferth. He may be, as some have thought, a serious, sinister character, but the evidence for this is weak, and it is at least as likely that he is a kind of jester, as *BTD* suggests, or that he is a fellow of low reputation in the court like Hottr in the saga. Given the uncertainty as to his character, it is impossible to argue with much conviction from the evidence of the swimming-tale which he introduces into the poem. It is conceivable that the Breca story is serious, but it could also be a wild yarn spun by the envious *þyle* or a flyting, or Unferth's effort to start a lying match.

The undue importance which has been accorded the Breca episode in the past is in part a legacy of the early mythologizing critics like Müllenhoff and Sarrazin, who viewed the swimming feat as a slightly veiled *Naturmythus* and hence thought it comparable in importance with the dragon fight and the contests with the Grendel kin.[43] The predisposition to see the Breca adventure as much bigger than life may have been nurtured by Panzer's carefully collected saga-parallels. Troubling aspects of the Unferth episode as a whole could always be shrugged off with the explanation that "they must be looked upon as an inheritance from the older legends which had come down from a ruder age,"[44] and this attitude may have discouraged close scrutiny of the

---

[43] See W. W. Lawrence, *Beowulf and Epic Tradition* (Cambridge, MA, 1928), pp. 151–2. Cf. Klaeber, *Beowulf and the Fight at Finnsburg*, p. 147, n. 2.

[44] Lawrence, *Beowulf and Epic Tradition*, p. 153.

textual mainstays of the received interpretation – such as the name and office of Unferth as well as his motivation, the precise terms in which Beowulf describes his own feat, and the manuscript evidence for his threat of hell in his retort. If the earlier interpretations of these matters have not been replaced here with indubitably surer and superior ones, I believe they have at least been shown to be less certain than scholars had previously assumed. If so, this must qualify one's interpretation of the evidence for astounding feats in the Breca episode, just as the textual realities of lines 1494–6 and 2354–68 must be taken into account in assessing the supposedly marvelous elements earlier in the poem.

Afterword 1992

Several scholars have contributed to the discussion of points raised in this essay. Karl P. Wentersdorf further examines the textual basis for supposed marvels in the Breca episode, as does James Earl.[1] These studies suggest a growing consensus for a less extravagant interpretation of the adventure with Breca than earlier scholars have offered. Roberta Frank provides a subtle and persuasive analysis of the semantic play involved in Unferth's taunting speech.[2] John C. Pope[3] accepts my restoration of *gehedde* and acknowledges that it can mean "cared for," as I suggest, but he says that the adoption of this meaning results in a reading which "is weighted toward a negative view of Unferth's concern for glory" (p. 179), and so he prefers to render it as a subjunctive meaning "could care for." He translates lines 503–5 "for he would not grant that any other man on earth could ever, under the heavens, care more for glorious deeds than he himself did" (p. 180), a rendering which allows a more positive view of Unferth.

Stanley B. Greenfield objects to my calling attention to textual problems underlying the supposedly marvelous elements in the characterization of the hero, for he prefers to read *Beowulf* as a "conflict between good monsters and bad monsters" (p. 297) rather than as the more sophisticated poem which I take it to be.[4] Essentially his argument seems to be that we can continue to read the poem as a simple conflict between good monsters and bad monsters if we will just return to the original interpretations of those words and passages whose long-assumed meanings I had shown to be questionable. John D. Niles dismisses my essay, which he characterizes as an "attempt to do away with marvelous elements in the poem."[5] Apparently he failed to read the first two sentences in the essay.

[1] Wentersdorf, "Beowulf's adventure with Breca," *Studies in Philology*, 72 (1975), 140–66, esp. pp. 162ff; Earl, "Beowulf's rowing-match," *Neophilologus*, 63 (1979), 285–90.
[2] Frank, "'Mere' and 'sund': two sea-changes in *Beowulf*," in *Modes of Interpretation in Old English Literature*, ed. Phyllis Rugg Brown et al. (Toronto, 1986), pp. 154–72, esp. pp. 159–65.
[3] Pope, "*Beowulf* 505, 'gehedde,' and the pretensions of Unferth," *Modes of Interpretation in Old English Literature*, pp. 173–87.
[4] Greenfield, "A touch of the monstrous in the hero, or Beowulf re-marvelized," *English Studies*, 63 (1982), 294–300.
[5] Niles, *"Beowulf": the poem and its tradition* (Cambridge, MA, 1983), p. 261, n. 5.

3
History, Religion, Culture: The Background Necessary for Teaching *Beowulf*

History

The scholar of *Beowulf* is concerned with three distinct chronological periods that bear on an understanding of the poem. First, there is the time and place of the poem's action, the late fifth and early sixth centuries in northern Europe. Then there is the period on the island of England centuries later when an English poet, looking back over the dark, estranging expanses of time, composed a heroic poem about his distant ancestors on the continent. Finally, there is the late Anglo-Saxon period, around AD 1000, when scribes copied the poem *Beowulf* into the manuscript that, among the many manuscripts of the poem that probably once existed, happens to survive today. Especially important for the student to remember is the time between the period of the poem's action and the period when it was composed, for this separation makes *Beowulf* a profoundly retrospective, archaistic poem. The gap between the time of composition and the time of the scribe's last recording of the poem is important mainly for a scholarly understanding of the state of the text rather than for an understanding of the poem itself. It is a gap to be noted by the teacher and the scholar but not dwelled on by students lest they lose their focus on that more important contrast of historical periods, the age of Beowulf and his people as opposed to the age of the *Beowulf* poet and his people.

How much detail about these periods do students need to master? Unless they are studying *Beowulf* as a vehicle for learning history rather than as a poem to be understood and enjoyed for itself, historical details are probably not as important as a general sense of each period. We are not sure just how much the poet knew about the earlier period. Francis B. Gummere believed that to the Anglo-Saxon poet "the figures of his continental legends, even when historical, had no chronology."[1] According to this view, the *Beowulf* poet would have

Reprinted from *Approaches to Teaching "Beowulf"* ed. Jess B. Bessinger, Jr, and Robert F. Yeager (New York, 1984), pp. 107–22.

[1] Gummere, *The Oldest English Epic* (New York, 1909), p. 192.

conceived of all the characters as having lived simply long, long ago, with no thought given to their specific and respective dates. Not all would agree with Gummere, but it is probably true that no strict chronology was sought by the poet for the characters of his narrative. As for the details of the period when the poem was composed, these will be impossible to establish before and unless we can establish the precise date of the poem's composition. And the date of composition now seems more maddingly uncertain than ever, Ashley Crandell Amos having demonstrated that traditional reliance on linguistic dating of Old English poems has been generally misguided,[2] and the symposium papers on *The Dating of "Beowulf"*, edited by Colin Chase, having shown that scholars of the highest authority can reach no agreement on even an approximate date of composition.[3] Indeed, some of these papers (notably that by Kevin Kiernan) move the date of composition forward so close to the date of the scribe's copying that we might have to say that there are, for students at least, but two historical periods that require consideration: northern Europe around the turn of the sixth century and Anglo-Saxon England in general. Such a broad conception of the historical background of poet and audience might seem inadequate for professional scholars, but for students it is preferable to a distracting immersion in the minutiae of scholarly debate over linguistic forms and paleographical details.

The Historical Background of the Poem's Action

According to contemporary historical accounts, a Scandinavian king named Hygelac lost his life between AD 521 and 526 in the course of a military expedition against West Germanic peoples (Franks, Frisians, and Hetware) living in the realm of Theodoric, king of the Austrasian Franks. This Hygelac is mentioned often in the poem *Beowulf* as the king whom Beowulf served loyally for many years, accompanied on his expedition against the Franks, and ultimately followed on the throne. Extrapolating from the date of this historical event described in the poem, we can determine that Beowulf would have been born around AD 495, become king of the Geatas in 533, and died in the last quarter of the sixth century. Hygelac's fatal raid is described four times in the poem, and the repetition and elaboration of the event give it symbolic resonance, as if it is meant to represent fate working through history, a tragic error that presages the doom of the nation. This artistic use of a historical event is representative of the poet's consistent use of the past as both the subject and the medium of his poetry and supports Morton Bloomfield's contention that

---

[2] Amos, *Linguistic Means of Determining the Dates of Old English Literary Texts*, Medieval Academy Books, 90 (Cambridge, MA, 1980).

[3] *The Dating of "Beowulf"*, ed. Colin Chase (Toronto, 1981).

Beowulf "belongs to the category of *historical* works and in its reciting, the tradition of society was being carried on."[4]

The Danish kingdom during the reign of Hrothgar is the setting of the poem after the prologue about Scyld Scefing. There are no reliable historical documents from this period, but a variety of medieval Scandinavian sources in prose and poetry discuss kings Scyld, Healfdane, and Hrothgar as well as the younger generation of Danes whom Beowulf meets in Heorot, such as Hrethric and Hrothulf. The legendary history concerning these characters interacts importantly with hints and allusions of the *Beowulf* poet and helps us complete the sense of what Wealhtheow says when she anxiously insists that Hrothulf will not forget his debt of gratitude toward the reigning king's family when Hrothgar's sons need support (1180–7). "By rather complicated, but quite unforced, fitting together of various Scandinavian authorities, we find that Hrothulf deposed and slew his cousin Hrethric."[5]

Attention to historical sources, then, reveals the tragic irony resident in Wealhtheow's speech and explains the *Beowulf* poet's (as well as the *Widsith* poet's) implicit statements that peace between Hrothgar and his nephew Hrothulf was but temporary. Scholars who, following Kenneth Sisam,[6] refuse to accept the dark implications here would seem determined to turn a deaf ear to the tone and words of the poem. Anyone who does not hear anxiety in Wealhtheow's speech about how Hrothulf will act toward her offspring must think that Mark Antony genuinely believes Caesar's murderers to be honorable men. In the legendary history of Denmark Hrothulf, not Hrethric, takes the Danish throne after Hrothgar, and Saxo Grammaticus notes that this happened only after Hrothulf slew Røricus (= Hrethric). Wealhtheow had good reason to be anxious.

Much of the circumstantial detail in the poem is shown by parallel sources from the continent to be part of the legendary history of Scandinavia and not the English poet's invention. Hrothgar (and later Hrothulf) ruled from a royal settlement whose present location can with fair confidence be fixed as the modern Danish village of Leire, the actual location of Heorot. The strife between Danes and Heathobards, which Beowulf predicts so astutely in lines 2020–69, was well known to Saxo Grammaticus and other medieval chroniclers on the continent, and these sources confirm the accuracy of Beowulf's prescient speculation as to the unhappy results of Freawaru's marriage to Ingeld. Modern readers of *Beowulf* must be aware that what happens in the Danish episode of *Beowulf* is part of traditional lore and that the lore at times

---

[4] Bloomfield, "Understanding Old English poetry," in *Essays and Explorations: studies in ideas, language, and literature* (Cambridge, MA, 1970), p. 70 (my emphasis).

[5] R. W. Chambers, *"Beowulf": an introduction to the study of the poem*, 3rd edn with a supplement by C. L. Wrenn (Cambridge, 1959), p. 26.

[6] Sisam, *The Structure of "Beowulf"* (Oxford, 1965), pp. 80–2.

spells out the full meaning of the actions in the poem. But a detailed study of early Danish history is hardly necessary for the student whose primary concern is *Beowulf*, since editors and translators of the poem place the crucial historical facts at the reader's disposal in notes and commentary. Those who are curious about fuller details of the Danish background can turn to Chambers's excellent syntheses in *"Beowulf": an introduction to the study of the poem* (see n. 5).

There seems to be widespread agreement now that Beowulf's tribe, the Geatas, are to be identified with the Götar, a people who lived in the southern portion of Sweden and who gave their name to the modern Swedish city of Göteborg, among other places. Early historians like Ptolemy (second century AD) and Procopius (sixth century AD) identify the Götar as a large and independent power, but in later reports they appear to have declined into a dependency of the Swedish nation. The *Beowulf* poet tells us that the Geatas are a flourishing power with Hygelac as their king, and another Anglo-Saxon source supplies the same information: the *Liber Monstrorum*, a Latin work of early English origin, tells us that Hygelac was king of the Geatas and that his body lies near the mouth of the Rhine, a detail that tallies with the *Beowulf* poet's description of Hygelac's death in the realm of Theodoric. Historical sources have nothing to say about a Beowulf being king of the Geatas, and the likelihood is that his is a fictional story inserted in the midst of a more sober historical narrative about a verifiable nation of Geatas who lived near the Swedes at the time of the action of the poem.

In *Beowulf* we read of much strife between the Geatas and the Swedes, and Scandinavian records verify both the conflicts of the Swedes at this time and the names of their rulers – Ohthere, Onela, Eadgils, and others. The records are not specific about the role the Geatas play in these wars or about their ultimate fate, but the speakers in the poem are very specific about the fate of the Geatas: Wiglaf, the messenger, and the woman mourning at Beowulf's funeral all agree that the nation faces disaster once King Beowulf is dead. Knowing the dismal future that history holds for the Geatas enables us to complete the poem's tragic meaning: heroic splendor and the values of the pre-Christian world are unavailing before the destructive forces of a brutal age; Beowulf's awesome achievement in protecting his people must end with his death, after which the forces of history so carefully delineated in the poem will turn inexorably against the nation whose moment of grandeur the poem has celebrated. Such knowledge as the Anglo-Saxons had of Geatish history would appear to have borne out this representation of events by the poet. As we have seen, the Anglo-Saxon author of the *Liber Monstrorum* affirms that Hygelac, king of the Geatas, was leading his army against powerful neighboring realms at the time when *Beowulf* also says he was doing so. But later, when the Latin history of Orosius was translated into Old English, during the period 890–9, the scholarly Anglo-Saxon who prepared the prefatory description of Europe "as it was known in the second half of the ninth century"[7] appears to know nothing of a Geatish realm, although in other respects his knowledge of Scandinavian lands and people is full and precise. Evidently the Geatas experienced a decline after the time of Hygelac and Beowulf and were absorbed into Sweden – as if in fulfillment of the prophecy in *Beowulf*, 2922–3007, that the Swedes and other enemies would fall upon the Geatish nation as soon as they heard that King Beowulf had fallen.

Kenneth Sisam, in an influential argument in *The Structure of "Beowulf"*,[8] has pointed out that some Scandinavian sources indicate an awareness of the Geatas "as a distinct people" well after the period when *Beowulf* seems to indicate that they were overrun by the Swedes. From this Sisam reasons that no tragic fate awaited the Geatas following Beowulf's fall and that hence the poem has a brighter ending than scholars had assumed. But for readers of *Beowulf*, late Scandinavian sources and even the facts of Scandinavian history are irrelevant: the history that matters for *Beowulf* is the history that the poet knew and used in the poem. Records surviving from Anglo-Saxon England, as we have seen, do not show any awareness of a flourishing nation of Geatas after the time of Beowulf. Moreover, the poet is more explicit about the fate of the Geatas than Sisam has allowed. Just before the messenger utters his long and circumstantial description of how the Geatas will be overcome by their enemies, the poet is careful to announce, in his own authorial voice, that the things the messenger is going to say are true: "he spoke to them all truthfully" (2899). Again, at the close of the speech, the authorial voice intrudes to declare, "nor did he much lie in his words or his prophecies" (3029–30) – that is, he spoke only the truth. (I use the translation by Donaldson, who renders *wyrda ne worda*, rightly I think, as "words or . . . prophecies.") Near the end of the poem the dire prophecies are repeated by the woman leading the funeral dirge, who laments that evil days, the horror of warfare, killings, and captivity await the nation now that the king is dead (3153–4). It is significant that this prediction is assigned by the poet to a woman, for in Germanic society (as Tacitus makes clear in his *Germania*) women were credited with special powers of prophecy, a belief exemplified by the *Beowulf* poet himself when he has Wealhtheow express such accurate forebodings about future trouble from Hrothulf.[9] Whatever late Scandinavian chroniclers may say, then, the *Beowulf* poet clearly assumed that history held a bleak future for the Geatas, and he used this assumed downfall of his hero's nation as an important part of his narrative strategy. If modern historians construct from sources at their disposal a different fate for the Geatas, their revisionism may have historical interest, but it has no bearing on our reading of *Beowulf*, just as it would have no bearing on

---

[7] *The Old English Orosius*, ed. Janet Bately, EETS s.s. 6 (London, 1980), p. 166.
[8] Sisam, *Structure*, pp. 51–9.
[9] See "The prescient woman in Old English literature," pp. 155–63 below.

our reading of *Macbeth* if modern historians should determine from documentary evidence that Duncan died of natural causes. The protagonist of Shakespeare's play would still be a regicide, and the play would still be a tragedy. Modern revisions of history are not retroactive to the old poets' uses of the history they knew.

The World of the Poet and His Audience

In order to understand *Paradise Lost* it is not enough to know about the biblical history out of which the poem was made; one needs to know something about John Milton's historical context in seventeenth-century England as well. The reader of *Beowulf*, for similar reasons, needs to have some sense of the thought world inhabited by the Anglo-Saxon poet and his audience. What attitudes and ideas did they share concerning paganism, kingship, runes, cremation, battle boasts, oaths of allegiance, vows of revenge, and other subjects that figure prominently in *Beowulf*? Here once again we are vexed by the problem of the poem's indeterminable date. Are we to concern ourselves with England of the early seventh century, when H. M. Chadwick thought the poem came into being,[10] or with a vastly different England of the eleventh century, when Kevin Kiernan thinks the poem was composed?[11] For present purposes it seems best, once again, to evade the question by limiting our attention to more general aspects of the period and eschewing details of history. All but a few partisans of extremely early or extremely late dating would in any event accept the limits AD 750 to 950 for the time of *Beowulf*'s composition, and most of the generalizations offered here would hold true for even this broad stretch of time.

For readers of *Beowulf*, the most important source of information about the values prevailing at the time the poem was composed is the poet himself, insofar as he declares his views. When in lines 178–88 he laments the horror and hopelessness of pagan worship, we may be sure he is expressing an attitude that his audience shared with him, whether they lived in the eighth, ninth, or tenth centuries. Sermons, penitentials, and other writings of the Anglo-Saxons, early and late, condemn all pagan practices. The poet's praise of loyalty to kin (for example, 2600–1), his admiration for good kings and loyal subjects (for example, 11, 20–5, 3174–7), his sense of the importance of being as good as one's word (758–60) are attitudes that accord with those expressed in many Anglo-Saxon writings outside *Beowulf*.

On the other hand, certain practices and speeches of characters in the poem would definitely not agree with the values of Christian Anglo-Saxons. Beowulf's speech to Hrothgar declaring that the best thing a person can do in this life is to achieve fame (1387–9) would jar rudely with the ideal of Christian

[10] Chadwick, *The Heroic Age* (Cambridge, 1912), p. 56.
[11] Kiernan, *"Beowulf" and the "Beowulf" Manuscript* (New Brunswick, NJ, 1981).

humility, as would Beowulf's concern that he be given a splendid funeral and a prominent resting place that will proclaim his name and renown to the seafarers passing by (2802–8, 3140). ("Let one not seek the empty renown of a famous name on earth," said Augustine, and many Anglo-Saxon homilists emphasize the vanity of worldly fame.) The description of Beowulf's cremation (as well as that of the dead warriors in the Finnsburg episode) may seem to the modern reader like mere vivid detail included to enhance the scenery, but to Christians living in the poet's time the implications of cremation were darkly ominous. Burning the dead is a pagan practice specifically forbidden to Christians, and Charlemagne's Saxon capitulary of 785 reveals just how determined Christian rulers were to prevent pagan cremations and burials:

> Whoever delivers the bodies of the dead to the flames, following the pagan rite, and reduces the bones to cinders, will be condemned to death. ... We ordain that the bodies of Christian Saxons are to be borne to our church's cemeteries and not to the tumuli of the pagans.[12]

Similarly, the sermons and penitentials of the Anglo-Saxons inveigh repeatedly against the pagan practice of observing omens, and this suggests that when the poet has Beowulf's first expedition launched with a reading of the omens (204), he is reminding his audience that the heroic society described in the poem is pagan.

Some aspects of Beowulfian society that modern readers might suspect to be at variance with the poet's Christian values, however, may not have been. Vengeance is urgently recommended as a noble course of action by Beowulf in lines 1384–5, and vengeance is practiced and praised elsewhere in the poem. Alien though this behavior is to strict Christian doctrine, Dorothy Whitelock, in her valuable study *The Audience of "Beowulf"*,[13] has shown that Christianity did not bring an end to vengeance-taking in Anglo-Saxon society, that such behavior came to be accepted as a necessity and received the express approval of the clergy as well as of the laity. Since runes originated in pagan Germanic times and have been associated with divination, the runes engraved on the sword hilt Beowulf gives to Hrothgar may be thought to carry alarming connotations of paganism. But while rune writing would be historically appropriate for Beowulf's pre-Christian society, the Christian Anglo-Saxon scribes and rune masters had adapted this writing system so completely to Christian uses that mention of runes in the poem would hardly bring gasps of horror from a contemporary audience. Even the audience's attitude toward paganism itself should not be conceived as simply one of horrified disgust. In an important essay called "The pagan coloring of *Beowulf*," Larry D. Benson

---

[12] Quoted in Pierre Riché, *Daily Life in the World of Charlemagne*, tr. Jo Ann McNamara (Philadelphia, 1978), pp. 181–2.

[13] Whitelock, *The Audience of "Beowulf"*, rev. edn (Oxford, 1958), pp. 13–19.

traces the growth and complication of Anglo-Saxon attitudes toward Germanic pagans as the English mission to the continent brought increasing contacts between Christian Anglo-Saxons and their non-Christian cousins in Europe.[14] Compassion rather than revulsion was often the dominant sentiment Anglo-Saxons felt toward the as yet unconverted, and occasionally they even expressed admiration for those who, without benefit of Christianity, still managed to comport themselves in a manner sometimes superior to that of the Christian English. Recent studies have shown further how the poet of *Beowulf* may have drawn on the pagan Viking society dwelling in parts of England as he formed his conception of the Germanic heroic age. The skillful essays by R. I. Page and Roberta Frank in *The Dating of "Beowulf"*[15] reveal how such intercultural contacts might have taken place. Yet other scholars have emphasized the possible influence on *Beowulf* of the traditional Irish tolerance of a pagan past.[16] None of this should be construed as meaning that the *Beowulf* poet may have had a nostalgic preference for paganism over Christianity; such a preference would have been as abhorrent to him as it was to the Anglo-Saxon churchmen who, from the beginning to the end of the period, denounced those who reverted to paganism or who aped the pagan customs of the Vikings resident in England. But we should also not assume that Anglo-Saxons were insensitive to the fact that pagans were civilized people capable of goodness despite their tragic ignorance of Christianity.

Beyond these general aspects of the thought world of Anglo-Saxon England, we should like to have specific knowledge of the cultural environment from which *Beowulf* emerged. Was the poet a churchman or a layman? For what audience was the poem intended? Did poet and audience conceive of the poem as relating primarily to contemporary Christian doctrine or to the themes and attitudes of the old heroic tradition? Scholars' answers to these questions show a rich disparity of opinion, of which the following three views may be representative.

First, some see *Beowulf* as essentially a secular English poem written for an audience knowledgeable about Christianity but not concerned exclusively with religion. Dorothy Whitelock, in *The Audience of "Beowulf"*, gives authoritative expression to the view that the poem was composed for a lay audience of the privileged class that, though not steeped in Christian doctrine, was familiar with the basic tenets of Christianity. In an important essay building on her

---

[14] Benson, "The pagan coloring of *Beowulf*," in *Old English Poetry: fifteen essays*, ed. Robert P. Creed (Providence, 1967), pp. 199–213.

[15] Page, "The audience of *Beowulf* and the Vikings," pp. 113–22, and Frank, "Skaldic verse and the date of *Beowulf*," pp. 123–39, in Chase, *The Dating of "Beowulf"*.

[16] See for example Charles Donahue, "*Beowulf*, Ireland, and the natural good," *Traditio*, 7 (1949–51), 263–77, and "*Beowulf* and Christian tradition: a reconsideration from a Celtic stance," *Traditio*, 21 (1965), 55–116.

work, Patrick Wormald argues that the secularized, aristocratic monasteries of which Alcuin, Bede, and other ecclesiastics complain were the institutions most likely to have provided the intended audience of the poem, and he shows that many if not all the basic elements of *Beowulf* are explicable in terms of such a context for the poem.[17] A second view, that *Beowulf* was intended to be read primarily as a Christian document and in terms of Christian allegory, is represented most fully by W. F. Bolton's *Alcuin and "Beowulf": an eighth-century view*, where we are given a thoroughgoing exposition of the way in which the learned cleric Alcuin would probably have read the poem. To some extent Alcuin's reading of literature, as Bolton presents it, seems to resemble that of D. W. Robertson, Jr, who feels that Christian instruction must be present in all serious literature of the Middle Ages and that where such instruction is not apparent in the literal narrative it must be present in allegorical form. Finally, Alain Renoir, in a series of wide-ranging literary-comparative studies, urges that *Beowulf* should be read in the context of western European heroic-age literature at large. Renoir's studies are in a way an oral-formulaic sophistication of the earlier contention of H. M. Chadwick that *Beowulf* needs to be judged alongside epic poetry from around the world. They constitute a needed reminder that we must see the poem in a transnational, generic context as well as in its historical context.[18]

No amount of irenic scholarly diplomacy will succeed in reconciling completely the approaches of Wormald, Bolton, Renoir, and the many other interpreters of *Beowulf*, but fair-minded students will probably find something persuasive in all of them. Readers coming to *Beowulf* for the first time should be made aware of the existence of competing conceptualizations of the poem in its own time and should be encouraged to measure each approach against their own experience of the text. Those who wish to make their own synthesis of the poem and its cultural context can learn about the historical background of Anglo-Saxon England by sampling the works listed in the chapter "The instructor's Library" in Bessinger and Yeager's volume on the teaching of *Beowulf*.[19]

---

[17] Wormald, "Bede, *Beowulf*, and the conversion of the Anglo-Saxon aristocracy," in *Bede and Anglo-Saxon England*, ed. Robert T. Farrell (Oxford, 1978), pp. 32–95.

[18] Bolton, *Alcuin and "Beowulf": an eighth-century view* (New Brunswick, NJ, 1978); Robertson, like Chadwick, argues his view throughout his publications; see especially Robertson's "The doctrine of charity in medieval literary gardens," *Speculum*, 26 (1951), 24–49. For a sense of Renoir's humane and witty scholarship, which is always distinguished by its sanity, fairness, and courtesy, see *A Key to Old Poems: the oral-formulaic approach to the interpretation of West-Germanic verse* (University Park, PA, 1988).

[19] *Approaches to Teaching "Beowulf"*, ed. Jess B. Bessinger, Jr, and Robert F. Yeager (New York, 1984), pp. 17–30.

Religion

As is clear from the historical context of the poem, two distinct religious systems are operative in *Beowulf*. The characters in the story are obviously pagan, but the poet narrating the story is manifestly Christian. The Germanic tribes on the continent in the fifth and sixth centuries had not yet come into contact with Christianity, as any Anglo-Saxon would have known. In lines 175-88 the poet tells us that the Danes to whose aid Beowulf comes prayed to heathen gods for assistance and would be damned for their ignorance. The Geatas' omen reading and Beowulf's cremation, as we have just seen, are other indications that the poet is careful to portray his characters as what they historically were: pre-Christian. On the other hand, he does not shock his audience by naming the pagan gods and portraying his characters engaged in the particular abominations that scandalized Christians throughout the Anglo-Saxon period. If he had shown his characters invoking Thor, casting spells, exposing unwanted children, or practicing ritual sacrifice, he could probably not have engaged sufficient audience sympathy for his story to win a hearing. Beowulf and Hrothgar accordingly refer to the deity with words like "god," "lord," or "the all-powerful one." They do not use designations that would be appropriate only for Christians, such as "Christ," "Savior," or "Redeemer," and they never refer to angels, the Virgin Mary, the Holy Ghost, the saints, and other specifically Christian subjects that Anglo-Saxon poets regularly treat in poems that have Christian settings. This deliberate blurring in the mode of religious reference allows the characters of *Beowulf* to attain some dignity and even nobility in the eyes of the Christian audience without belying their pre-Christian status.

When he speaks in his own voice, the poet alludes to the Bible, to salvation and damnation, to the devil, and to other Christian topics, but even then he is usually not specific and emphatic in his allusions to Christianity. His biblical references are limited to the pre-Mosaic Old Testament, and his allusions to the deity are muted and general. By making them so, he avoids emphasizing the contrast between his own religion and that of his characters. This dictional restraint in no way implies that the poet's Christian belief is primitive or half-hearted; it is a matter of literary skill and tact used to unite rather than divide the audience and its ancestry.[20]

Commentators on *Beowulf* usually allow Alcuin to represent Anglo-Saxon Christianity in its confrontation with *Beowulf*. In a letter to monks of Lindisfarne in AD 797 reprimanding them for listening to ancient pagan tales rather

---

[20] For a fuller treatment of the complex religious situation in the poem, see my *"Beowulf" and the Appositive Style* (Knoxville, TN, 1985), especially chapter 2.

than to Bible readings when they supped, the stern churchman from York says,

> Let the word of God be read at the meal of the clergy. There it is proper to hear a reader, not a harp-player; to hear sermons of the church fathers, not songs of the laity. What has Ingeld to do with Christ? The house is narrow; it cannot hold both. The King of Heaven will have nothing to do with so-called kings who are heathen and damned, for that King reigns in Heaven eternally, while the heathen one is damned and laments in Hell.[21]

This uncompromising, Augustinian view of Christian salvation was no doubt widely held among Anglo-Saxon ecclesiastics, and Alcuin's specific reference to Ingeld, a character who figures in the poem *Beowulf*, as being the kind of subject in which devout Anglo-Saxons should take no interest, gives cause for wonder that a poem like *Beowulf* should have survived at all in such an inhospitable intellectual climate. But we should perhaps not think of the religious views of all Christian Anglo-Saxons as being uniformly identical with those of Alcuin. Benson's demonstration that a saintly man like Boniface could admire the virtues of Germanic heathens should be recalled, as should Charles Donahue's essays mentioned above, where we learn that Irish thinkers contemporary with the *Beowulf* poet took a much more hopeful view of the destiny of pagans who, though deprived of revelation, behaved well according to an instinctive sense of what is good in human conduct.[22] Morton W. Bloomfield has observed that the poet's limitation of his biblical references to pre-Mosaic times implies a kind of analogy between patriarchs like Abraham (who lived before the revelation of the law to Moses as well as before New Testament revelation) and the virtuous pagans of the Germanic world.[23] Both Abraham and Beowulf led their lives as well as they could without Judeo-Christian revelation; if the one gained salvation, is it not possible that the other might?

If such questionings seem overbold for a medieval poet, we might recall that *Beowulf* was composed in "the privacy of the vernacular," as Thomas D. Hill, in a different connection, has interestingly termed Old English poetic language.[24] That is, serious theological reasoning was normally conducted in Latin and was subject to the scrutiny of Christian scholars throughout the Western world.

[21] For the Latin original see *Bibliotheca rerum Germanicarum*, ed. Philipp Jaffé, 6: *Monumenta Alcuiniana*, ed. W. Wattenbach and E. Dümmler (Berlin, 1873), p. 357.

[22] For the essays by Benson and Donahue see above, nn. 14 and 16.

[23] Bloomfield, "Patristics and Old English literature: notes on some poems," *Comparative Literature*, 14 (1962), 36–43.

[24] Hill, "The fall of angels and man in the Old English *Genesis B*," in *Anglo-Saxon Poetry: essays in appreciation for John C. McGalliard*, ed. Lewis E. Nicholson and Dolores Frese (Notre Dame, IN, 1975), p. 290.

But when one wrote poetry in a vernacular like Old English, one was addressing a much more intimate audience, an audience prepared for the relaxed explorations of local poetry rather than the rigors of theological debate in an international language. Residents in the aristocratic and secularized monasteries where Wormald conjectures that *Beowulf* had its origin and its audience would be naturally inclined to speculate wistfully over the destiny of their pagan ancestors despite the stern orthodoxy to which Alcuin summons them in his Latin epistle.

Culture

Among the questions often raised by scholars concerning the cultural background of *Beowulf* are: Was the text orally composed, or was it composed in writing, which implies the possibility of long reflection and revision? Was the poet's method and matter influenced by Celtic literature? Did he know and use Vergil? Important though these questions are, discussion of them would probably do little to improve students' comprehension and appreciation of the poem in a literature class. Exponents of oral composition, who are fewer in number and increasingly on the defensive, have never succeeded in proving their case that *Beowulf* is the result of more or less instinctive oral improvisation rather than a highly conscious literary composition, but neither have the skeptics been able to disprove it conclusively. Pierre Le Gentil's response to disputes over the possible oral origin of *Roland* may suffice for the general reader of *Beowulf*: "Since it is so sure, it hardly matters whether this [poet's] intelligence is more instinctive than conscious."[25] The question of Celtic influence, too, remains unresolved: only loose parallels have been adduced as internal evidence, and speculation over possible cultural contacts constitutes almost the only explanation as to how the Celtic themes would have reached the *Beowulf* poet. Similarly loose parallels have been cited to prove Vergilian influence, but few scholars have found them convincing. The most interesting discussion is Theodore Andersson, *Early Epic Scenery*, which finds suggestive similarities in the modes of narration in the two poems.[26] But scholars at large do not regard the connection between *The Aeneid* and *Beowulf* as proved.

Instead of reviewing scholarly investigations of the cultural background of *Beowulf*, the general reader may find it useful to examine a few of the instances where a theme or subject in *Beowulf* had markedly different cultural significance for the poet and his audience than it has for the modern student of the poem. Consideration of six such topics will help readers free themselves from their own cultural preconceptions and project themselves into the imaginative

[25] Le Gentil, *The Song of Roland*, tr. Francis F. Beer (Cambridge, MA, 1969), p. 101.
[26] Andersson, *Early Epic Scenery* (Ithaca, NY, 1976).

world of *Beowulf*: love and friendship, shame culture and guilt culture, vengeance, gift giving, descriptions of artifacts and nature, and fate.

Our first instance of a cultural conflict between Anglo-Saxon and modern worlds is not precisely a subject dealt with in *Beowulf* but one that is conspicuously missing from it. Although women as well as men figure importantly in the narrative and although a husband's love (or the cooling of his love) is mentioned once (2065–6), romantic passion between the sexes is absent from *Beowulf*, as it is absent from most Old English poetry, while feelings of friendship and loyalty between men are surprisingly intense. C. S. Lewis in *The Allegory of Love* has characterized the Germanic attitude toward love and friendship in the Middle Ages:

> "Love," in our sense of the word, is as absent from the literature of the Dark Ages as from that of classical antiquity.... The deepest of worldly emotions in this period is the love of man for man, the mutual love of warriors who die together fighting against odds, and the affection between vassal and lord. We shall never understand this last, if we think of it in the light of our own moderated and impersonal loyalties.... The feeling is more passionate and less ideal than our patriotism.... Of romance, of reverence for women, of the idealizing imagination exercised about sex, there is hardly a hint. The centre of gravity is elsewhere – in the hopes and fears of religion, or in the clean and happy fidelities of the feudal hall. But, as we have seen, these male affections – though wholly free from the taint that hangs about "friendship" in the ancient world – were themselves lover-like; in their intensity, their wilful exclusion of other values, and their uncertainty, they provided an exercise of the spirit not wholly unlike that which later ages have found in "love."[27]

Lewis may overdramatize the distinction between medieval and modern attitudes, but the distinction is there and must be remembered when we read of Beowulf's farewell from Hrothgar (1870–80) or of his expression of affection for Hygelac (2149–51). We should also remember Lewis's words when we read the description of Beowulf at the end of the poem. Readers have often assumed that since the hero has no heir and since no wife is mentioned we are to understand that he remained solitary and celibate throughout his life. It is quite possible, however, that the poet simply felt that Beowulf's marital status was of insufficient interest to warrant mention in the poem.

In *The Greeks and the Irrational*[28] E. R. Dodds adopts the anthropologists' terms "shame culture" and "guilt culture" to explain an important difference between the outlook of the heroic age and a later day. The highest good in a society like that of Homer or Beowulf is public esteem and the greatest evil is

---

[27] Lewis, *The Allegory of Love* (London, 1936), pp. 9–10.
[28] Dodds, *The Greeks and the Irrational* (Berkeley, CA, 1951), pp. 17–18.

public disgrace. *Dom biðˀ selest*, according to an Old English maxim, which one might translate "Favorable judgment by others is the best thing there is." Beowulf says as much in lines 1386–9. The public dispute with Unferth, the obsession with fame, the hero's concern for his memorial after his death, all should be viewed in the light of the fact that Beowulf lived in a shame culture. The Christian society of the poet and his audience, on the other hand, is a guilt culture, where the highest good is the enjoyment of a quiet conscience. In the poem *Beowulf*, then, we have a shame culture as viewed through the eyes of a guilt culture, and at one point the contrast between the two comes to the surface. When Beowulf asks himself whether the dragon's attacks can be the result of some unrecognized wrongdoing on his part, the poet observes, "His breast within was troubled with dark thoughts, *which was not usual with him*" (2331–2). The heroic world is a world of action and of public recognition for deeds performed, not of brooding and soul searching.

One form of public esteem sought by Germanic man is revealed in the ritual of revenge. Each man sought to demonstrate that injury done to him or to any of his people would have to be remedied or vengeance would be taken. Francis Bacon defined revenge as "a kind of wild justice," but in the ancient Germanic world it was an exceedingly precise and elaborate kind of justice.[29] Traditional laws prescribed that if a person is killed or injured by another, then the injuring party must offer to the victim's lord an amount of compensation precisely calibrated according to the predetermined worth of the victim. Otherwise life will be taken in talion for life. This system of organized retribution protected the weak against injury and the strong against loss of esteem. When the system breaks down, the result is extreme anguish – as when the Danes have to suffer Grendel's depredations without restitution (154–8) or when Hrethel must see his son die unavenged (2442–3). In these instances the survivors must bitterly accept their bereavement with no outlet for grief.

Another feature of Beowulfian society that is related to the importance of public esteem is the giving of gifts. Scene after scene in the royal halls shows king and retainer giving and receiving gold, weapons, horses, accoutrements, grants of land, and other items of great value. Early in the poem (20–5) the poet remarks how important it is for young kings to be generous with gifts, and much of Hrothgar's long speech to Beowulf in lines 1700–84 is devoted to the importance of generosity. In large part this emphasis is a function of a culture oriented toward fame and shame. Receiving a splendid gift is a visible sign of a man's worth, and since visible recognition is the central good in this society, the deserving men must receive rewards. It is the act of giving and receiving that is important more than the actual possession of the gift. Often in *Beowulf* a gift received is promptly presented to another person, as when Queen

[29] See William Ian Miller, "Choosing the avenger: some aspects of the bloodfeud in medieval Iceland and England," *Law and History Review*, 1 (1983), 159–204, esp. 194–203.

Wealhtheow gives Beowulf a splendid torque and he, on his return to Geatland, promptly gives it to the Geatish royal family. Gift taking also had social and ceremonial significance, being an overt symbol of the social contract implicit in the heroic world. When a man receives a gift from his lord or queen, for example, he solemnizes his allegiance to the dispenser of the gift. For a man to accept a gift and then fail his benefactor in time of need would not merely be ingratitude; it would be a violation of the social code. Beyond these symbolic aspects of gift giving, moreover, the *Beowulf* poet seems to imply an even more elemental good in openhandedness, as if it were a measure of one's well-being. There is warmth and joy in the scenes of gift giving and a reassuring sense that social harmony is attainable. Negative examples like the niggardly Heremod, on the other hand, suggest that stinginess is a sign of almost pathological unhappiness. The *Beowulf* poet would have found it fitting that the modern English word "misery" is derived from "miser".

Any reader of *Beowulf* will be struck by the poet's frequent and enthusiastic descriptions of artifacts: sword-hilts, saddles, shields, jewelry, and helmets are all carefully depicted, and the building of Heorot is described as if it were the crowning achievement of Hrothgar's kingship. While it is true that archeological discoveries like Sutton Hoo have revealed remarkable craftsmanship among Anglo-Saxon smiths, jewelers, and metalworkers, one might think nonetheless that so much attention to artifacts in *Beowulf* bespeaks an almost childish preoccupation with material objects. But this impression would result from a conflict in medieval and modern cultural values. Rousseau and the English Romantic writers have taught us to mistrust the artificial products of a calculating mind and to put our trust in nature – an external nature that is benign and instructive and a human nature that is inherently good. But to medieval people and the poet of *Beowulf* nature is chaotic and menacing. The few descriptions we get of nature are almost entirely of storms, fire, and the frightening mere. Grendel emerges from fens that are swarming with natural and reptilian life. Each artifact that the *Beowulf* poet describes is reassurance that mankind can control the natural world, can constrain its brute substance into pattern and order. The Anglo-Saxons would have understood Alfred North Whitehead's observation that "art is the imposing of a pattern on experience, and our aesthetic enjoyment is recognition of the pattern." The zoomorphic capital letters in Anglo-Saxon manuscripts are perfect examples of this mind-set. The illuminator forces vegetation, animals, and fantastic creatures to assume the abstract patterns and shapes that are beautiful and meaningful to human beings. The conduct of human beings is formalized into banqueting rituals, social forms, traditions, and patterns of allegiance, thus bringing human nature as well as external nature into reassuring patterns. It is in the light of this desire for rational order as a defense against the anarchy of nature that we should read the description of artifacts in *Beowulf*. Each celebration of a damascened sword or a well-constructed helmet recapitulates in miniature that moment early in the poem when Hrothgar builds Heorot – when a good king brings order to a people and a place by walling out the beasts and fens and darkness and constructing a place of control and assembly whose "light shone over many lands."[30]

The common Old English word for "fate" is *wyrd*, a word that is still used by Shakespeare when he refers to the "weird sisters" (that is, the sisters of fate) in *Macbeth*. *Wyrd* is mentioned repeatedly in *Beowulf* as the force determining lives, and some scholars have thought that behind these usages lurks the old pagan idea of the Germanic goddess of fate. The plural of *wyrd* is used by other writers to translate Latin *Parcae*, the name of the Roman mythological goddesses of fate, so clearly *wyrd* did have this association, but most scholars think that in *Beowulf* the term refers to fate in a more abstract sense. In his translation of Boethius's *Consolation of Philosophy* King Alfred reasons from a Christian viewpoint that *wyrd* is the accomplishment of God's providence. That is, *wyrd* is subject to God, it is what God determines shall be. In *Beowulf*, *wyrd* and God are mentioned as parallel and simultaneous forces at times, which would seem to support the Boethian reading of the concept in the poem. But quite possibly the term is to be understood according to context. To the characters in the poem, their lives seem to be governed by a stern and implacable fate. Both the poet and his audience knew that that fate, *wyrd*, was simply the accomplishment of God's will, but they also knew that to Beowulf and his contemporaries, who were deprived of Christian revelation, *wyrd* represented something more obscure and disquieting.

These aspects of the world of *Beowulf* that have meanings different from those our modern culture would lead us to expect are only representative of a larger number of such subjects requiring modern readers to question their cultural assumptions as they read the poem. Understanding literature from another time and land is an exercise in projecting ourselves imaginatively into other people's minds and lives and language. It is this exercise that constitutes one of the greatest rewards of literary study, as one thinks one's way into a different time and a different world from one's own. The world of *Beowulf* is worth the effort.

Afterword 1992

For a spirited protest against my judgment of Sisam's view of Hrothulf (p. 40 above) see now Bruce Mitchell, "Literary lapses: six notes on *Beowulf* and its critics," *RES* n.s. 43 (1992), 10–14.

[30] In *"Beowulf" and the Appositive Style*, pp. 70–4, I have dealt in more detail with the significance of artifacts in the world of *Beowulf*.

4
An Introduction to *Beowulf*

Beowulf is one of the relatively few major poems from the distant past which, upon first reading, still capture the attention of the modern reader and leave him changed when he puts the book down. Even those who have felt the narrative method to be flawed have usually responded to the poem's bracing severity, its awesome conflation of dignity and horror, and its strange, autumnal close. To an extent the poem transcends the slow revolutions in literary taste which have taken place since the eighth century: any modern reader can feel its moving power.

But readers require more from a serious poem than to be vaguely moved by it. The poet of *Beowulf* had a strategy and a purpose in moving readers, and to understand – rather than just feel – the poem the reader must have some sense of how the poet adjusted his medium to his narrative and his narrative to his purpose. At least three things are necessary for such an understanding. He must overcome the linguistic barrier of a form of English so archaic as to strike the modern reader as a foreign tongue. He must accustom his mind to a narrative method different from that of most literature read today, a narrative method which has little in common with that classical poetic which underlies post-medieval European literatures. And finally, he must gain some insight into the thought-world of England in the heroic age.

The Language of *Beowulf*

For readers of Marijane Osborn's translation of *Beowulf* the barrier of language has been removed. Wisely aware that translation is the art of taking as few losses as possible in a losing battle, Dr Osborn tells us that she is surrendering density of language in order to give the reader easy access to the narrative. Her decision was the right one. The story itself is translatable, and the dignity of its telling can be suggested. But the morphemic richness, the artfully congested syntax, and the odd, continually resumptive movement of the original poetry

Reprinted from *"Beowulf": a verse translation with treasures of the ancient North* by Marijane Osborn (Berkeley, CA, 1983), pp. xi–xix. Copyright © 1984 Marijane Osborn.

would be intolerable to modern minds accustomed to having stories developed through lucid predications. A full and literal translation of the first sentence of the poem may help to illustrate the problem. The original Old English is as follows.

> Hwæt, we Gar-Dena   in geardagum,
> þeodcyninga   þrym gefrunon,
> hu ða æþelingas   ellen fremedon!

And the approximate sense in modern English is

> Lo! Of Spear-Danes in yore-days
> of nation-ruling scions of the family,
> – concerning their surging power our
> questions have been answered:
> how sons of landed nobility
> fulfilled their competitive zeal then.

Add to this mish-mash the constraints of the elaborate Germanic metrical form, and we are lost in a poetic language so distractingly dense and self-conscious as to be beyond modern comprehension.

For the translator one of the most difficult features of Old English poetry is the pervasive phenomenon of syntactic juxtaposition. The sentences do not move from subject to verb to object. One element of the sentence is expressed and then, in mid-sentence, the poet stops to offer an alternative statement of the same element: "of Spear-Danes, of nation-rulers, we have heard the power, have heard how they fulfilled" and so on. Not only the sentences, but the very words of the poetic language are constructed upon this principle of juxtaposition. The poet does not say "spear-bearing Danes" but poses instead the simple juxtaposition "Spear-Danes," leaving it to us to discover the relationship between the two elements, a relationship which is not always as simple as it would seem at first glance: Danes skillful with spears? Danes stalwart as a spear? Danes well-provided with spears? Because this fondness for suggestive juxtaposition permeates the Old English poetic method at every level (as we shall see below), it will be well to pause here to examine a few of the poetic compounds which test the translator's skill.

In line 159 the Old English word *deað* "death" and the word *scua* "shadow" are combined to produce *deaðscua*, a word referring to the monster Grendel. The full meaning of the compound is "a shadowy, death-dealing creature" or perhaps "a death-dealing creature who dwells in the shadows." Later (703) Grendel is called *sceadugenga* "shadow-walker," an epithet with similar suggestiveness. In her translation Dr Osborn is able to retain these compounds intact. But elsewhere such juxtapositions of words are too cryptic for modern English. In the Finnsburg episode the wounds on the bodies of the slain are called *bengeato* "wound-doors" (1121), and Dr Osborn translates "gashes" since no modern equivalent could encapsulate the intricate associations of the Old English word. For *bengeato* draws its significance from a complex of epithets in Beowulf and other Old English poetry which describe the human body as a house: *banhus* "house of bone," *feorhhus* "life's house," *gasthus* "house of the spirit," and *sawelhus* "house of the soul." The human body is a house of flesh and bone in which the spirit sojourns for an interval before its departure for the next world. Mortal wounds, therefore, are doors in this house through which the spirit escapes. The complex of these images develops a major subtheme in *Beowulf*, the theme of the sudden transience of man's life on earth. It would take an entire poem to develop the full sense of "wound-door" and "bone-house." And in "The Caged Skylark" Gerard Manley Hopkins produced such a poem after reinventing the compound "bone-house." Poems *in nuce* are precisely what these verbal juxtapositions are, and one of the translator's most difficult challenges is to resist their lure, to avoid clogging the narrative with hopeless attempts at reproducing juxtapositional effects which were natural to Old English but are alien to Modern. *Gleobeam* "glee-wood" must yield to the colorless "harp," *breostwylm* "breast-whelming" to "emotion," and *hiorodrincas* "sword-drinks" to "loss of blood through sword-wounds." Our modern polyglot English with its streamlined structures of predication and modification can never achieve the effects of a highly stylized poetic diction deeply rooted in ancient Germanic habits of verbal juxtaposition.

That modern translators should not ape the diction of Old English was demonstrated conclusively by a disastrous rendering of *Beowulf* undertaken by the poet William Morris near the turn of the century. A passage like lines 280–1 –

>   gyf him edwenden   æfre scolde
>   bealuwa bisigu   bot eft cuman –

can only be rendered in something like the way Dr Osborn has done it:

>   – if change from this evil affliction
>   can ever grant him relief again –

The unwitting hilarity of Morris's

>   the business of bales, and the boot come again

(which seems to suggest wholesaling footwear rather than relieving affliction) is fatal to any passage, and such examples are common on nearly every page of his poem. And yet, one sympathizes with his effort to suggest those qualities of the poetry that are lost to the person who reads *Beowulf* in translation. A better way to achieve this end might be to indicate an approximate analogue of the Old English poetic method in a modern poem which succeeds (at least stylistically), and to urge the reader to keep that analogue in mind as he reads the smoothly paced rendering of Dr Osborn. The closest one can come to the ancient forms in modern English verse, I believe, is the opening stanza of Hopkins' "The Wreck of the Deutschland":

> Thou mastering me
> God! giver of breath and bread;
> World's strand, sway of the sea;
> Lord of living and dead;
> Thou has bound bones and veins in me,
> fastened me flesh,
> And after it almost unmade, what with dread,
> Thy doing: and dost thou touch me afresh?
> Over again I feel thy finger and find thee.

The startling images, the juxtapositional syntax, and the exuberant verbal power of this stanza suggest something of the manner of the Old English longline at work. As a vehicle for a three-thousand line narrative this kind of verse would never do for a modern English reader. But for the Anglo-Saxon hearing *Beowulf* it worked splendidly, and the students of this translation should try to imagine for themselves something of the Anglo-Saxon's experience as they encounter the ancient story in its newest modern dress.

The Narrative Method in *Beowulf*

A tactful translation can help the reader over linguistic and stylistic barriers, but it can do little to condition his mind to unfamiliar narrative devices. Without some preliminary attention to these the reader may mistake an unaccustomed literary strategy for a literary defect and may look in the wrong direction for poetic achievement. Following are some of the more prominent differences between ancient and modern narrative methods.

The poet's opening statement that "we have heard of the glory of the great folk-leaders, how those athelings did arduous deeds" should not be dismissed as merely a convention for getting the poem underway. The poet means what he says. His audience has already heard the tales he is about to tell. They know the figures of Germanic legend and what they did. This fact liberates the poet from any obligation to tell his story in exhaustive detail with who, what, when, where, and how spelled out at every point in chronological order. It enables him to be allusive, to give hints and gists of episodes outside his main plot line. Indeed, from this point until the end of the narrative the story of Beowulf unfolds amid rumors of heroism and tragedy from the Germanic Heroic Age. Sigemund the dragon slayer is mentioned briefly as the subject of the minstrel's song in honor of Beowulf's defeat of Grendel. The most renowned of all Germanic heroes, Sigemund is the subject of Scandinavian legends, and his story emerges again in the later Middle High German *Nibelungenlied*. The *Beowulf* poet expects us to recognize him and to see the aptness of the comparison of Sigemund with the victorious Beowulf. He also expects us to sense the tragic overtones in the minstrel's joyous reference to Sigemund's triumph over the dragon: Beowulf too shall slay a dragon, but unlike Sigemund he shall then die of the wounds the dragon inflicts upon him. Such foreshadowing is possible when the audience shares the poet's knowledge of his characters' fates. Later we hear of Hengest and Hnæf, two precursory defenders of the Danes, and we are reminded of the fabled King Offa, one of several kings in the poem whose characterization provides us with a common model against which to measure the stature of Beowulf when he becomes king. Beowulf is contrasted with Heremod, a notorious tyrant who serves as a foil to the noble hero, just as the shadowy lady named Thryth serves as a foil to the good Queen Hygd. To the modern reader these allusions to names and events which are then dropped rather than developed can seem distracting or enigmatic. But in fact they are precisely in keeping with the stated terms of the poet's narrative. They provide his central characters with a context in a reverently remembered past, and that past lends poignant meaning to each contrast that the allusions offer.

Even those episodes that are presented in full rather than allusively may strike the modern reader as somewhat lacking in visual realization. We have come to expect in long narrative poems a wealth of description – the graphic details that Homer lavishes on his characters and their settings, the careful setting-of-the-scene in *Roland*, or the plethoric word-pictures in medieval romance. Of this there is little in *Beowulf*. We are never told what Beowulf or Hygelac or Grendel look like. The "high hall" Heorot is alluded to again and again but never really described. Scholars argue inconclusively over the topography of the poem, so vaguely does the poet suggest it. Instead of description the poet tells us the *effects* people and things have on those who encounter them. Beowulf is a man so impressive that a wary shore-guard is overawed by his appearance. Heorot attracts men from distant regions and casts its light over many lands. The haunted mere (which, in an exceptional set-piece, *is* described somewhat) is so frightening that the stag at bay yields up his life to the hunting dogs rather than take refuge there. Hrothgar seems moved to an impassioned exhortation by the ornamented sword-hilt he holds in his hand. (How different is the poet's brief account of the rune-carved sword-hilt from Homer's leisurely depiction of Achilles's shield!)

Almost systematically the poet ignores the superficies of things to dwell instead on their profound effects on those around them, and in doing so he reveals a set of mind characteristic of the Germanic culture he is portraying. In the dark time before Christianity arrived, the main positive good Germanic men found in life was the artifact of a life well lived – and the fame that follows such a life. A man or a thing enters memorial afterlife not because of appearances but because of effects. A man is remembered because he made friends love him and enemies fear him, a royal hall because it drew men from far around and touched their lives. In a culture where appearances pass away utterly while deeds are remembered, why should Beowulf's beard or Grendel's girth be measured? Anyone who reads the noble death speech of Beowulf and then complains that the location of his wounds and the expression on his face were insufficiently particularized has not yet understood the world-view of the Germanic heroic age.

The poet's proclivity for selective presentation and his emphasis on effects more than appearances lead to another unusual aspect of his poem – its narrative structure. A modern reader might feel that *Beowulf* has (as Johnson complained of *Samson Agonistes*) a beginning and an end but no middle. The first long section of the poem presents the youthful hero entering upon his first great exploit, the slaying of the Grendel kin. Then, at line 2200, in no more than ten lines of verse the poet says, in effect, "and then fifty years passed," and we are suddenly plunged into the last day of the hero's life. The poet does tell us many of the hero's triumphant achievements during the intervening period, but these are all woven piecemeal into the many reminiscences and recollections that crowd upon Beowulf's memory as he marches towards his fatal encounter with the dragon. Structurally what the poet has done is to collapse end against beginning. Instead of allowing us to see his *Heldenleben* as a procession of events he forces us to view Beowulf's career as a stark juxtaposition of dawn and twilight, of hero's arrival and hero's departure. One effect of this narrative strategy is to direct our attention toward origins and destiny and to make us wonder whence the hero comes and whither he goes. That this is one intention of the poet is strongly suggested by the fact that we are introduced to this same structural pattern *in parvo* at the very beginning of *Beowulf*. The prologue concerning Shield Shefing tells us how a troubled nation saw a young hero emerge from the unknown, grow to manhood and secure his subjects and then, full of years, depart across the waters toward an obscure destiny. The prologue closes with the assertion that no one could say what his fate would be. The structure of *Beowulf* as a whole is in a way a restatement of that question, and the poem itself is a response – as the final section of this essay will try to suggest.

Other explanations have been offered for the two-part structure of the poem, and no doubt there is some validity in them. Juxtaposing the hero's youth with the hero's age provides the poet with many opportunities for suggesting the pathos of human life, and the poet makes use of those opportunities with delicacy and restraint. The aged Hrothgar in the first part of the poem is a sad presage of what Beowulf will become; the youthful Wiglaf at the end is a poignant reminder of what Beowulf has been. The poet emphasizes these contrasts by shifting the epic formulas he had earlier attached to old Hrothgar to the aged Beowulf at the end and by shifting the formulas he had applied to the youthful Beowulf at the beginning to the youthful Wiglaf at the end. The result, of course, is to contrast as well as compare these figures: young Beowulf is greater than young Wiglaf, old Beowulf greater than old Hrothgar. Another effect of the two-part structure is to keep the essential moments in the hero's life before the reader's attention and to subordinate the less crucial events. And the essential moments are the moments of testing, the moments of ultimate stress. The youthful hero proving himself in his first great battle; the aged hero facing certain death – these are the moments that interest the poet. Anglo-Saxon poets are concerned to study man *in extremis* (compare the elegiac monologue *The Wanderer* or the great battle-poem *Maldon*), just as their Germanic cousins on the continent were. How do good men comport themselves at the critical moment? This had always been a favorite theme. And no doubt there are other literary interests served by the poet's choice of a two-part structure over the more familiar (to modern readers) "beginning, middle, end." The latter is an Aristotelian, not a Germanic formulation, and, as Samuel Daniel has well said, "All our understandings are not to be built by the square of Greece and Italy." A close examination of Germanic "monuments of truth," adds Daniel, "argues well their worth and proves them not without judgment, though without Greek or Latin" (*Defense of Rhyme*).

It was noted above that the root principle of Old English word-formation and syntax in the poetry was juxtaposition, and in the immediately foregoing paragraphs juxtaposition was seen to be the basic structural principle at the highest level of aesthetic organization in the poem. The conclusion seems inescapable that *significant juxtaposition* is a device that readers must watch for in reading Anglo-Saxon poetry. I believe this is true to a much greater degree than is usually recognized. Just as the poet constantly combined two independent words with independent meanings and then expected his audience to ponder their relationship and appreciate the *tertium quid* that emerges from their juxtaposition, so also he placed one episode alongside the other or one scene in juxtaposition to another and expected us to divine their mutual relationship. Perhaps the best advice one can give to a reader who has come to *Beowulf* for the first time is to urge a constant alertness to the significance of juxtapositions within the poem.

One striking example of significant juxtaposition in *Beowulf* is the most famous single passage in the poem – Hrothgar's account of the ghastly mere where Grendel's mother dwells. The ogress has just slain Hrothgar's favorite retainer in talion for Beowulf's killing of Grendel, and the old King hopes that the hero might be willing to undertake the forbidding challenge of tracking her to her lair and doing battle with her there. The account of the deadly tarn where she lives, with its almost unique use of descriptive detail, is usually cited as a "purple passage" in the poem:

> In a secret land
> they dwell, among wild fells, wolf-slopes,
> windy headlands where a waterfall
> hurtles down through the mist into darkness
> under the fells. Not far away
> in miles lies hidden that lonely mere
> overhung by trees covered in hoar-frost,
> a deep-rooted wood that shadows the water.
> They say every night there appears a strange
> fire on the lake! – And no man lives
> so wise as to know that water's depth.
> Though the stag on the heath, pressed hard by hounds,
> should make for the forest with his mighty antlers,
> put to flight from afar, he will forfeit his life
> on the shore rather than swim in that lake
> to protect his head. Not a happy place!
> There the wind stirs up sudden storms
> where clashing waves ascend to the clouds
> and the sky presses down, dark and smothering,
> weeping from above.
>
> (1356–76)

Every reader of *Beowulf* has admired this scenic tour de force, but rarely does anyone ask why it is there. (E. B. Irving, in his sensitive *Reading of Beowulf*, pp. 76ff does ask, and his comments merit close study.) That the king should tell Beowulf where the Grendel kin live is quite natural, but why should the poet be at pains to heighten the poetry so, making this passage so unforgettably evocative of the horrors that lie beyond Heorot? Thinking in terms of characterization, we might conjecture that the passage is there as a reflection of the king's desperation. His imagination has been captured by the horrors that face him, and in describing a landscape so sad and menacing that it seems to have a soul Hrothgar is in fact displaying the desolate landscape of his own mind. Although plausible, perhaps, this explanation does not seem wholly adequate to the occasion. It is more to the point, I believe, to notice that the speech of Hrothgar is one element in a collocation of two passages that form a dynamic juxtaposition. For immediately following the description of the tarn appears Beowulf's clearest enunciation of the heroic code of the North:

> Grieve not, wise ruler! A man should rather
> avenge his friend's murder than mourn him too much.
> Death comes to all. Let him who is able
> achieve in the world what he wants for himself
> of fame and glory before he must die –
> for the atheling, that is afterwards best!
> Arise, great king.
>
> (1384–90)

And the response to Beowulf's stirring speech is dramatic:

> The gray-haired king leapt up, thanking God,
> the mighty Sky-Lord, for what that man said.
> Then a horse was bridled for Hrothgar,
> a stallion with braided mane. In splendor
> the king rode.
>
> (1397–1401)

What we have witnessed is a valiant young warrior regenerating a despondent king and his grieving nation with an affirmation of the heroic view of life. But the glory of the passage is the juxtaposition of Beowulf's words with the graphic horrors against which he is asserting his code. For the Anglo-Saxon audience, the real purple passage is Beowulf's vigorous articulation of the heroic principle. Or, better stated, the supreme moment in this scene is the point of juncture between the two speeches – that ignition point that releases the power and meaning of what is perhaps the most important single statement by Beowulf in the poem.

Another significant juxtaposition occurs early in the poem. Lines 64–81 describe the happy flowering of Hrothgar's reign. Men work in harmony to build the fair hall Heorot, and in harmony they occupy it, with king and court observing their mutual vows of love and loyalty. But harmony prevails only so long as men can repress the hatred, disloyalty, and violence to which human nature is prone. The dark impulses are introduced with startling suddenness in lines 82–5, and what follows immediately – almost as if triggered by the human violence just mentioned – is the introduction of Grendel. There is a suggestion that the evil spirit without is brought to life by the evil within. And we may even see in the juxtaposition a hint of the old truth that while men always imagine that the greatest threat to their security is the enemy attacking from without, in truth they are more threatened from within. And the narrative at large makes clear what the juxtaposition suggests: Grendel with all his horror made a nightmare of Heorot, yet he could not finally destroy it, thanks to the help of Beowulf. But Heorot *was* violently destroyed by a force against which Beowulf was powerless to defend it – the hatreds which lurked within the hearts of the Danes themselves.

Finally, consider the close of the Finnsburg lay (1159ff). After Beowulf's successful avenging of the Danes against Grendel, the royal minstrel sings of an earlier occasion when the Danes avenged themselves against an enemy – Hengest's destruction of Finn and his restoration of Finn's widowed queen to her ancestral home in Denmark. The minstrel's account is joyous, but oddly the poet of *Beowulf* gives a melancholy emphasis to the story, repeatedly focussing our attention on the sorrows of the queen, who lost brother, son, husband, and her entire world in the violent encounter. Why this odd emphasis? The answer seems to lie in a juxtaposition artfully arranged at the close of the episode: "The lay was sung," says the poet, and almost immediately thereafter, "Then Wealhtheow came forth." The poet is calling our attention to an analogy between the two queens: like Hildeburh, Wealhtheow shall witness internecine warfare culminating in the burning of the royal hall Heorot. It appears from analogues outside the poem that the Danes were victorious in this warfare, as in the Finnsburg battle, but we are reminded by the poet's juxtaposition that victories do not end sorrows. The ill-starred Wealhtheow knows that the defeat of Grendel still leaves Heorot vulnerable to the envy and hatred in the hearts of men around her and seems almost to read the meaning of the poet's juxtaposing her entrance with the close of the Finnsburg lay, for she hastens to seek protection from the trouble she fears will arise from her ungrateful nephew. But her efforts will be unavailing. Dynastic struggles of tragic dimension lie ahead, and she, like Hildeburh, shall lose her dearest kin in the dispute. Here as elsewhere in the poem a simple juxtaposition of passages conveys presentiments of disaster which reverberate throughout the remainder of the narrative.

The Thought-World of the *Beowulf* Poet

Beowulf is about many things, and the intellectual concerns that the poet shared with his milieu were no doubt numerous, complex, and beyond total recall. But it may be useful here to act out some of the more easily recognizable concerns of his culture, especially those which seem to have a bearing on his poem.

Many of these points of agreement between the poem and its cultural setting will be obvious. That a Christian poet writing only a century after his nation was converted from paganism should express pious views such as those in lines 180–8 will be a surprise to no one. That a poem describing the warrior class in the Heroic Age preceding that conversion should have little to say about the farmers and craftsmen upon whom any society depends will also seem normal to anyone who has ever read an epic or romance. But other attitudes in the poem can be understood only if we pause to consider the difference between our modern thought-world and that of the *Beowulf* poet. Consider the respective roles of nature on the one hand and man's artifice on the other. Anyone living after Rousseau and the English Romantic poets will be familiar with the view that man is born with a natural inclination towards wholesome conduct but that he is often corrupted by the artificial forms with which society surrounds him, such as inhibitions, social customs, and city life. To restore the soul we must return to Nature, for

> One impulse from a vernal wood
> Can teach you more of man,
> Of moral evil and of good,
> Than all the sages can.

No attitude could have been more alien to the pagan Germanic society depicted in *Beowulf* or to the early Christian society in which the *Beowulf* poet lived. Men in that day found no more comfort in nature *per se* than a thoughtful modern man finds in typhoons, black holes, or atomic fission today. Nature seemed anarchic, inimical, and life was endurable only in so far as man had imposed rational order upon it. The vernal woods were menacing, beset with fens and wolf-slopes, fires and storms, and uncontrolled, monstrous life. Against this aimless, teeming world man poses his rational craft. He strikes roads through the wilderness and dispells the natural darkness with lighted mead-halls. His ships conquer the turbulent wave and his ringmail and weapons keep sea-monsters at bay. Readers of *Beowulf* must be conscious of this attitude when they see throughout the poem the many references to cunningly made armor, artfully curved ships, damascened swords, and well-wrought buildings. Each artifact is a celebration of man's triumph over the hostile wilderness that surrounds the islands of order such as Heorot. The many artifacts pictured at intervals throughout the ensuing translation were not merely utilitarian objects: they were reassuring signs that man's rational order can be made to prevail over a formless and malignant nature.

Nor is the *Beowulf* poet's delight in rationalizing nature limited to external nature. Human nature, when it escapes man's control, is perhaps the most dangerous force of all, as some of the preceding discussion has suggested. We find much in *Beowulf*, therefore, about the forms and customs by which men ordered their lives. Greetings, speeches, preparations for battle are performed almost ritualistically. The herald who takes Beowulf's message to King Hrothgar does so standing "before his shoulder, according to the noble custom." All this is not mere *mise en scène*; it expresses a major theme in the poem, reminding us that men must ever strive for control, not yield to impulse. The same is true of the mead-serving ceremony and the formalities of seating guests and taking food. We never hear of feasts without ceremony – except when Grendel falls to his gruesome repast, or when the evil Heremod explodes with anger and slays his table companions. To the *Beowulf* poet such conduct as this is not human. It is natural.

The characters in *Beowulf* and the poet himself do not shrink from moral judgments. A man who slays his own kin is treacherous, not (as such a man might be judged today) in need of psychological counseling. A man who deserts his comrades in battle is a coward, not a respectable dissenter marching to a different drummer. A ruler who usurps the wealth that is owed to his followers is condemned and expelled; he is not, like some modern embezzlers, excused on the grounds that he was working under an emotional strain. A king whom old age has crippled may be excused as blameless even though he can no longer protect his people; but otherwise one is held responsible for one's actions. Some modern critics have resisted this stern strain in the Anglo-Saxon outlook. They believe Beowulf's heroic stature is qualified by the poet, and the monsters, though evil, have something to be said in their defense. Such views smack of the modern world, not of the world of *Beowulf*.

And yet, moral judgments in the poem are not merely simplistic. In a sense, the entire narrative is a subtle questioning of the prevailing (eighth-century) moral judgment of the Heroic Age. But to understand this we must examine one further aspect of the thought-world of *Beowulf*, the confrontation of Christian and pagan beliefs in Dark Age England.

The standard Christian authorities in the time of the *Beowulf* poet left no room for uncertainty in assessing the confrontation of Christian and pagan: Christianity was the Truth and paganism was a treacherous network of lies and deceptions fabricated by the Devil. Any devout Christian, including the *Beowulf* poet, would presumably have accepted this view without question. A logical corollary to this view, which Christians would also have been expected to accept, is the dictum expressed most clearly by St Cyprian: "There is no salvation outside the Church." Most Anglo-Saxons who wrote on this subject espoused Cyprian's view without difficulty, but for some the implications were troubling. For to accept this view meant that one was willing to see one's ancestors consigned to eternal damnation. To kings who traced their lineage back to Woden and aristocrats who took pride in the works and wisdom of their continental forebears, the consequences of accepting the Christian view could involve some pain. Many, no doubt, tried not to dwell on the past, turning their minds instead toward the Christian present and future.

And yet it is precisely this condemned ancestry of the English to which the *Beowulf* poet has devoted his poem. Though himself a Christian, and probably the son and grandson of Christians, he does not write of the Christian heroes celebrated by many of his fellow poets but turns his gaze back to the continent in the fifth and sixth centuries, back to his ancestors in the dark and hopeless past. He knows of their desperate situation in the Christian scheme of things, for he refers to the heathen practices of his characters (lines 175ff):

> At times they vowed in idol-tents
> to sacrifice,

and to the consequences of their heathenism:

> Woe be to him
> who because of strife must shove his soul
> to the heart of the fire! He cannot hope
> for help or change, ever.
>
> (183–6)

But having acknowledged that his heroes lived in the days of heathen ignorance and having recognized the consequences of their benighted condition, he proceeds to tell their story with the deepest respect, admiring their generosity, praising their dignity, and exalting their prowess, right up to the moment that Beowulf departs this life.

Such treatment of his subject by the *Beowulf* poet was in a way daring, for churchmen in his day (and before) were emphatic in their declarations not only that pagan ancestors should be consigned to damnation but that they should also be forgotten. In his letter to the monks of Lindisfarne the eighth-century cleric Alcuin states the matter clearly when he exhorts the brothers to stop listening to stories of pagan heroes like Ingeld:

> Let the words of God be read at the meal of the clergy. There it is fitting to hear the lector, not a harp-player; the sermons of the Fathers, not songs of the laity. For what has Ingeld to do with Christ? Narrow is the house; it cannot hold both. The King of Heaven will have nothing to do with so-called kings who are heathen and damned. For the One King rules eternally in Heaven, while the heathen is damned and laments in Hell.

Is it impermissible, then, even to acknowledge that heathens were capable of good acts? Tertullian had an answer: "The virtues of the heathen, being devoid of grace, can only be looked upon as splendid vices" (*De Carne Christi*).

Not every voice concurred in this harsh judgment. Anglo-Saxon missionaries on the continent in the eighth century reported to their countrymen that the conduct of Germanic heathens was sometimes admirable, even though they were deprived of Christian revelation. In the neighboring Celtic regions Christian thinkers wondered whether truly virtuous men might not find salvation outside the Church if they intuitively sensed God's precepts and followed them. But these were minority voices, and the poet of *Beowulf* does not invoke their doctrines, if he knew them. Rather, through literary strategies he seeks to make a place for the noble ancestors in the memory of his nation. On the one hand he is forthright in acknowledging that Beowulf and his contemporaries were pagans. The speech Beowulf makes to Hrothgar following the description of Grendel's mere is from the pagan Germanic world and could never be reconciled to Christianity. The omens the Geats seek to read by casting lots (204–5), the totemic animals that protect their armor, and the allusions to Weland and Wyrd are all elements of pagan Germanic culture. And at his death Beowulf is cremated (an abomination to eight-century Christians) and the tumulus reared over his remains seems almost a *heroön*, so reverent are the praises that his comrades chant to his memory.

And yet, along with these pagan details in Beowulf's characterization, the poet has in other respects portrayed his hero as a man of such virtue as to suggest, at times, the example of Christ himself. Beowulf's entire career is one of self-sacrifice, as he repeatedly risks (and ultimately gives) his life for the salvation and protection of his people. While not a Christian, Beowulf is nonetheless deeply religious, for although he never refers to Christ or to anything pertaining to the church, he does refer often to an allpowerful Higher Being which rules the world and men's actions. He thanks this Being for his triumphs, he ascribes his strength to Him, and near the end of the poem he worries over the possibility of his having offended this Higher Being in some way of which he is unaware. He attains to virtue by adhering to the tenets of the old Germanic code, but he does so with such piety that he seems to approach the Christian ideal. His kindness is revealed when he refuses to accept the throne which Hygd offers him, preferring out of Germanic loyalty and love to help a young, weaker man to rule. At his death, Beowulf never condemns the cowardly retainers who deserted him in his hour of need; his thoughts are always and exclusively on the survival of his people. In their conception of nature (as was discussed above) and in many other things the pagan and the Christian views converged, and the poet emphasizes these points of convergence.

The poet's most imaginative device for portraying the pagan Beowulf as deserving of an honorable place in the Christian thought-world is in his conception of evil in the poem. It is in the monsters, as J. R. R. Tolkien has pointed out, that we find an objective realization of all that is evil in heroic life and, at the same time, the center of evil in the Christian view. The accommodation of the two is clearest in the poet's tracing of the genealogy of Grendel in lines 105–14 (and again in lines 1261ff). He tells us that Grendel is the descendant of Cain, thus giving him Judeo-Christian ancestry. But the line of descent includes giants and elves and walking dead – creatures that have no place in biblical lore but rather are from the demonology of the pagan Germanic peoples. These creatures, according to northern mythology, were the enemies of gods and men, the forces of chaos and brute violence seeking always to undo the order that good men and good gods have brought to the world. Grendel and his mother (and later the dragon) are embodiments of the evil force as it was conceived by Christians and, simultaneously, of the evil side of the Germanic heroic life.

By pitting the hero Beowulf against the monsters thus defined, the poet has his hero join forces, unwittingly, with the Christian Anglo-Saxons of later years. This enables Christian Anglo-Saxons to identify positively with their pagan forefathers and thus retain pride of ancestry despite the theological gulf that divides them: Beowulf, though ignorant of Christian revelation, is nonetheless fighting against the same enemy that Christians of the poet's own day are fighting. While we can understand the Good only through Revelation and conversion, Evil is always the same. Cruelty and violence, whether manifested in Heremod or Cain, in the dragon of the Apocalypse or the dragon of Germanic mythology, are peculiar to no creed or culture. With this sad truth the poet of *Beowulf* was able to establish a place for the noble pagan in the collective memory of Christian Anglo-Saxons.

The *Beowulf* poet is not the first to build with poetry a place for his nation's past, but he has done it in a manner that is uniquely moving. There is an air of mystery and pathos in *Beowulf* that readers rarely forget. In part this is because the question of Beowulf's destiny beyond life is never clearly resolved. "His soul went forth," the poet says, "to seek the judgment of the just." The vagueness is deliberate, for the stern voices of early Christian dogma cannot be imagined away. Perhaps we must regard all the virtues of Beowulf as nothing more than "splendid vices"; perhaps the only just judgment for him after his pagan funeral *is* damnation. No word in the poem denies this. But the poet's tone – a tone of unqualified admiration for the hero maintained throughout three thousand lines of poetry – protests against such a judgment. We are thus left at the end of *Beowulf* with a delicately poised contradiction and a sad uncertainty. It is an uncertainty which for many centuries has darkened men's broodings over life and afterlife.

A modern example of such brooding provides an illuminating analogue to the conflicting feelings with which the poet closes *Beowulf*. The twentieth-century Spanish thinker Miguel de Unamuno engaged the subject of life after death in a moving philosophical meditation called "Del sentimiento trágico de la vida" ("On the Tragic Sense of Life"). After several agonized chapters on man's need for a belief in personal immortality, Unamuno finally acknowledges that there may after all be no afterlife, and hence no meaning in human existence. This terrible realization urges the author to the finest sentence in this book: "Y si es la nada lo que nos está reservado, hagamos que sea una injusticia esto!" ("And if it is oblivion that is reserved for us at the end of this life, then let us act in such a way that this will have been an injustice!") The devout Christian who composed *Beowulf* could never have uttered directly such a desperate sentiment as this, but through the indirections of poetry he has suggested something very like it. For the tone and emphasis of his poem seem to tell us no less forcefully than Unamuno could have done that if it is oblivion that is reserved for such heroes as Beowulf, then these men lived their lives in such a way that this will have been an injustice.

Part II

Literary Interpretation: Several Poems

5
Two Aspects of Variation in Old English Poetry

Discussion of Old English stylistic devices is problematic from the outset, for we have no contemporary treatises on style to aid us in establishing historically valid definitions. There is no *Ars poetica* of Old English verse; there is not even a *Skáldskaparmál*. The technique of "variation" is a case in point.[1] Since the term has no authority in Anglo-Saxon tradition but is an invention pure and simple of modern scholarship, any definition offered now by a student of Old English poetry must be regarded as little more than stipulative.[2] I claim no more than this for the definition I set out below, although I have tried to include within it those features which most scholars have associated with the term, and I have contrived to gain some small status for my definition by locating it briefly within the mainstream of scholarly debate on variation since the term was introduced in the nineteenth century. If I appear to pass hurriedly and selectively through the accumulated commentary on the nature of the figure, it is because my primary concern in this essay is not with definition *per se* but rather with scrutinizing two of the generally recognized types of variation in order to deepen in some small measure our understanding of how Old English poets used this stylistic device.

When John Milton described the style of the Old English poem *Brunanburh*, contrasting it with the style of the surrounding prose of the *Chronicle*, he

---

Reprinted from *Old English Poetry: essays on style*, ed. Daniel G. Calder (Berkeley, CA, 1979), pp. 127–45.

[1] The phrase *wordum wrixlan* in *Beowulf*, 874, has been interpreted by some scholars as a contemporary allusion to the technique of variation, but since *wordum wrixlan* occurs elsewhere with the unambiguous meaning "to speak, converse," a meaning which yields acceptable sense in *Beowulf*, 874, this isolated occurrence would seem insufficient evidence for the technical sense. Cf. German *Wortwechsel* "discussion, dispute."

[2] Consequently, any dispute over which scholar's definition of the figure is "right" is meaningless. My own definition excludes Roy F. Leslie's "conceptual variation" and Kemp Malone's "outer variation," for I do not find these usages helpful; but their formulations are no less "right" than my own. See Roy F. Leslie, "Analysis of stylistic devices and effects in Anglo-Saxon literature," in *Stil- und Formprobleme in der Literatur*, ed. Paul Böckmann (Heidelberg, 1959), pp. 129–36, and Kemp Malone, "The old tradition: poetic form," in *A Literary History of England*, ed. Albert C. Baugh, 2nd edn (New York, 1967), pp. 28–9.

chose the term "over-charg'd" to characterize the poetry.³ Since his paraphrase of *Brunanburh* "in usuall language" tends to excise the frequent restatements in the poem, it seems likely that "over-charg'd" refers to those carefully massed tautologies which later critics would denominate "variation". Similar comments were made by other early readers of Old English, but little can be made of these observations. They prove only that the characteristic restatements of Old English poems are a prominent feature which cannot fail to attract the attention of even the most casual observer.⁴

"A strong tendency toward apposition" is the way Henry Sweet described Old English poetic style in 1807,⁵ and here we move toward a more precise characterization of variation. But "apposition" is not quite adequate to describe poetic restatements which involve not only nouns and pronouns, but also verbs, adjectives, phrases, and even entire sentences. Recognizing the need for a special term, Richard Heinzel, in 1875, introduced the word "variation" to describe the phenomenon.⁶ His definition was somewhat vague, however, and subsequent scholars such as Rudolf Kögel and Paul Pachaly⁷ blurred the concept further when they explained Heinzel's term as a loose metaphor derived from musical composition – theme and variation. The original statement of a concept or referent would be the theme, presumably, and subsequent appositional restatements would be the variations. But this metaphorical interpretation of the term seems fanciful. Heinzel, I feel certain, was adopting a Latin rhetorical term (although he does not say so) and applying it to Germanic poetry. The term appears to have been developed for the most part by post-classical writers; one finds a typical use, with definition, in the *Carmen de figuris vel schematibus* edited by Karl von Halm in 1863.⁸ James Henry coins the term anew in the first volume of his edition of the *Aeneid* published two years before Heinzel's treatise,⁹ and "variation" was also popular among

---

³ *Complete Prose Works of John Milton*, ed. Don M. Wolfe (New Haven, 1953–1982), 5.308–9. Milton would have read the Old English poem in the edition of Abraham Wheloc, relying heavily, no doubt, on the Latin translation provided therein.

⁴ Thus Sharon Turner gave some attention to "the repetition of synonymous expressions" in *The History of the Anglo-Saxons*, 3, 4th edn, 3 vols (London, 1823), pp. 258–65, as did John J. Conybeare in his *Illustrations of Anglo-Saxon Poetry* (London, 1826), pp. xxviii–xxxii and 6; see Daniel G. Calder, "The Study of style in Old English poetry: a historical introduction," *Old English Poetry: essays on style*, ed. Calder (Berkeley, CA, 1979), pp. 1–65.

⁵ Sweet, "Sketch of the history of Anglo-Saxon poetry," in W. Carew Hazlitt's edition of Thomas Warton's *History of English Poetry from the Twelfth to the Close of the Sixteenth Century*, 2, 4 vols (London, 1871), p. 5.

⁶ Heinzel, *Über den stil der altgermanischen Poesie* (Strasbourg, 1875), pp. 3–9, 49.

⁷ Kögel, *Geschichte der deutschen Litteratur bis zum Ausgange des Mittelalters* (Strasbourg, 1894), p. 334; Pachaly, *Die Variation im Heliand und in der altsächsischen Genesis* (Jena, 1899), p. 2.

⁸ *Rhetores latini minores*, ed. von Halm (Leipzig, 1863), pp. 67, 70.

⁹ *Æneidea*, ed. Henry, 4 vols (Leipzig, 1873–89), vol. 1, pp. 745–51.

German writers on prose style in the eighteenth century. That the word was from the beginning a technical rhetorical term is a point worth establishing, for the alternative assumption of a musical metaphor underlying the concept "variation" can only serve to impede clear definition of the term.

My own definition, which is a respectful modification of that proposed by Walther Paetzel in his treatise *Die Variationen in der altgermanischen Allitterationspoesie*,[10] is as follows: "syntactically parallel words or word-groups which share a common referent and which occur within a single clause (or, in the instance of sentence-variation, within contiguous clauses)." Simply stated, I regard variation as apposition (Sweet's old term), if apposition be extended to include restatements of adjectives, verbs, and phrases as well as of nouns and pronouns. This definition is objective and formal and, as a result, somewhat narrow. Some would complain that it excludes too many collocations that share certain qualities with the phenomena I do include.[11] To this objection I would answer that I do not deny that variations strictly defined share fundamental characteristics with other elements of diction and narrative. But I find it more useful not to declare every similar element a variation but rather to recognize that there are some common features shared by stylistic devices which bear different names.

The stylistic functions of variation in Old English poetry are manifold. A cluster of variations can prolong dramatically a crucial moment in a poem. A single variation can effect a swift rhetorical transition without the interrupting mechanics of hypotactic linkage. Variations can register subtle shifts in perspective, a function which Stanley Greenfield has described with particular skill.[12] Variation can introduce rhetorical suspense into a sentence through its effect of artful retardation. And in the best poetry it achieves these effects while simultaneously and effortlessly fulfilling the metrical and alliterative requirements of the verse form. If there were time and space, I should like to examine and admire a selection of variations illustrating each of these functions, but, as it is, I shall deal with only two types, hoping thereby both to sharpen our understanding of the figure and to illustrate how the local tactics of Old English poetic style sometimes reflect the larger strategies of variation.

In the first type of variation to which I shall turn, a referent is designated at least once in literal terms and once by a figurative expression which might be

---

[10] Paetzel, *Die Variationen in der altgermanischen Allitterationspoesie* (Berlin, 1913).

[11] Ewald Standop is especially skillful in demonstrating the close interrelationship between a wide variety of stylistic devices which he includes under the term *Variation*; see his "Formen der Variation im *Beowulf*," *Festschrift für Edgar Mertner*, ed. Bernard Fabian and Ulrich Suerbaum (Munich, 1969), pp. 55–63.

[12] Greenfield, *The Interpretation of Old English Poems* (London and Boston, 1972), pp. 68–72.

mystifying were it not for the clarification provided by the second, unmetaphorical element. Consider, for example, *Beowulf*, 1368–9:

> Ðeah þe hæðstapa   hundum geswenced,
> *heorot hornum trum*,   holtwudu sece

"Although the heath-stalker, pressed by the dogs, the hart strong in horns should seek the forest."[13] The "heath-stalker" (*hæðstapa*) could be a wolf, or a man, or even a grasshopper, since the compound refers to a single vivid action characteristic of all these creatures. The specifying variation *heorot hornum trum* resolves the synecdochic ambiguity. A similar effect may be seen in *Beowulf*, 1745–7:

> þonne bið on hreþre   under helm drepen
> *biteran stræle*   (him bebeorgan ne con),
> *wom wundorbebodum*   *wergan gastes*

"Then he is struck in his heart beneath his helmet with a sharp arrow – he knows not how to protect himself – with the crooked mysterious urgings of the evil spirit." In this highly metaphorical passage from Hrothgar's sermon, clarifying variations repeatedly help the audience through the quasi-allegorical language, explaining that the *weard* of line 1741 is *saweles hyrde*, and so forth. In the passage before us, the symbolic meaning of the metaphorical arrow is spelled out in detail.

A slightly subtler example is the variation in *Beowulf*, 1143–4:

> þonne him Hunlafing   *hildeleoman,*
> *billa selest,*   on bearm dyde

"Whenever the son of Hunlaf placed the battle-flame on his lap, the best of swords." Here the ambiguous metaphor *hildeleoman* is clarified by the variation following. Some learned readers of Old English might question whether there really is any ambiguity to be clarified, since swords are frequently spoken of as flames or flashes of battle (*Swurdleoma stod, swylce eal Finnsburuh fyrenu wære* will come to many readers' minds). But the text of *Beowulf* itself shows us that the literal meaning of *hildeleoma* was still very much alive, and hence the epithet *was* ambiguous. For lines 2582–3 contain the same compound used literally to refer to fire:

> wearp wælfyre;   wide sprungon
> *hildeleoman*

"[The dragon] threw forth deadly fire; the hostile flames leapt far and wide." Thus the specifying, clarifying variation in lines 1143–4 is not otiose.

Another example raises the old question as to how much dictional skill we

[13] All quotations in this essay are, unless otherwise identified, from *ASPR*.

can expect from an Old English poet. We have just seen that in *Beowulf*, 1143, the root meaning of *hildeleoma* is intact, and thus the word has authentic figurative force. And yet, when we see the same figurative term used of a word in the following passage (*Beowulf*, 1522-4), the poet seems to treat the epithet as a dead metaphor, for he combines the flame figure with imagery of biting or eating:

>   Ða se gist onfand
> þæt se *beadoleoma*   bitan nolde,
> aldre sceþðan,   ac seo ecg geswac

"Then the stranger discovered that the battle-flame would not bite, injure the vitals, but the blade failed." A doctrinaire oral-formulaist would crow with delight over such an apparent lapse of attention as this, for line 1523 would seem to argue that the poets were too hurried in their composition to notice the literal meanings of their formulas. But we cannot be sure that this is the case. For in an earlier passage where he spoke of the sword's hostile bite on an enemy's body, the poet artfully combines this image with fire-imagery which also involves biting, or at least devouring. The context is the funeral scene in the Finnsburg episode (*Beowulf*, 1121-4):

>   ðonne blod ætspranc,
> laðbite lices.   *Lig* ealle forswealg,
> *gæsta gifrost*,   þara ðe þær guð fornam
> bega folces

"The blood spurted forth from the body's hostile bite. Fire, the greediest of creatures, devoured all of those of the two armies whom war had destroyed there." Is it possible, then, that *Beowulf*, 1523, involves a *double metaphor*, one prepared for by an earlier variation in which the image of fire as a ravenous devourer is joined with a metaphor of a sword's biting? If so, then in *beadoleoma bitan* we have two bold metaphors resolved harmoniously into one through the agency of the common term *bitan*.

Before answering this question in the affirmative, the cautious critic, mindful of E. G. Stanley's suggestion that little is knowable and nothing is certain in the study of Old English style,[14] should pause and ask himself whether he is perhaps reading conscious artistry into a happy accident of traditional poetic diction. I have paused long over this instance, but what prompts me after all to grant the poet at least the possibility of conscious design here is, on the one hand, the superior sensitivity with which he uses traditional diction throughout *Beowulf*, and, on the other, the particular care with which he seems to use fire-imagery in the poem. From the opening prelude where we are told that the

[14] Stanley, "Two Old English poetic phrases insufficiently understood for literary criticism: *þing gehegan* and *seonoþ gehegan*," in *Old English Poetry*, ed. Calder, pp. 67-90.

house Heorot stands in wait of the hostile fervor of destroying fire until the end where fire is awakened one last time to destroy the *banhus* of the hero's body, the poet seems attentive and deft in his frequent use of fire-imagery. When Grendel makes his last raid on Heorot, for example, we are surprised to hear that the hall stands *fyrbendum fæst* (722) "secure in the bonds of fire" only shortly after we were told that hostile fire would destroy the hall (and my own surprise is not entirely allayed by the editors' footnotes assuring us that the reference is to "fire-forged metal braces" or the like). And lest we rush unheeding past this curious description of the fire-doomed hall, the poet introduces at this point, in obvious proximity with *fyrbendum fæst*, a striking simile: Grendel's eyes, as he fixes his gaze on the warrior he will seize and devour, are *ligge gelicost* (727) "most like to fire." I find it difficult not to believe, then, that *fyrbendum fæst* carries a discreet but powerful irony. Or again, when, in his speech of advice to Beowulf, Hrothgar enumerates the various ways men may die, one of which, he says, will end Beowulf's life, are we being over-subtle to notice it is the *fyres feng* that actually does destroy Beowulf, and to savor the sad irony that fire's *feng* – its "grip" – will prove greater even than the mighty grip of the hero?

The hostile fire that seizes, bites, and devours throughout the poem seems to me a consistently portrayed, living entity in *Beowulf* – one might almost say a character in the narrative. Its portrayal and meaning are even more consistent than is that of the fire-imagery in Homer, a subject which has been discussed so well and at such length in Cedric Whitman's *Homer and the Heroic Tradition*.[15] And because I am so impressed by the deftness with which the *Beowulf* poet uses fire-imagery, I am susceptible to persuasion that the last two passages quoted above may be related and meaningful, rather than a thoughtless bungle.

Turning to another group of "clarifying" variations, a group dealing with warrior bands, I would first call attention to the Old English *Exodus*, 180–2:

>Ymb hine wægon   *wigend unforhte*,
>*hare heorowulfas*   hilde gretton,
>þurstige þræcwiges,   þeodenholde

"Around him moved fearless warriors, grey, deadly wolves; loyal to their prince and thirsting for battle, they welcomed war." Here the literally denominated warriors are characterized further with the somewhat metaphorical variation

---

[15] Whitman, *Homer and the Heroic Tradition* (Cambridge, MA, 1958), pp. 128–45. Whereas Whitman finds references to fire in the *Iliad* forming a "pattern of associations, all centering around the theme of heroic passion and death," (p. 129), the *Beowulf* poet seems to make the symbolism even more explicit: the heroes of the Old English poem seem always to be pitted against a fire-like inimicality (e.g., the fiery-eyed Grendel who dwells in a fire-lit cave beneath a mere on which appears fiery light, a fiery dragon, the fire that consumes the two royal halls in the poem, the dark fires of the funeral pyre, and the fires of hell).

describing them as wolves. A similar but more problematic example occurs in *Beowulf*, 1829–35, where Beowulf vows twice to Hrothgar that he will bring an army to his assistance if need should befall. He says,

        ic ðe þusenda   þegna bringe,
        hæleþa to helpe . . .
                      . . . ic þe wel herige
        ond þe to geoce   garholt bere,
        mægenes fultum,   þær ðe bið manna þearf

"I shall bring to your aid a thousand thanes, heroes . . . ; I shall honor you [*or* provide you with an army?] and bring to your aid a wooden spear, the support of an army, if you have need of men." I have always thought there was a touch of bathos in Beowulf's promise to bring along a wooden spear with the multitudes of warriors he will lead to Denmark, and Klaeber too was troubled, asking with an uncertain query whether *garholt* is perhaps a plural and should be rendered "wooden spears," an improvement which seems somehow not to solve the problem. Some may well wonder why this passage is included at all among a list of variations purporting to contain a figurative expression explicated by a literal term.

The answer is that I do take *garholt* as a figurative term: I believe that the baseword *holt* may not mean "wood" in the sense of "material" but "wood" in the sense of "forest." Beowulf, I suggest, is saying, "I shall bring to your support a *forest* of spears!"[16] I make this suggestion not merely because it seems to me to improve the tone and sense of the passage, but also because the metaphor comparing a spear-bearing army to a forest is a traditional trope, one occurring, for example, in line 47 of the Latin version of the *Waldere* legend, where the subject is Attila's army:

        Ferrea silva micat totos rutilando per agros[17]

"A forest of iron glistens, gleaming red through all the fields." Behind this, of course, are references to cornfields of spears and acres of bristling iron in the *Aeneid* and other Latin writings.[18] Lucan (a favorite of Aldhelm's) refers to a warrior with a hyperbolic "forest of spears" in his breast, and William of Malmesbury works this turn of phrase into his account of the wars with

---

[16] Caroline Brady has kindly called my attention to the fact that my interpretation of *garholt* was anticipated by Arthur G. Brodeur in *The Art of Beowulf* (Berkeley, CA, p. 1959), 30. See also Phyllis Hodgson's review of Brodeur in *Modern Language Review*, 55 (1960), 426, and Brady's study, "Weapons in *Beowulf*: an analysis of the nominal compounds and an evaluation of the poet's use of them," *Anglo-Saxon England*, 8 (1979), 79–141, esp. 130–1.

[17] See Karl Strecker's edition of *Waltharius* in *MGH: Poetarum Latinorum Medii Aevi*, 6, no. 1, 26.

[18] Strecker cites *Aeneid*, book XI, lines 601–2, and book III, lines 45–6. Cf. also book VII, line 516.

Penda.[19] Looking to the Germanic side, we see that the later tradition of the Icelanders has an entire system of kennings based on warriors imagined as trees: *hildimeiðr, vighlynr, geira viðr*, and so on. The same image is used, if I am not mistaken, elsewhere in Old English poetry. *Exodus*, 155–9, describes the advance of Pharoah's host in these terms:

> siððan hie gesawon   of suðwegum
> *fyrd* Faraonis   forð ongangan,
> *oferholt* wegan,   *eored* lixan,
> (garas trymedon,   guð hwearfode,
> blicon bordhreoðan,   byman sungon),

"Then they saw the host of Pharoah advance from the south, an overwhelming forest move, the army glitter (the spears were arrayed, the shields shone, trumpets sang, war approached)," where the thickly arrayed spears are pictured as "an overwhelming forest" (*oferholt*). Actually, my reading of this passage was anticipated by *BTD*, where we find entered with queries the suggestion that the word *oferholt* might possibly be read here as "a forest of spears which rise over the heads of those who bear them." This reading has found little favor with recent editors, who apparently feel that to translate the simple element *ofer-* as "over the heads of those who bear them" is supplying a little more than the bare prefix warrants. I would suggest, however, we need only take the prefix in the sense which it clearly has in this sentence from a confessional manual detailing the penalty for rape: *Gyf hwa mid his* ofercræfte *wif oððe mæden neadinga nymð to unrihthæmede hire unwilles, beo he amansumod* "If someone by his *overpowering strength* take a woman or maiden forcibly in fornication against her will, let him be excommunicated."[20] The prefix would seem to carry the same signification in *Beowulf*, 2916–17:

> þær hyne Hetware   hilde genægdon,
> elne geeodon   mid *ofermægene*

"There the Hetware assailed him with war, boldly brought it about with an overwhelming army," and in *Elene*, 63–4, we are told that Constantine feared he could never withstand the *mægen unrime* (61) of the Huns because he

> hæfde wigena to lyt,
> eaxlgestealna   wið *ofermægene*

"He had too few warriors, comrades, against the overwhelming army." Occurrences of *ofer-* with the sense "overpowering, overwhelming" are in fact

---

[19] *Willelmi Malmesbiriensis Monachi: De Gestis Regum Anglorum*, ed. William Stubbs, 2 vols (London, 1887–89), vol. 1, p. 52. Cf. Lucan, *Pharsalia*, 6, 205.

[20] Roger Fowler, "A late Old English handbook for the use of a confessor," *Anglia*, 83 (1965), 23.

fairly frequent,[21] and if we assume that the prefix carries this meaning in the *oferholt* of *Exodus*, 157, the emendation *eoforholt*, the strained meaning "phalanx of shields,"[22] and other desperate measures may be unnecessary.

The overall effect of the "clarifying" variations is to impart to Old English poetry a lucidity and accessibility which distinguishes its style sharply from the more cryptic and mystifying effects of the Old Icelandic poets, who prefer as a rule to designate their referents only once and metaphorically, leaving the reader to puzzle out the meaning as best he can. Something deep in the Anglo-Saxon tradition seems to relish both the metaphorical statement and the clarity which metaphor sometimes lacks, a division of aims illustrated vividly in an Old English glossator's response to a verse of Aldhelm's Anglo-Latin *Ænigma*, 95. Speaking of the song which Circe chanted over a pool of water, the flamboyant Aldhelm says, "fontis liquidi maculabat flumina verbis" ("she stained with words the flowing stream of the liquid spring"), which the downright glossator paraphrases, *þæt is, sang on þæt wæter* ("that is, she sang on the water").[23]

At times this impulse toward double statement seems to find reflexes in the narrative art of the Old English poets. The *beamas twegen* of *Exodus* 94 is a cryptic and puzzling allusion until, in a second account thirteen lines later, we are given clarification. At a higher level of narrative structure, we may think of the *Beowulf* poet's representation of Hrethel's grief through an elaborate analogy – that of the hanged man's father and his pathetic lament – which is made clear by the poet's preceding literal statement of the event. Beowulf's report to Hygelac (2000–151) and the reiterated prophecies of the fall of the Geats offer yet larger-scaled examples of this repetition of identical facts in contrasting terms, while elaborate repetitions in the description of the dragon's hoard (2210–323) have been shown by Christopher Knipp to be a deliberate and characteristic narrative device.[24] In the past such instances have often been regarded as inadvertencies or lapses of skill. Yet the same mental habit that produced the clarifying variations seems to be at work in these larger structural repetitions, and we might suspect that in all these instances the poets were proceeding by a consistent stylistic principle and were not just aimlessly repeating themselves.

The next and last type of variation to be considered is exemplified by the ensuing list of ten apparently corrupt passages from the Old English poetic corpus. Each passage in the list violates a well-known rule of Old English

---

[21] See the citations in *BTD*, s.v. *ofermægen*.

[22] *CHM*, s.v. *oferholt*.

[23] Thomas Wright, *Anglo-Saxon and Old English Vocabularies*, ed. Richard Wülcker, 2nd edn, 2 vols (London, 1884), vol. 1, p. 447).

[24] Knipp, "*Beowulf* 2210b–2323: repetition in the description of the dragon's hoard," *Neuphilologische Mitteilungen*, 73 (1972), 775–85.

variation technique: *a poet may not repeat a major word in the two parts of a variation.* If the purpose of variation is to *vary*, to say the same thing in *different* words, then the repetition of a key word contradicts the very motive principle of the figure. Therefore, textual criticism has come to the rescue of these spoiled variations, and in the selection of ten representative examples below I have tried to review some of those rescue missions. I quote the variation as it stands in the unemended manuscript and then indicate to the right the suggested improvements.

1 *Beowulf*, 2283–4:

      Ða wæs *hord* rasod,   *hlæw*[25]
onboren beaga *hord*   *dæl*[26]

"Then the hoard was rifled, the hoard of rings plundered."

2 *Exodus*, 91–2:

      þæt þær *drihten* cwom   *dihtan*[27]
weroda *drihten*   *waldend*[28]

"That the Lord came there, the Lord of hosts."

3 *Riddle 60*, 12–14:

hu mec seaxes *ord*   and seo swiþre hond,
eorles ingeþonc   ond *ord* somod,   *ecg*,[29] *oroð*[30]
þingum geþydan

"How the point of the knife and that right hand, the man's deep thought and the point together, purposely imprinted me."

4 *Elene*, 214–17:

      ond þa his modor het
feran foldwege   folca þreate

---

[25] Ferdinand Holthausen, "Beiträge zur Erklärung des altengl. Epos," *Zeitschrift für deutsche Philologie*, 37 (1905), 120; Walter J. Sedgefield, *Beowulf*, 2nd edn (Manchester, 1913).

[26] Sophus Bugge, "Zum Beowulf," *Zeitschrift für deutsche Philologie*, 4 (1873), 212.

[27] Elliott V. K. Dobbie, review of Edward B. Irving, *The Old English Exodus, JEGP*, 53 (1954), 230.

[28] "In view of the usual OE principles of variation," Edward B. Irving, *Exodus* (New Haven, 1953), p. 74, is led "to suspect strongly that the original may have had *weroda Waldend*." But in "New notes on the Old English *Exodus*," *Anglia*, 90 (1972), 300, Irving defends the manuscript reading, supporting this decision with persuasive parallels from scripture.

[29] Georg Herzfeld, *Die Räthsel des Exeterbuches und ihr Verfasser* (Berlin, 1890), p. 69.

[30] James M. Hart, "Allotria II," *MLN*, 17 (1902), 463.

to Iudeum,   georne secan
wigena *þreate*   hwær se wuldres beam   *werode*,[31] *heape*[32]

"And then he commanded his mother to travel over the earth-way with a band of people to the Jews, to seek with a band of warriors where the tree of glory [was hidden]."

5 *Elene*, 313-15:

Gangaþ nu snude,   snyttro geþencaþ,
weras wisfæste,   wordes *cræftige*,   *gleawe*[33]
þa ðe eowre æ   æðelum *cræftige*   *gode*[34]

"Go now quickly, think with prudence of men versed in wisdom, skillful of speech, skillful by their nature, who [know] your law."

6 *Daniel*, 33-4:

þa wearð reðemod   rices *ðeoden*,
unhold *þeoden*   þam þe æhte geaf   *þeodum*[35]
                                                        drihten,[36] *þeode*[37]

"Then the prince of the realm, the hostile prince, became angry with those to whom he had given dominion."

7 *Daniel*, 36-7:

wæron mancynnes   metode *dyrust*,
dugoða *dyrust*,   drihtne leofost   *drymust*[38]
                                                        demend[39]
                                                        dryhta[40]

---

[31] Bernhard A. K. ten Brink, "Cynewulfs Elene mit einem glossar herausgegeben von Julius Zupitza," *Anzeiger für deutsches Alterthum*, supp. vol. 5 (1879), 59.
[32] Ferdinand Holthausen, *Cynewulfs Elene* (Heidelberg and New York, 1914).
[33] Albert S. Cook, ed., *The Old English Elene, Phoenix, and Physiologus* (New Haven, 1919), p. 13.
[34] Holthausen, *Cynewulfs Elene*; cf. Julius Zupitza's note in *Cynewulfs Elene* (Berlin, 1899), p. 14.
[35] *ASPR*, vol. 1, p. 112; Wilhelm Schmidt, *Die altenglische Dichtung 'Daniel'* (Halle, 1907); Ernst A. Kock, "Jubilee jaunts and jottings: 250 contributions to the interpretation and prosody of Old West Teutonic alliterative poetry," *Lunds Universitets Årsskrift*, new ser. sect. 1, vol. 14, no. 26, p. 12.
[36] Peter J. Cosijn, "Anglosaxonica II," *Beiträge zur Geschichte der deutschen Sprache und Literatur*, 20 (1895), 107.
[37] Karl W. Bouterwek, *Caedmon's des Angelsachsen biblische Dichtungen* (Gütersloh, 1854), p. 324. Cf. Thorpe's reading *þeodne* in his edition of the Junius MS, *Cædmon's Metrical Paraphrase of Parts of the Holy Scriptures* (London, 1832).
[38] Christian W. M. Grein, *Bibliothek der angelsächsischen Poesie*, ed. Richard P. Wülcker, 3 vols (Leipzig, 1881-98), vol. 2, p. 478.
[39] Cosijn, "Anglosaxonica II," p. 107.
[40] Kock, "Jubilee jaunts."

"They were to God the dearest of mankind, the dearest of peoples, most cherished by the Lord."

8 *Daniel*, 321–2:

     oððe *brimfaropes*,   *brimflodes*[41]
sæfaroða sand   *sæwaroða*[42]

"Or the sand of the ocean shore, of the shores of the sea."

9 *Durham*, 7–8:

wuniad in ðem wycum wilda *deor* monige,   [no
in deope dalum *deora* ungerim   emendations]

"Many wild beasts dwell in those places in the deep dales, beasts beyond number."

10 *Charm*, 9, 14–15:

Binnan þrym nihtum cunne ic his *mihta*,
his mægen and his *mihta* and his mundcræftas   Delete
                          and his
                          mihta[43]

"Within three days I shall know his might, his might and his main, and the powers of his hand."

It should be noticed that the passages requiring emendation appear in a variety of Old English poetic genres and that more than one passage of this type can be found in the same poem. Two of the examples from *Daniel* occur within the scope of only five verses. It should also be noticed that the verbal repetitions which editors have removed never involve any breakdown in meaning, meter, or grammar. The emender's knife has in each instance been wielded solely in the name of a presumptive rule of variation technique. Only the *Durham* passage has been allowed to stand, presumably because there are two independent witnesses to this reading in *Durham*,[44] and scholars were hesitant to assume the same corruption in both lines of transmission. Perhaps

---

[41] Hertha Marquardt, *Die altenglischen Kenningar* (Halle, 1938), p. 175. (The manuscript reads *brimfaropæs*.)

[42] Christian W. M. Grein, "Zur Textkritik der angelsächsischen Dichter," *Germania*, 10 (1865), 416–29, at 419; Grein, *Bibliothek*, p. 492; Schmidt, *Die altenglische Dichtung 'Daniel'*.

[43] Felix Grendon, "The Anglo-Saxon charms," *Journal of American Folklore*, 22 (1909), 105–237; Godfrid Storms, *Anglo-Saxon Magic* (The Hague, 1948), p. 210.

[44] The repeated *deor...deora* appears in both University Library, Cambridge, MS Ff.i.27 and in the version which George Hickes printed in his *Linguarum vett. septentrionalium thesaurus grammatico-criticus et archaeologicus*, 1, 3 vols (Oxford, 1705), pp. 178–9, from the now lost Cotton MS Vitellius D.xx.

editors consoled themselves with the hypothesis that since this is a very late Old English poem, the strength of the prior tradition must have been failing. Such a poet might well have forgotten the classical principle that repetition within variation is impermissible in Old English verse.

But another thought must also suggest itself to the reader who studies this list of putative blunders: the well-known principle of the impermissibility of repetition within variation has been upheld only by virtue of some rather extraordinary exertions on the part of editors and textual scholars. Is it not perhaps possible that these and other passages in which such repetition occurs[45] are perfectly sound as they stand and that there is no rule forbidding repetition within variation?

In considering this question one should also notice that repetition within variations would hardly be an isolated phenomenon in Old English verse. An examination of any fairly extensive section of the corpus will reveal verbal repetition within coordinate series linked by conjunctions, repetition of the same word or morpheme to establish the alliterative stave of a longline (although these, like repetitions within variations, will often be removed by editorial emendation), repetition within a single sentence or within contiguous sentences, paronomastic repetition of the kind that Roberta Frank explores,[46] and ornamental polyptota such as *æðele be æðelum, werige mid werigum, wundor æfter wundre, stan from stane, halig haligne, cyninga cyning, of dæge on dæge*, and *in worulda woruld*, all of which occur within the poem *Andreas*. As an example of how the presence of other types of repetition might suggest that repetition within variations was not as abhorrent to the Anglo-Saxon ear as we have long assumed, we may examine once again the tenth passage in the above list. Preceding this passage in the ninth charm are the following verses (7-9):

> find þæt feoh   and fere þæt feoh
> and hafa þæt feoh   and heald þæt feoh
> and fere ham þæt feoh

"Find that herd, and convey that herd, and keep that herd and hold that herd, and bring that herd home." Immediately following the variation containing repetition, moreover, is this line:

> Eall he *weornige,*   *swa syre wudu weornie*

"May he all wither, as dry wood may wither." That successive scholars should pause amid this din of incantatory repetition in order to excise a single

---

[45] I have noted four further passages with such repetition in *Beowulf*, two in *Maldon*, and a sprinkling of occurrences in the elegies, the gnomic poetry, the *Paris Psalter* (where the parallelism and repetitions of the Vulgate no doubt reinforced the tendency), and in *Instructions for Christians*.

[46] Frank, "Some uses of paronomasia in Old English scriptual verse," *Speculum*, 47 (1972), 207-26.

repetition from a variation bears impressive witness to the strength of our belief in the conjectural rule that variation can never involve repetition.

That rule, I believe, is an invention of modern scholars, not of the scopas. Repetition within variation, like repetition within other, similarly close syntactical structures, would appear to have been a consciously cultivated stylistic device, and the manuscript reading in each of the passages cited above should be allowed to stand without further challenge. We should try, moreover, to sense the special effect the poet is intending when he adopts such repetitions in his variations. Sometimes the repetition seems to throw emphasis on the word repeated, as in the third example, in which *ord* appears twice. At other times, paradoxically, the repetition of a noun seems to give greater emphasis to a modifier which occurs with but one of the occurrences of the repeated word. In the second example above, for instance, the iteration of *drihten* seems somehow to lay stress on *weroda*, the effect being to emphasize God's role as Lord of hosts. If the second *drihten* is changed to *Waldend*, as Edward B. Irving originally suggested in his edition, the contrastive force of the variation would be dissipated among the two different elements of the variation rather than focussed on the one differing element *weroda*. Other repetitive variations in the list may well have been intended for yet other effects.

There is in Old English poetry such pervasive use of artful synonymy, of contrastive restatement in different words, that we sometimes overlook just how extensive and various are the stylistic uses of exact verbal repetition. But repetition is used, and in many different ways. An obvious example is those rhetorical units which Adeline C. Bartlett has called "envelope patterns."[47] Here the repetition of words or groups of words at the beginning and at the close of self-contained segments of narrative effectively and functionally marks these sections off from the surrounding text. Another use of repetition within similar compass is in those fugal patterns of recurrence which John O. Beaty long ago called "echo-words" and which James L. Rosier has more recently characterized as "generative composition."[48] These uses of repetition produce

---

[47] Bartlett, *The Larger Rhetorical Patterns in Anglo-Saxon Poetry* (New York, 1935), p. 9. A special case is the repeated epithet *ece dryhten* in Caedmon's *Hymn*, a repetition which John C. Pope, *Seven Old English Poems* (Indianapolis, 1966), p. 52, sees as a kind of burden marking off the poem into stanza-like units. Another special case is the *dúnadh* pattern (as in "The Capture of the Five Boroughs") discussed by Patrick L. Henry, "A Celtic-English prosodic figure," *Zeitschrift für Celtische Philologie*, 29 (1962), 91–9.

[48] Beaty, "The echo-word in *Beowulf* with a note on the *Finnsburg Fragment*," *PMLA*, 49 (1934), 365–73; Rosier, "Generative composition in *Beowulf*," *ES*, 58 (1977), 193–203. The phenomenon is also explored by Eugene R. Kintgen, "Echoic repetition in Old English poetry, especially *The Dream of the Rood*," *Neuphilologische Mitteilungen*, 75 (1974), 202–23, who argues that such repetitions are conscious artistic effects which function as both stylistic and structural devices in the poem. His argument would seem to gain strength from the demonstration by a later scholar that Old English poets were capable of eschewing such repetition when they found it artistically preferable

a verbal intertexture which contributes more than we consciously realize, I suspect, to the unity of style and harmony of phrase that we all sense in the best Old English poetry.

A more specifically pointed use of repetition may be seen in the Unferth intermezzo of *Beowulf*, where the hero's repetition of Unferth's own words in his reply to the hostile *þyle* gives force and sting to the rejoinder. Here repetition functions dramatically within the narrative action itself. But the poet also uses repetition as a way of making implicit comments on his narrative, as when he embellishes the description of Beowulf's funeral rites at the end of the poem with echoes and epithets from the Scyld funeral which introduced the narrative.[49] Being convinced, as I am, that the formulaic quality of Old English poetry did not deaden the ear to nuances, I sense stylistic effect and poetic meaning in these echoes. A similar effect and meaning result, I believe, from the way Beowulf, in his old age, falls heir to the epithets which had earlier described Hrothgar – *eald eþelweard*, *folces hyrde*, *gumcystum god*, *har hilderinc*, *frod cyning*, *rices hyrde*, and so on – while Wiglaf inherits the epithets for the youthful Beowulf, such as *hæle hildedeor* and *feþecempa*.[50] The pathos of aging and the mystery of the hero's inevitable departure from this life acquire deeper poignancy through these verbal echoes that emphasize the rhythmic recurrence of such events in the heroic past. Verbal repetition plays a part, it would seem, in some of the poem's best moments, and if this is true of the larger structure of *Beowulf*, we should perhaps be all the readier to accept repetition in the smaller structures, such as variation.[51]

In isolating for analysis two of the many types of variation in Old English poetry, I have tried to illustrate more than one way in which we can profit from study of this kind. This scrutiny may lead to a finer discernment of the local effects which a poet sought with a certain kind of variation if we examine these variations in aggregate. Indeed, by examining them together, we can at times even throw light on the textual interpretation of a difficult passage. Taking a broader view, we can perceive analogies between the poet's strategies in his use of variation and his procedures at other levels of diction, and on occasion, in

---

to do so; see Geoffrey R. Russom, "Artful avoidance of the useful phrase in *Beowulf*, *The Battle of Maldon* and *Fates of the Apostles*," *SP*, 75 (1978), 371–90.

[49] See *Beowulf and the Fight at Finnsburg*, ed. Fr. Klaeber, 3rd edn with 1st and 2nd supplements (Boston, 1950), p. 228, note to lines 3108ff.

[50] See William Whallon, "Formulas for heroes in the 'Iliad' and in 'Beowulf,'" *MP*, 63 (1965), 102.

[51] Nor should we look askance on emendations which introduce repetition into variations if other considerations warrant the change. See, for example, the meritorious emendation of *adloman* to *aðlogan* (with the attendant repetition of *-logan* in *wærlogan* and *aðlogan*) in *Guthlac*, 912, proposed by Herbert D. Meritt, *Fact and Lore about Old English Words* (Stanford, 1954), pp. 5–6.

the larger narrative structures.⁵² Such analogies should not be pressed too far, but they can be a helpful guide to understanding the stylistic intentions in a body of poetry for which we have no *Ars poetica* and no *Skáldskaparmál*.

⁵² In arguing this point my method has been the reverse of Joan Blomfield's, who, in "The style and structure of *Beowulf*," *RES*, 14 (1938), 396–403, tried to demonstrate how "analysis of style is ... a justifiable approach to analysis of structure" (p. 397).

6
Understanding an Old English Wisdom Verse: *Maxims II*, Lines 10ff

The verse *soð bið swicolost* in *Maxims II*[1] has become a kind of shibboleth for Old English scholars. Those who argue that Old English poetry is subtler and more complex than its early editors have usually assumed retain the manuscript reading and try to justify the arresting sense "truth is most tricky." Scholars who are wary of oversubtle literary interpretations and impatient with editorial pusillanimity before the authority of medieval scribes welcome the emendations *switolost* or *swutolost*, which allow the simpler, cheerier meaning "truth is most evident." To a certain extent, the division of opinion falls along national lines. Favoring emendation and the simpler meaning are the English scholars Sweet, Sedgefield, Whitelock, Wyatt, and Hamer, who emend to *swutolost*,[2] and the Americans Williams, Dobbie, Cassidy and Ringler, Greenfield and Evert, who emend to *switolost*.[3] Favoring the manuscript reading and the more complex sense are the Germans Brandl, Ettmüller, Grein, Kluge, and Wülcker, who retain *swicolost*, rendering it "Wahrheit ist sehr trügerisch" or something similar.[4] There are of course exceptions to the rule,[5] but the general

---

Reprinted from *The Wisdom of Poetry: essays in Early English literature in honor of Morton W. Bloomfield*, ed. Larry D. Benson and Siegfried Wenzel (Kalamazoo, MI, 1982), pp. 1–11, 261–4.

[1] Line 10a. The full context is quoted below, p. 94, from *The Anglo-Saxon Minor Poems*, ed. Elliott Van Kirk Dobbie, ASPR, 6 (New York, 1942), pp. 55–6, but I restore the manuscript reading *swicolost* both here and there.

[2] Henry Sweet, *An Anglo-Saxon Reader in Prose and Verse* (Oxford, 1876), p. 183; Walter J. Sedgefield, *An Anglo-Saxon Verse-Book* (Manchester, 1922), p. 104; *Sweet's Anglo-Saxon Reader*, rev. throughout by Dorothy Whitelock (Oxford, 1967), p. 174; A. J. Wyatt, *The Threshold of Anglo-Saxon* (Cambridge, 1926), p. 34; Richard Hamer, *A Choice of Anglo-Saxon Verse* (London, 1970), p. 110. John Earle was troubled by the maxim because it "has a strange Machiavellian look" (*Two of the Saxon Chronicles Parallel* [Oxford, 1865], p. xxxv).

[3] Blanche Colton Williams, *Gnomic Poetry in Anglo-Saxon* (New York, 1914), p. 148; Dobbie, *The Anglo-Saxon Minor Poems*, p. 175; Frederic G. Cassidy and Richard N. Ringler, eds., *Bright's Old English Grammar and Reader* (New York, 1971), p. 374; Stanley B. Greenfield and Richard Evert, "*Maxims II*: gnome and poem" in *Anglo-Saxon Poetry: essays in appreciation for John C. McGalliard*, ed. Lewis E. Nicholson and Dolores Warwick Frese (Notre Dame, 1975), p. 341.

[4] Alois Brandl, *Vom kosmologischen Denken des heidnisch-christlichen Germanentums: der frühangelsächsische Schicksalsspruch der Handschrift Tiberius B. I und seine Verwandheit mit Boethius* (Berlin, 1937), pp. 8–9; Ludwig Ettmüller, *Engla and Seaxna Scôpas and Bôceras* (Quedlinburg, 1850), p. 283;

[*See p. 88 for n. 4 cont. and n. 5*]

division between German and Anglo-American readings of the passage should be noted, for Anglo-American scholars often pride themselves on their textual conservatism and their openmindedness to poetic complexity and nuance, while criticizing Germans for being incurably literal-minded and prone to needless emendation. In this case the roles are reversed, reminding us of the folly of such characterizations in the first place.

My concern here is to determine, insofar as possible, which of the two readings of the *Maxims* verse is more likely to represent the compiler's intentions and to reflect the Anglo-Saxons' conception of the nature of truth. Can a case be made for the more imaginative German reading, which allows us to retain the words the scribe transmitted to us, or is the circumstantial evidence for "truth is most evident" so compelling that we must abandon the manuscript and settle for the simpler, more hopeful conception of truth? A case can be made for either interpretation, as I shall try to show, but my preference in the end (since suspense is not part of my strategy) will be for the somber German rather than the bright Anglo-American meaning. Primarily this is because of the contextual evidence which has come to my attention and which I set out below; but I also prefer the more somber reading of this wisdom verse because it conforms better with the character of wisdom literature as it has been described by Morton Bloomfield, our undisputed authority on the subject: "Its general tone is pessimistic and worldlywise."[6]

However blandly optimistic it may seem to some modern readers, an Old English maxim "truth is most evident" is by no means inherently implausible. The medieval proverb "veritas semper certa et perspicua est"[7] provides a Latin model, and the Anglo-Saxons themselves are known to have made observations of this order. *The Durham Proverbs* include *soþ hit sylf acypeð* (translating "veritas seipsam semper declarat" ["Truth always reveals itself"])[8] and the same

---

Christian W. M. Grein, *Bibliothek der angelsächsischen Poesie* (Göttingen, 1857), vol. 1, p. 346; Friedrich Kluge, *Angelsächsisches Lesebuch* (Halle, 1915), p. 141; Richard Paul Wülcker, *Bibliothek der angelsächsischen Poesie neu bearbeitet* (Kassel, 1883), 1:339.

[5] Walther Fischer, in a review in *Anglia Beiblatt*, 48 (1937), 364, takes issue with Brandl's spirited defense of the manuscript reading *swicolost*. J. K. Bollard, in a very good edition and discussion of the poem, preserves *swicolost*, like the German editors, because "we should not reject the MS. reading merely because we cannot immediately comprehend its full significance. . . . I have chosen to retain the MS. reading rather than run the risk of eliminating what could well be an insight into a very elusive subject"; see his article "The Cotton Maxims," *Neophilologus*, 57 (1973), 185. The American James R. Hulbert, on the other hand, adopts Sweet's *swutolost* rather than Williams's *switolost* in his revision of *Bright's Anglo-Saxon Reader* (New York, 1935), p. 177.

[6] Bloomfield, "Understanding Old English poetry," *AnM*, 9 (1968), 18; rpt in Bloomfield's *Essays and Explorations: studies in ideas, language, and literature* (Cambridge, MA, 1970), p. 73.

[7] Hans Walther, *Proverbia Sententiaeque Latinitatis Medii Aevi* (Göttingen, 1967), vol. 5, no. 33157.

[8] See the edition by Olof Arngart, "The Durham Proverbs," *Speculum*, 56 (1981), 288–300, esp. p. 293. See also Bartlett Jere Whiting and Helen Wescott Whiting, *Proverbs, Sentences, and Proverbial*

maxim is quoted, apparently, in *Blickling Homily* XV ("The Story of Peter and Paul"): *Nu mæg soð hit sylf gecyþan* ("Now truth can reveal itself").[9] In context, however, the quotation is ironical, for the speaker is Nero, who is expressing confidence that the spectacle he has just arranged with the delusive sorcerer Simon will reveal once for all the truth of Simon's claims and the falsity of Peter's and Paul's. In the event it is the truth of the two saints that is vindicated, of course, while Simon's tricks are exposed as frauds, and yet Nero persists in believing the sorcerer's false truth, to his ultimate doom. The tale exemplifies the extreme difficulty a man can have in discerning the truth when he is faced with alternative versions of it. Indeed, one could epitomize the plot of "The Story of Peter and Paul" in terms of Old English maxims by saying that whereas Nero thinks deludedly that *soð hit sylf gecyþeþ* ("Truth reveals itself"), the events of the narrative show that in fact *soð bið swicolost* ("Truth is most tricky") – at least for those who do not share the Christian illumination enjoyed by Peter and Paul.

The simple meaning "truth is most evident" is possible, then, but *Blickling Homily* XV shows that Anglo-Saxons could view this cheerful interpretation of truth with a measure of irony. This should encourage a pause at least before we emend *swicolost*, and in pausing we might note that the emendation is not quite so simple a matter as some of the emenders have implied. The difference between *c* and *t* being so slight in Insular script, one might conclude that the emended form has virtually equal authority with the manuscript reading. "Why not *switolost*?" asks Blanche Colton Williams. "Palæographically this form is quite possible, *c* and *t* often being mistaken for each other."[10] Cassidy and Ringler, among others, concur: "The emendation is suggested by common sense and supported by the fact that scribal confusion of *c* and *t* is widespread."[11] The American emenders may well have been puzzled as to why Sweet and his English compatriots prefer the more complicated reconstruction *swutolost* when the minimal change to *switolost* apparently produces the same results. But there is good reason for Sweet's *swutolost*: back umlaut of *i* by *o* is to be expected when the intervening consonant is *t*, and a preceding *w* frequently caused the resulting diphthong to become *u*. Thus I find in the Healey-Venezky concordance[12] a total of 313 occurrences of the adjective

---

Phrases From English Writings Mainly Before 1500 (Cambridge, MA, 1968), p. 533. The Whitings cite this maxim (as Arngart notes) and list ten subsequent variations on the phrase in English writings from Chaucer to Horman's *Vulgaria*. They do not notice the occurrence of the maxim in *Blickling Homily XV*.

[9] *The Blickling Homilies of the Tenth Century*, ed. Richard Morris, EETS, 58, 63, 73 (London, 1874–80), p. 187.   [10] Williams, *Gnomic Poetry*, p. 148.

[11] Cassidy and Ringler, *Bright's Old English Grammar and Reader*, p. 374.

[12] *A Microfiche Concordance to Old English* compiled by Antonette di Paolo Healey and Richard L. Venezky and published by the Dictionary of Old English Project, Centre for Medieval Studies, University of Toronto (Toronto, 1980). For the figures cited here I have used the "Word and

sweotol in its various forms and derivatives, and the root is spelled *swit-* only ten times. The commonest spelling is *sweot-* (163 times), next is *swut-* (109 times), and the spellings *swyt-, su(u)t-, swot-, swiot-,* and *swet-* occur a total of thirty-one times. The form *switolost*, then, while not impossible, is a statistically abnormal form, and therefore a somewhat dubious emendation. Sweet's *swutolost* would be much more likely to occur in an eleventh-century manuscript like Cotton Tiberius B.i, and, indeed, in the only other occurrence of the adjective in this codex (in the poem *Menologium*, 129), the spelling is *swutelra*.

The unemended manuscript reading *swicolost*, on the other hand, is the statistically normal spelling of that word, since back umlaut of *i* by *o* is very rare when the intervening consonant is *c*. Of a total ninety-four occurrences of *swicol* in its various forms and derivatives recorded in Healey-Venezky, ninety-three have the spelling *swic-*, while only one has *sweoc-*. (There are no spellings *suic-, su(u)c-, swuc-,* or *swyc-*.) The isolated spelling with *eo* occurs in the word *sweocolan*, which is a variant reading for *diglan* in one of the manuscripts of King Alfred's translation of *The Pastoral Care*.[13] Another such spelling (*ofersweocola*) is recorded by Alistair Campbell in his supplement to the Bosworth-Toller *Dictionary*,[14] but this is in fact a deviant and erroneous reading in one of the manuscripts of the Old English *Benedictine Rule*, and its inclusion in Campbell's *Addenda* was a mistake. *Ofersweocola* occurs in Corpus Christi College, Oxford, MS 197 where other manuscripts have *ofersprecola*.[15] Since the Latin word being translated is *linguosus*, it is obvious that *ofersprecola* is correct and the apparent *hapax legomenon ofersweocola* is in fact nothing but a careless scribe's miscopy of *ofersprecola*. *Swicol* being, then, the correct and practically invariable spelling of the adjective, we have in the manuscript reading a legitimate word. The emendation *switolost* is statistically dubious: if we are to emend at all, we must adopt Sweet's *swutolost*, and this form requires a more elaborate rationale than the mere citation of close similarity between *t* and *c* in Insular script.

If we retain the reading of the manuscript, what is to be made of the resulting maxim *soð bið swicolost*? Bosworth-Toller offers a very tentative suggestion that *swicol* might carry, in this one occurrence, the sense "occasioning offense."[16] A

---

frequency lists" at the end of the microfiche concordance, but for other data in this essay I have drawn on the concordance proper.

[13] *The Pastoral Care*, ed. from British Library MS Cotton Otho B.ii by Ingvar Carlson, completed by Lars-G. Hallander et al. (Stockholm, 1978), pt. 2, p. 89, n. to line 6.

[14] Campbell, *Enlarged Addenda and Corrigenda* (Oxford, 1972), to *BTS*, s.v. *oferswicol*. Another spelling of *swicol* is recorded by Campbell in his *Old English Grammar* (Oxford, 1959), p. 92, par. 218, where he records *swiocol* as a frequent form in Old English. Since I could not find one documentation of this spelling in the microfiche concordance, I have taken no account of it in my calculations.

[15] *Die angelsächsischen Prosabearbeitungen der Benediktinerregel*, ed. Arnold Schröer, zweite Auflage mit einem Anhang von Helmut Gneuss (Darmstadt, 1964), p. 30, n. to lines 5–6.

[16] *BTD*, s.v. *swicol*, II.

maxim "truth is most offensive" would not be implausible if viewed within the context of popular proverbs such as "whoso says the sooth shall be shent" or "all sooth is not to be said."[17] The latter saying, as the Whitings note, is attested in the Old English *Durham Proverbs*, no. 19: *Ne deah eall soþ asæd ne eall sar ætwiten*." If one Anglo-Saxon thought truth could give offense, then clearly another could think so as well. But the evidence for *swicol* meaning "offensive" is unfortunately thin (hence Bosworth-Toller's warning queries around the conjecture). The well-attested senses of the word are in the semantic areas of delusion and deception.

Blanche Colton Williams, before deciding that emendation was unavoidable, tried briefly to make a case for "truth is treacherous" by referring to Chantepie de la Saussaye's account of how Norsemen, in order to give themselves freedom of action without violating their word of honor, used ambiguous language in phrasing their treaties:

> truthfulness did not by any means preclude everything that we are accustomed to regard as deceit. If truth was only adhered to from an external and formal point of view and the feeling of personal honor thereby preserved, there was felt to be no objection against relying upon the deceit contained in an equivocal word, or a dissembling mien, by which the enemy was misled. Such shrewdness was viewed as redounding to a man's honor and glory rather than to his shame. Keeping this distinction in mind, it will be seen that the notorious faithlessness with which so many medieval writers charge the Norsemen is not at all incompatible with their love of truth. With great subtleness and acumen, they made use, in the terms of a treaty, of ambiguous expressions: their honor thus remained unstained, their word unbroken.[18]

Among some Scandinavians, it may be added, one can find an actual aversion for the truth. Stanza 45 of the *Hávamál* tells us

> Ef þú átt annan, þannz þú illa trúir,
> vildu af hánom þó gott geta:
> fagrt skaltu við þann mæla, en flátt hyggia
> ok gialda lausung við lygi.[19]

---

[17] Whiting and Whiting, *Proverbs, Sentences, and Proverbial Phrases*, pp. 532–3. The sentiment is common in various languages and in various forms: "Veritas odium parit," "Il n'y a que la vérité qui offense," "Non c'è niente che offenda come la verità," "Wahrheit bringt Hass," "Quien dice las verdades, pierde las amistades," etc.

[18] Pierre Daniel Chantepie de la Saussaye, *The Religion of the Teutons*, tr. Bert J. Vos (Boston, 1902), pp. 409–10. Williams refers to this book in *Gnomic Poetry*, p. 148.

[19] *Edda: die Lieder des Codex Regius nebst verwandten Denkmälern*, ed. Gustav Neckel, 4th rev. edn Hans Kuhn (Heidelberg, 1962), p. 23.

"If you have another [friend], whom you mistrust, and yet you want to receive good from him, you must speak fair to him and think false and pay back lying with lies." And Saxo Grammaticus at one point refers to himself and his people as "We who do not account lying and deceiving as wicked and despicable."[20] But the Norsemen's occasional approbation of lying or duplicitous phrasing seems not to have been shared by the Anglo-Saxons, and the maxim's adjective *swicolost*, moreover, seems to suggest a dangerous uncertainty or unreliability in truth rather than approval of skillful lying.

The most probable meaning of the maxim would seem to be that suggested above in the discussion of the Blickling Homily on Sts Peter and Paul. That is, truth is tricky, or deceptive, or perhaps elusive (cf. *swice*, "escape," and *swīcan*, "to escape") because it is difficult to recognize, the distinction between truth and falsehood being a subtle one. This idea is by no means alien to western thought. The Book of Proverbs emphasizes the value of truth (3: 3, 23: 23), but it acknowledges at the same time that one may have difficulty in recognizing it: "There is a way that seemeth to a man right, and the ends thereof lead to death" (16: 25). Diogenes Laertius's somber observation on truth has become proverbial in many European tongues: "We know nothing certain; for truth is hidden at the bottom of an abyss."[21] Wander records a wealth of *Sprichwörter* on the difficulty of discerning the truth: "Zwischen Warhrheit und Lüge ist ein schlüpfriger Pfad" ("Between falsehood and truth is a slippery path," p. 1763, no. 410); "Wer die Wahrheit sehen will, muss gute Augen haben" ("He who wishes to see the truth must have sharp eyes," p. 1761, no. 365); "Auch Wahrheit ist eine Lüge, zur Unzeit geredet" ("Even truth is a lie when told out of season," p. 1747, no. 4); "Wahrheiten hier sind Irrtümer dort" ("Truths here are errors there," p. 1758, no. 292); etc. The last of these, emphasizing the relativity of truth, finds an analogue in Pascal: "Chacun suive les mœurs de son pays.... Vérité au deçà des Pyrénées, erreur au delà" ("Each follows the customs of his country.... Truth on this side of the Pyrenees is error on the other side").[22] Later, Pascal, adds the almost despairing observation, "La vérité est si obscurcie en ce temps, et le mensonge si établi, qu'à moins que d'aimer la vérité, on ne saurait la connaitre" ("Truth is so obscure now and lying so entrenched that unless one loved the truth one would not be able to recognize it," p. 412). Such skepticism espoused within the context of religious faith was as easy for a medieval cleric as for the seventeenth-century Christian apologist. The Italian canon Tommasino dei Circhieri, in line 1126 of his German poem *Der Welsche Gast* (composed between 1215 and 1216), defends courtly literature

---

[20] Quoted by Chantepie de la Saussaye, *The Religion of the Teutons*, p. 409.

[21] *The Oxford Dictionary of English Proverbs*, 3rd edn, rev. by F. P. Wilson (Oxford, 1970), p. 844. Cf. Karl Friedrich Wilhelm Wander, *Deutsches Sprichwörter-Lexikon* (Leipzig, 1876), volume 4, p. 1756, no. 257. Centuries before Diogenes the Greek skeptic Carneades had expressed similar views.

[22] Blaise Pascal, *Pensées*, Librairie Générale Française (Paris, 1972), p. 142.

with the observation that "wâr man mit lüge kleit" ("Truth is clothed with lies").[23] Similarly, the intense religiosity of Spinoza, derived in part from Jewish medieval philosophy, did not prevent his remarking the fine line between truth and deception.[24] Cynical assertions about the nature of truth can (especially in modern times) take on the tone of jesting Pilate, of course, as in Campoamor's

> Y es que en el mundo traidor
> Nada hay verdad ni mentira;
> Todo es según el color
> Del cristal con que se mira.[25]

"And in the deceitful world there is no truth or falsehood; everything depends upon the color of the glass through which it is viewed." The *cristal* of the poet has little in common with the lenses of Spinoza, and yet the perception of truth articulated by the two writers is mutual, suggesting how wide and flexible is the applicability of this motif of the deceptiveness of truth.

Allusions to the deceptiveness of truth or to the successful subreption of truth by evil schemers occur in Old English documents in a variety of contexts. Two Wulfstanian tracts refer to a past era when those men were thought wisest who could most craftily transform untruth into truth: *þuhte hwilum wisast se þe wæs swicolost and se þe lytelicost cuðe leaslice hiwian unsoð to soðe*.[26] Elsewhere Wulfstan says that it is arch-liars instructed by Antichrist who are capable of overpowering truth with untruth: *And swa doð þa þeodlogan eac þe taliað þæt to wærscype þæt man cunne and mæge lytelice swician and mid unsoðe soð oferswiðan*.[27] To distinguish between truth and untruth, one needs special understanding bestowed by God's grace: *And he hæfð god ingehygd þurh Godes gyfe þe . . . can him gescead betweox soðe and unsoðe*.[28] What may seem truth and wisdom to men of this world, says another homilist, is folly to God: *Ærest ealre þingen æighwylce mæn is to secene, hwæt seo se soðe wisedom, oððe hwylc seo seo soðe snytere, for þan þe se wisedom*

---

[23] Thomasin von Ziclaria, *Der Welsche Gast*, ed. H. Rückert (Berlin, 1965).

[24] "Was nennt ihr Wahrheit? Die Täuschung, die Jahrhunderte alt geworden. Was Täuschung? Die Wahrheit, die nur eine Minute gelebt." Quoted in Martin Hürlimann, *Stimmen der Völker im Sprichwort* (Zurich, 1945), p. 167.

[25] Ramón de Campoamor, "Las dos linternas" in Doloras y Humoradas, 3rd edn (Buenos Aires, 1947), pp. 98–9. Contrasting with this formulation and yet leading to a similar conclusion is Louis Aragon's observation, quoted in *The New York Review of Books*, March 19, 1981, p. 43. "Surely it must be realized that the face of error and the face of truth cannot fail to have identical features."

[26] *Wulfstan: Sammlung der ihm zugeschriebenen Homilien*, ed. Arthur Napier, rpt with a bibliographical supplement by Klaus Ostheeren (Weidmann, 1967), p. 268. Cf. p. 128, lines 7–10. These two texts are compilations of phrases from other works by Wulfstan rather than independent compositions by him.

[27] *The Homilies of Wulfstan*, ed. Dorothy Bethurum (Oxford, 1957), p. 190, lines 133–5; cf. p. 277, lines 23–5, for a similar formulation.

[28] Bethurum, *Homilies*, p. 186, lines 42–4. Cf. Napier, *Wulfstan*, p. 57, line 20, to p. 58, line 2.

þyssere wurlde is dysignysse beforen Gode.[29] For a more philosophical meditation on the nature of truth, one might turn to the Old English version of Augustine's *Soliloquies*, where the relationship between *soþ* and *soþfæstnes* is debated.[30]

Truth and its simulacra were, then, a current topic among the Anglo-Saxons, who dealt with the subject in various contexts. This would seem to support the contention that the unemended maxim meaning "truth is most tricky" accurately represents one line of thought on the nature of truth in early England. What remains to be asked is whether it is possible to specify the context of the verse and thus narrow the reference of *soð bið swicolost* in *Maxims II*. Since maxims are by nature more general in their reference than specific, to raise this question may be a mistake. And yet, more than one scholar has adverted to the interconnectedness of the items in the opening section of this collection of maxims,[31] so it may be advisable, in closing this analysis, to consider at least tentatively whether *soð bið swicolost* stands in meaningful relation with juxtaposed elements in the passage. The full context of our verse is a series of superlatives:

> Winter byð cealdost,
> lencten hrimigost (he byð lengest ceald),
> sumor sunwlitegost (swegel byð hatost),
> hærfest hreðeadegost, hæleðum bringeð
> geres wæstmas, þa þe him god sendeð.
> Soð bið swicolost, sinc byð deorost,
> gold gumena gehwam, and gomol snotorost,
> fyrngearum frod, se þe ær feala gebideð.
>
> (5–12)

"Winter is most cold, spring most frosty (it is cold for the longest time), summer most radiant with sunshine (the sun is most hot), autumn most glorious – it brings to men the fruits of the year, which God sends to them. Truth is most tricky; treasure, gold, is most precious to every man, and the old man full of years who experiences much early is the wisest." The superlatives are logically sequential, the cold of winter being followed by the frost of spring, the frost then being explained by the verses on the duration of cold in spring. Mention of summer is followed by the verse on the sun's heat, of autumn by

---

[29] *Early English Homilies from the Twelfth-Century MS. Vespasian D.XIV*, ed. R. D.-N. Warner, EETS, 152 (1917), p. 91, line 25.

[30] *King Alfred's Version of St. Augustine's Soliloquies*, ed. Thomas A. Carnicelli (Cambridge, MA, 1969), pp. 81–2.

[31] See, for example, P. L. Henry, *The Early English and Celtic Lyric* (London, 1966), p. 97, and R. MacGregor Dawson, "The structure of the Old English gnomic poems," *JEGP*, 61 (1962), 14–22.

verses on harvest time. The expectation is thus established that a statement of a superlative will be followed by a verse or verses mentioning a cause or consequence of that statement. This being so, we might reasonably ask whether *soð bið swicolost* is in some way related to the immediately ensuing verses about riches being the most precious of things to man.

A frequent theme in Old English moralistic writings is the corruption of truth by lucre. Ælfric, in a letter to Wulfstan, sees money as the thing that prompts men to turn lies into truth and truth into lies: *Wa ðam, ðe for sceattum forsylþ hyne silfne and awent soð to leasum and leas to soðum.*[32] He returns to this theme in his homilies: *man ne sceal . . . for nanum sceatte þæt soðe awægan;*[33] *fela manna . . . nellað forwandian þæt hi ne syllon soðfæstnysse wið sceattum.*[34] He sees the theme personified in the character of Judas: since Christ is the Truth, and Judas betrayed the Truth for money, where is the traducing of truth better exemplified than in *ðam swicelan Judan* ("the deceitful Judas")? *Se ðe soðfæstnysse beceapað wið feo, he bið Iudan gefera* ("He who sells truth for money is the comrade of Judas").[35] Judges who sell truth for bribes, on the other hand, will have the *swicolan deofle* ("deceitful devils") for their companions through eternity: *eall swa þa unrihtwisan deman þe . . . habbað æfre to cepe heora soðfæstnysse . . . þonne habbað hi on ende for heora unrihtwisnysse mid þam swicolan deofle þa ecan susle* ("Likewise the iniquitous judges who always have their truth for sale . . . will in the end experience everlasting torment with the deceitful devil because of their iniquity").[26] One admonition of this kind which appears in both Ælfric and in the Old English *Dicts of Cato* (in one of the Anglo-Saxon translator's expansions of his Latin exemplar) goes back ultimately to a biblical verse. The Old English version of Deut. 16: 19 reads, *Ne wanda ðu for rican ne for heanum ne for nanum sceatte, for ðam medsceattas ablendað wisra manna geðancas and awendaþ rihtwisnessa word* ("Do not have regard for the powerful or for the poor or for any payment, for bribes blind the thoughts of wise men and pervert the words of righteousness").[37] The Old English *Dicts* follows this formulation fairly closely: *ne nym þu medsceattes, for heo ablændeð wisra manna geðancas and wændeð rihtwisra word* ("Do not accept bribes, for they blind the thoughts of wise men and pervert the words of the righteous").[38] Ælfric's version is looser but still strongly reminiscent of Deuteronomy: *ða sceattas ablendað swa swa us bec secgað þæra manna mod þe hi manfullice nimað and ða domas awendað to wohnysse swa* ("Bribes, as books

---

[32] *Die Hirtenbriefe Ælfrics*, ed. Bernhard Fehr, rpt with a supplement by Peter Clemoes (Darmstadt, 1966), p. 202, lines 6–9.
[33] *Homilies of Ælfric: a supplementary collection*, ed. John C. Pope, EETS, 260 (London, 1968), p. 501.
[34] *Ælfric's Catholic Homilies: the second series*, ed. Malcolm Godden, EETS, s.s. 5 (London, 1979), p. 139, lines 58–60.
[35] Ibid., lines 61–2.
[36] *Ælfric's Lives of Saints*, ed. Walter W. Skeat, EETS, 82 (London, 1885), p. 430, lines 233–8.
[37] *The Old English Version of the Heptateuch*, ed. S. J. Crawford, EETS, 160 (London, 1922), p. 353.
[38] R. S. Cox, "The Old English Dicts of Cato," *Anglia*, 90 (1972), 16.

tell us, blind the mind of men who wickedly accept them and thus pervert judgements into error").[39]

Most of these citations are from late texts, but the antagonism between money and truth can be traced back to the earlier periods of Old English as well. The discussion of the qualities of a good judge (called "Judex") published by Liebermann includes repeated admonitions against allowing money to corrupt the truth. *Seo anfengnes medsceata on domum ys soðfæstnesse forlætnes* ("The acceptance of bribes in [making] judgments is the perdition of truth")[40] is one formulation. Another appears to be yet another version of the verse from Deuteronomy: *þa medsceattas ablendað þæra wisra manna heortan and hi forcyrrað ðæra rihtwisra manna word* ("Bribes blind the hearts of wise men and pervert the words of righteous men").[41] Roland Torkar has demonstrated that the entire text of "Judex" is translated from Alcuin's *De virtutibus et vitiis*, chapter 20.[42] The Latin originals of the two passages just quoted are as follows: "Acceptio munerum in judiciis, prævaricatio est veritatis"; "munera excæcant corda prudentium, et subvertunt corda justorum."[43] This idea of men's thoughts or hearts being overthrown by wealth may lie behind one of the maxims in *Beowulf*:

> Sinc eaðe mæg,
> gold on grund(e)   gumcynnes gehwone
> oferhigian,   hyde se ðe wylle![44]

"Treasure, gold in the ground, can easily delude [overpower?] any man, hide it who will." The conjecture of some scholars that the *hapax legomenon oferhigian* is etymologically related to *hyge*[45] agrees particularly well with this reading of the verses. Another poem may contain a cryptic allusion to this motif. The laconic half-line *sinc searwade* in *The Rhyming Poem* (37) has been translated "treasure did treachery" by Mackie[46] and "treasure was deceitful" by Alexandra Olsen.[47] Either interpretation could be read in the context of riches distorting truth in the minds and thoughts of men.

---

[39] Skeat, *Ælfric's Lives of Saints*, p. 430, lines 241–3. For yet another version, see n. 41 below.
[40] *Die Gesetze der Angelsachsen*, ed. Felix Liebermann (Halle, 1903), vol. 1, p. 476.
[41] Ibid., p. 474.
[42] Torkar, "Eine altenglische Übersetzung von Alcuins 'De virtutibus et vitiis, Kap. 20'" (Ph.D. diss., Göttingen, 1976). I am grateful to Dr Torkar for kindly sending me Xerox copies of relevant pages of his dissertation.
[43] *PL*, 101: 628–9.
[44] *Beowulf and the Fight at Finnsburg*, ed. Fr. Klaeber, 3rd edn with 1st and 2nd supplements (Boston, 1950), lines 2765–7.
[45] Ibid., n. to lines 2764b–6, p. 220.
[46] *The Exeter Book*, part 2, ed. Mackie, EETS, 194 (London, 1934), p. 59.
[47] Olsen, "The heroic world: Icelandic sagas and the Old English *Riming Poem*," *PCP*, 14 (1979), 54. Olsen sees the possibility of a second meaning as well: "treasure was made with skill."

It may be then that "truth is most tricky" because man's inordinate love of money is constantly inducing him to make falsehoods look like truth and truth like falsehoods. Money being as beloved by men as it is, truth is most tricky. Or, as another medieval poet phrases it, "Mucho faz' el dinero, mucho es de amar" ("Money does much, it is much to be loved"). Juan Ruiz's *Libro de buen Amor* has much to say about the miraculous powers of money, and one of his stanzas sums up with wry Spanish wit the concern which we have seen to have prompted so much heavy moral denunciation from the Anglo-Saxons:

> Fazié muchos priores,   obispos ë abades
> arçobispos, dotores,   patriarcas, potestades;
> muchos clérigos necios   dávales denidades;
> fazié verdat mentiras,   e mentiras, verdades.[48]

"It made many curates, bishops and abbots, archbishops, savants, patriarchs, potentates; it gave high honors to many simpleton priests; it turned truth into lies, and lies into truths." That the half-line from *Maxims II* is the Anglo-Saxons' version of this sentiment that money makes truth out of lies and lies out of truth seems to me possible and even appealing, but since this interpretation depends in part upon inferences drawn from juxtaposition of ideas, I cannot claim to have proven the point beyond all doubt. What does seem to me virtually certain, however, is that the general sense of the unemended verse should be accepted, for it codifies in typical gnomic language a well-attested Anglo-Saxon attitude toward truth, an attitude that is "pessimistic and worldlywise."

---

[48] Juan Ruiz, *Libro de Buen Amor*, ed. Joan Corominas (Madrid, 1967), p. 227.

7
Artful Ambiguities in the Old English "Book-Moth" Riddle

> Thy words were found, and I did eat them.
> Jeremiah 15: 16

Since 1968, several scholars have identified intentional verbal ambiguities in Old English verse, thus challenging effectively an earlier assumption that Anglo-Saxon poets did not indulge in this stylistic device.[1] The present essay suggests that in the well-known "Book-Moth" Riddle of the Exeter Book (Krapp-Dobbie no. 47)[2] a poet has used a series of related and highly functional verbal ambiguities to develop a specific poetic theme. If this suggestion is correct, then not only will our understanding of a single minor poem have been increased, but we will also have a fuller awareness of the range of dictional subtlety which we may reasonably expect in other poems of the Anglo-Saxon period, a range which includes not merely occasional isolated punning but successions of interconnected puns organized around a central subject.[3]

The six lines of the "Book-Moth" Riddle read as follow in the *Anglo-Saxon Poetic Records*:

Reprinted from *Anglo-Saxon Poetry: Essays in Appreciation for John C. McGalliard*, ed. Lewis E. Nicholson and Dolores Warwick Frese (Notre Dame, 1975), pp. 355–62.

[1] Marijane Osborn, "Some uses of ambiguity in *Beowulf*," *Thoth*, 10 (1969), 18–35; M. J. Swanton, "Ambiguity and anticipation in 'The Dream of the Rood,'" *NM*, 70 (1969), 407–25; P. B. Taylor, "Text and Texture of 'The Dream of the Rood,'" *NM*, 75 (1974), 193–201; Fred C. Robinson, "The significance of names in Old English literature," pp. 185–218 below, and "Lexicography and literary criticism: a caveat," pp. 140–52, esp. pp. 149–50, below. For an excellent general survey of the background and varieties of word-play in Old English poetry, see Roberta Frank, "Some uses of paronomasia in Old English scriptural verse," *Speculum*, 47 (1972), 207–26.

[2] *ASPR*, III, 205. All subsequent quotations from Old English poetry are taken from this collective edition.

[3] Sixteen years after the original publication of this essay, Seth Lerer, *Literacy and Power in Anglo-Saxon England* (Lincoln, NE, 1991), pp. 100–25, draws perceptively on some of its conclusions and on other details of the "Book-Moth" Riddle itself to expand significantly the context of the poem.

> Moððe word fræt.   Me þæt þuhte
> wrætlicu wyrd,   þa ic þæt wundor gefrægn,
> þæt se wyrm forswealg   wera gied sumes,
> þeof in þystro,   þrymfæstne cwide
> ond þæs strangan staþol.   Stælgiest ne wæs
> wihte þy gleawra,   þe he þam wordum swealg.

Aside from some uncertainty as to the referent of *þæs strangan staþol*, the verses offer no lexical difficulties, and R. K. Gordon's literal translation presents a fair consensus of the poem's interpreters to date: "A moth ate words. That seemed to me a strange event, when I heard of that wonder, that the worm, a thief in the darkness, should devour the song of a man, a famed utterance and a thing founded by a strong man. The thievish visitant was no whit the wiser for swallowing the words."[4] The only problem that commentators have found with the poem is that it seems embarrassingly unproblematic. Since it begins and ends by stating the answer to the riddle (*Moððe word fræt ... he þam wordum swealg*), it appears to be no riddle at all. "Here," says Kemp Malone, "the riddle form was stretched to include something merely paradoxical, and even this only by identification of the ink-marks with the words they symbolize."[5] The trick question of conventional riddlers is indeed excised, and yet, if I am not mistaken, the poet has reintroduced a richly equivocal quality to the poem through a pattern of puns which achieve the "identification of the ink-marks with the words they symbolize" in a way that is both imaginative and meaningful.

Since the poet's strategy is to begin with a literal statement of his subject and develop it to its conclusion with a progression of words used in two senses, I shall begin with the last word, *swealg* and from there work back through its other key puns. The first sense listed in *BTD* under *swelgan* is "to swallow," and this is the meaning which editors and translators have uniformly assigned to the verb in the riddle. But equally relevant in the context is the dictionary's second sense for *swelgan* – "to take into the mind, accept, imbibe (wisdom)." Among the sample quotations cited under this meaning is one from the Old English *Azarias*, 179–80, which resembles the phrasing of the sentence of the riddle: *Ða þam wordum swealg/brego Caldea* "when the lord of the Chaldeans had understood those words." When *swealg* is construed in this sense, the final clause of the riddle becomes more than just an impudent rebuttal to the old

---

[4] *Anglo-Saxon Poetry*, selected and tr. R. K. Gordon (London, 1954), p. 303. Gordon's translation of *gied* as "song" has no more foundation in the text than has the suggestion by other scholars that the word refers to a biblical passage. *Gied* could refer to any speech, narrative, or proverb and could even mean "riddle."

[5] Malone, "The Old English period (to 1100)" in *A Literary History of England*, ed. Albert C. Baugh, 2nd edn (New York, 1967), p. 89.

maxim "Difficile est vacuo verbis imponere ventri" "It is hard to impress an empty stomach with words"; it becomes a genuine paradox: "He understood the words and yet was no wiser."[6]

Parallel with the pun on *swealg* is a pun on *staþol* in the preceding sentence. Interpreters have occasionally been troubled by this slightly odd use of *staþol* "foundation" (cf. Gordon's evasive "a thing founded"), but most agree on a literal meaning "foundation on which the words stand" – that is, "the manuscript."[7] This no doubt is one of the senses intended. But occurrences of the word elsewhere in contexts similar to that in the riddle show that *staþol* was also used in an abstract sense to refer to intellectual foundations or to the content of a thought or an argument. In Thorpe's *Ancient Laws and Institutes of England*, it occurs in a familiar locution which (like lines 4 and 5 of the riddle) brings together the words *cwide* and *staþol*: *on ðissum cwydum is se staðol ealles geleafan*[8] "In these sayings is the foundation of all belief." A similar shade of meaning is suggested by *hiera geðohtes staðol*[9] "the foundation of their thought" and by the fact that the derivative *staðolung* has the sense "ordinance, precept" in the Old English *Benedictine Rule*.[10] The riddle's phrase *þæs strangan staðol* finds an echo in Solomon's answer to the book-riddle which Saturn proposed to him: *Gestrangað hie* [that is, *bec*] *and gestaðeliað staðolfæstne geðoht*[11] "they strengthen and confirm a steadfast thought." In the Exeter riddle *þæs strangan* refers to *þrymfæstne cwide* "the mighty utterance," the entire phrase *þæs strangan staðol* "the basic argument of the mighty one" referring on one level to the intellectual content of the mighty utterance. At another level, of course, it refers to the page on which the mighty utterance stands written. The two meanings "parchment" and "intellectual content" are in equipoise, the former sense patterning with the concrete meaning of *swealg*, the latter with the abstract meaning: the insect (1) ate the parchment (2) understood the argument.

In line 4 the word *cwide* also seems to have simultaneous associations with the two levels of corporal ingestion and intellectual inquiry. The obvious

---

[6] The riddler's statement that a creature was none the wiser for having understood the book may well have had special force since it denies a maxim which specifically asserts that the man who masters book-learning will always be the wiser: *Bald bið se ðe onbyregeð   boca cræftes; / symle bið ðe wisra   ðe hira geweald hafað* (*Solomon and Saturn*, 243-44). "He who tastes the power of books will have confidence; he who masters them will always be the wiser."

[7] Malone, p. 89; F. G. Cassidy and W. Ringler's revision of *Bright's Old English Grammar and Reader* (New York, 1971), p. 342, and Dorothy Whitelock's revision of *Sweet's Anglo-Saxon Reader* (Oxford, 1967), p. 279, all agree on "parchment, vellum." C. L. Wrenn, on the other hand, translates *þæs strangan staþol* as "which had given strength to the strong." See Wrenn, *A Study of Old English Literature* (London, 1967), p. 174.

[8] Thorpe, *Ancient Laws and Institutes of England* (London, 1840), vol. 2, p. 426.

[9] See *BTD*, s.v. staðol II.

[10] *Die angelsächsischen Prosabearbeitungen der Benediktinerregel*, ed. Arnold Schröer (Kassel, 1888), p. 112, line 24.

[11] *Solomon and Saturn*, 240.

meaning is "sentence, statement," but *cwide* taken in isolation could also be a form of *cwidu* "what is chewed." At first reading the grammar of the sentence directs readers' attention away from this sense of the word,[12] but the ensuing puns on *stapol* and *swealg* would very likely suggest in retrospect this other highly appropriate meaning of *cwide*.

In *þystro* (4) would also have yielded separate meanings in response to the simultaneous contexts of studying books and eating books. On the physical level it simply means that the moth ate the book "in the dark." On the level of studying, however, the phrase becomes paradoxical, for words cannot be read "in the dark." If *þystro* also had had some of the metaphorical meaning of "ignorance" (as it often did when translating biblical *caligo* and *tenebrae*), it may pattern contrastively with *gleawra* in line 6: the benighted creature was none the wiser for having taken in so much wisdom. Precisely this same play on darkness and ignorance may be seen in Aldhelm's eighty-ninth *Ænigma* on "arca libraria" ("bookcase"), where the bookcase complains that although his "præcordia" ("stomach/mind") is stuffed with sacred volumes, he can learn nothing from them "since the dire Fates deny me the light of books."[13]

As the puns increasingly specify a second level of activity (a man seeking wisdom) coexisting with the literal level (an insect eating parchment), the poet's terms for the book-moth become correspondingly anthropomorphized: *moðð̃e*, *wyrm*, *þeof*, *stælgiest*. He is at first a simple moth eating words, and the prosaic Old English compound *moðfreten* "moth-eaten" suggests that *moðð̃e word fræt* is about as literal a statement of this act as was possible. In the next allusion to the moth he is *se wyrm*, which has the more general meaning "insect, mite," a sense which was extended to that of "poor creature" in Old English translations of the twenty-first Psalm.[14] In the last two terms the personification is complete: he is *þeof* in the fourth line and *stælgiest* in the fifth. This last term occurs nowhere else in Old English, but the second element *giest* can only mean "guest" or "stranger." The first element is always assumed to mean "thievish," presumably because of the preceding *þeof*. But it is also possible that it could mean "place," as it does, for example, in the compound *stælwyrðe*

---

[12] As a neuter *wa*-stem *cwidu* should have -*u* or -*o* rather than -*e* in the accusative singular, and its gender would not agree with the masculine inflection of *þrymfæstne*. It should be noted, however, that elsewhere in the Exeter Book there is some wavering between -*u*, -*o* on the one hand and -*e* on the other; see, for example, *gewædu* for *gewæde* in Riddle 35, line 14; *heore*- for *heoru*- in *Phoenix* 217; *æpele* for *æþelu* in *Widsith* 5. This orthographic confusion suggests that the distinction between -*u* and -*e* was moribund by the time the Exeter Book scribe was writing, and it may already have been weakened in the Riddle-poet's day.

[13] R. Ehwald, *Aldhelmi Opera Omnia*, MGH, Auctores Antiquissimi, xv (Berlin, 1919), p. 138.

[14] See Psalm 21: 7 in the various Old English Psalter translations. This verse is quoted in the *Benedictine Rule*: the Old English version (edited by Schröer, p. 29, lines 3–4) reads: *Ic soðlice eom wyrm and no man, manna hosp and folces æwyrp* "Truly, I am a worm and no man, the reproach of men and an outcast of the people."

according to *BTD*. Or it could be a form of *steal(l)* and refer to the place which an abbot sets apart for the negligent members of a monastic house.[15] In the absence of other contexts for *stælgiest*, however, it is best to observe only that *-giest* indicates a complete personification of the insect and this personification enables the creature to serve as the logical subject of the punning senses of *swealg*, *stapol*, *cwide*, and *þystro* which refer to the moth as an unsuccessful scholar or dimwitted bookworm.

A final instance of word play on *wrætlicu wyrd* in line 2, although it does not participate directly in the dual development of the book-moth's role, nonetheless embraces the course and theme of the entire poem. Commentators have uniformly assumed that *wyrd* in this occurrence has the sole meaning "event, fate," and it is indeed the curious event to which the poet is directing our attention. But as the rest of the poem shows, it is also and particularly the words describing the event that become the real subject of his poem, for the poet's words in their double meanings both develop and resolve the paradox suggested by the event. In this context another meaning of *wyrd* comes into play, that of the etymologically unrelated homophone *(ge)wyrd* which *BTD* (s.v. *gewyrde*, *-wyrd*) defines as "speech, conversation, collection of words, sentence" and *BTS* further defines as "copiousness of speech, verbosity." Thus *wrætlicu wyrd* means that both the event and the words reporting the event are "wondrous, curious,"[16] and the remainder of the poem demonstrates the validity of this *double entente* by using artfully equivocal words to explore the curious paradox of the event.

This second meaning of *wyrd* has passed unremarked, I suspect, first because *wyrd* "fate, event" is such a familiar and famous word in Old English and, second, because *wyrd* "speech, sentence," although it is commonly documented in derivatives and compounds,[17] occurs only here as an independent word. This latter consideration would weigh heavily against the likelihood of a pun, I believe, were it not for other factors which suggest that there was a rather close psychological association of these two words in the minds of literate Anglo-Saxons. First, both in copying of manuscripts[18] and in derivative

---

[15] See Schröer, p. 68, line 11; cf. p. 12, line 19.

[16] The gender of *wyrd* "sentence" is apparently feminine (see F. Holthausen's *Altenglisches etymologisches Wörterbuch*, 2nd ed. [Heidelberg, 1963], s.v. [*ge*]*wyrd* 2), so that *wrætlicu* agrees equally with *wyrd* "event" and *wyrd* "speech, sentence."

[17] Most common is *gewyrd*, which is documented in phrases such as *wisra gewyrdum* "by the statements of wise men" (*Menologium*, 66) and *ðæt ic mæge becuman to bræddran gewyrde* "that I may attain to more copious speech" (see *BTD*, s.v. *gewyrde*, *-wyrd*, where both passages are cited). But the root also occurs in compounds: *fægerwyrde* "smooth-speaking", *gearowyrde* "fluent of speech", *gewyrdelic* "verbatim", *hrædwyrde* "hasty of speech", *scandwyrde* "slanderous", *wærwyrde* "cautious of speech", etc.

[18] For substitutions of *word* for *wyrd* in the copying of manuscripts, see the variant readings in *Bischof Wærferths von Worcester Übersetzung der Dialoge Gregors des Grossen*, ed. Hans Hecht (Hamburg,

formations from *wyrd*[19] there was a tendency to interchange *word* and *wyrd*. In the poetic context of the riddle, moreover, an association between the two words may well have been fostered by the pre-existing verse-formula *wrætlicum wordum*.[20] There is no corresponding formula linking *wrætlic* and *wyrd* "fate" (so far as the extent records show), and so the poet of the "Book-Moth" Riddle may have been playing on the expectation set up by *wrætlicum wordum*.

Aside from these points of contact, however, there was in the Anglo-Saxon period a specific philological association of *wyrd* "fate, event" and *wyrd* "speech" based on the etymology of the Latin word *fatum* "fate." *Fatum* is derived from the past participle of Latin *fari* "to speak," the original meaning of *fatum* being "the sentence (of the gods)." Isidore of Seville explained this relationship between "fate" and "speech" in his *Etymologies*, VIII, xi, 90:

> Fatum autem dicunt esse quidquid dii fantur, quidquid Iuppiter fatur.
> A fando igitur fatum dicunt, id est a loquendo.[21]

"Now they aver that *Fate* is whatever the gods *say*, whatever Jupiter *says*. Thus from *saying*, that is from 'speaking,' they say *Fate*." This surprisingly accurate information is reflected, perhaps, in the Latin-Old English glossaries, which include such entries as these:

> Fatis . gewyrdum
> Fatum . dictum, locutio
> Fata . i. fortuna, euentus, uel dicta; locuta, gewyrda[22]

In a gloss like *fatis - gewyrdum* one cannot even be certain whether the primary sense intended in the Old English word was "fate" or "speech," and such uncertainties arise in other contexts involving *(ge)wyrd*. BTS lists the gloss "Conditio *gecwide* vel *gewyrd*" under *Gewyrd* "fate," for example, but then adds that it could equally well be taken as *gewyrd* "speech." If *gewyrd* as an individual word was as ambiguous as Toller's note implies, then it hardly seems improbable that a pun was intended in the Riddle-poet's *wrætlicu wyrd*.

In one sense, the "Book-Moth" Riddle simply collapses the terms of a

---

1907), p. 185, line 19, and p. 223, line 20, and *BTS*, s.v. *wærwyrde*, where *swiðe wær on his wordum* is given as one variant reading of *wærwyrde*.

[19] See for example *andwordan, -wyrdan*; *foreword, -wyrd*; *scandword, -wyrde*; *wærword, -wyrd*.

[20] See *Andreas*, 1200, and *Christ*, 509; cf. *Andreas*, 92–3.

[21] *Isidori Hispalensis Episcopi Etymologiarum sive Originum*, ed. W. M. Lindsay (Oxford, 1911), vol. I.

[22] The first and last glosses are quoted from Thomas Wright's *Anglo-Saxon and Old English Vocabularies*, ed. and collated Richard Paul Wülcker (London, 1884), p. 235, lines 35 and 37. The second is from *The Harley Latin–Old English Glossary*, ed. Robert T. Oliphant (The Hague, 1966), p. 177, line 128. All three glosses are found in the Harley Glossary.

familiar metaphor into a paradox. The metaphor is that found, among other places, in the Old English translation of the *Liber Scintillarum*:

> swa soþlice of flæsclicum mettum byþ gefedd flæsc, swa of godcundum spæcum inra mann byþ festrud and byð gefedd.[23]

"Now just as the body is fed from corporal food, so the inner man is nurtured and fed from spiritual language." In his "Tinea" enigma Symphosius presented a real-life situation which reduced the simile to literal fact.[24] The Old English poet then took the third step of retranslating the living paradox back into the verbal realm by using a concatenation of puns to develop the subject. More than just a Mannerist experiment, his puns make the poem self-referential in a complex and sophisticated way, forcing the words themselves to display the simultaneous reality and insubstantiality of language. In doing so, he has not only achieved what Herzfeld long ago accused him of failing to do ("Neue Seiten," said Herzfeld, "hat er seinem Gegenstande allerdings nicht abzugewinnen vermocht"[25] "He was not able to give any new twists to his subject"; he has also given us grounds for suspecting that the use of a succession of related puns as an artistic device could well have been within the capacities of other poets in the Anglo-Saxon period. If a study of other Old English riddles should reveal similar uses of pun-complexes (rather than just the isolated puns which previous commentators have from time to time identified), we will then be in a better position to assess several recent and attractive suggestions that even the more serious poets of the period may have used sustained *double entente* as a means of developing complex themes.[26]

---

[23] *Defensor's Liber Scintillarum*, ed. E. W. Rhodes, EETS, o.s., 93 (London, 1899), p. 222. Cf. Jeremiah 15: 16, my epigraph.

[24] The Old English poet's source is generally presumed to have been Symphosius's sixteenth riddle: "Litera me pavit, nec quid sit litera novi. / In libris vixi, nec sum studiosior inde. / Exedi Musas, nec adhuc tamen ipsa profeci" "Writing has fed me, and I don't even know what writing is. I have lived among books, and yet I am no more learned thereby. I have devoured the Muses, and yet thus far I have not profited from it." See *The Enigmas of Symphosius*, ed. R. T. Ohl (Philadelphia, 1928), p. 48.

[25] Georg Herzfeld, *Die Rätsel des Exeterbuches und ihr Verfasser* (Berlin, 1890), p. 29. Consecutive punning is not the poet's only improvement on his source. Especially noteworthy is his unusual employment of alliteration on initial *w*- to knit up the poem, uniting the initial statement and closing restatement of the paradox by a phonic continuum which includes the key terms *word*, *wyrd*, and *wordum*. (The alliteration of accented *w* words is metrically functional in lines 2, 3, and 6; incidental in lines 1 and 5.)

[26] See the studies by Marijane Osborn, Michael Swanton, and P. B. Taylor cited above, n. 1. See further Ida L. Gordon's edition of *The Seafarer* (London, 1960), p. 30.

8
God, Death, and Loyalty in *The Battle of Maldon*

In *The Battle of Maldon*, said Humphrey Wanley, "celebratur virtus bellica Beorhtnothi Ealdormanni, Offae et aliorum Anglo-Saxonum, in praelio cum Danis,"[1] and two and a half centuries later another great Anglo-Saxon scholar summed up the traditional interpretation of the poem in terms which, though fuller, are not essentially different: "The words of Beorhtwold [*Maldon*, 312–19] have been held to be the finest expression of the northern heroic spirit, Norse or English; the clearest statement of the doctrine of uttermost endurance in the service of indomitable will. The poem as a whole has been called 'the only purely heroic poem extant in Old English.'"[2] Most (though not all)[3] readers still view the poem as primarily a celebration of heroism rather than a homiletic or hagiographical exercise, and yet this view involves some theoretical difficulties which have hitherto been dealt with, as far as I am aware, only indirectly if at all. The first difficulty is that *Maldon* was written out of a culture whose fundamental assumptions about God and death were incompatible with a heroic sense of life. The second is that the ideal which motivates the heroes'

Reprinted from *J. R. R. Tolkien, Scholar and Storyteller: essays in memoriam*, ed. Mary Salu and Robert T. Farrell (Ithaca, NY, 1979), pp. 76–98.

[1] *Antiquae Literaturae Septentrionalis Liber Alter seu Humphredi Wanleii Librorum Vett. Septentrionalium, qui in Angliae Bibliothecis extant, ... Catalogus Historico-Criticus* (Oxford, 1705), p. 232.

[2] J. R. R. Tolkien, "The homecoming of Beorhtnoth Beorhthelm's son," *Essays and Studies*, 6 (1953), 13–14. This statement of the traditional view of the poem is the starting point for Tolkien's own argument that *Maldon* specifically celebrates "the heroism of obedience and love" which is "the most heroic and the most moving" of all heroic gestures (p. 16), a view which is accepted and expanded in the closing pages of this essay.

[3] Bernard F. Huppé, *Doctrine and Poetry: Augustine's influence on Old English poetry* (New York, 1959), pp. 23–38; N. F. Blake, "*The Battle of Maldon*," *Neophilologus*, 49 (1965), 332–45; and W. F. Bolton, "Byrhtnoth in the wilderness," *MLR*, 64 (1969), 481–90, all argue in varying ways that Christian doctrine has displaced concern with secular heroism in the poem, a view which is vigorously opposed by, among others, George Clark, "*The Battle of Maldon*: a heroic poem," *Speculum*, 43 (1968), 52–71. J. E. Cross supports Clark's position in general, although he differs with him over some particulars, in "Mainly on philology and the interpretative criticism of *Maldon*", in *Old English Studies in Honour of John C. Pope*, ed. E. B. Irving and R. B. Burlin (Toronto, 1974), pp. 235–53. See also Cross's essay "Oswald and Byrhtnoth: a Christian saint and a hero who is Christian," *ES*, 46 (1965), 93–109.

sacrifice seems (from previous interpreters' accounts of it) too narrow and parochial to sustain *Maldon*'s significance beyond its own age, a great heroic poem requiring a theme of more universal significance than "comitatus loyalty." By confronting these difficulties in the present essay, I hope to confirm *Maldon*'s status as "the finest expression of the northern heroic spirit" and to deepen in some measure our understanding of the poem's meaning.

I

The battle of Maldon was fought and the poem about it was written at a time when the Heroic Age of England and the conditions which made that age possible lay in the distant past. The Anglo-Saxons had embraced Christianity centuries before, and the period of monastic reform which preceded the battle had been effective in rejuvenating men's faith and in renewing Christianity's pervasive enrichment of the vernacular literature of the Anglo-Saxons. In the range of literary conventions at their disposal, however, their commitment to the church entailed losses as well as gains. The Christian world-view, with its assumption of a just God presiding over the affairs of men and its promise of a joyous life after death for all believing and obedient Christians, was not a world-view congenial to heroic narrative. Among the cultural historians who have observed this fact, R.W. Southern, in his essay "Epic and romance," has stated the matter with particular clarity:

> [T]he monastic life – or for that matter the Christian life in any form – could never be merely "heroic" in its quality. That fatal struggle of man against superior forces, that meaninglessness of fate, and the purely resigned, defensive and heroic attitude of man in the face of fate could not, on a Christian view, be the whole story. As Europe became Christianized the epic was bound to decline, for it left out the personal and secret tie between man and God.[4]

Viewed through the uncolored lens of history, the Anglo-Saxons at Maldon in August of 991 would appear to have been anything but resigned, heroic men waging a struggle in the face of a meaningless fate. They were Christians fighting heathens, and they were led by a man who was exceptionally devout. The personal tie between these men and their God would seem to have been indissoluble, and we could imagine their looking forward to the happy afterlife which, as the Anglo-Saxon homilists so often proclaimed, awaits those who suffer martyrdom for the Lord. Indeed, as we reflect on the men at Maldon in 991, their deaths seem less and less like acts of heroic daring and more and more like a joyous witness to the faith.

[4] Southern, *The Making of the Middle Ages* (New Haven and London, 1953), p. 224.

But when we turn our eyes from the historical battle and consider its depiction in the poem, the dying soldiers do not seem to be Christian martyrs on the threshold of paradise but valiant warriors enacting a grim and terribly meaningful heroic sacrifice for heroic ideals. They appear to be oblivious of the Christian assurances which were available to men in their predicament, and it is this that gives the poem that curiously ancient quality remarked so often by the critics. "But for a few phrases it might, as far as the matter is concerned, have been written before the conversion of England," observed W.P. Ker in 1896,[5] and a later critic amplifies his statement to absurdity: "In *Maldon* for the last time in our literature the old epic strain is ... revived. Once again flames out in a Christian epoch the spirit of the old pagan lays. It was doubtless the work of a Christian, but of a Christian in whom the defence of home and kindred against the Danish sea-robbers, 'the wolves of blood,' had roused the smouldering pagan fires."[6] Almost everyone who has meditated over the poem has sensed something archaic and stern in it – "the old epic strain," if you will. But the "smouldering pagan fires" are an embarrassing relic from nineteenth-century Romantic scholarship. Indeed, the central question, both for the *Maldon* poet and for us, is how can a poem revive an "old epic strain" (posited on the fatal struggle of man against superior and unfriendly forces) when there are no pagan fires smouldering? I believe an answer to this question may lie in the poet's portrayal of God and death in his narrative, for it is a portrayal which evokes an aspect of the Christian thought-world congenial to the heroic temper.

There is in the poem only one detailed account of a warrior's death, and that is the slaying of Byrhtnoth, which therefore becomes a type and emblem of all the many death-agonies suffered by Englishmen in the battle. Lines 130–72 recount the manner of Byrhtnoth's slaying, and in lines 173–80 appears his much-discussed death-prayer:

> Geþancie þe, ðeoda waldend,
> ealra þæra wynna þe ic on worulde gebad.
> Nu ic ah, milde metod, mæste þearfe
> þæt þu minum gaste godes geunne,
> þæt min sawul to ðe siðian mote
> on þin geweald, þeoden engla,
> mid friþe ferian. Ic eom frymdi to þe
> þæt hi helsceaðan hynan ne moton.[7]

"I thank thee, Lord of hosts, for all the good things I have experienced in the world. Now, gracious Creator, I have the greatest need that thou shouldst grant

---
[5] Ker, *Epic and Romance* (London and New York, 1897), 2nd edn (Oxford, 1908), p. 55.
[6] W. MacNeile Dixon, *English Epic and Heroic Poetry* (London, 1912), p. 86.
[7] Quotations from *Maldon* and other Old English poems are drawn from *ASPR*.

favor to my spirit so that my soul may travel into thy keeping, Lord of angels. I implore thee that the fiends from hell not be allowed to bring it down [into hell]." Before Morton Bloomfield's discerning essay "Patristics and Old English literature,"[8] readers paid scant attention to what this speech actually says, regarding it as no more than a vaguely pious prayer. In fact, it is a specific allusion to the *judicium particulare* – a literal, physical struggle between devils and angels for possession of the soul as it leaves the body of a dying man. Having identified the motif, Bloomfield goes on to suggest that this evocation of the "patristic" notion of the death-struggle bespeaks a religious dimension in the characterization of Byrhtnoth and that the "speech would suggest a consciousness of [Byrhtnoth's] martyrdom." Proceeding from Bloomfield's conclusion, other scholars have arrived at allegorical or hagiographical interpretations of the entire poem.[9] In contrast to this view, I shall argue that the motif which Bloomfield identified has the opposite effect, that instead of Christianizing the poem the death-speech of Byrhtnoth subtly de-Christianizes the cosmic setting of *Maldon* and in doing so helps to create the conditions necessary for a heroic narrative.

While it is true that the supernatural struggle for a dying man's soul may be found in the writings of the Fathers,[10] it is by no means limited to patristic contexts. To the *Maldon* poet, I suspect, this curious conception would have seemed a popular rather than a patristic tradition and hence would have introduced no particular suggestion of formal Christian theology into the poem. For the motif occurs much more widely than has been noticed heretofore. It is the subject of a text called "Freondlic Mynegung" which appears in Bodleian MS Ashmole 328 at the end of Byrhtferth's *Manual*, and it is developed vividly in an eighth-century Latin letter from Wynfrith to Eadburga, which was translated into Old English in the late tenth century.[11] Many Old English homilists describe how the soul will be attacked when it

---

[8] Bloomfield, *Studies in Old English Literature in Honor of Arthur G. Brodeur*, ed. Stanley B. Greenfield (Eugene, OR, 1963), pp. 37–8.

[9] Bolton, "Byrhtnoth in the wilderness," p. 489; Blake, "*Battle of Maldon*," p. 339. Cf. Huppé, *Doctrine and Poetry*, pp. 237–8. The first scholar to suggest a hagiographic reading of *Maldon*, however, was Bernhard ten Brink, and it is interesting to note that in his translation of Byrhtnoth's death-prayer he silently deletes any reference to the devils who will strive with the angels for Byrhtnoth's soul. See his *Geschichte der englischen Litteratur* (Berlin, 1877), vol. I, p. 120. Very likely ten Brink sensed that the squabbling demons detracted from the religious dimension which he wanted to see in the poem.

[10] See G. Rivière, "Rôle du démon au jugement particulier chez les Pères," *Revue des Sciences Religieuses*, 4 (1924), 43ff., and Alfred C. Rush, "An echo of Christian antiquity in St Gregory the Great: death a struggle with the devil," *Traditio*, 3 (1945), 369–80. For a wider survey of the occurrences of the theme, see Ute Schwab, "*Ær-Æfter*. Das Memento Mori Bedas als Christliche Kontrafaktur. Eine philologische Interpretation," in *Studi di Letteratura Religiosa Tedesca in Memoria Sergio Lupi* (Florence, 1972), pp. 91–100.

[11] See Kenneth Sisam, *Studies in the History of Old English Literature* (Oxford, 1953), pp. 199–224.

passes from the body,[12] sometimes in phrasing reminiscent of Byrhtnoth's prayer in *Maldon*.[13] Several accounts of the death-struggle occur in Old English translations of Apocrypha,[14] and of Gregory's *Dialogues*,[15] while formulas alluding to it appear in the penitential texts published by Max Förster.[16] Bede's *Historia Ecclesiastica* depicts the struggle for the soul in his accounts of Furseus and Dryhthelm, and these were excerpted and translated into Old English as exempla by his countrymen.[17] Vernacular poems allude to the death-struggle, as does at least one entry in the *Anglo-Saxon Chronicle* – that for AD 959 containing the half-metrical obituary for King Eadwig.[18] A vivid illustration of St Peter fighting with a devil over the soul of a dead Christian appears in an Anglo-Saxon manuscript which has been dated to 1031 – just forty years after the battle of Maldon.[19] There are many descriptions of the death-struggle in Latin works from the British Isles,[20] and the theme is attested in vernacular literature across the English Channel. The ninth-century Old High German *Muspilli*, 1–30, gives a particularly somber description of the clash of angels and devils, and there is a reference to it in *Gíslasaga*. Jacob Grimm cites numerous occurrences of the motif in later vernacular literature and suggests parallels between the Christian version of the death-struggle and pagan Germanic visions of the Valkyries descending

---

[12] See *Wulfstan: Sammlung der ihm zugeschriebenen Homilien*, ed. Arthur Napier (Berlin, 1883), pp. 140–1, 235–7, 249–50 (also in *Byrhtferth's Manual*, ed. S. J. Crawford, EETS o.s. 177 [London, 1929], pp. 249–50); *Homilies of Ælfric*, ed. Benjamin Thorpe (London, 1846), vol. II, pp. 336–8, 350–2; *Early English Homilies from the Twelfth-Century Manuscript Vespasian D.XIV*, ed. R. D.-N. Warner, EETS o.s. 150 (London, 1917), 110–13; *Ancient Laws and Institutes of England* (London, 1840), vol. II, pp. 466–9; *The Blickling Homilies*, ed. R. Morris, EETS o.s. 73 (London, 1880), p. 209, and cf. pp. 149–51. See also *Homilies of Ælfric: a supplementary collection*, ed. John C. Pope, EETS o.s. 260 (London, 1968), vol. II, pp. 776–9.

[13] Compare, for example, *Maldon*, 173–4, and *Wulfstan*, ed. Napier, p. 237, lines 4–6; *Maldon*, 180, and *The Blickling Homilies*, ed. Morris, p. 209, line 28.

[14] Rudolph Willard, *Two Apocrypha in Old English Homilies*, Beiträge zur englischen Philologie, 30 (Leipzig, 1935), pp. 38ff, 126ff, and passim; and Milton McCormick Gatch, "Two uses of apocrypha in Old English homilies," *Church History*, 33 (1964), 379–91 (esp. his discussion of the Apocalypse of Paul).

[15] *Bischof Wærferths von Worcester Übersetzung der Dialoge Gregors des Grossen*, ed. Hans Hecht, Bibliothek der angelsächsischen Prosa 5 (Hamburg, 1907), pp. 316–21.

[16] Förster, "Zur Liturgik der angelsächsischen Kirche," *Anglia*, 66 (1942), 29 and 35.

[17] *Venerabilis Baedae Opera Historica*, ed. C. Plummer (Oxford, 1894), vol. I, pp. 164–7, 303–10. For the Old English versions see *Homilies of Ælfric*, ed. Thorpe, vol. II, pp. 332–58.

[18] *Two of the Saxon Chronicles Parallel*, ed. C. Plummer (Oxford, 1892–9), vol. I, p. 115, lines 14–16. Among the poems, see *Resignation*, 49–56, and *A Prayer*, 74–6; cf. *Guthlac*, lines 6–7, 22–5.

[19] British Library MS Stowe 944, fol. 7ʳ. The setting in this instance, it should be mentioned, is the last judgment.

[20] Rudolph Willard, "The Latin texts of the Three Utterances of the Soul," *Speculum*, 12 (1937), 147–66; *Adomnan's Life of St. Columba*, ed. Alan Orr Anderson and Marjorie O. Anderson (London, 1961), pp. 477–9; see also n. 17, above.

to catch up the souls of the slain.[21] Though never as widespread as the more conventional Christian conceptions of death and judgment,[22] the contest of angels and devils at a *judicium particulare* was clearly an alternative explanation which was available in popular tradition.[23]

What is most striking about these various accounts of devils and angels struggling over the souls of the dying is the stark terror which they bring to the experience of death and their apparent negation of the usual Christian consolations for death. The souls of good men as well as of evil ones are repeatedly described as cowering in the corpses which they ought to have abandoned,[24] afraid to venture outside where "all this air is filled with hellish devils which travel throughout the world."[25] A frequent motif is the dying Christian's fear that during his lifetime he may have committed sins of which he was unaware – unwitting sins which could tip the balance of the battle between the angels and the devils in the direction of the swarming demons. This is especially noticeable in the poem *Resignation*, 75–82, where the speaker's mention of *þara synna þe ic me sylf ne conn / ongietan gleawlice* brings to a climax his anxieties over the fortunes of his departing soul.[26] It is these same anxieties which moved the saintly Bede to speak "de terribili exitu animarum e corpore" when he utters his *Death-Song*,[27] and which add poignancy to the

---

[21] *Teutonic Mythology*, tr. J. S. Stallybrass, vol. II (London, 1883), pp. 836–8; vol. IV (1888), p. 1551.

[22] The prevailing view, as expressed repeatedly by Ælfric and others, was that the souls of good to mediocre Christians repose with God or in some kind of vaguely conceived purgatory until the last judgment, while evil Christians await everlasting punishment in hell. (See, for example, *Homilies of Ælfric*, ed. Pope, vol. I, pp. 425–8, and *Byrhtferth's Manual*, ed. Crawford, p. 249.) Milton McCormick Gatch has rightly observed that the contrary view suggested by Byrhtnoth's prayer was somewhat eccentric. "By far the more usual sort of prayer," says Gatch in *Loyalties and Traditions: man and his world in Old English literature* (New York, 1971), p. 143, "is that which Cynewulf wove into the conclusion of the *Ascension*: that men would pray for him so that he might be accepted at the Judgment as a thegn of Christ."

[23] The point of uncertainty which lay between the two explanations of the soul's passage to the next life was the question as to where the soul abided between death and judgment. Gregory deals with this question at some length in book IV of the *Dialogues*. For a survey of Anglo-Saxon views, see Milton McCormick Gatch, "Eschatology in the anonymous Old English Homilies," *Traditio*, 21 (1965), 124–8.

[24] See for example *Wulfstan*, ed. Napier, pp. 140–1, and *Homilies of Ælfric*, ed. Pope, vol. II, pp. 776–9. Cf. *Das altenglische Martyrologium*, ed. Günter Kotzor (Munich, 1981), vol. 2, pp. 237–8.

[25] *Wulfstan*, ed. Napier, p. 250: *eall þis lyft ys full hellicra deofla, þa geondscriðað ealne middangeard*. The statement occurs in the context of a description of the *mycel gewinn betweox deoflum and englum* on the day of one's death. Cf. *Byrhtferth's Manual*, ed. Crawford, p. 249.

[26] Anxiety over sins unconsciously committed is also a motif in some of the prose accounts of the war with the demons for a man's soul. Thus in Wynfrith's letter (Sisam, *Studies*, p. 216) a dying man saw that *manige synna þær cirmdon swiðe egeslice wið hine þa þe he næfre ne wende þæt hio to synnum oðlengdon; and þa awyrigdan gastas wæron geswege eallum þam synnum*. See n. 31 below.

[27] *Venerabilis Baedae Opera Historica*, ed. Plummer, vol. I, p. clxi.

melancholy forebodings in his *De die judicii*. If a pious man like Bede feared the moment of divine decision, then how much more terrible should that moment be to a soldier at Maldon with his enemy's lifeblood on his hands?

In the other accounts of Byrhtnoth's slaying which have come down to us along with *The Battle of Maldon* there is nothing like the disturbing image of struggle which darkens his last moments in the English poem. The nearly contemporary *Vita Oswaldi* draws on the more conventional religious doctrines when it tells us that at Maldon Byrhtnoth was supported by "the manifold love of the Lord – because he was deserving." All "the alms and holy masses he had donated comforted him," and his "prayers and his [former] good deeds lifted him up."[28] The later *History of Ely* also emphasizes his "righteous life and deeds," and, most interestingly, observes that he was "free from the fear of death" ("sine respectu et timore mortis"). The account of the monks' tender care for the corpse of "this active and pious man" brings the narrative to a close with distinct overtones of the conventional saint's life.[29] Indeed, it is the strikingly similar death of St Boniface which comes most readily to mind when we read the Latin accounts of Byrhtnoth's death. Boniface's joyous death-speech to his comrades as they are about to be cut down by the pagan Frisians is just what we might have expected Byrhtnoth to say: "Now is the day for which we have long yearned, and the moment of our release, which we have desired, is at hand. . . . Do not be frightened by these who kill our bodies, for they cannot slay the soul, which is immortal; rejoice, rather, in the Lord, . . . because in a moment He will give you a reward of everlasting recompense and a seat with the angels in the heavenly hall."[30]

Instead of these reassurances, the poet of *Maldon* evokes the anxieties of the supernatural struggle for the soul as Byrhtnoth takes leave of his life, and his last words are a pathetic plea to God not to let the demons prevail in the contest. We are not told why this good and generous benefactor of monasteries should feel so uncertain about the fate of his soul. Perhaps we are to assume

---

[28] "Stabat ipse, statura procerus, eminens super caeteros, cujus manum non Aaron et Hur sustentabant, *sed multimoda pietas Domini fulciebat, quoniam ipse dignus erat. . . . elemosinae et sacrae Missae eum confortabant. . . . Protegebat se . . . quem orationes et bonae actiones elevabant*." See *Historians of the Church of York and Its Archbishops*, ed. James Raine, vol. I (London, 1879), p. 456.

[29] *Liber Eliensis*, ed. E. O. Blake, Camden 3rd series, XCII (London, 1962), p. 134.

[30] *Vitae Sancti Bonifatii Archiepiscopi Moguntini*, ed. Wilhelm Levison in *Scriptorum Rerum Germanicarum in usum scholarum ex Monumentis Germaniae Historicis separatim editi* (Hannover and Leipzig, 1905), pp. 49–50 (my translation). Other good Christians of the period end their lives like Boniface and Oswald "with a happy slaying" ("felici cede" in ibid., p. 50). Thus St Edmund, who, like Byrhtnoth, was slain by Vikings and beheaded, sees his "happy soul travel to Christ" the moment he is cut down (*Ælfric's Lives of Saints*, ed. W. W. Skeat, EETS o.s. 114, vol. II, p.32). Felix, in *Life of Saint Guthlac*, ed. Bertram Colgrave (Cambridge, 1956), p. 159, says that Guthlac at his death declared that "the spirit is eager to be carried away to joys without end," while the Old English poet in lines 1266–8 describes the saint's soul as "yearning for its exit hence to nobler homes." On every hand the contrast with Byrhtnoth's death as it is described in *Maldon* is striking.

that he, like the speaker in *Resignation*, feared that he might have committed unawares some grievous sins which would leave his soul prey to the rapacious devils.[31] Or again, he may have had a more immediate cause for anxiety. Anglo-Saxon penitentials state that homicide on the field of battle is not exempted from all ecclesiastical censure but must be atoned: even soldiers who have fought "pro aecclesiastica justitia" or who were defending their homeland against pagan invaders ("incursio paganorum") are forbidden entry to the church for specified periods of time.[32] Byrhtnoth and his troops had good reason to fear death at Maldon, and the poet was not violating the letter of current beliefs when he adopted as his image of death in the poem a conception which emphasizes all man's uncertainties and anxieties over dying and thus recalls a thought-world more like that of Homer or the sagas. The poet was careful, moreover, in his timing of the allusion. It is immediately after he has evoked the image of the *judicium particulare* that the cowards break and run for their lives; it is in the face of this disturbing vision of death that the heroes of the poem make their decision to stand and die.

Even before we come to Byrhtnoth's death-prayer, however, the poet has begun to hint subtly at an ominous uncertainty in God's disposition of events in this world. Besides Byrhtnoth's prayer there are but three allusions to the deity. The first occurs when Byrhtnoth, having rashly granted the Viking horde free passage through the Panta to his own army's position, muses over the outcome of the battle to which he has committed his troops: *God ana wat / hwa þære wælstowe wealdan mote* (94–5). At first glance this statement seems to be a mere formula for acknowledging an uncertainty, but in the context of the poem and of history it is darkened with tragic irony, for readers of *Maldon* have always shared God's foreknowledge of how the battle was to end: he granted victory to the heathens and allowed his faithful Christians to be massacred. This bitter irony restores to the formula some of the meaning which it bore in an earlier gnomic phrasing:

---

[31] Such morbid fears are but an extreme expression of the orthodox Christian view that mortals must never presume to know what God's judgment of any human being will be. Gregory the Great's interlocutor Peter gives expression to this feeling in book IV of the *Dialogues*, the Old English translation of which is this: *Hwylc man is, þe him ne ondræde, þonne he cymð to ænde, swa unasecgendlicne cwyde þære hynðe ond þæs wites, þe þu rehtest, sy swa hwylces weorces ond geearnunge man swa hit sy, forþon þe þeah he eallunga wite, hu he lifde ond hwæt he dyde ær, he swa þeah nat þonne gyt, hu smealice his dæde sceolon beon gedemde beforan Godes eagum?* to which Gregory answers, *Swa hit is swa þu sægst.* See *Bischof Wærferths Übersetzung*, ed. Hecht, p. 377.

[32] See J. E. Cross, "The ethic of war in Old English," in *England before the Conquest: studies in primary sources presented to Dorothy Whitelock*, ed. Peter Clemoes and Kathleen Hughes (Cambridge, 1971), pp. 280–1. It should also be mentioned that in the instances of the war for dying men's souls which are cited above, one of the commonest motifs is the warning that men who had not confessed their sins were especially vulnerable to the host of demons who came for the soul. It seems unlikely that the men at Maldon had all been safely shriven before the battle.

>   Meotod ana wat
> hwyder seo sawul sceal   syððan hweorfan ...
> æfter deaðdæge. ...
>   Is seo forðgesceaft
> digol and dyrne;   drihten ana wat.
>
>   (*Maxims* II, 57–62)

The next allusion to God occurs at the moment when Byrhtnoth drives his spear through the heart of a Viking. He rejoices briefly[33] and thanks God for the success he has had. And then, as if in sardonic reply to his prayer of thanksgiving, the next line of the poem tells us that a Viking spear immediately pierced the Christian, wounding him mortally. Here again a startling juxtaposition of narrative details throws an ominous shadow on a prayer of Byrhtnoth's. The final allusion to God is near the end of the poem where the Christian warriors offer prayers to God that he allow them to punish the heathen slayers of Byrhtnoth – prayers which, once again, God seems not to have granted. These allusions to God in the poem, along with the dying prayer of Byrhtnoth, suggest a world devoid of the certainties which orthodox Christianity is usually thought to bring and one in which heroism is achieved at a dear price and is rich with meaning.

The poet's artful evocation of a cultural attitude which makes heroic narrative possible in no way implies that he criticized or rejected standard Christian beliefs. His strategy, rather, is to select from the available Christian attitudes those which depict the world in the bleakest possible way. We should remember that pessimism and uncertainty over the divine scheme of things were not uncommon around the year 1000 and in the immediately succeeding centuries. The entries in the *Anglo-Saxon Chronicle* from the time of the battle of Maldon to the end of the twelfth century make surprisingly few references to God working through history, and such allusions as do occur often carry a tone of bewilderment at the deity's permitting the horrors which seem to prevail throughout that period. "A more sorrowful deed was not done in this country since the Danes came and peace was made with them here," says the *Chronicle* poem for the year 1036 (referring to Godwin's mutilation and murder of Alfred's retainers), and the Chronicler adds uncertainly, "Now one must trust to the beloved God that they will be happy and peaceful with Christ who were

---

[33] The poet says (147) *hloh þa, modi man*, and both the phrasing and the situation are echoed elsewhere in early English literature in a way that suggests that the words are a narrative formula. In *Judith*, 23–6, Holofernes *hloh ond hlydde, ... modig ond medugal* before Judith decapitates him. Later, in *Layamon's Brut*, ed. F. Madden (London, 1847), vol. II, p. 203, line 13, we are told that *þa king loh* at the very moment when, unbeknownst to him, Rowenna is pouring poison into his cup. This laugh may be a conventional dramatic signal that a mortal blow is imminent at the moment when the threatened person least expects it.

so miserably murdered without any guilt."[34] Three times in this period an entry closes with a form of the gloomy refrain, *God hit bete þa his wille beð*, and this mood culminates in the Peterborough chronicler's observation on the prevailing despair of the English: "And the land was all destroyed by such deeds, and men were saying openly that Christ and his saints were asleep."[35] Henry of Huntingdon (who is among the chroniclers who recorded the story of Byrhtnoth's death) also speaks of Englishmen saying that God slept,[36] while William of Newburgh reports the view that "the Deity seemed to be sleeping and not caring for the things of men."[37]

God's apparent condonation of human suffering had long troubled the Anglo-Saxons, of course, and the homilist Wulfstan is typical of many churchmen in his frequent insistence that England's calamities were God's punishment for the sins of the English. But as the innocent appeared increasingly to be those who suffered most, this explanation of God's purpose lost persuasiveness among some writers. The *Peterborough Chronicle* of Hugh Candidus contains a powerful description of the horrors of the Viking invasions, in which innocent Christians were butchered by bloodthirsty pagans, and then, at the close of his account, the author turns indignantly on "men of perverse mind who persist in saying that these things are visited upon men because of their own sins." Hugh seeks among seven alternative reasons why God might afflict the innocent, but in the end he concludes stoically that Christians must assign calamities "to the mysterious judgments of God"[38] – a view which seems to bring us back to the Anglo-Saxon gnomic reflection cited above: "God alone knows ... future destiny is hidden and mysterious; God alone knows."

It was in this world where God was inscrutable – or simply asleep – that the poet of *Maldon* recognized a viable analogue to the cosmic outlook of a Heroic Age. He portrayed the actions of his heroes against a background of divine remoteness and indifference which many Englishmen were at that time beginning to sense, and which gave deep meaning to heroic sacrifice. In doing so, the *Maldon* poet was solving in a new way the problem that an earlier

---

[34] "The Death of Alfred," lines 11–15. Although Dobbie (*ASPR*, vi, 24), following Plummer (*Two of the Saxon Chronicles Parallel*, vol. I, p. 158, and vol. II, p. 211), prints the first part of this entry as prose, it is clear that the Chronicler intended it all to be poetry, the first lines in alliterative verse (of very poor quality) and the rest in a combined alliterative-rhyming form.

[35] *The Peterborough Chronicle*, 1070–1154, ed. Cecily Clark (Oxford, 1958), p. 56.

[36] *Henrici Archidiaconi Huntendunensis Historia Anglorum*, ed. Thomas Arnold (London, 1879), p. 277.

[37] *Historia Rerum Anglicanum*, in *Chronicles of the Reigns of Stephen, Henry II, and Richard I*, vol. I, ed. Richard Howlett (London, 1884), p. 45.

[38] *The Chronicle of Hugh Candidus, a Monk of Peterborough*, ed. W. T. Mellows (London, 1949), pp. 23–7. Hugh lived more than a century after the battle of Maldon, but, as the editor has shown in his introduction, his Chronicle often draws on Old English sources.

English poet had solved with equal success in a quite different way. The author of *Beowulf*, who was also a Christian, used the simple device of placing his heroic narrative in the lost world of Germanic paganism, thereby lending a dark grandeur and heroic meaning to deeds which, had they been performed by devout Christians in a Christian setting, would have been merely exemplary.[39]

II

While the poet's portrayal of God and death may provide the conditions necessary for a heroic poem, it does not in itself provide a heroic poem. For no matter how bravely men die, they do not achieve heroic stature unless they sacrifice themselves for some purpose which readers can recognize as significant and worthy. To most readers there has never been doubt that it is loyalty that inspires the English to fight and die in *The Battle of Maldon*, but the poet has stressed and characterized that particular ideal of loyalty more fully, I believe, than previous students of the poem have noticed.[40] By focussing on the Viking messenger's speech, the speeches of the dying Englishmen, and other narrative details in the poem, I shall try to show first how central the theme of loyalty is in *Maldon* and second how the poet has expanded the significance of that theme so that it justifies the heroic sacrifices of the English.

It is the superb arrogance of the Viking's challenge (29–41) which is usually noticed, and that arrogance may have been given an especially sharp edge by the poet's use of Scandinavicisms to characterize the speaker (a device which

[39] The classic work on this subject is J. R. R. Tolkien's "*Beowulf*: the monsters and the critics," Sir Israel Gollancz Memorial Lecture, 1936, *Proceedings of the British Academy*, 22 (1936), 245–95.

[40] Most previous discussion of the ideal of loyalty in *Maldon* has centered on the question whether it was a poetic anachronism (suggestive of the customs described in Tacitus's *Germania*) or an actuality of the late tenth century. Edward B. Irving, "The heroic style in *The Battle of Maldon*," *SP*, 58 (1961), 460, speaks of "the antique virtues husbanded over the centuries in the worn formulas of poetic diction," and this seems to me to account adequately for the highly traditional form which the theme assumes in the poem. T. D. Hill, "History and heroic ethic in *Maldon*," *Neophilologus*, 54 (1970), 291–6, and M. J. Swanton, "*The Battle of Maldon*: a literary caveat," *JEGP*, 67 (1968), 441–50, see the ideals governing the heroic action as genuinely anachronistic and argue that the poet is critical of Byrhtnoth for adhering to them. Hans Kuhn, on the other hand, feels that the comitatus was a living system which the Essex Englishmen had adopted from their Scandinavian neighbors in the Danelaw: see "Die Grenzen der germanischen Gefolgschaft," *Zeitschrift der Savigny-Stiftung für Rechtsgeschichte*, Germ. Abt. 86 (1956), 1–83, esp. p. 45, as well as the rejoinder by Walter Schlesinger, "Randbemerkungen zu drei Aufsätzen über Sippe, Gefolgschaft und Treue," *Alteuropa und die Moderne Gesellschaft: Festschrift für Otto Brunner*, Herausgegeban vom Historischen Seminar der Universität Hamburg (Gottingen, 1963), pp. 21–41. František Graus's startling claim, "Eine typische germanische Treue gibt es (ausser in der Historiographie) nicht," in "Über die sogenannte germanische Treue," *Historica*, 1 (1959), 120, is effectively rebutted by Schlesinger, pp. 41–59.

would make this the first instance of literary dialect in English).[41] But these features merely supplement the central point of the speech, which is to challenge the Englishmen's loyalty to their leader. This challenge becomes clear when we attend to those grammatical forms in the speech which have troubled scholars in the past. "The use of singular and plural in this passage is puzzling," says Margaret Ashdown, and in her translation she uses modern English *you* for both singular and plural.[42] But the poet's shifts in number are his sign that the Viking does not address himself exclusively to the leader Byrhtnoth, as protocol would dictate, but speaks alternately to Byrhtnoth and to his men. Taking for granted that all Englishmen are disloyal cowards at heart, he presumes to negotiate directly with the troops themselves. The opening sharp demand is directed to Byrhtnoth alone (*þu most sendan raðe beagas wið gebeorge*), but the speech softens as the messenger turns way from the leader to speak directly with the troops (*eow betere is*...). At line 34, or possibly even at line 33, the Viking actually slips into a comradely first-person plural (*ne þurfe we us spillan*), implying that the soldiers in the field, both Viking and English, are united in their desire for peace, which is obstructed only by the selfish leader Byrhtnoth. When he returns to the second-person singular and addresses Byrhtnoth again, he talks as if he were the spokesman for both English soldiers and Vikings: *Gyf þu þat gerædest, þe her ricost eart*..., and his plea with the leader to "deliver" or "ransom" his men (*lysan*) is barbed with a stinging double entente: The sense of *ricost* addressed to Byrhtnoth is "most powerful" (that is, the one in authority), while the sense addressed to the Englishmen under arms is "wealthiest" – insinuating that it is Byrhtnoth, not they, who stands to lose the most if peace is purchased from the Vikings. The last clause in the speech is once again a friendly plural addressed over Byrhtnoth's head to his men: *We willaþ... eow friþes healdan*.

To these divisive innuendoes Byrhtnoth replies appropriately in the name of his army,

            Gehyrst þu, sælida,   hwæt þis folc segeð?

The ensuing plurals of his rejoinder unite the English and their leader decisively and thus answer the challenge to his men's honor. Byrhtnoth underscores the strength of the bonds of loyalty by emphasizing that he is himself but the loyal servant of his own lord, Æthelred (53), and thus expects no more from his troops than his own lord expects from him. Byrhtnoth's assertion (51), "here stands an undishonored earl with his army," affirms that the traditional bond between men and leader remains intact.

The exchange of speeches is, then, a rhetorical prelude rehearsing the test of

[41] My evidence for this supposition is set forth in "Some aspects of the *Maldon* poet's artistry," which follows this essay in this volume.

[42] Ashdown, *English and Norse Historical Documents* (Cambridge, 1930), p. 74.

loyalty soon to be enacted on the battlefield in deadly earnest. At another passage of high rhetoric near the end of the poem the dramatics of speech-making serve again as a vehicle for the poet's central theme. The sequence of the speakers in lines 209–60 has evoked several alternative explanations. R. W. V. Elliott perceived the speeches as "a picture of confused hurling of words as of spears" and thought of "the random style of the cine-camera."[43] N. F. Blake surmised that the variety of warriors from various regions and social stations was intended "to imply that the defenders in the battle were a microcosm of the whole of England," while O. D. Macrae-Gibson sees the speeches at the end of the poem progressing steadily from active cries for vengeance to passive statements of the speaker's willingness to die.[44] It seems to me, however, that the speeches from lines 209–60 are arranged in a sequence determined by the poem's theme of loyalty, a sequence which dramatizes the increasing power which the ideal of loyalty exerts among the loyal English at the close of the poem. The first speaker, Ælfwine, explains that in his case the claims of loyalty are the most tangible and urgent of all, for *he wæs ægðer min mæg ond min hlaford* (224). The rhetorical emphasis upon *min* forced by the meter emphasizes Ælfwine's special obligations to live up to the heroic ideal.[45] Offa, the next speaker, does not share Ælfwine's double tie of kinship and fealty, but he is clearly the most overtly obligated of all the other retainers, being portrayed throughout the poem (esp. 198–201, 289–93) as a specially close friend and lieutenant of Byrhtnoth's – probably even his second in command. Leofsunu is a less distinguished retainer, and his homely boast is that the steadfast soldiers whom he knows back at the pool near Sturmer[46] will find no reason to taunt him for disloyalty. He shares neither kinship nor close friendship with Byrhtnoth, but the principle of loyalty, conceived of in broad social terms rather than personal terms, motivates him to make the same noble sacrifice as Ælfwine and Offa have vowed to make. Next, the churl Dunnere, a fyrd man who is not even a member of Byrhtnoth's *comitatus*, is fired by the idea of loyalty and, in two simple verses, demonstrates that the inspiring example of the previous speakers has elevated him to the company of Byrhtnoth's comrades in performance of duty.[47] There is yet one further climax in

---

[43] Elliott, "Byrhtnoth and Hildebrand: a study in heroic technique," in *Studies in Old English Literature*, ed. Greenfield, p. 64.

[44] Blake, "*Battle of Maldon*," p. 338; Macrae-Gibson, "*Maldon*: the literary structure of the later part," *NM*, 71 (1970), 192–6.

[45] See John C. Pope, *Seven Old English Poems* (Indianapolis, 1966), p. 78.

[46] See Gordon, ed., *Battle of Maldon*, Methuen's Old English Library (London, 1937), p. 85, on the meaning of *Sturmere*.

[47] The name *Dunnere* may be related to *Dunne*, which Henry Bosley Woolf cites as the name of a peasant in his *Old Germanic Principles of Name-Giving* (Baltimore, 1939), p. 140. W. J. Sedgefield, *The Battle of Maldon* (Boston, 1904), inadvisedly emends the name to Dunhere, thus obscuring its humbler origins.

this sequence, for the example of Dunnere seems to have been infectious itself. First, the noble *hired* is inspired by his example (261), and then the one man among the Anglo-Saxons who had least obligation of all to die with Byrhtnoth joins the loyal heroes: the Northumbrian hostage Æscferth at this point surges forward to fight and die for the fallen Essex leader.[48] At the end of this sequence of speeches the poet has demonstrated in strong dramatic terms that the remaining Englishmen on every hand have withstood the challenge to their loyalty, and we know precisely the motivation for the deaths in the remaining lines of the poem, where the poet records the name of each of the Englishmen as they fall under the Vikings' axes.

The force of the heroes' commitment to the ideal of loyalty is further dramatized by the poet in quite another way. Throughout the poem there emerge several partial justifications for an Englishman's taking flight. First, Byrhtnoth is clearly stated to have made an error when he committed his troops to a battle in which the enemy were allowed to have free passage across the river and take up positions before the Englishmen could begin their defense. One may argue over the meanings of *lytegian* and *ofermod* (although Professor Helmut Gneuss has provided virtually certain evidence that the latter word means "pride" and that the poet's use of *ofermod* signals a criticism of Byrhtnoth's generalship),[49] but the phrase *landes to fela* admits of no doubt. Byrhtnoth erred, and the men at Maldon were free to meditate over this fact as they considered whether or not to remain and die out of loyalty to the man whose misjudgment had brought them to this hard decision. They might further have reflected that Byrhtnoth's misjudgment was probably the basis for his retainers' decision to flee. At least some of the cowards were among Byrhtnoth's closest household thanes (see 200–1), and if these high-ranking men thought it right to leave the field, then surely the hostage Æscferth and humble fellows like Dunnere might be excused for leaving. Finally, the poet's pointed references to Æthelred throughout the poem would clearly have carried some irony, for Æthelred was at this time becoming the national symbol for English unwillingness to stand and fight.[50] A king who set an

---

[48] Sedgefield, finding it incredible that a hostage held by Byrhtferth should die fighting for him, reasons that "Æscferð was doubtless a hostage who had escaped from the enemy" (*Battle of Maldon*, p. 38). That a hostage could be inspired by the example of his captor's loyal retainers to join in the fight for their leader is demonstrated, however, by the British hostage in the famous *Chronicle* entry for 755.

[49] See H. Gneuss's discussion in "*The Battle of Maldon* 89: Byrhtnoth's *ofermod* once again," *SP*, 73 (1976), 117–37.

[50] In the essay that follows in this volume, I argue that *The Battle of Maldon* was composed long enough after the death of Byrhtnoth for its audience to have appreciated the historical ironies created by Æthelred's ineffectual warfaring in succeeding decades. The frequent assumption that *Maldon* was composed almost before the dust of battle had settled has little to support or recommend it. As Tolkien observed ("Homecoming," p. 16), the poem "is certainly not a work of hot haste."

example for cravenness, a leader who had blundered, and lieutenants who withdrew from the field might well provide soldiers with a basis for reassessing the force of their own sworn loyalties. But the heroes at Maldon, though presumably aware of these possible justifications for flight, scorned them, and the nobility of their stand is accordingly enhanced.

However inspiring their gesture, it remains to be asked whether the "narrow Germanic convention of honor and loyalty"[51] is a sufficiently serious theme to warrant the poet's celebration of it. Soldiers fighting loyally to the death are not necessarily an exalting spectacle; indeed, without some clearly perceived higher purpose their struggles might be, as Milton disdainfully observed, no "more worth ... then to Chronicle the Wars of Kites, or Crows, flocking and fighting in the Air."[52] Why was the loyalty of the Maldon Englishmen worth the poet's writing a poem on the subject, and what is that poem's claim on our interest and sympathy today?

More than a mere tribal custom, the interlocking bonds of loyalty were the principle on which Anglo-Saxon civilization rested, the only bulwark against primitive chaos and anarchy.[53] Wulfstan's most famous sermon is in large part a catalogue of the horrors that befall a people once the principle of loyalty is forgotten,[54] and the *Chronicle* entry for 1010 illustrates how the absence of loyalty between leaders and men induces anarchy: "Ultimately," says the Chronicler, "no captain would raise an army, but each man took flight as best he could, and at the last one shire wouldn't even support the other."[55] Like respect for the law today, loyalty in pre-Conquest society was the *sine qua non*, and its absence marked the difference between civilization and primeval disorder. The concept in this enlarged sense was extended by poets even into the theological realm. As has often been remarked, portrayals of Christ in *The Dream of the Rood* and other Old English poems suggest that it was not merely love, but rather that unique combination of loyalty and affection which Anglo-Saxons felt for their chosen leaders that seems to bind the Christian to his Lord. And as the poem *Genesis* makes clear, Satan emerges in the Anglo-Saxon

---

[51] *The Oxford Anthology of English Literature*, vol. I, ed. J.B. Trapp et al. (London, 1973), p. 106: "The poet's theme turns on this narrow Germanic convention of honor and loyalty." See n. 40 above.

[52] *The History of Britain* in *The Works of John Milton*, ed. F. A. Patterson et al. (New York, 1932), p. 191. The reference is to earlier wars of the Anglo-Saxons.

[53] See Dorothy Whitelock, *The Beginnings of English Society* (Harmondsworth, Middlesex, 1952), pp. 29–47, and Gatch, *Loyalties and Traditions*, pp. 129–41. Gatch's discussion of *Maldon* on pp. 129–35, which anticipates in part some of my own arguments, seems to me to be the best existing account of the theme of loyalty in the poem.

[54] *Sermo Lupi ad Anglos*, ed. Dorothy Whitelock, reprinted with additions to the bibliography (New York, 1966).

[55] *Two of the Saxon Chronicles Parallel*, ed. Plummer, vol. I, pp. 140–1. Clark, "*The Battle of Maldon*," p. 59, cites this passage.

view as an unworthy thane whose disloyalty to God introduced disorder and evil into the world. To Christians elsewhere, the primal sin of Lucifer was pride; to the Christian Anglo-Saxon it seems more often to have been disloyalty.

That disloyalty reduces human society to ungoverned misery is stated overtly by more than one poet. The doom-laden prediction of Wiglaf makes the connection directly:

> Londrihtes mot
> þære mægburge monna æghwylc
> idel hweorfan, syððan æðelingas
> feorran gefricgean fleam eowerne,
> domleasan dæd.
>
> (*Beowulf*, 2886–90)

In *Maldon* the connection is dramatized rather than stated. As long as the Anglo-Saxons stand fast in their loyalty to Byrhtnoth, the English line holds, and the English warriors are as one. But at the climax of the poem, where the cowards break and run, all is suddenly transformed. The cowards' behavior is depicted not merely as a panic but specifically as personal disloyalty leading to anarchic disorder: Godric usurps the horse and trappings of his leader, and this induces immediate chaos in the English ranks, for, as Offa explains in lines 237–42, some men mistook the fleeing Godric for their lord and so were deceived into thinking Byrhtnoth was leading them in a retreat. "The people were dispersed," laments Offa, "and the shieldwall was shattered" by Godric's violation of the oaths that bound him to Byrhtnoth.

The shieldwall itself is another eloquent symbol of the link between personal loyalty and social order, for this formation was the perfect physical expression both of loyalty to the leader and of mutual loyalty among men. At the leader's command, "the front rank of men held their shields before their breasts and the ranks behind held theirs over their heads to protect both those in front and themselves."[56] As long as each man stands fast (as Byrhtnoth repeatedly urges his men to do), the formation is virtually impregnable,[57] but if a section of the rank gives way, the battle order is lost and the soldiers become isolated and helpless, vulnerable to massacre. Twice in the poem we see Byrhtnoth ordering the men to form and hold the shieldwall (19–21, 101–2), and twice we are told how it was broken by the disloyal retreat of the cowards (193–5, 241–2). The cowards' disloyalty not only severs the bond of love and obedience between

---

[56] Gordon, ed., *Battle of Maldon*, p. 50.

[57] Albert S. Cook, *Judith* (Boston, 1904), p. 26, collects passages from Roman historians attesting to the difficulty of penetrating a Germanic shieldwall. (Gordon, ed., *Battle of Maldon*, p. 50, calls attention to Cook's note.)

men and their leaders; it also disrupts the bonds between men and men and reduces a harmonious community to primitive anarchy.

It is a comprehensive principle of human loyalty and civilized order which the English heroes choose to preserve on the battlefield of Maldon when they regroup to fight the enemy in a last desperate stand. They uphold this ideal despite the plausible rationalizations for flight which the poet suggests were available to them, and they uphold it in the face of a death to which the poem has lent renewed and ominous meaning. When the Englishmen decide to die, each man reasoning out his decision in a speech, they are not dying under orders, for their leader is dead. They are not dying in a frenzy of hatred for the enemy, for the poet has been careful to portray the Vikings as anonymous rather than hateful.[58] They are not even dying for victory, since it is clear after the rout of the cowards that no hope of victory remains. As the details and emphases of the poem make clear, the soldiers are dying together,[59] loyal both to their lord and to each other, for the principle which underlay all that was positive and good in life as they understood it.[60] The principle can be upheld on the field of battle only if man's mind and spirit are brought to assert the superior importance of the ideal over physical life and physical strength. And it is this assertion that Byrhtwold makes in the name of the fallen and falling Englishmen in words that are more meaningful the more literally they are understood: "The mind must be the firmer, the heart the stronger, the spirit must be the greater, as our body's strength declines."[61] In making this statement against the background of cosmic uncertainty which the poem's details suggest, *Maldon* is a supremely heroic poem, in a sense more heroic than the poems with which it is so often compared – the *Iliad*, the Eddic lays, and *The Song of Roland*.

---

[58] Clark ("*The Battle of Maldon,*" p. 58) has stated this point well: "The vikings are simply a force impelling the decisions to pay or fight, to flee or die; they are not objects of interest in themselves." See also my remarks in "Lexicography and literary criticism: a caveat," pp. 141–2 below, and in "Some aspects of the *Maldon* poet's artistry," following.

[59] The orderly solidarity of the dying heroes stands in eloquent contrast with the pell mell, *sauve qui peut* flight of the deserters. Brave men die in good company; the oldest proverb in English tells us how cowards die: *suuyltit thi ana*.

[60] In their speeches the Englishmen do not, of course, enunciate an abstract principle of loyalty. They speak rather to the particular vows which are the concrete manifestations of that principle of loyalty within their own lives.

[61] *Maldon*, 312–13. F. Th. Visser, *An Historical Syntax of the English Language*, part 1 (Leiden, 1963), pp. 162–3, makes the interesting suggestion that *sceal* is gnomic in this passage. But his translation of the verb ("is proper," "ought to be") seems weak. Context implies the normal meaning "must be." I have benefited from suggestions and encouragement generously offered by Professors Robert Farrell, Thomas D. Hill, and Robert E. Kaske of Cornell University.

9
Some Aspects of the *Maldon* Poet's Artistry

"A great subject and a narrative most worthy of our forefathers" – thus does the twelfth-century compiler of the *Liber Eliensis* assess the story of Byrhtnoth's fall at Maldon, and his words might well refer to the extant Old English poem on the subject.[1] Modern readers continue to see greatness of subject and style in *Maldon*, and the poem has not lacked acute interpreters.[2] But a work so rich is not easily exhausted, and several features of the poet's artistry appear to have escaped notice thus far, or at least merit fuller treatment than they have received. My observations vary in scope and in length and treat such diverse subjects as date, language, manuscript, and textual criticism. No overall unity among the nine sections below is intended, but each does share the common aim of revealing a new facet of the poem's artistry and meaning.[3]

I

>   Me sendon to þe   sæmen snelle,
>   heton ðe secgan   þæt þu most sendan raðe
>   beagas wið gebeorge;   and eow betere is
>   þæt ge þisne garræs   mid gafole forgyldon,
>   þon we swa hearde   hilde dælon.
>   Ne þurfe we us spillan,   gif ge spedaþ to þam;

Reprinted from *JEGP*, 75 (1976), 25–40.

[1] "Res enim magna est et maiorum relatio dignissima." See *Liber Eliensis*, ed. E. O. Blake, Camden, 3rd series, 92 (London, 1962), pp. 133–4. Blake believes that "the compiler of the *Liber Eliensis* may have known and misunderstood the Old English poem on the battle of Maldon" (p. xxix; cf. pp. 134–5, nn. 1 and 4).

[2] Edward B. Irving's essay "The heroic style in *The Battle of Maldon*." *SP*, 58 (1961), 457–67, was the first in a series of literary studies on the subject. Among noteworthy succeeding treatments are Thomas D. Hill's "History and heroic ethic in *Maldon*," *Neophilologus*, 54 (1970), 291–6; Cecily Clark's "Byrhtnoth and Roland: a contrast," *Neophilologus*, 51 (1967), 288–93; and George Clark's "The Battle of Maldon: a heroic poem," *Speculum*, 43 (1968), 52–71.

[3] Quotations from *Maldon* are drawn from the text in vol. 6 of *ASPR*, *The Anglo-Saxon Minor Poems*.

> we willað wið þam golde   grið fæstnian.
> Gyf þu þat gerædest,   þe her ricost eart,
> þæt þu þine leoda   lysan wille,
> syllan sæmannum   on hyra sylfra dom
> feoh wið freode,   and niman frið æt us,
> we willaþ mid þam sceattum   us to scype gangan,
> on flot feran,   and eow friþes healdan.
>
> (29–41)

Readers have long appreciated the poet's subtle conception of the Viking's message to Byrhtnoth, but I do not believe it has been noted before that these thirteen lines may contain the first literary use of dialect in English. Locutions of Scandinavian origin as well as locutions that are simply unique in Old English are prominent in the speech, and it seems likely that these features were intended to suggest to an Anglo-Saxon ear the menacing voice of a foreigner.

Grið (35) is a Scandinavian loanword not recorded in the language before the time of the battle of Maldon. Its subsequent use in Old English is limited generally to contexts involving dealings with the Danes, and so the word would have retained its foreign associations throughout the late Anglo-Saxon period. The poetic compound *gārræs* (32) is found nowhere else in Old English, but its exact counterpart *geirrás* is found in Old Norse.[4] Because *þon* meaning "than" is quite rare in Old English, the occurrence of this form in line 33 is usually emended to *þonne* by editors of *Maldon*; but the poet's *þon* could have been intended to suggest Old Norse *þan* "than".[5] Bertha Phillpotts, in a quite different connection, observed long ago that *mōst* in line 30 has the marks of a Scandinavicism, and *hilde dǣlan* "to contend in battle" (33) is an unusual collocation of Old English words which seems to be modeled on Old Norse phrases like *deila heiptir* and *deila sakar*, the specialized meanings "feud, quarrel, contend" being prominent in the Old Norse form of

---

[4] See *Heimskringla, Nóregs konunga sögur af Snorri Sturluson* I, udgivne for Samfund til udgivelse af gammel nordisk litteratur ved Finnur Jónsson (Copenhagen, 1893–1900), p. 300, l. 16, where the word appears in a quotation from the late tenth-century Icelandic poem *Vellekla*. Jónsson translates the compound as "spear-torrent" or "rush of spears" (his note in vol. 4, p. 81, renders *geirrásar* as "spyd-strömmens"), and this literal meaning fits equally well the context in *Maldon*, 32. It is difficult to see why Old English lexicographers and editors of *Maldon* have in the past always generalized the meaning of *gārræs* to "battle"; *Maldon*, 108–11, makes clear that the first stage of a battle at this time is the hurling of spears (called *beaduræs* by the Old English poet in l. 111).

[5] This is the early form of the conjunction which, through assimilation in enclitic use, later appears as *an* and then *en*. See Finnur Jónsson, *Lexicon poeticum antiquae linguae septentrionalis*, 2nd edn (Copenhagen, 1931), s.v. 2 *en. þan* occurs in an inscription from the Isle of Man dated ca.1100, and E. V. Gordon, *An Introduction to Old Norse* (Oxford, 1957), p. 259, notes that it "occurs elsewhere in runic inscriptions, e.g. on stone 4 of Aalum, Denmark, *ca.* 1000–25," while Old Swedish retains it even into the later language.

the verb.⁶ The phrase *syllan* ... *sylfra dōm* (38) parallels exactly the Old Norse legal term *selja sjálfdœmi*, and, although it is true that other (less exact) parallels can be found elsewhere in Old English,⁷ it seems likely that at this period the English phrase would have taken a strong Scandinavian coloring from usage in the neighboring Danelaw.⁸

In addition to these foreignisms, the Viking's challenge contains two collocations which are syntactically peculiar and so may have suggested the speech of a non-native. In line 34 *gif gē spēdaþ tō þām* has no parallel elsewhere in the corpus, and scholars are divided over its precise meaning. The sense of *ēow friþes healdan* (41) seems clear, but the grammar is odd since *friþ* used with *healdan* should be in the dative or accusative case rather than the genitive.

While it must be conceded that the emergence of hitherto undiscovered Old English texts might show one or another of these features to be less peculiar than it now appears to be, it seems unlikely that the entire cluster of Scandinavicisms and unidiomatic phrases in so short a space should be either illusory or accidental. And the foreign accent which such features would give to the Viking's speech would do more than merely contribute toward verisimilitude. As readers have noticed before, the poet is careful throughout *Maldon* to portray the Vikings not as heinous villains but as a vague inimical force – merely the occasion for the Englishmen to display the varying moral qualities within their own ranks. The Vikings exist in the poem simply to provide the challenge to heroism which initiates the action and leads to the issue of *Maldon*. This being so, it is artistically just that the one moment in the poem when the Norsemen emerge from their anonymity and achieve dramatic realization is when the messenger utters their arrogant challenge to English honor. If the challenge was delivered in the alien accents of a living, speaking Norseman, this would be a particularly vivid element in that dramatic realization.

---

⁶ Bertha Phillpotts, "*The Battle of Maldon*: some Danish affinities," *MLR*, 24 (1929), 188 and 187. Editors of *Maldon* have sometimes cited *eofoðo dǣle* in *Beowulf*, 2534, as a parallel to *Maldon*, 33, but the difference in meaning between *eafoð* and *hilde* weakens the supposed correspondence.

⁷ See Fritz Mezger, "Self-judgment in Old English documents," *MLN*, 67 (1952), 106–9.

⁸ Scholars have often remarked that contacts between the Essex English and the Norse Danelaw must have been close in Byrhtnoth's time, and Hans Kuhn even argued that the very concept of comitatus loyalty which Byrhtnoth's men are upholding was borrowed by the English from their Scandinavian neighbors in the Danelaw. See *Zeitschrift der Savigny-Stiftung für Rechtsgeschichte* (Germanische Abteilung), 73 (1956), 1–83. If sustained, Kuhn's theory would have an important bearing upon the ironies at work in the poem, but see W. Schlesinger, "Randbemerkungen zu drei Aufsätzen über Sippe, Gefolgschaft und Treue" in *Alteuropa und die moderne Gesellschaft, Festschrift für Otto Brunner* (Gottingen, 1963), pp. 21–41. If Bertha Phillpotts was correct in thinking that the *Maldon* poet was "someone whose native language was Anglo-Saxon, who was well acquainted with Anglo-Saxon ... verse, but who was also able to draw on Danish poetical tradition," then it would be particularly easy to explain his artful use of Scandinavicisms in the Viking's speech. But even a casual acquaintance with Scandinavian words and ways would have enabled an English poet to give a Norse coloring to the Viking's speech.

II

...Æþelredes eard,   ealdres mines,...

(53)

...þurh ðone æþelan   Æþelredes þegen.

(151)

þa wearð afeallen   þæs folces ealdor,
Æþelredes eorl;

(202–3)

Each of the poet's allusions to Ethelred the Unready carries a rich and powerful irony if we can assume that the poem was composed long enough after the battle for the audience to know that the king had proved unworthy of the sacrifices that were made in his name. Most bitterly ironical is the fact that Byrhtnoth's election of an honorable death over the ignominy of paying tribute to the Danes took place almost simultaneously with Ethelred's adoption of tribute-payment as a national policy. The coincidence seems to have been savored by more than one chronicler of the events;[9] thus it is tempting to think that the *Maldon* poet shared their sense of royal betrayal. Other events subsequent to the battle, such as Ethelred's reception of Olaf Tryggvason at the court and the apparent freedom with which Viking ships preyed on England following the stand at Maldon, would also tend retrospectively to deepen the tragedy and enhance by contrast the nobility of the heroes who died for *Æþelredes eard*. Rarely in the literary history of England has so great a gain or loss of poetic meaning depended upon the establishment of a poem's approximate date of composition.

Most readers have assumed that *Maldon* was composed almost before the dust of battle had settled, and the basis for this assumption is strikingly naïve: "The vividness of the poet's memories," says Dobbie, "suggests ... that the poem was written very shortly after the battle, and it is generally agreed by scholars that such was the case."[10] Scholars have indeed agreed to an early date and have accepted the ingenuous connection between vivid detail and

---

[9] See below.
[10] *ASPR*, vol. 6, p. xxx; cf. E. V. Gordon, *The Battle of Maldon* (London, 1937), p. 21, and Margaret Ashdown, *English and Norse Documents Relating to the Reign of Ethelred the Unready* (Cambridge, 1930), p. 9. For one argument challenging the early dating of the poem, see George Clark ("*The Battle of Maldon*," p. 56), who is in turn challenged by J. E. Cross, "Mainly on philology and the interpretative criticism of *Maldon*," *Old English Studies in Honour of John C. Pope*, Ed. E. B. Irving and R. B. Burlin (Toronto, 1974), pp. 252–3. It does not seem necessary to me to place the poem's date as late as Clark proposes, but neither does it seem impossible.

topicality.[11] But since several prose accounts of the battle are extant even now, and since it is known from the *Liber Eliensis* that others once existed, it could be that a detailed chronicle of Byrhtnoth's last engagement gave the poet his first knowledge of the battle – perhaps decades after 991 – and moved him to compose a poem on the subject. He would not have been the first Anglo-Saxon who was inspired to great and vivid poetry by a written source. Such a poet, moreover, need not have been a native of Essex but could have been a West Saxon of comprehensive sympathies who wished to express admiration for the noble stand which his neighbors' elders had made against the Dane. If so, this would obviate the dilemma previous scholars faced in trying to explain how a poem that is "so consistently and characteristically West Saxon" in its language could have originated in the Essex region.[12] In the past, of course, it has usually been posited that the poet could only be a patriotic Essex man, but the assumption will hardly bear scrutiny. (Who would argue that the *Beowulf* poet could not have written so movingly about his subject unless he were a Geatish exile?)

That the surviving text of the poem is late is attested by the meter as well as the language, but the text provides no evidence on which to base a more precise date. Nor is there much to be gained from such evidence as exists about the now burned manuscript. Gordon, in a resourceful but not finally compelling argument, urged that since the folios containing *Maldon* originally "stood between a text copied early in the eleventh century and others copied in the last half (or, more probably, the last quarter) of the century," therefore "the text of

---

[11] A salutary warning aganst confusing historical poetry with history is that of J. B. Bessinger in "*Maldon* and the *Óláfsdrápa*: an historical caveat" in *Studies in Old English Literature in Honor of Arthur G. Brodeur*, ed. S. B. Greenfield (Eugene OR, 1963), pp. 23–35. Perhaps this same distinction between the claims of poetry and the claims of history might be summoned in answer to the argument that *Maldon* must have been composed soon enough after the event for the audience to have been familiar with all the people mentioned in the poem. (For this and other conjectures about date and authorship, see Liebermann's discussion in "Zur Geschichte Byrhtnoths, des Helden von Maldon," *Archiv*, 101 [1898], 20–1, 23–5. Although reasonable, his observations are, as he says, "eine Hypothese nur!") An audience might know of the characters mentioned only through chronicle or legend – or may not know some of them – and still understand and value the poem. It seems curious that those modern scholars whose comprehension and appreciation of Old English poetry have been most impressively profound (despite unidentified names and references throughout that poetry) persist in assuming that *Maldon* would have been meaningless to its first audience if it were not "composed sufficiently close to the event for the poet to rely on his audience's familiarity with the persons concerned" (*Sweet's Anglo-Saxon Reader*, 15th rev. edn, ed. Dorothy Whitelock [Oxford, 1967], p. 116).

[12] The words are Gordon's (*The Battle of Maldon*, p. 38); he goes on to say, "Almost the only certainly eastern form is one which editors have always removed – *gofol* in line 61." This is slender evidence indeed, and the emending editors may have been right in assuming *gofol* to be a mere scribal error for *gafol*. In *Maldon* the word occurs twice in its usual West Saxon spelling *gafol* (32, 46) and only once as *gofol* (61). See B. J. Timmer's remarks on *Maldon* in his edition of *Judith* (London, 1951), pp. 5–6.

Maldon can accordingly be assigned to the eleventh century."[13] But he overlooked the significance of the fact that in the manuscript as Wanley described it both the beginning and the end of *Maldon* were missing, a condition which suggests the likelihood that the poem was an alien text salvaged from another manuscript and inserted into this highly miscellaneous codex. Since the second half of the manuscript contained texts which can have been copied no earlier than the end of the twelfth century, the possibility suggests itself that *Maldon* could have been inserted into the codex very late indeed and could have originated at virtually any date after 991 that is consistent with the language of the text.

Some might feel that if the scribal hand of *Maldon* had differed from that of the other texts in the manuscript, then Wanley would have noted this fact. But Wanley says nothing in the *Catalogus* about the differing dates and character of other hands in the codex (although in another place he does discuss the varying hands in the Asser text which appeared early in the manuscript).[14] Moreover, at other points in the *Catalogus* Wanley does not mention such details. For example, in his account of Bodley Hatton 115 on pages 39 to 40 of the *Catalogus* he neglects to mention that article XXXII (article 34 in Neil R. Ker's *Catalogue of Manuscripts Containing Anglo-Saxon*) is, as Ker notes, "in a hand of quite different" type and date and, though "long bound with the rest, ... was not originally so."[15] Wanley's and other early reports on the manuscript leave us, then, with even less to go on than has been previously assumed.

How long after the battle must the poem have been written if the allusions to Ethelred and the refusal to pay tribute were to have ironic force? Probably only a few years. The *Anglo-Saxon Chronicle* entries for 991 make the essential connections. The annal for that year preserved in BM MSS. Cot. Tiberius B.i, Cot. Tiberius A.vi, and Cot. Tiberius B.iv tells of Byrhtnoth's death and then adds that it was in that year that the payments to the Danes were begun. The fact that payments had actually been made before this year adds significance, perhaps, to the annalist's juxtaposing this assertion with the report of Byrhtnoth's sacrifice, and the author of the early eleventh-century chronicle usually assigned to Florence of Worcester apparently appreciated the wry meaning of the juxtaposition, for he preserved it in his own account of the battle.[16] The Parker Chronicle gives in the annal for this year an equally telling juxtaposition

---

[13] Gordon, *The Battle of Maldon*, p. 33.

[14] See Kenneth Sisam, *Studies in the History of Old English Literature* (Oxford, 1953), pp. 148–9.

[15] Ker, *Catalogue of Manuscripts Containing Anglo-Saxon* (Oxford, 1957), pp. 403, 399.

[16] *Florentii Wigorniensis Monachi Chronicon ex Chronicis*, ed. Benjamin Thorpe (London, 1848), p. 149. Payments to the Vikings before 991 are listed in Cross, "Mainly on philology and the interpretative criticism of *Maldon*," p. 241. The annalist for 991 was either ignorant of these previous payments or conveniently forgot them in order to introduce the irony of Ethelred's pusillanimous "inauguration" of tribute payments in the very year when Byrhtnoth had died rather than yield to Viking extortion.

of events. Identifying Olaf Tryggvason as the leader of the Danish force which slew Byrhtnoth, it tells us that after the battle Ethelred made peace with Olaf and subsequently sponsored the Viking at his confirmation. (Scholars once doubted this statement that Olaf was at Maldon, but more recent observations by Alistair Campbell add to the mounting evidence that Olaf was indeed a commander there.)[17] The comment about Ethelred's receiving Olaf is for the most part entered in the margin of the Parker manuscript, and this leads Dorothy Whitelock to conclude that it was "added as an afterthought."[18] So it may be: but it seems equally plausible that the remark was added purposefully as a bitter comment on how miserably Ethelred honored the memory of the men who had died in his name. Subsequent *Chronicle* entries – beginning especially strongly with the entry for 999 – suggest increasing disappointment with Ethelred's conduct, and by the time of the entry for 1011 the annalist's criticism of the king is explicit.

The Battle of Maldon is not a glossy and relatively uncomplicated occasional poem like the *The Battle of Brunanburh*; it is a long, thoughtful account which takes the measure of its subject and celebrates with artful restraint that which is most significant in it. Its vivid details are not merely rich but are meaningful, both individually and collectively, and each contributes toward the articulation of the poem's major theme.[19] Such details and such art do not suggest a hasty improvisation soon after the event or a versified dispatch from the battlefield; they bespeak a poem wrought and revised over a considerable period of time by a poet whose moral judgment is undisturbed by the passions that usually excite the minds of men who assess a massacre by predatory foreigners shortly after the event. In the total absence of external evidence for dating the composition of the poem, it seems far more reasonable to assume that an interval elapsed between the time of the battle and the time that the poet – perhaps in a distant city in Wessex reading a sad chronicle of the defeat – began to reflect upon the sacrifice that Byrhtnoth and his men had made. During the interval a decade or

[17] The Parker Chronicle entry identifying Olaf as Byrhtnoth's antagonist was long under suspicion because the account of the battle seemed to be misdated to 993. But Campbell noted that a hitherto unremarked caret mark by the Anglo-Saxon scribe correctly referred the entry to the year 991. (His discovery is reported by Whitelock in *Sweet's Anglo-Saxon Reader*, p. 265, and in her revised translation of *The Anglo-Saxon Chronicle* [London, 1965], p. 82, n. 3.) In his lecture *Skaldic Verse and Anglo-Saxon History* (London, 1971), pp. 7–8, Campbell offers circumstantial evidence from Norse verses attributed to Olaf's own court poet which suggest the likelihood of Olaf's having been present at the battle of Maldon.

[18] *The Anglo-Saxon Chronicle*, p. 82, n. 4. Whitelock notes that the comment would have been added to the original entry "after the entry for 994 had been made." Perhaps this suggests that the *Maldon* poet was not the only Anglo-Saxon who, some years after the battle had taken place, meditated over the significance of Byrhtnoth's last stand in the light of Ethelred's subsequent conduct.

[19] I attempt to define this theme and to suggest how the various details of the poem contribute to its expression in the preceding essay in this volume.

so of history would have made available just the perspective that the poet achieved in viewing his heroes and just the sense of Ethelred's failings which seem, ironically, to add meaning and dignity to the heroic gesture of the men who died defending the land and honor of their unworthy king.[20]

III

Ða se eorl ongan   for his ofermode
alyfan landes to fela   laþere ðeode.

(89–90)

That *ofermōd* means "pride" and concedes a flaw in Byrhtnoth's judgment has now been established beyond serious doubt by Helmut Gneuss.[21] The lapse of judgment is further confirmed in the explicit statement *se eorl ongan... alyfan landes to fela* (89–90), and it seems to me that the leader's error is an important element in the poet's celebration of the Englishmen's heroic conduct. Their decision to die out of loyalty to Byrhtnoth appears all the more admirable when we realize that they knew he had erred seriously in his leadership of them. And yet, though inexcusable, his error must nonetheless be understandable, for the poem's meaning depends on his character being noble though flawed. The poet therefore portrays Byrhtnoth as thoroughly noble in manner and intention, and presumably we are expected to appreciate the complexity of the decision faced by the ealdorman when the battle reached an impasse.[22]

One consideration that helps explain Byrhtnoth's excessive zeal for a battle on any terms seems to me to have been insufficiently emphasized. Critics usually refer to the island on which the Vikings had encamped as if it were an unpopulated holm. But this view overlooks the significance of the causeway. Such a link between the island and the mainland would have been built only if there were some reason for traffic between island and shore: the island was

---

[20] When this essay was in galley proof before its first publication, John McKinnell's essay "On the date of *The Battle of Maldon*" appeared in *MÆ*, 44 (1975), 121–36. McKinnell argues that the poet's use of *eorl* in the Scandinavian sense (which developed only during Cnut's reign) shows "that the poem is unlikely to have been composed before about 1020 at the earliest" (p. 128).

[21] Gneuss, "*The Battle of Maldon* 89: Byrhtnoð's *ofermod* once again," *SP*, 73 (1976), 117–37.

[22] Byrhtnoth's noble qualities and the factors that would have tempted him to his disastrous error have misled some scholars into viewing him as flawless in judgment and character. This view ignores the inescapable meaning of the poet's words in lines 89–90, to say nothing of the disastrous outcome of the battle. It is true that the flight of the cowardly retainers precipitated the massacre and was wholly reprehensible, but the retainers had reason for their cowardice: Byrhtnoth had committed his forces to a battle on the Vikings' terms. The poem celebrates men who rise above such justifications for cowardice and die for love and loyalty.

apparently under cultivation and may even have been under permanent settlement. In either case the probability of there being helpless English civilians trapped on the island with the brutal marauders[23] extenuates somewhat Byrhtnoth's proud and fatal rashness in granting his enemy free passage to his own position. He was wrong, and the poet properly condemns his error and his pride. But it is well to remember that his judgment may have been clouded by humane considerations more immediately pressing than the one usually cited: *viz.*, that "had he refused, the Danes would presumably have sailed away and ravaged out of reach of his army."[24]

IV

"... god ana wat
hwa þære wælstowe   wealdan mote."
Wodon þa wælwulfas.

(94–6)

It seems unlikely that the poet's use of *wæl-* compounds in two consecutive lines was inadvertent and meaningless. By referring to the Vikings as *wælwulfas* immediately after Byrhtnoth has asserted God's foreknowledge of who will possess the *wælstowe* the poet seems to be presaging ominously that it is the Vikings to whom the battlefield naturally belongs. The repetition also lends special emphasis to the second of the compounds, *wælwulfas*. The element *-wulf*, as J. E. Cross has demonstrated, is not in itself a depreciatory epithet in Old English battle poetry.[25] On the other hand, the use of the epithet here, just ten lines before the scavenging animals are introduced (106–7), does suggest an inevitable association between the *wælwulfas* and the beasts of battle, among which wolves are so often numbered. Perhaps the poet wishes to imply that although the Vikings are to triumph and rule the field of slaughter they will be victors merely in the physical sense in which scavenging animals are the only ultimate victors in any battle. The victory that matters most to men – the triumph of intellect and human principles over animal instincts – is reserved to the English, who prove by their deaths that "mind is firmer, heart more powerful, and spirit mightier" than mere bodily strength (312–13).

---

[23] The *Chronicle* entries for 980, 981, 982, 993, 994, 997, and elsewhere reveal what citizens might expect at the hands of the Vikings.

[24] *Sweet's Anglo-Saxon Reader*, p. 267. Even Samouce, who is the most determined of the scholars who would exonerate Byrhtnoth of any error of judgment whatever, overlooks the significance of the causeway. See Warren A. Samouce, "General Byrhtnoth," *JEGP*, 62 (1963), 129–35.

[25] Cross, "Oswald and Byrhtnoth: a Christian saint and a hero who is Christian," *ES*, 46 (1965), 107–8.

V

stihte hi Byrhtnoð,
bæd þæt hyssa gehwylc   hogode to wige
þe on Denon wolde   dom gefeohtan.
Wod þa wiges heard,   wæpen up ahof,
bord to gebeorge,   and wið þæs beornes stop.

(127–31)

The referent of *wiges heard* and *þæs beornes* is confusing, and different editions of *Maldon* offer either of two interpretations of the passage, both of which presuppose a lapse in narrative skill on the part of the poet. Some editors (for example, Sedgefield; Anderson and Williams)[26] assume quite logically that *wiges heard* can only refer to Byrhtnoth since he is the subject of the foregoing sentence. But this would make *þæs beornes* refer to the Viking opponent, and the use of the definite article must then "be explained by supposing the narrator to be unaware that he has not previously mentioned the *ceorl* whom Byrhtnoth attacks."[27] Other editors take *wiges heard* as referring to a Viking warrior hitherto unmentioned and regard *þæs beornes* as Byrhtnoth, but this presupposes an unmarked shift of subject which would have confused the poem's early readers and listeners as much as it has modern editors.

The difficulty, I suspect, results from scribal inattention rather than from a lapse in poetic skill. Quite likely either the Old English scribe or the eighteenth-century transcriber has omitted a line or two which introduced the Viking warrior referred to as *þæs beornes* in line 131, the omission occurring between lines 130 and 131. A similar scribal omission has long been recognized at line 172, and J. C. Pope discovered another at line 284.[28] Such information as we have about the original manuscript, moreover, may offer a modicum of evidence about the process of error in this instance. In Cotton Otho A.xii, folio 59^v could have begun at approximately the area where I am assuming a loss of text, a coincidence which suggests that scribe or copyist may have lost track of some words in turning the page. According to Hearne's marking of the foliation, folio 59^r began at about line 108 and 60^r at line 162.[29] The transcriber neglected to mark the transition from 59^r to 59^v, and so we have no indication of the change of page in Hearne, who simply copied the foliation from the transcriber's transcript in the Bodleian Library (MS.

---

[26] *The Battle of Maldon*, ed. W. J. Sedgefield (Boston, 1904), p. 36; M. Anderson and B. C. Williams, *Old English Handbook* (Cambridge, MA, 1935), p. 347.

[27] Sedgefield, *The Battle of Maldon*, p. 36.

[28] *Seven Old English Poems*, ed. J. C. Pope (Indianapolis, 1966), p. 78.

[29] Thomas Hearne, *Johannis Confratris et Monachi Glastoniensis, Chronica sive Historia de Rebus Glastoniensibus* (Oxford, 1762), vol. 2, p. 573.

Rawlinson B.203).³⁰ However, the problematic passage falls roughly midway between the two markings that we do have.³¹

VI

> he gehleop þone eoh   þe ahte his hlaford,
> on þam gerædum   þe hit riht ne wæs.
>
> (189–90)

The syntax seems to falter in line 190, and some editors have accordingly emended *þe* to *þeah*. It is tempting to assume that the break in syntax is a deliberate anacoluthon, the poet's restrained understatement of the scandalous flight of the deserters giving way to a momentary choke in the sentence structure which reveals the true depth of his feeling. (One might compare the artful use of aposiopesis in Satan's speech in the Old English *Genesis*, 370.) But some might regard such a dramatic use of syntax as suspiciously modern in character, and it must be mentioned that Hearne's edition indicates that folio 60ᵛ of the original manuscript began at just this point in the poem, a coincidence which, once again, suggests the likelihood that the textual awkwardness results from the loss of some letters at the turning of the page. Future editors of the poem might mention the attractive possibility of a deliberate and meaningful roughening of the syntax in line 190, but they should also concede the circumstantial evidence which supports those who would assume that either the Old English scribe or the eighteenth-century transcriber copied *þe* where he should have copied *þeah* or *þeah þe*.

VII

> "Gemunan þa mæla   þe we oft æt meodo spræcon,
> þonne we on bence   beot ahofon,
> hæleð on healle,   ymbe heard gewinn;
> nu mæg cunnian   hwa cene sy.
> Ic wylle mine æþelo   eallum gecyþan,

---

³⁰ As my colleague Antonette diPaolo Healey kindly informs me after checking the transcripts in Oxford.

³¹ Gordon (*The Battle of Maldon*, p. 52) assumes that 59ᵛ began at l. 136 rather than at l. 131, presumably because folio 9ᵛ of the transcript begins with this line. But the first lines of these pages do not always concur with the first lines of the folios in the original manuscript (as these are recorded in the transcriber's foliation of the manuscript). He marks folio 59ʳ, for example, as beginning at the third line of his own folio 9ʳ. If the loss of text occurred in the copying of the original manuscript (Otho A.xii), then the foliation of the transcript would of course be irrelevant.

> þæt ic wæs on Myrcon   miccles cynnes;
> wæs min ealda fæder   Ealhelm haten,
> wis ealdorman,   woruldgesælig.
> Ne sceolon me on þære þeode   þegenas ætwitan
> þæt ic of ðisse fyrde   feran wille,
> eard gesecan,   nu min ealdor ligeð
> forheawen æt hilde.   Me is þæt hearma mæst;
> he wæs ægðer min mæg   and min hlaford."
>
> (212–24)

The speech of Ælfwine (212–24) is predominantly in the first person singular: *Ic wylle... ic wæs... wæs min... þæt ic... Me is*, etc. This is fitting, for the purpose of Ælfwine's speech is to emphasize that Byrhtnoth's death is to him a peculiarly grievous personal loss, the slain man being both his leader and his kinsman. J. C. Pope has noticed that this emphasis on the first person is heightened by a calculated use of the verse form to give prominence to the repeated pronoun *min* in the closing line of the speech (224).[32]

The only sentence in the speech which does not have a strong first-person emphasis is the initial one, which editors indicate must be read as a command or exhortation instructing the warriors to remember discussions with Byrhtnoth in the mead-hall. But in the only other occurrence of this formulaic reference to a warrior's remembering mead-hall pledges made to a leader (the occurrence in *Beowulf*, 2633ff) the speech begins not with a command but with a first-person statement such as we might have expected in the *Maldon* speech:

> Ic ðæt mæl geman,   þær we medu þegun,
> þonne we geheton   ussum hlaforde
> in biorsele,   ðe us ðas beagas geaf,
> þæt we him ða guðgetawa   gyldan woldon.[33]

If we return to the text of the poem as it has come down to us through transcript and Hearne, we will see that the speech does begin in the first person there and that it is the editors who have changed the verb-form to an imperative or subjunctive plural, *gemunan* and *gemunaþ* being the most popular emendations. The transmitted text says,

> gemunu þa mæla   þe we oft æt meodo spræcon

which we may translate, "I remember the occasions on which we often spoke at the mead. ..."[34] Though rare, *gemunu* is an attested first-person singular

---

[32] Pope, *Seven Old English Poems*, pp. 77–8.

[33] Quoted from *Beowulf and the Fight at Finnsburg*, ed. Fr. Klaeber, 3rd edn with 1st and 2nd supplements (Boston, 1950). I have deleted Klaeber's macrons.

[34] Most editors have interpreted *mæla* as the occurrence of an otherwise unattested Old English

present indicative form in the *Vespasian Psalter*, while *gemune*, showing weakening of the inflectional vowel, occurs repeatedly in late West Saxon. It is the omission of the personal pronoun, no doubt, which brought the original reading under editorial suspicion, but such ellipsis of pronoun subject is paralleled precisely in line 172 (where we have *Geþance þe* for *Ic geþance þe*)[35] and in line 275 (where we have *mæg cunnian* for *man mæg cunnian*). The clustering of these ellipses in battlefield speeches may even be a deliberate stylistic device for suggesting the rush and urgency of the warriors' words of encouragement to one another in the middle of a battle.

VIII

Her lið ure ealdor   eall forheawen,
god on greote.

(314–15)

Ða hine heowon   hæðene scealcas
and begen þa beornas   þe him big stodon

(181–2)

Both here and in the earlier description of Byrhtnoth's slaying (181–2), the poet refrains from mentioning the most shocking detail of the English leader's death, the fact that the Vikings decapitated him as he was fighting and then bore his head away as a trophy. The atrocity is recorded in the *Liber Eliensis*[36] and appears to have been confirmed by the report to the Society of Antiquaries

---

word *mǣl* "speech" instead of the common word *mǣl* "occasion," but the repeated collocation of *mǣl* "occasion" with forms of the verb *gemunan* elsewhere in Old English poetry argues strongly against this view. See, for example, James L. Rosier, "*Instructions for Christians*: a poem in Old English," *Anglia*, 82 (1964), 15, l. 124, *Vainglory*, 83, and especially the closely parallel passage from *Beowulf* quoted above. It may be noted that in uttering such a sentence as this Ælfwine would be responding appropriately to the *bon mot* which Byrhtnoth is reported to have made when the abbot of Ramsey invited him to dine with him but refused to extend the invitation to Byrhtnoth's soldiers: "Sciat dominus abbas, quod solus sine istis nolo prandere, quia solus sine illis nequeo pugnare" (*Liber Eliensis*, ed. Blake, p. 135). But cf. Liebermann's remarks in "Zur Geschichte Byrhtnoths," 26–7.

[35] For the frequency of the omission of pronoun subjects in Old English, see Alois Pogatscher, "Unausgedrücktes Subjekt im Altenglischen," *Anglia*, 23 (1900), 261–301. Some editors emend *geþance* to the normal form *geþancie* (just as they emend *ferian* to *feran* in l. 179), but it seems clear that such distinctions in verbal endings were being lost at the time when *Maldon* was committed to parchment. Cf. also the phonetic weakening revealed in such spellings as *modelice* (200), *forlætun* (208), *frymdi* (179).

[36] "caput pungnantis vix cum magno labore secuerunt" (p. 136).

on the exhumation of Byrhtnoth's body in 1769.[37] It is possible, of course, that the poet did mention the decapitation in some portion of the poem now lost, but it is hard to imagine in what context he would mention it if not in the account of Byrhtnoth's death and the subsequent allusions to his body, which are preserved in the text as it has come down to us. On the other hand, one might argue that the poet was simply ignorant of the mutilation, and it must be noted that the briefer accounts of Byrhtnoth's death in chronicles and in the *Vita Oswaldi* do not mention it. But in all other respects the poet's sources seem to have provided him with such a wealth of detail that it is hard to imagine their omitting the horrifying climax of Byrhtnoth's slaying. There is, moreover, in the surviving text of the poem a possible hint of the poet's awareness of the mutilation, for he describes Byrhtnoth's corpse twice as *forheawen* (223, 314). While this verb does not carry the specific meaning "mutilate, decapitate," it does seem to occur in contexts where something other than just "kill" is intended. In glosses it renders Latin *caedo* and *concido*, while its only other poetic occurrence is in *Widsith*, 49, where the Danes *forheowan æt Heorote Heaðobeardna þrym*. Since Saxo Grammaticus informs us that the Heathobards' bodies were denied burial and scattered to rot in the fields,[38] some suggestion of dismemberment may be present in the verb here too. The Old Saxon cognate *farhauwan* occurs but once in the *Heliand* (4877), and there it describes St Peter's mutilation of Malchus's ear.[39] The documentations are few, to be sure, but barring an unusual coincidence, they suggest that there is internal as well as external evidence that the *Maldon* poet was aware of the Danes' peculiarly brutal slaying of Byrhtnoth.

Assuming for the moment that he did know of the decapitation but suppressed it, how are we to interpret the poet's reticence? It seems to me that this would be precisely characteristic of his care throughout the poem to avoid denigrating the Vikings, and, instead, to portray them as an inimical, impersonal force. If he played up the brutality of the invaders, he would "misdirect ... readers into viewing the narrative as primarily a conflict between virtuous Englishmen and evil Vikings," a polarization of sympathies that

---

[37] Gordon, *The Battle of Maldon*, p. 21.

[38] Saxo Grammaticus, *Gesta Danorum*, VI, 213–14.

[39] The amputation of Malchus's ear in the Old High German *Tatian* is also described with a form of this verb, though with a different prefix: Latin *amputavit* is rendered *abahio*. See *Tatian, Lateinisch und Altdeutsch*, ed. Eduard Sievers (Paderborn, 1872), p. 307. The exact Old High German cognate of *forheawan*, *furhouwan*, appears in a glossarial list printed by E. G. Graff, *Diutiska* (Stuttgart and Tubingen, 1826), p. 341, glossing the Medieval Latin word *capulare* "cut off, mutilate" (*cappulauerit : firhouuuid*). Elsewhere *furhouwan* occurs with the meanings "wound, cut off, cut down (a tree)."

If Old English *forheawan* does mean "cut, mutilate" rather than "kill," then it must carry this meaning in *Maldon*, 288, where it refers to Offa, who came to "die of his wounds" (293) and to Wulfmær, who the poet says is *wund ... forheawen* in ll. 113–15.

"would divert attention from the important conflict – the tensions within the English ranks."⁴⁰ A sensational detail like the beheading of Byrhtnoth would have spoiled entirely the poet's artful restraint in depicting the Vikings as nothing more than the embodiment of a challenge to heroism, the anonymous occasion for each Englishman's moral decision to stand or to flee. If the omission from the poem is merely an accident of manuscript losses or of defective sources, it is an accident which accords surprisingly well with the poet's narrative strategy throughout the poem as we have it.

IX

Byrhtwold maþelode,　　bord hafenode
(se wæs eald geneat),　　æsc acwehte.

(309–10)

The words *eald geneat* in line 310 persuade most readers that Byrhtwold is a man advanced in years, and *frod feores* in line 317, although not conclusive proof of the point (cf. *Beowulf*, 1844, for example), tends to confirm the impression. But several scholars have thought otherwise. Liebermann argued that *eald geneat* means "true follower" rather than "old retainer";⁴¹ Gordon says that *eald* means only "trusty, of long service"; Ashdown says, "Perhaps the term may be taken to indicate a member of the *dugoþ* in contradistinction to the *geogoþ*; and Wyatt, in a note to an earlier line, asks, "Of what use is an old man in battle?"⁴²

That an old man can be effective in battle is demonstrated by King Beowulf, King Onela, and Byrhtnoth himself. What makes it especially likely that Byrhtwold was intended to be an old warrior, moreover, is the apparent fact that it is a standard convention of Germanic heroic literature for an aging warrior to assume responsibility for reminding his younger comrades of the sacred duty of loyalty and revenge which the ancient code prescribes for them. In *Beowulf* there is the *eald æscwiga, se ðe eall geman* (2042), who exhorts the younger warriors to remember their duty toward the fallen leader Froda, and his Scandinavian counterpart Starcatherus is similarly portrayed as an old man by Saxo Grammaticus (*Gesta Danorum*, VI, 189–214). An even more remarkable parallel to Byrhtwold's eloquent declamation is the speech of the aged Saxon warrior Hathagat recounted in Widukind of Corvey's *Rerum*

---

⁴⁰ See "Lexicography and literary criticism: a caveat", p. 141 below.

⁴¹ Liebermann, "Zur Geschichte Byrhtnoths," 19, n. 35: "*eald geneat*, obwohl von altem Manne gesagt, heißt vielleicht 'echter Gefolgsmann', eher als 'alter (Kampf)genosse' und gewiß nicht 'Altersgenosse'." Later scholars have not always noticed that Liebermann conceded, despite his interpretation of *eald geneat*, that Byrhtwold was an old man.

⁴² Gordon, *The Battle of Maldon*, p. 61; Ashdown, *English and Norse Documents*, p. 90; *An Anglo-Saxon Reader*, ed. Alfred J. Wyatt (Cambridge, 1919), p. 282.

Gestarum Saxonicarum Libri Tres, a historical narrative completed in 973 which draws heavily on Germanic songs and heroic legends for its matter.

> Erat autem tunc in castris quidam de veteranis militibus iam senior, sed viridi senectute adhuc vigens, qui merito bonarum virtutum pater patrum dicebatur, nomine Hathagat. Hic arripiens signum, quod apud eos habebatur sacrum, leonis atque draconis et desuper aquilae volantis insignitum effigie, quo ostentaret fortitudinis atque prudentiae et earum rerum efficatiam, et motu corporis animi constantiam declarans ait: "Hucusque inter optimos Saxones vixi, et ad hanc fere ultimam senectutem aetas me perduxit, et numquam Saxones meos fugere vidi; et quomodo nunc cogor agere quod numquem didici? Certare scio, fugere ignoro nec valeo. Si fata non sinunt ultra vivere, liceat saltem, quod michi dulcissimum est, cum amicis occumbere. Exempli michi paternae virtutis sunt amicorum corpora circa nos prostrata, qui maluerunt mori quam vinci, inpigras animas amittere quam coram inimicis loco cedere. Sed quid necesse habeo exhortationem protrahere tantisper de contemptu mortis? Ecce ad securos ibimus, ad caedem tantum, non ad pugnam. Nam de promissa pace ac nostro gravi vulnere nichil suspicantur adversi, hodierno quoque prelio fatigati quemadmodum sunt, sine metu, sine vigiliis et solita custodia manent. Irruamus igitur super inprovisos et somno sepultos, parum laboris est; sequimini me ducem, et hoc canum caput meum vobis trado, si non evenerit quod dico."[43]

Of course, in *Maldon* no less than in Widukind what the writer presents is intended as "true history," not as fiction. But it is equally clear that in *Maldon* (as in Widukind) the ordering of details, the portrayal of characters, and the phrasing of speeches are all shaped according to the demands of aesthetic conventions, not of literal reportage.

[43] *Widukindi Monachi Corbeinsis Rerum Gestarum Saxonicarum Libri Tres*, ed. George Waitz, Scriptores Rerum Germanicarum in Usum Scholarum ex Monumentis Germaniae Historicis, Separatim Editi (Hannover and Leipzig, 1904), p. 16.

This study is dedicated to the distinguished scholar and teacher Norman E. Eliason on the occasion of his retirement as Kenan Professor of English at the University of North Carolina at Chapel Hill.

10
Literary Dialect in *Maldon* and the Casley Transcript

       and eow betere is
þæt ge þisne garræs mid gafole forgyldon
þon we swa hearde (hi)lde dælon.
       The Battle of Maldon, 31–3

"And it is better for you that you avoid this battle by paying tribute than that such brave ones as we should contend in battle." The words *þon* and *hilde dælon* are two among several expressions in this speech by the Viking messenger (29–41) which I have elsewhere identified as expressions of Scandinavian origin which the poet uses here to suggest the tone and accent of the Norsemen delivering this speech.[1] In his edition of *The Battle of Maldon* D. G. Scragg notes without comment my argument for the Scandinavian quality of *hilde dælon*, but on *þon* (which Scragg emends to *þonne*), he has this to say:

> 33 *þonne*. Dobbie keeps Elphinston's *þon* as a "permissible variant", and Robinson, "Some Aspects", p. 26, argues for its retension [*sic*] as a deliberate imitation of ON *þan*. But Elphinston omits the abbreviation mark from this word a number of times in his transcription of Cotton Tiberius A.xiii.[2]

That is, since the abbreviatory superscript is omitted form *þoñ* "a number of times" in the transcription of Hemming's Cartulary in Tiberius A.xiii made by Elphinstone (as he himself spelled his name), Scragg assumes that Elphinstone must have made the same transcriptional error in his transcription of *The Battle of Maldon*. Hence *þon* cannot be, as I have suggested, a Scandinavicism.

But Scragg's basis for rejecting my defense of the transmitted form *þon* is now exploded by H. L. Rogers's demonstration that Elphinstone was not the transcriber of *The Battle of Maldon* at all. *Maldon* was transcribed by David Casley, who had an altogether different set of scribal characteristics and who,

---

Reprinted from *American Notes and Queries*, 26 (1986), 103–4.

[1] See above, "Some aspects of the *Maldon* poet's artistry," pp. 122–4.
[2] *The Battle of Maldon*, ed. D. G. Scragg (Manchester, 1981), pp. 69–70.

in his transcription of another vernacular Old English manuscript (Vespasian B.xxiv) "does correctly copy the abbreviation over *þon*."[3] Therefore, those who find merit in my contention that there is conscious artistry in the *Maldon* poet's use of *þon* and other terms of Scandinavian flavor in the Viking's speech should not be deterred by Scragg's deletion of this reading from the text, since that deletion is based on a mistaken identification of the copyist of the manuscript.

This note is but a single example of the importance of H. L. Rogers's discovery. Not only must Scragg's various textual arguments based upon his comparison of supposed transcripts by Elphinstone be re-examined; all scholars who have drawn inferences from this long-held misattribution must now reconsider the cases in a new light.[4]

[3] H. L. Rogers, "*The Battle of Maldon*: David Casley's transcript," *NQ*, 32 (1985), 147–55.

[4] Rogers himself provides a reassessment of many of Scragg's textual decisions based on the transcriptional habits of Elphinstone (ibid., 152–3). Although the evidence Rogers cites supports my retention of *þon*, he concludes by saying, without explanation, "I would read *þonne* myself."

11
Lexicography and Literary Criticism: A Caveat

> Once a word is placed in a dictionary, the very fact of its niche there tends to induce its inclusion in later dictionaries and to give it a usually quite fitting garb of authenticity; not all of them deserve it.
>
> Herbert D. Meritt, *Fact and Lore About Old English Words*

No one familiar with the literary history of English would be so rash as to suggest that lexicography and literary study are incompatible pursuits. Admired writers as different from one another as Coleridge, James Boswell, and Alexander Pope all involved themselves in lexicographical projects,[1] and it cannot be wholly fortuitous that three of the greatest prose stylists in English – Ælfric, Addison, and Samuel Johnson – have also been lexicographers.[2] The two roles would seem to coincide harmoniously, and one might well question the wisdom of the caveat announced in the title above.

The warning I wish to raise, however, is not against versatile lexicographers doubling as men of letters; rather it is against subconscious confusion of the two roles by both those who compile dictionaries and those who use them. For sometimes when a lexicographer is assessing the meaning of a word in a given occurrence, he slips unawares into the role of literary interpreter, recording a meaning for a word not on the basis of lexicographical evidence but purely because his particular critical interpretation of the passage requires such a meaning. Scholars who then encounter his judgments in the dictionary often fail to distinguish between what is lexicographical fact and what is the dictionary-maker's momentary indulgence in literary criticism. In some instances, these unsubstantiated *ad hoc* meanings can fix the critical interpretation of a passage in a permanent course of error; for, so long as they

---

Reprinted from *Philological Essays: studies in Old and Middle English language and literature in honour of Herbert Dean Meritt*, ed. James L. Rosier (The Hague, 1970), pp. 99–110.

[1] See A. W. Read, "Projected English dictionaries, 1755–1828," *JEGP*, XXXVI (1937), 193, 360-1, and Samuel Johnson's *Plan* for his *Dictionary* (*Works* [Oxford, 1825], vol. V, p. 20).

[2] Ælfric's and Johnson's places in the history of English lexicography are well known; for Addison's "design to make a dictionary," see Johnson, *Works*, vol. VII, p. 442.

remain unchallenged, the dictionary definitions of words are necessarily the starting point for any critical explication of the literature which uses those words. What follows here is an exploration, by way of example, of the various ways in which unconscious literary interpretation masquerading as lexicographical fact can impair literary understanding of passages in early English poetry.

An important consideration in any critical reading of *The Battle of Maldon* is the precise meaning of the epithets applied to the Vikings in the poem. It has often been noted that the poet's terms for the foe seem curiously restrained and dispassionate, a remarkable feature when we remember that these marauders constitute the nemesis of the heroic English. Yet, for the most part the poet describes them in approximately the same way as they describe themselves in lines 29–38, that is, as "seamen": *brimliþend, brimmen, flotan, lidmen, sælidan, sæmen, særincas*. Elsewhere he calls them "Vikings" (*wicingas*), "the enemy" (*fynd*), "strangers" (*gystas*), "hated or hostile people" (*laðe leode*), or "heathens" (*hæðene*), all of which are simply descriptive. In a number of instances he uses the same terms to refer to the Norsemen as he uses to refer to the English themselves: *hyssa, leode, werod*, and *ceorl*.

A quite reasonable explanation for this choice of epithets would seem to be that the *Maldon* poet deliberately avoids vilifying terms for the Vikings because he does not want to misdirect his readers into viewing the narrative as primarily a conflict between virtuous Englishmen and evil Vikings. Such a polarization of sympathies would divert attention from the important conflict – the tensions within the English ranks. (It would lead, in fact, to a simplistic narrative like *The Battle of Brunanburh*, which has the moral subtlety of a Wild West film.)[3] But many readers seem not to share this conception of *Maldon*. They feel that some indignation on the part of the poet is required, and consequently they search the dictionaries for evidence that at least some of the poet's epithets for the Vikings are in fact pejorative. In the case of one epithet they are not disappointed. The word *scealcas*, applied to the Vikings in line 181, is "a term of reproach" according to *BTD*.[4] If this is correct, then we must adjust our interpretation of the narrator's tone accordingly.

But what is the dictionary's authority for saying that in *Maldon* the word *scealcas* is "a term of reproach"? In most of its occurrences *scealc* means "man, soldier, sailor, servant," in which sense it is applied to Beowulf, David, and

---

[3] For a perceptive discussion of how the early Germanic writer achieved moving effects by resisting facile moral judgments when describing human conflicts, see Jorge Luis Borges's essay on the confrontation of King Harold and Tostig in "El pudor de la historia," in *Otras Inquisiciones* (Buenos Aires, 1960), pp. 229–33.

[4] The following abbreviations are used in this essay in addition to those listed on p. x. *GKH* stands for *Sprachschatz der angelsächsischen Dichter* by C. W.M. Grein with the assistance of F. Holthausen, revised by J. J. Köhler (Heidelberg, 1912); *B* is *A Short Dictionary of Anglo-Saxon Poetry* by J. B. Bessinger (Toronto, 1961).

other admirable personages. There are, on the other hand, only two documentations in *BTD* for the supposed pejorative sense of *scealc*: one is the *Maldon* passage in question; the other is *Christ and Satan*, 132-3, which *BTD* quotes as *hwilum ic gehere helle scealcas, gnorniende cynn*. This second example requires close scrutiny. To be sure, the characters described here as *scealcas* are Satan's fellow-victims, but this does not necessarily imply a pejorative sense for unmodified *scealcas* any more than it does for *cynn*, which stands in apposition with *scealcas*. And in any case, modern editions no longer read *scealc* in this passage as an independent word. The line is now taken by editors universally as

> hwilum ic gehere   hellescealcas,
> gnornende cynn

thus removing this piece of evidence altogether from the picture. Indeed, *BTD* records the compound *hellescealc* some three hundred pages before the *scealc* entry, citing as the sole occurrence of the word *Christ and Satan*, 133! One can only assume that the entry "*scealc* . . . II. as a term of reproach" is based entirely upon the lexicographers' literary critical interpretation of *Maldon* and that the *Christ and Satan* passage was brought in (somewhat absent-mindedly) as a desperate means of giving that interpretation some documentary support. The fact is, however, that it has no support. The supposed pejorative sense of *scealc* is merely a bit of literary criticism posing as lexicographical fact. There is, then, no objective evidence that the *Maldon* poet expresses open contempt for the Vikings, and regardless of whether one agrees that he is a better poet for dramatizing without asserting their iniquity, one must accept the fact that he apparently did not assert it.[5]

Similar instances are not far to seek elsewhere in the dictionaries. The famous example of *lofgeornost* in *Beowulf*, 3182, comes readily to mind. Our entire conception of the poet's attitude toward his hero rests to a considerable extent upon our decision whether this term is wholly complimentary in Christian terms (as are the three adjectives preceding and paralleling it) or whether it is a frank acknowledgment of the secular Germanic side of the hero's character. Both *BTD* and *BTS* assure us that the word is used here "in a good sense" meaning "eager to deserve praise" and *BTS* sets up a special entry

---

[5] Other epithets from *Maldon* which scholars have tried to interpret pejoratively are shown by J. E. Cross, "Oswald and Byrhtnoth: a Christian saint and a hero who is a Christian," *ES*, XLVI (1965), 14-16, to be in fact connotatively neutral. Cross does concede a slight pejorative sense for *scealc*, however, on grounds of the Old Icelandic cognate *skálkr* "rogue," but this seems to me an unnecessary concession. If an English writer today referred to "knights" in a story dealing with German gentry, this term would hardly take on pejorative connotations simply because the German cognate of *knight* is *Knecht*. The *Maldon* usage of *scealc* is also declared pejorative by G. C. Britton in "The characterization of the Vikings in *The Battle of Maldon*," *NQ*, n.s. XII (1965), 85-7, where the word is rendered "louts" (on the strength of the *BTD* entry which I have challenged above).

for this semantic category. But when the reader notices multiple documentations for the word's use "in a bad sense" meaning "ostentatious, boastful" and only the single *Beowulf* occurrence to support the "good sense," the inevitable question arises. What evidence beyond the lexicographers' benevolent literary interpretation of *Beowulf* warrants the lexicographic authority which the "good sense" now enjoys? Their interpretation may, of course, be right, but the responsible student must insist upon full access to the evidence for it.[6]

One *Beowulf*ian nonce-word which the dictionaries have interpreted dubiously is of considerable interest in understanding the role of Grendel. In the poet's single detailed description of the monster's cannibalistic attacks, we are told that he seized a warrior and

> bat banlocan,   blod edrum dranc,
> synsnædum swealh.
>
> (742–3)

"he bit the bone-lockings, drank blood from the veins, swallowed the *synsnædum*." At first glance, *synsnædum* looks like a word meaning "sinful morsels," but the dictionaries reject this possibility, preferring to see *syn-* here as a form of the prefix *sin-* "perpetual, permanent," which is then assigned the *ad hoc* meaning "huge, immense" so that it will make acceptable sense in this occurrence.[7] This interpretation was offered very tentatively in *BTD*, but subsequent dictionaries have long since given it the full authority of an unqualified entry, and editors and translators have, without exception, followed their lead.

But I am convinced that there is much to be said for the less complicated interpretation of *synsnædum* as "sinful morsels," an alternative which seems never to have been explored. (The dictionaries' confident agreement that the word here means "huge morsels" would suggest that there is nothing to explore.) In Anglo-Saxon times the mention of blood-drinking would probably have suggested a specific and horrifying sin, a sin which would match on a

---

[6] An analogous example from *Beowulf* is that of *forpringan* in l. 1084. The expected meaning of this verb would be "to crowd out" and it is documented with this meaning in BasPr., vol. 2, pp. 114, 115. But the *Beowulf* occurrence is glossed by the dictionaries with a precisely opposite meaning, "protect" (*BTD*), "*defendere ab aliquo*" (*GKH*), purely on the grounds that satisfactory literary interpretation of the episode seems to require such a meaning. But see *Beowulf with the Finnesburg Fragment*, ed. C. L. Wrenn (London, 1953), pp. 204–5.

[7] From time to time one or another of the numerous other *sin-* compounds has been entertained as possibly constituting a second instance of *sin-* "immense" (e.g. *sinfrea, sindolh, sinhere*), but all are equally well explained in terms of the usual meaning of *sin-*, "perpetual, permanent." *Sinfrea* means "permanent lord, husband." *Sindolh* is adequately interpreted in Moritz Heyne's edition of *Beowulf*, rev. Adolf Socin (Paderborn, 1898), p. 254, as meaning "immerwährende, d.i. nicht zu heilende Wunde." *Sinhere* would seem to mean "permanent army" – i.e. the standing retinue of the prince as opposed to an emergency levy. There is no justification in the context for the assumption that the force referred to was an "immense army": see *Beowulf*, 2936.

spiritual, theological level the physical horror of Grendel's feast. A casual examination of Old English prose writings reveals an almost obsessive concern with the Old Testament injunction against the drinking of blood.[8] Ælfric and Wulfstan, as well as other homilists, reiterate the warning both in Latin and in vernacular writings,[9] and it is a constant theme in penitential writings.[10] Alfred the Great incorporated the blood-proscription into his law-code,[11] and Bede dealt with it in his theological writings.[12] It even turns up elsewhere in Old English poetry: *Genesis A*, lines 1518-20, contains the injunction

> Næfre ge mid blode   beodgereordu
> unarlice   eowre þicgeað,
> besmiten mid synne   sawldreore.

Here the mention of blood is followed, as in the *Beowulf* passage, by an elaborative epithet. The two collocations may be thought of as roughly proportional:

blode: besmiten mid synne sawldreore = blod: synsnædum

The true meaning of *synsnæd*, I suspect, is closer to the *Genesis* poet's *besmiten mid synne sawldreore* than it is to the dictionaries' gloss "huge morsels."

The reasons which medieval commentators offered for the blood-prohibition suggest some interesting tie-ins with the characterization of Grendel elsewhere in the poem and also with some of the poet's other terms for "blood."

[8] For Biblical statements of the prohibition, see Gen. 9: 4-5; Lev. 3: 17, 7: 26-7, 17: 10-14, 19: 26; Deut. 12: 15-16, 12: 23-5, 15: 23; I Sam. 14: 32-4; and the important New Testament allusion to the law in Acts 15: 19-21, 28-9. For a generous sampling of the copious patristic and canonical writings on the subject, see Karl Böckenhoff's *Das apostolische Speisegesetz in den ersten fünf Jahrhunderten* (Paderborn, 1903), esp. pp. 93ff, and his *Speisesatzungen mosaischer Art in mittelalterlichen Kirchenrechtsquellen des Morgen- und Abendlandes* (Münster, 1907), pp.37-49. Pages 62 to 107 of the latter work deal abundantly with the especially large literature on the subject in Britain during the early Middle Ages. (It has been convincingly argued that the remarkably vigorous tradition of the blood-prohibition in Anglo-Saxon England resulted from dual Eastern Christian influences transmitted through Celtic agents on the one hand and through Theodore and Hadrian on the other.)

[9] See *Angelsächsische Homilien und Heiligenleben*, ed. Bruno Assmann, BasPr., vol. 3 (Kassel, 1889), p. 84, and *Die Hirtenbriefe Ælfrics*, ed. Bernhard Fehr, BasPr., vol. 9 (Hamburg, 1914), p. 223. See *The Homilies of Wulfstan*, ed. Dorothy Bethurum (Oxford, 1957), p. 205, and *Wulfstan. Sammlung der ihm zugeschriebenen Homilien*, ed. Arthur Napier (Berlin, 1883), p. 136. A rather detailed vernacular account of the prohibition is cited by Friedrich Kluge in *Englische Studien* 8 (1885), 62-3.

[10] *Die altenglische Version des Halitgar'schen Bussbuches*, ed. Josef Raith, BasPr. vol. 13 (Hamburg, 1933), pp.57, 62, provides vernacular examples, and the repetition of the blood-proscription in *Wulfstan's Canons of Edgar*, ed. Roger Fowler, EETS o.s. 266 (London, 1972), pp. 12-13, the Irish penitentials, and the penitentials of Pseudo-Theodore and Pseudo-Bede suggest that it was a regular feature of the confessional. See also "Be Blodþigene" in *Die Gesetze der Angelsachsen*, ed. Felix Liebermann (Halle, 1903), vol. II, pp. 130, 18.

[11] Liebermann, *Gesetze*, vol. I, p. 44.

[12] Bede, *Patrologia Latina*, vol. XCII, pp. 977, 1024.

It was widely held, of course, that blood was identical with the soul. This notion, which was current in vernacular Old English writings,[13] probably lies behind both the compound *sawldreore* in *Genesis* 1520 and the *Beowulf* poet's striking expression

                Ða wæs heal roden
feonda feorum.

"Then the hall was reddened (or stained) with the souls of the foes."[14] It also explains the compound *feorhlast* "bloody track (lit., track of the soul)" in line 846:

      fæge ond geflymed   feorhlastas bær;
      ðær wæs on blode   brim weallende

(For the extraordinary difficulties of the dictionaries in assessing the meaning of *feorhlast*, see entries in *CHM* and *BTS*.) It was largely because of this assumption that the blood was the seat of the soul that blood-drinking was regarded as such a heinous offense. To imbibe the blood of any creature was worse than merely to kill it; to do so was to consume life itself, which is reserved properly to the Lord (see esp. Lev. 17: 10–14 and Deut. 12: 15–16).

In view of this identification of the blood with the soul, it is not surprising that a number of early commentators (for example, Tertullian, Origen, Justin, Athenagoras) should explain that blood-drinking was specifically characteristic of certain corporeal demons descended from the evil giants who inhabited the world before the Flood. (The giants, as we are told in the Apocryphal Book of Enoch, turned violently on mankind, devoured flesh, and drank the blood; it was precisely in consequence of their violating the blood-prohibition, according to the Pseudo-Clementine *Recognitions*, I, xxx, that God sent the punitive Deluge.) The giant-sprung demons who persisted in the antediluvian blood-craving continued to seek out blood in any form, and it is for this reason as much as for any other, explains Origen, that human beings are strictly forbidden to consume it: blood is the food of demons.[15]

Bloodthirsty monsters from secular pagan literature could be brought into

[13] See Ælfric's metrical *Letter to Wulfget* (BasPr., vol. 3, p. 12), 302–3: *ic wylle ofgan æt ðe his blodes gyte, / þæt is sawul*. In the prose *Solomon and Saturn* the question *hwar resteð þas mannes sawul þone se lychaman slepð?* is answered, *on þam bragene, oððe on þere heortan, oððe on þam blode*. See *The Prose Solomon and Saturn and Adrian and Ritheus*, ed. James E. Cross and Thomas D. Hill (Toronto, 1982), p. 31. Ælfric's assertion *heora blod is heora lif* refers to animals alone (*Sermo de initio creaturae* in *The Homilies of the Anglo-Saxon Church. The First Part, Containing the Sermones Catholici, or Homilies of Ælfric*, ed. Benjamin Thorpe [London, 1843–6], vol. 1, p. 14).

[14] *Beowulf*, 1151–2. Cf. the identical use of *feorh* in *Juliana*, 476–8: *þæt him banlocan blode spiowedon / þæt hi færinga feorh aleton / þurh ædra wylm*.

[15] For a succinct survey of these early patristic expositions, see Böckenhoff, *Das apostolische Speisegesetz*, pp. 36–64.

the context of Christian interpretation without difficulty. Thus Clemens of Alexandria identified as one of the postdiluvian demons those shades of Hades who, in the *Odyssey*, XI, 34ff, rush in to drink the blood of an animal slain by Odysseus. It is not wholly improbable, then, that a Christian Anglo-Saxon poet might view one of the monsters from his own heroic literature in terms of the Christian Fathers' abhorrence of blood-drinking. That Grendel is not the only such ogre in Germanic tradition is amply attested, of course, by numerous parallels, one of the most interesting being the evil figure Grímr in the Old Icelandic *Göngu-Hrólfs saga*, who drinks the blood of both men and beasts and is endowed with supernatural powers, such as the ability to dull the edges of the Danes' swords. (He is called *Grímr ægir* because his mother was a sea-monster.)

This rather lengthy exposition of the possible implications of *synsnædum* in *Beowulf*, 743, may serve to illustrate what complex and important allusions can be concealed by a lexicographer's untimely indulgence in literary interpretation. If dictionaries had from the start recorded the literal meaning of *synsnæd*, then the need for literary scholars to establish a rationale for the compound would have been apparent. But the compilers judged the literal meaning aesthetically unacceptable and substituted an unwarranted sense which merged blandly into the context. As a result, scholars and editors have been distracted from what might be an important, functional allusion.

Yet another instance of lexicographical obfuscation is mentioned in an article by Ernst Leisi.[16] Leisi suggests that the dictionary definitions of the Old English verb *geweorðian* have long obscured an important cultural function of treasure and rewards in pre-Conquest times. He argues ingeniously that sumptuous gifts and precious objects were valued by the Anglo-Saxons not for any intrinsic worth but rather because they were an objective measure of the recipient's human achievement and prestige – of his *Manneswert*. This, Leisi explains, is the reason for the poet's frequent use of the verb *(ge)weorðian* in phrases like *since geweorðod, geofum geweorðod,* and *maðmum geweorðod*.[17] Dictionaries are wrong to enter special contextual meanings like "adorn, reward" for these occurrences, suggests Leisi; the verb should be read in its primary sense of "honored, distinguished, ennobled," and we should discern in its usage with words like *sinc* and *gifa* a clear indication of the Anglo-Saxons' symbolistic concept of gold and gifts, a concept which, if firmly authenticated,

---

[16] Leisi, "Gold und Manneswert im *Beowulf*," *Anglia*, LXXI (1953), 259–73, esp. p. 262.

[17] Cf. *Beowulf*, 1901–2, *he syðpan wæs / on meodubence maþme þy weorþra*, where the adjective suggests the full meaning of *weorðian* in similar contexts. The primary sense of the word is also clearly attested in the following *Boethius* passage: *ge beoþ on gedwolan, þonne ge wenað þæt ænig mæg mid fremdum welum beon geweorþod. Gif hwa nu bið mid hwelcum welum geweorþod . . . hu nu ne belimpð se weorðscipe þonne to þam þe hine geweorðað?* (*King Alfred's Old English Version of Boethius De consolatione philosophiae*, ed. Walter John Sedgefield [Oxford, 1899], p. 32).

would be of considerable importance in any general interpretation of *Beowulf*.[18]

The examples cited thus far illustrate how the lexicographer can unwittingly blind his reader to denotations and allusions which are important to a full understanding of the specific work in which they occur. Another kind of lexicographical obfuscation results when the dictionaries conceal from the reader the full force of the poetic style and particularly of the figurative language used in the early texts. If a word occurs in a slightly unusual application, the lexicographer's tendency is to introduce into the dictionary entry a special meaning for the occurrence, a definition which will fit in a literal way the context in question. This propensity often leads lexicographers to flatten out figurative language and to resolve intended ambiguities. Effects like synaesthesia, paronomasia, and personification are, I believe, far more frequent in Old English than our dictionaries and glossaries permit us to see.

In *Beowulf*, 1160–2, the poet describes the sounds of revelry which fill the hall:

> Gamen eft astah,
> beorhtode bencsweg, byrelas sealdon
> win of wunderfatum.

The force of this description, as I read it, lies in the synaesthetic representation of the convivial sounds "glittering" through the hall as the wine streams out of the bright chalices.[19] But the dictionaries, which are dutifully followed by editors and translators, explicitly deny this effect. Without exception, they list copious instances of the verb *beorhtian* in the visual sense ("glisten, shine, brighten") and then list a second meaning to accommodate the one occurrence in *Beowulf*, 1161: "to sound clearly" (*CHM*), "to sound clearly or loudly" (*BTD*), "*clare sonare*" (*GKH*), "sound clearly" (*B*). No evidence is cited by the dictionaries in support of this decision to reduce an arresting figure of speech to a commonplace descriptive phrase; one can only assume that lexicographers have at some point judged synaesthetic metaphor to be uncharacteristic of Old English poetic style. But the judgment seems hasty. We know from *Soul and Body*, 15, that Old English poets could speak of human voices in tactile terms:

> Cleopað þonne swa cearful   cealdan reorde

---

[18] In passages where (*ge*)*weorðian* is used of inanimate objects (e.g. *Beowulf*, 1038: *sadol... since gewurþad*) we should perhaps sense a slight personifying effect: "saddle ennobled by treasure." See Neil D. Isaacs, "The convention of personification in *Beowulf*" in *Old English Poetry: fifteen essays*, ed. Robert P. Creed (Providence, RI, 1967), pp. 215–48, for a careful demonstration of the pervasiveness of personification in Old English poetry.

[19] In an earlier description of a similar scene (494–7) the poet also juxtaposes this synaesthetic image (*scop hwilum sang / hador on Heorote*) with the description of a steward pouring bright wine (*þegn... scencte scir wered*).

and the presence of the same figure in the *Atlakviða* (7) suggests that the trope was a traditional Germanic one:

> kallaði þá Knefrœðr   kaldri rǫddo

The synaesthetic expression "a cold voice" continues into modern times, of course, but then so does the image of *beorhtode bencsweg*, as is attested by the seventeenth-century "till my music shine" and Swinburne's "light of sweetest songs" and "music heard as light." It is hard to see what line of reasoning led the lexicographers to credit a synaesthetic figure in the one case (they enter no aural meaning for *ceald*) and to reject it in the other.

Actually, the Anglo-Saxon poets appear to have been unusually bold in their use of synaesthetic imagery. Certainly the *Exodus* poet did not shrink from mingling the senses in order to gain a striking dictional effect: describing the horror and confusion of the overwhelmed Egyptian soldiers, he says,

> lyft up geswearc
> fægum stefnum[20]

"The air above grew dark with doomed voices." Frank recognition of the Anglo-Saxon poets' capacity for this kind of literary language might even help us to resolve some of the textual puzzles which have perplexed critics of Old English literature. The famous crux in *The Battle of Brunanburh* (12–13)

> feld dennade
> secga swate

has provoked a multitude of conjectures as to what *dennade* (v.l. *dæn[n]ede*) may be. One of the least strained interpretations is the view that it represents the common verb *dynade* "resounded," but this reading, of course, presupposes a remarkable synaesthetic image, "the field resounded with the blood of men." Before rejecting this interpretation as too bizarre, however, careful attention should be given to the battle-scene described in lines 28, 357ff of Layamon's *Brut*:

> feldes beoueden eke;
> gurren þa stanes   mid þan blod-stremes[21]

---

[20] *Exodus* 462–3. Cf. *Aeneid*, X, 895: "clamore incendunt caelum."

[21] Cited by Fr. Klaeber in *Palaestra*, CXLVIII (Leipzig, 1925), pp. 1–7. Bennett and Smithers, *Early Middle English Verse and Prose* (Oxford, 1966), p. 152, print, without comment, *ȝurnen* for *gurren*. I do not know the authority for this reading. G. L. Brook, *Selections from Layamon's Brut* (Oxford, 1963), p. 114, reads, like the generally accurate Madden, *ȝurren* (*Laȝamons Brut, or Chronicle of Britain*, ed. Sir Frederic Madden [London, 1847], vol. 3, p. 133.) Assuming the traditional reading, some may still feel that the sense is sufficiently strained to require further authentication in some independent allusion. This may be at hand in Orosius's *Historia*, IV, 2: "Triste adeo id bellum fuit, ut merito dicatur tantum humanum sanguinem susceptura terra tremuisse," which Alfred renders,

"the fields also trembled; the stones resound with the streams of blood." Our own sense of the limits of synaesthetic imagery may not have been that of the earlier writers, and we should remember this when evaluating the dictionaries' numerous *ad hoc* entries which implicitly deny synaesthetic effects in Old English poetry.

Another area where modern lexicographers are reluctant to acknowledge dictional complexity in Old English writings is that of deliberate verbal ambiguity. There is, in fact, a general assumption among Old English scholars that the use of puns or *double entente* "does not seem consistent with Anglo-Saxon poetic method."[22] The basis for this assumption is hard to determine, for paronomasia was a favorite device among the writers most familiar to the Anglo-Saxons,[23] and the Old English writers themselves discussed and used puns both in their vernacular and in their Latin writings.[24] Yet, even the most explicit puns in Old English are denied recognition by the dictionaries, which arbitrarily select one or the other of two intended meanings in a given occurrence, enter it in the article for the word, and omit mention of the other simultaneously intended meaning. Consider, for example, three puns from the Old English verse *Riddles*: *wonge* (31: 14) "in the field" and "in the cheek"; *blæd* (37: 7) "breath" and "prosperity"; *hæfte* (73: 22) "handle" and "confinement."[25] The standard dictionaries deal with these puns (all of which are explicitly cited by editors of the *Riddles*) as follows. BTD and GKH agree in identifying *wonge* as signifying only "earth, *campus*"; GKH indicates that *blæd* in *Riddle* 37 means only "ubertas, prosperitas, *etc.*" and not "breath"; GKH enters the citation for *hæfte* in *Riddle* 73 under the meaning "manubrium, Heft," excluding the sense "confinement." (*BTD* and *BTS* do not cite the last two.)

A good example of the difficulties which artful ambiguity can pose for the lexicographer is a single line in *Exeter Riddle* 20. This riddle is spoken

---

with only slight inaccuracy, *seo eorþbeofung tacnade þa miclan bloddryncas þe hiere mon on þære tide to forlet* (*King Alfred's Orosius*, ed. Henry Sweet, EETS, 79 [1883], pp. 160-2). See Carl T. Berkhout, "*Feld dennade* – again," *ELN*, 11 (1974), 161-2.

[22] J. D. A. Ogilvy, "Unferth: foil to Beowulf?," *PMLA*, LXXIX (1964), 372-3.

[23] See, for example, Christine Mohrmann, "Das Wortspiel in den augustinischen Sermones," *Mnemosyne*, 3rd ser., III (1935), 33-61, and A. Guillaume, "Paronomasia in the Old Testament," *Journal of Semitic Studies*, IX (1964), 282-90.

[24] Bede discusses and illustrates paronomasia in *De schematibus et tropis*, and Aldhelm uses puns in his *Ænigmata* (e.g. no. 99: *Camellus – camillus*) and elsewhere. For Alcuin's punning, see Peter Dale Scott, "Alcuin as poet," *UTQ*, XXXIII (1964), 248 and n. 27. Bethurum, *The Homilies of Wulfstan*, p. 92, refers to Wulfstan's fondness for puns, and in "Artful ambiguities in the Old English 'Book-Moth' Riddle," pp. 98-104 above, I have suggested that there is a pattern of wordplay in an OE verse riddle. For a discussion of paronomasia in OE, see *Byrhtferth's Manual*, ed. S. J. Crawford, EETS o.s. 177 (1929), p. 176.

[25] These are all noted by Tupper, *The Riddles of the Exeter Book* (Boston, 1910), pp. 158, 145, and 213. In my references, however, I use the Krapp-Dobbie numbering of the riddles: *The Exeter Book*, ed. George Philip Krapp and Elliott Van Kirk Dobbie, *ASPR*, vol. 3 (New York, 1936).

prosopoetically by a sword which, since it is assigned the dignified formulas of Old English heroic poetry, is automatically transformed by that diction into a noble warrior. It is just this double sense of the poetic language which creates the riddling quality as well as the light humor of the poem, a humor not wholly different from that in Chaucer's characterization of Chaunticleer, who, while speaking the language of a courtly knight, reveals unmistakably his essential roosterhood. Just so the sword, as it speaks of serving its *frean* with its *byrne* and *compwæpnum*, nevertheless leaves no doubt that it is merely an inanimate weapon accustomed to the restraining grip of its owner's hand. This fine equivocation is brought to perfect balance in line 23 of the poem, where the sword speaks of its relationship to

> þam healdende   þe me hringas geaf.

Healdend means "ruler, lord," but it is also the present participle of *healdan* "to hold, grasp." *þe me hringas geaf* refers to the literal fact that the sword's owner had outfitted it with rings – the ornamental devices by which it is attached or suspended; but at the same time it is a poetic formula commonly spoken by a warrior who receives rings (gold circlets used as money) from his lord in reward for service. The two meanings of the phrase stand here in precise equipoise, and one turns with interest to the dictionaries to see how the occurrence is glossed. *BTD* and *BTS* in their entry for *hring* pass over the *Riddle* usage in silence; *GKH* enters it hesitantly under the meaning "vinculum," posting a query alongside. Under *healdend GKH* enters an *ad hoc* meaning "possessore" to accommodate the passage in question, while *BTD* suggests "guardian." The effect in each case is to deny the puns intended.[26]

It must be acknowledged, of course, that deliberate ambiguities present an especially delicate problem for the compiler of a citatory dictionary. She must enter a meaning which is suitable for each occurrence of the word, but she cannot register every stylistic subtlety of each occurrence. Perhaps the best way to deal with explicit ambiguities would be for the lexicographers to avoid citing passages involving puns (if the dictionary is not exhaustively citatory), or else to enter a punning occurrence twice, once under each relevant meaning. Either expedient would avert implicit disavowal of this prominent feature of Old English poetic style.

[26] Another kind of dictional richness not unrelated to punning is the use of a word in both its abstract and concrete senses simultaneously, a device which dictionaries do not adequately recognize. Thus the *Beowulf* verses *Ic him þenode / deoran sweorde* (560-1), which *GKH* explicates bluntly as meaning "erschlug sie damit," has been shown by James L. Rosier, "The uses of association: hands and feasts in *Beowulf*," *PMLA*, LXXVIII (1963), 9-10, to carry concrete, metaphorical force, the verb *þenode* meaning "to serve up (food)" as well as "to strike down." This reading is strongly supported by one of Layamon's expansions of Wace in the description of Pascent's death: *He smat hine uuenen þat hæued þat he adun halde / and þat sweord putte in his muð: swulc mete him wes uncuð* (18090-3 [*Layamon's Brut* ed. Madden, vol. 2, p. 334]).

Poetic effects other than synaesthesia and paronomasia are sometimes inadvertently obliterated when they pass through the medium of lexicographic explication. The characteristic Germanic understatement in phrases like *wop wæs wide, woruld-dreama lyt* (*Exodus*, 42) and *þis sweord . . . þæt mec ær ond sið oft gelæste* (*Beowulf*, 2499–500) is entirely lost for the reader whose dictionary defines *lyt* and *oft* as meaning, respectively, "not at all" and "constantly, regularly, continually."[27] Similarly, one wonders whether the poetic word *feasceaft* is rightly rendered (as in *CHM* and *B*) "destitute, miserable, helpless, poor," with no inkling of the wry meiosis lurking in the element *fea-*. Yet another kind of interference with stylistic effect occurs in recent dictionary entries for the word *fus* "eager, hastening" as it is used in *Dream of the Rood*, 21: *Geseah ic þæt fuse beacen / wendan wædum ond bleom*. The normal meaning of *fus*, which would imply strong personification here, has been denied by many editors of the poem who insist instead on a special meaning "bright," although there is no firm evidence for such a meaning elsewhere. This tenuous conjecture has now passed into lexicographic fact, for some dictionaries give it sanction in their entries for the word.[28] But the adjective *fus* is used elsewhere repeatedly to modify personified inanimate objects – such as a military banner in *Exodus*, 129, an arrow in *Beowulf*, 3119, a cloud in *Riddle*, 3: 43 – and considering the extraordinary degree of personification vested in the speaking cross in *Dream of the Rood*, one wonders whether it is wise for the dictionaries to validate such a slenderly evidenced meaning and dismiss the possibility of *fus*'s being used in its customary sense with personifying effect: the cross is "eager and hastening" as it moves through its awesome transmutations into the dreamer's ken.

The examples I have cited here are neither exhaustive nor exhaustively representative, and the fact that they all come from Old English dictionaries should not, of course, be taken to imply that lexicographic interference with literary interpretation is a phenomenon unique to Old English textual criticism: though less noticed, it is no less pervasive in the scholarly study of later English literature.[29] The obvious way to reduce the interference would seem to

---

[27] The words are so glossed in Martin Lehnert's *Poetry and Prose of the Anglo-Saxons: dictionary* (Berlin, 1956), a generally excellent student dictionary which deserves to be better known among students of Old English despite the minor lapses cited here.

[28] See Lehnert, *Dictionary*, and *B*, s.v. *fūs*.

[29] The *OED* and even the currently appearing *Middle English Dictionary* contain many instances. One example from the latter may serve for many here. The final verse of the famous lyric *Foweles in þe frith* is "For beste of bon and blod," which could be taken to mean either "for (a) beast of bone and blood" or "for (the) best of bone and blood" – i.e. "for the best lady in human form." The *MED* decides unhesitatingly in favor of the first alternative, citing this line prominently as its first quotation under "*bēst/e n. . . .* One of the animal kingdom." One wonders, however, at the lexicographers' confidence in ruling out the second alternative, for the *MED* itself quotes in its entries for *blod*, *bon*, and the superlative adjective *best* such quotations as "þe feyrest on þat euer

be to study with a cold eye all the dictionaries on which we rely, pointing out, as I have tried to do here, the various points at which lexicographers trespass on literary critics' ground. This method cannot be ultimately successful, however, for there must always be some element of literary interpretation involved in lexicographic judgments, and experts will sometimes differ as to what is excessive and what is appropriate. Perhaps the best course would be for the users of dictionaries to become more fully aware of the proper limits of lexicographic speculation and to develop a healthy suspiciousness in evaluating the dictionaries' information on any vocabulary item affecting literary interpretation. A thoughtful recollection from time to time of the words quoted as the epigraph of this essay, and frequent reference to H. D. Meritt's numerous publications exposing error in lexicographic entries, would be a good way of cultivating in our own minds that proper balance of grateful admiration and affectionate skepticism with which we should approach the venerable dictionaries upon which literary study of our early texts is ultimately based.

---

wes mad of blod ant bon," "nys non so feyr of blod ant bone," "þe fairest leuedi . . . þat miȝt gon on bodi and bones," "so brighte a barne of bane and blode," "leuedi, best of alle þing," and "lauerde, þe is best of us."

Part III

Women in Old English Literature

12
The Prescient Woman in Old English Literature

In a passage which has been cited by generations of Germanic scholars the Roman historian Tacitus describes how highly the men of Germania revered their women:

> They even believe that there is in women a certain holiness and power of prophecy, and they do not neglect to seek their advice, nor do they disregard their replies.[1]

This occurs in *Germania*, book 8. In his *Historiae* Tacitus repeats this observation:

> By ancient custom among the Germans powers of prophecy (and, as the superstition increased, even divinity) are ascribed to many of their women.[2]

Earlier Julius Caesar had noted that the Germans turned to their women for advice on whether to engage in combat:

> Among the Germans it is a custom for the matrons of the household to declare by means of lots and divinations whether or not a battle should be undertaken.[3]

Reinhold Bruder cites nineteen passages in classical authors alluding to Germanic women as seeresses,[4] and there is ample testimony in the surviving records of the various Germanic tribes themselves that women were regarded

Reprinted from *Philologia Anglica: essays presented to Professor Yoshio Terasawa on the occasion of his sixtieth birthday*, ed. Kinshiro Oshitari et al. (Tokyo, 1988), pp. 241–50.

[1] "inesse quin etiam sanctum aliquid et providum putant, nec aut consilia earum aspernantur aut responsa neglegunt."
[2] "vetere apud Germanos more, quo plerasque feminarum fatidicas et augescente superstitione arbitrantur deas" (*Historiae*, 4, 61).
[3] "apud Germanos ea consuetudo esset, ut matres familiae eorum sortibus et vaticinationibus declararent" (*De Bello Gallico*, 1, 50).
[4] Bruder, *Die germanische Frau im Lichte der Runeninschriften und der antiken Historiographie*, Quellen und Forschungen zur Sprach- und Kulturgeschichte der germanischen Völker 57 (Berlin, 1974), pp. 151–2.

as being often gifted with prophetic powers and therefore especially valued for their advice on matters of importance. The Old Icelandic dictionary of Cleasby and Vigfusson has this to say under the entry for "völva," "a prophetess, sibyl, wise woman":

> The ancient Sagas contain many remarkable records of the heathen wise-women or sibyls, who were held in honour and reverence; at the great feasts and sacrifices in the autumn, the völva (often a woman of rank) went with her troop of maidens through the country, where she, so to say, crowned the feast: she was seated on a high seat (seiðhjallr) in the hall, where she wrought her spells and sang her "weird-songs" (varðlokur), after which the guests went past her one by one, and she told each his fate, or whatever else one wanted to know. [5]

The generalization about wise-women or sibyls "in ancient sagas" is borne out by Inger M. Boberg's *Motif-Index of Early Icelandic Literature* which cites twenty-two passages where old women or "völur" prophesy future events, and elsewhere women referred to as "spádis," "spákona," or "seiðkona" also foretell events to come.[6] The idea of second-sighted women is prominent in mythological contexts as well: in *Njalssaga*, chapter 157, for example, the outcome of the battle of Clontarf is foretold in the verses chanted by Valkyries observed by Dorrud. The most sublime representation of the prescient woman, however, is in the *Völuspa*, where the sibyl foretells the future of her entire race, culminating with the Doom of the Gods. This motif of a woman prophesying the destruction of her people is, we shall find, a recurring one.

Allusions to the prescience of women are to be found in virtually all Germanic cultures. E. Mogk illustrates this fact selectively but well in an article beginning with the sentence, "Nach Anschauung aller germanischen Stämme besassen die Frauen besondere prophetische Gabe."[7] A much fuller survey tracing the theme from its earliest documentations down through the medieval and early modern centuries (with copious examples) is provided by Grimm.[8] Naturally one example or another of this Germanic view of women's powers has been challenged or variously interpreted from time to time. For example, Reinhold Bruder questions the accuracy of Tacitus's comment in his *Germania*.[9] But the evidence

---

[5] *An Icelandic-English Dictionary* initiated by Richard Cleasby, revised by Gudbrand Vigfusson, 2nd edn with a supplement by Sir William A. Craigie (Oxford, 1957), pp. 721–2.

[6] Bibliotheca Arnamagnæana 27 (Copenhagen, 1966), p. 194 (M301.2, M301.2.1, M301.2.2).

[7] Mogk, "Weise Frauen," in *Reallexikon der Germanischen Altertumskunde*, ed. Johannes Hoops (Strassburg, 1911–19), pp. 504–5; see also the article "Weissagung", pp. 505–7.

[8] Jacob Grimm, *Teutonic Mythology*, tr. James Steven Stallybrass (Dover reprint of 4th edn [Berlin, 1875–88]) (New York, 1966), vol. 1, pp. 95–8, 396–437; vol. 4, pp. 1396–1406.

[9] Bruder, *Die germanische Frau*, pp. 152–62. Actually this skepticism had been expressed before – e.g. in *P. Cornelii Taciti De Germania*, ed. Alfred Gudeman (Berlin, 1916), p. 86 – but it has not found general acceptance.

for the concept in Germanic cultures is so widely attested that it is not significant that one or another isolated reference has been questioned.

Among the Anglo-Saxons one finds evidence of the Germanic view of women in daily life as well as in literature. Hild, the abbess of Whitby who presided over the inception of a Christian poetic tradition in English, is said by Bede to have been so wise that kings and princes as well as commoners sought her advice, and the same is said of her successor Ælffled. The eighth-century English nun Lioba, who did missionary work on the continent and became abbess of Bischofsheim, "was an adviser to royalty and was venerated for her wisdom by all."[10] Repeatedly pagan kings accepted the advice of their Christian queens and converted to Christianity, both in England and in other Germanic lands.[11] The surprisingly high status enjoyed by women in Anglo-Saxon England generally probably has something to do with the fact that they were so venerated for their wisdom.[12]

Old English literature also attests to the view of women as farsighted counsellors. The poet of the Exeter Book *Maxims* (86-92) describes the ideal wife as one who can

> rune healdan ... ond him ræd witan
> boldagendum bæm ætsomne

"keep counsel ... and have advice for the two masters of the home [that is, the husband and wife]." It has often been noted that the women characters in *Beowulf* are counsellors and even prophetesses of the kind Tacitus describes.[13] Wealhtheow's advice to Hrothgar to be mindful of their sons and her anxiety over the future (1177-87, 1226-31) are proved by subsequent events to have

[10] Richard J. Schrader, *God's Handiwork: images of women in early Germanic literature* (Westport, CT, 1983), p. 51. See also p. 48.

[11] Jane Chance, *Woman as Hero in Old English Literature* (Syracuse, NY, 1986), p. 58. This pattern may be seen in Germanic lands other than the Anglo-Saxon: e.g. the pagan Frankish king Clovis is converted by his Christian wife Clotild, who continues to exercise major influence on events in the kingdom both during and after Clovis's life. See, e.g., *Liber Historiae Francorum* (where major roles as advisers and participants in events are also played by the women Fredegund and Brunhild). In the Icelandic *Laxdæla Saga* Unn the Deep-Minded, who prophesies her own death, is seen to have superior wisdom because she is a Christian in pagan Iceland (Schrader, *God's Handiwork*, pp. 109, 110-11).

[12] Christine Fell, *Women in Anglo-Saxon England* (London, 1984), demonstrates conclusively the high status of women in Anglo-Saxon times. Cf. F. M. Stenton's observation that "there is no doubt that Old English society allowed women not only private influence, but also the widest liberty of intervention in public affairs" (quoted in Alexandra Hennessey Olson, "Women in *Beowulf*," in *Approaches to Teaching Beowulf*, ed. J. B. Bessinger, Jr and R. F. Yeager (New York, 1984), p. 150. See further Dorothy Whitelock, *The Beginnings of English Society* (Harmondsworth, Middlesex, 1952), pp. 93-5, 151-2.

[13] For example, Youko Imaizumi, "The women in *Beowulf*," *Studies in Language and Culture* (Nagoya University), 5 (1984), 1-9.

been well-founded.[14] When Hygd asks Beowulf to accept the throne of the Geatas because she does not believe that her son Heardred will be able to protect the kingdom against foreign armies, the hero refuses out of loyalty to the royal family, and Heardred becomes king. But events prove Hygd's sense of the situation to have been precisely correct: the Swedes invade the Geatish kingdom, Heardred is slain, and Beowulf agrees to accept the throne, just as Hygd had wanted in the first place. Finally and most important, we are told that at Beowulf's cremation an old woman predicts that evil days will now come upon the Geatish nation with the horror of military invasion, slaughters, humiliations, and captivity for the people (3150–5).[15] Twice before in the poem men have predicted the doom of the Geatas, and twice the poet in his own authorial voice confirmed that what they said is true.[16] The third prediction by a prophesying woman is, then, the climactic and ultimate corroboration that doom is at hand, for, as Grimm observes, "To the German way of thinking, the decrees of destiny assume a greater sacredness in the mouth of a woman."[17] And we should note further that a woman prophesying (accurately) the doom of a people is itself a recurring motif in the annals of the Germanic peoples. Veleda, a maiden of the Bructeri, prophesied the destruction of the legions arrayed against her people,[18] and a woman of the Cheruscians foretells the imminent doom of Drusus.[19] In the *Nibelungenlied* (stanzas 1533, 1539–42) the *wisiu wip* "wise-women" predict the downfall of the Burgundians. The archetype of these scenes would seem to be the mythical motif of a seeress predicting the doom of the gods and all the world, as we see in the *Völuspa*. It is important to note the Germanic cultural background of the prophesying woman at the close of *Beowulf*, for some scholars have not given sufficient weight to her words and have even doubted whether the *Beowulf* poet intended us to understand that the Geatish nation is doomed following the death of Beowulf.[20]

There are many other passages or works in Old English that we should reassess in the light of the Germanic motif of the prescient woman. Salient

---

[14] Fred C. Robinson, "History, religion, culture: the background necessary for teaching *Beowulf*," p. 40 above.

[15] The passage is damaged, but there seems to be general agreement that the surviving words indicate that an old woman (*bundenheorde*) is predicting evil days and an invasion. See Tilman Westphalen, *Beowulf 3150–55: Textkritik und Editionsgeschichte*, Bochumer Arbeiten zur Sprach- und Literaturwissenschaft 2 (Munich, 1967), esp. p. 286.

[16] Robinson, "History, religion, culture", p. 36 above.

[17] Grimm, *Teutonic Mythology*, p. 397.

[18] Tacitus, *Historiae*, 4.61.

[19] Dio Cassius, *Romaika*, 55.1. Gregory of Tours describes a seeress who foretells the deaths of kings Charibert and Chilperic: see *Historia Francorum*, 5, 11; cf. 7, 44 for an account of another seeress.

[20] Robinson, "History, religion, culture", pp. 40–1 above.

among these is the description of the temptation and fall of man in *Genesis B*. As has long been noticed, the Germanic poet[21] gives a unique twist to the biblical story, emphasizing the fateful deception of Adam and Eve rather than their sinfulness. The process of deception is greatly elaborated. Whereas the Bible states simply that the serpent persuaded Eve to eat the apple, and then Eve gave it to Adam, and he ate it as well (Genesis 3: 6), the Old English (and, presumably, Old Saxon) poem introduces several new features: the tempter first approaches Adam and urges him to eat the fruit, but Adam is unpersuaded by his arguments and refuses. Then the tempter turns to Eve and presses her "to think of counsel in abundance" (*rume ræd geþencan*, 561) for Adam, and says to her, "Urge him earnestly to carry out your advice" (*span þu hine georne þæt he þine lare læste*, 575–6). He persuades her to eat the apple and then provides her with a vision of heaven that seems to confirm his reassurances that God's will is being served.[22] Armed with the evidence of her vision and with the arguments the tempter has supplied her, Eve approaches Adam and urges him at length to follow her counsels (655–83), emphasizing that her supernatural vision proves that the command to eat the apple does come from God and that the tempter is truly God's emissary (666–81). Adam is persuaded by the woman (as he had not been by Satan's henchman) and eats the apple.

The Germanic poet's innovations have resulted in Adam's being persuaded by the counsels of a woman claiming divine insight, and we should reflect on the impact this would have on a Germanic audience. Adam's role, as the poet has developed it, resembles that of all the Germanic men of the past who accepted the advice of second-sighted women and seemed always to find that advice sound. Such an audience would see a kind of inevitability in Adam's decision to accept Eve's advice, and this goes a long way toward explaining why the fall of man in *Genesis B* seems to be a tragedy of fate more than a moral lapse and why "the nemesis which overtakes [Adam and Eve] is determined by a causal rather than a moral law."[23] To a people who believed in prescient women, the story of the fall told in this manner could hardly have meant anything else.

Another Old English poem which needs to be examined with reference to our motif is *Judith*. This poem is an Anglo-Saxon poet's versification of a portion of the colorful Old Testament Book of Judith:[24] an Assyrian army

---

[21] I.e. the Old Saxon poet of the original poem which is then redacted in Old English by the Anglo-Saxon poet.

[22] Scholars who in the past have interpreted *wacran hige* in l. 590 to mean that Eve had inferior intelligence are mistranslating. Chance, *Woman as Hero*, p. 74, is correct when she says that "Eve fails here not because she is unintelligent or inferior to Adam but because she has not been trained to resist, to fight, to remain strong against an adversary."

[23] J. M. Evans, "*Genesis B* and its background," *RES*, n.s. 14 (1963), 115.

[24] Just how large a portion cannot be specified since text is missing at the beginning of the surviving poem. Here and throughout this paper Old English poems are quoted from *ASPR*.

under the command of Holofernes is beseiging the Hebrews in Bethulia, and so the Jewish heroine Judith gains entry into the Assyrian camp, bewitches Holofernes with her beauty, encourages him to drink himself senseless, and then beheads him. She returns with the head to her people, who then triumph over the Assyrians. The Anglo-Saxon poet introduces into his telling of the story two noteworthy embellishments. First, as B. J. Timmer noted, "The poet has given Judith the features of an Anglo-Saxon woman," and of these features, he says, "she is ... above all wise (*gleaw, snotere, searoðoncel, gleawhydig, gearoponcol*)."[25] Second, the Old English poet adds at the end of his poem a long and lively description of a battle between the Jews and the Assyrians, a battle which is not even mentioned in the Vulgate Book of Judith.[26] In the Old English poem Judith advises her nation's army to march against the Assyrians and prophesies the outcome of the ensuing battle:

> Fynd syndon eowere
> gedemed to deaðe,   ond ge dom agon,
> tir æt tohtan,   swa eow getacnod hafað
> mihtig dryhten   þurh mine hand
>
> (195-8)

"Your foes are doomed to death, and you will have fame, glory at battle, as the mighty Lord has signified through my hand." Then at the end of the battle we are told that the Jews had reaped the spoils of victory "through the wise instruction of the courageous woman Judith" (*þurh Iudithe gleawe lare, mægð modigre* (333-4). This shaping of events clearly projects Judith into the role of the typical Germanic wise-woman advising her nation on whether to go to war and prophesying the outcome. We should bear this in mind when we engage the questions of what led the Old English poet to introduce his changes and of how his audience would have perceived the resulting poem.

The Germanic preconception about the wisdom and clairvoyance of women would probably have affected the way an Anglo-Saxon audience would have viewed the parts women play in both native Germanic stories and in imported narratives, in individual scenes and in characterization at large. In *Waltharius*, for example, when Walter's absence is reported to Atilla he mistakenly assumes that Walter is still asleep somewhere on the premises, but his wife Osperin,

---

[25] *Judith*, ed. B. J. Timmer, 2nd edn (London, 1961), p. 13. R. E. Kaske expands on this aspect of the characterization of the Old English heroine in "*Sapientia et fortitudo* in the Old English *Judith*," in *The Wisdom of Poetry: essays in Early English literature in honor of Morton W. Bloomfield*, ed. Larry D. Benson and Siegfried Wenzel (Kalamazoo, MI, 1982), p. 13. Similarly in Ælfric's treatment of the story Judith's violence "is overwhelmed by the symbolism and is not as significant as her wisdom, her wise counsel" (Schrader, *God's Handiwork*, p. 23).

[26] In the Vulgate the Assyrians flee without a fight after discovering their leader slain. The Old English poet has apparently seized on the barest hint of a possible skirmish or two in 15: 4 as a pretext for his battle-scene.

when she is told that Hildegund is absent, instantly and uncannily knows all that has happened and will happen: Walter has escaped and abducted Hildegund just as Osperin had foretold, and the empire of Atilla has lost its strength (*Waltharius*, 358–79).[27] Considering women's roles on a larger scale, we may suspect that the Germanic attitude toward women might have made an Anglo-Saxon audience more receptive than some modern readers to the long and windy speeches of Juliana and Elene, especially since Cynewulf has in both poems heightened the saints' characterizations as wise spokesmen.[28] Woman as wise teacher is a strong image in much literature of the Anglo-Saxons, and in both Aldhelm and in Old English saints' lives women are prominent and are often praised for their wisdom and learning.[29]

My last example of the effect of the Germanic conception of women on an Anglo-Saxon audience's understanding of a work of literature is in some ways the most far-reaching. When King Alfred translated (or rather paraphrased and adapted) Boethius's *De consolatione philosophiae*, he produced in Old English a sustained dramatic narrative in which a man receives instruction from a woman with supernatural insight. He does not transform the late Roman setting into a Germanic one by any means, but he does make fundamental changes in the dramatic situation and the characters. Instead of Boethius's personified Lady Philosophy, Alfred presents a female figure called *Gesceadwisnes* "Reason" or *Wisdom*.[30] Boethius, whom she instructs, is usually referred to as *Mod* "Mind," and *Wisdom* is said to be the mother of this more generalized interlocutor. As Kurt Otten has observed, the relationship between the two in the Old English work is different from that in the original Latin:

> Bei Boethius herrscht der Ton des platonischen Dialogs, der die Verehrung des Lehrers mit einer Gleichberechtigung des Partners zu paaren versteht in der sachlichen Gemeinsamkeit des Fragens, und eben das war für Alfred nicht verständlich. So hat er in der Veränderung der Partner auch den Ton des Dialogs geändert und der neuen Situation

[27] *Ekkehardi Primi Waltharius*, ed. Rodulfus Peiper (Berlin, 1873).

[28] Schrader, *God's Handiwork*, pp. 19–20, notes that Cynewulf adds to his source in characterizing Juliana, assigning to her "wisdom and fortitude," "wisdom and resourcefulness," and a *deop gehygd* "deep mind." Daniel Calder, *Cynewulf* (Boston, 1981), pp. 81–2, observes that "any reader sufficiently attuned to the purposes of Cynewulf's expansive rendering should realize at once that ... Juliana, and no other character, possesses the 'judgment of wise men' (*wigena dom*)." Thomas Hill, "Sapiential structure and figural narrative in the Old English 'Elene'," *Traditio*, 27 (1971), 159–77, argues that Elene is characterized as true wisdom in conflict with the learned but literal-minded reasoning of the Jews.

[29] Schrader, *God's Handiwork*, p. 17.

[30] Although *philosophia* is glossed by Old English *wisdom* in two word-lists, the more specific word for "philosophy" was *uðwitigung*, for "philosopher" *uðwita*. In the Old English *Orosius* the translator renders Latin *philosophus* with the loanword *philosoph*. *Gesceadwisnes* never renders *philosophia*.

angepasst. Es fehlen die Vertrautheit und die persönliche Nähe, aber in seiner Art gründet Alfred die Beziehungen der Dialogpartner tiefer, in der Sehnsucht des Himmlischen. Die Dialogpartner sind nicht nur weit davon entfernt, einander ebenbürtig zu sein, sondern sind voneinander geschieden wie Himmlisches und Irdisches.[31]

That is, there is in the Old English version more emphasis on the fact that the man is receiving truth from a higher authority (*heofencund wisdom* "celestial wisdom") rather than engaging in a dialogue with an equal.

A Germanic audience, it would seem, might be peculiarly predisposed to accept this situation as a natural one, especially as Alfred has reshaped it.[32] The Germanic theme of the farsighted woman imparting valuable truths to men of lesser vision is, as we have seen, one which the Anglo-Saxons would have encountered often in traditional lore and literature. Indeed, the wise Queen Hygd of *Beowulf* even bears a name (like Alfred's Wisdom) which attests to her mental powers.[33] Not only the traditional Germanic literature, but also the new literature that came in with the conversion, continues, as we have seen, to make the association between women and wisdom. Ælfric's St Daria is "wise in philosophy" (*uðwitegunge snoter*), while another homilist's St Eufrasia inspires wonder with her wisdom and quick understanding.[34] And Judith, both in the Old English poem discussed above and in Ælfric's homily on the Book of Judith, is portrayed as a wise counsellor to men.[35] Scholars in the past have been concerned to detect details of Alfred's rendering of Boethius which reflect here and there his Anglo-Saxon background – homely similes, a Germanic-heroic sentiment about fame, the apt allusion to Welund. Perhaps we should also acknowledge that an Anglo-Saxon audience would probably have perceived almost unconsciously a much broader and more deeply felt cultural syncretism in Alfred's work as well, one which gave added force to the dramatic situation of the *Consolatio* and subtly integrated it with an old and familiar preconception.

In pointing out passages and works where the Germanic concept of the

---

[31] Otten, *König Alfreds Boethius*, Studien zur englischen Philologie, n.f. 3 (Tübingen, 1964), p. 89.

[32] The German nun Hrotsvitha of Gandersheim, who lived and wrote in the century after that of Alfred's reign, composed an allegorical drama (*Sapientia*) in which a mother named "Wisdom" lectures the Emperor Hadrian and others on Christian truths. See William Provost, "The Boethian voice in the dramas of Hrotsvit," in *Hrotsvit of Gandersheim: rara avis in Saxonia?*, ed. Katharina M. Wilson, Medieval and Renaissance Monograph Series 7 (Ann Arbor, MI, 1987), pp. 71–8. For a charming translation of *Sapientia* see *The Dramas of Hrotsvit of Gandersheim*, tr. Katharina M. Wilson (Saskatoon, Saskatchewan, 1985), pp. 115–31.

[33] See R. E. Kaske, "'Hygelac' and 'Hygd'," in *Studies in Old English Literature in Honor of Arthur G. Brodeur*, ed. S. B. Greenfield (Eugene, OR, 1963), pp. 200–6.

[34] For these and other examples, see Schrader, *God's Handiwork*, p. 17.

[35] Ibid., p. 23.

prescient woman might affect the way Anglo-Saxon authors treated their subjects and the way Anglo-Saxon audiences perceived those subjects, one runs the risk of appearing to ride a thesis excessively hard: to focus on a subject is necessarily to isolate and perhaps exaggerate it. Every woman in Anglo-Saxon England was not a seeress, and Anglo-Saxon men did not view women one-dimensionally as personifications of wisdom or clairvoyance. Various Anglo-Saxons, moreover, were no doubt mindful of old traditions like this one in varying degrees. The inherited associations of women with wisdom was but one element, recurrent but not constant, in an elaborate and ever-changing Anglo-Saxon *Weltanschauung*. But it *was* an element in that outlook, and one which differentiates it from later attitudes in England and in the world at large. Nothing is to be gained and something will be lost if we pretend that our modern way of viewing women in the role of counsellors and prophets is the same as an Anglo-Saxon's would have been. Remembering the difference between the two will improve our understanding of a literature which, though it has often been described as quintessentially masculine, is in fact concerned extensively with women.

13
Old English Poetry: The Question of Authorship

Near the beginning of this century a book which helped form much of our thinking about Old English literature in the twentieth century suggested that so far as Old English poems are concerned "there is some reason for believing that, for the most part, they are the work of minstrels rather than of literary men."[1] Today there is probably less confidence in the belief that minstrels were the authors of most of the poetry that survives. The majority of Old English verse is devoted to saints' lives, biblical narrative, the Psalter, and poems to which scholars have assigned titles like "Homiletic Fragment" (I and II), "The Lord's Prayer" (I, II, and III), "The Gloria" (I and II), "The Judgment Day" (I and II), "Soul and Body" (I and II), "The Creed," "A Prayer," "An Exhortation to Christian Living," "The Kentish Hymn," "The Seasons for Fasting," "Alms-Giving," and "A Summons to Prayer." Most readers now would probably think that members of the Anglo-Saxon religious establishment are more likely to have written poems like these than are the minstrels and *scopas* who were so active in the imaginations of scholars of an earlier day. When we turn to those few Anglo-Saxon poets whose identity is known to us (despite the prevailing anonymity of most work in the period), the impression that Old English poetry is to be associated more with the pulpit and the refectory than with the mead-hall gains strength. The author of Bede's *Deathsong* apparently never stirred far from his monastery at Wearmouth-Jarrow. Aldhelm, who is known mainly for his Latin works since his vernacular compositions seem to have perished, was a distinguished churchman who rose to be bishop of Sherborne. Cædmon entered a monastery as soon as he became a poet and spent the last, literary portion of his life as a brother at Whitby. Cynewulf, who wrote from Latin sources and whose signed poems are all devoted to religious subjects, is almost certain to have been a churchman.[2] If one were to generalize from this handful

Reprinted from *American Notes and Queries*, n.s. 3 (1990), 59–64.

[1] H. Munro Chadwick, "Early national poetry," in *The Cambridge History of English Literature*, ed. A. W. Ward and A.R. Waller (New York and London, 1907), vol. 1, p. 21.

[2] Daniel G. Calder observes in *Cynewulf* (Boston, 1981), p. 16, "Whether monk, priest, or bishop, Cynewulf's extensive acquaintance with many different religious texts – the Bible, the liturgy, sermons, and a vast body of patristic writings – links him directly with the church."

of Old English poets whose names we know, one might surmise that Old English verse was largely produced by people connected with the church, most of whom composed in Latin as well as in Old English. One reason why poetry and religion would seem to go hand in hand so much of the time is that "a clerical author had ways of getting his compositions written down, even if he did not write them down himself."[3]

As the quotations in the first and last sentences of the preceding paragraph make clear, the one point on which there seems to be general agreement is that the authors of all Old English verse were men – whether religious or secular. Even poems in which the grammar and subject matter make it unambiguously clear that the speaker is a woman are confidently assigned male authorship, since "a male author might perfectly well make a woman his mouthpiece."[4] If it is unthinkable that poems spoken by women could have been composed by women, then it is easy to reject as well the possibility that women might have composed verse riddles about kneading dough, weaving at a loom, or churning butter; and there is no reason to believe that a poem transmitting various kinds of folk wisdom to one's people, including a sensitive comment on child-rearing and an account of a Frisian woman welcoming her husband home from the sea, could be the work of a woman.[5] So far as I know, no one has even been willing to attribute to female authorship the three-line Old English poem on an eleventh-century woman's brooch found on the Isle of Ely and claiming ownership by a lady named Æduwen. (One wonders whether we must also assume that the inscription "husband embrace me," carved in Old High German on a brooch found in Bülach, Switzerland, can only have been composed by a male.)[6]

---

[3] Kemp Malone, "The Old English period (to 1100)," in *A Literary History of England*, ed. Albert C. Baugh (New York, 1948), vol. 1, p.22.

[4] Ibid. In "Two English *Frauenlieder*," *Studies in Old English Literature in Honor of Arthur G. Brodeur*, ed. Stanley B. Greenfield (Eugene, OR, 1963), p. 117, Malone repeats that these are poems "that the poets put in the mouths of women," and he refers to the poets accordingly: "He composed for an audience" (p.111), "He showed the same independence when he restricted himself" (p. 117), etc. Malone's phrasing in the first of these quotations may be a reminiscence of Ernst Sieper, *Die altenglische Elegie* (Strassburg, 1915), p.217, who observes "dass das Lied ["The Wife's Lament"] einer Frau in den Mund gelegt ist."

[5] *Maxims*, I, ll. 45–9, 93–106. All quotations from Old English verse refer to the editions in *ASPR*. A notable exception is Paull F. Baum, "The *Beowulf* poet," *PQ*, 39 (1960), 389–99, especially pp. 393–4, who suggests tentatively that the poet of *Beowulf* might have been a woman. Richard J. Schrader, *God's Handiwork: images of women in early Germanic literature* (Westport, CT, 1983), pp. 49–50, cites Baum's hypothesis with favor but adds, "Admittedly, the literature seldom presents images implying that women were poets in the vernacular" (p. 49). Schrader's book is a valuable discussion primarily of female characters in the literature rather than of authorship, but a number of the examples cited in this paper appear *passim* in Schrader's study.

[6] For the Old English inscription see Elisabeth Okasha, *Hand-List of Anglo-Saxon Non-Runic Inscriptions* (Cambridge, 1971), p.117; for the Old High German inscription see Brian O. Murdoch, *Old High German Literature* (Boston, 1983), p.15.

It may be pointed out that the brief list of Anglo-Saxon poets known to us by name and reviewed above would itself suggest that authors of Anglo-Latin and vernacular verse, in addition to being members of the religious establishment, are most probably men, since there is not a woman's name among them. If we broaden the scope of our search to include Anglo-Saxon writers whose known writings happen to be in Latin, however, we find that authorship is not an exclusive male preserve. Two eighth-century lives of Wynnebald and Willibald (relatives of St Boniface) were composed by an Anglo-Saxon nun of Heidenheim named Hygeburg (spelled *Hugeburc*).[7] Another contemporary of Boniface, a nun named Berhtgyð, also wrote poems.[8] Edward the Confessor's queen Edith was described by later sources as "celebrated and distinguished for verse and prose."[9] And Boniface received from his female correspondent St Leoba verses whose composition she modestly acknowledges as her own, explaining that her teacher, a woman named Eadburg, had taught her how to write poetry.[10] From this one gains the impression that a woman writing poetry in Anglo-Saxon England was not so much an oddity as a cultural tradition passed on from one generation of women to the other.

One might object, of course, that all this evidence of literary creativity by women is limited to composition in Latin and that (despite the fact that the known male poets from the Anglo-Saxon period who wrote vernacular verse all wrote verse in Latin as well or else worked from Latin sources) we have no reason for assuming that women could also have been vernacular poets. It is difficult, of course, to establish anything specific about authorship in the vernacular when virtually the entire corpus is anonymous, and there is precious little put down in writing anywhere describing who wrote popular poetry. But we are not totally without leads. The Latin poem in an eleventh-century Cambridge manuscript describing a boy and an educated girl (*docta puella*) composing songs to be sung to the harp is probably not referring to Latin songs, and, as Fell says, it shows that the idea of a woman composing popular poetry was not alien to the Anglo-Saxons.[11] Also, as Fell further notes, it is hard to explain the existence of Old English terms like *wifhearp* "a woman's harp," *fiðelestre* "a female fiddler," and *sangestre* "a female singer" if women did not have something to do with the *performance* of vernacular song.[12] Across the

---

[7] Wilhelm Levison, *England and the Continent in the Eighth Century* (Oxford, 1946), pp. 43, 81, 294.

[8] Christine Fell, *Women in Anglo-Saxon England* (London, 1984), p. 114. Berhtgyð and many other female writers in the Middle Ages are discussed in Peter Dronke, *Women Writers of the Middle Ages: a critical study of texts from Perpetua (†203) to Marguerite Porete (†1310)* (Cambridge, 1984). See also Katharina M. Wilson, ed., *Medieval Women Writers* (Athens, GA, 1984).

[9] *Vita Ædwardi Regis qui apud Westmonasterium requiescit*, ed. Frank Barlow (London, 1962), p. 14 – quoted and translated in C. R. Dodwell, *Anglo-Saxon Art: a new perspective* (Ithaca, NY, 1983), p. 48.

[10] Fell, *Women in Anglo-Saxon England*, pp. 114–15; cf. Schrader, *God's Handiwork*, p.51.

[11] Fell, *Women in Anglo-Saxon England*, p. 55.

[12] Ibid., p. 54.

English Channel, Charlemagne forbade abbesses in his realm to compose and circulate *uuinileudos*, a word which clearly refers to some kind of vernacular songs, perhaps lovesongs.[13] Knowing as we do Alcuin's anxious prohibitions against "songs of the people" in his famous letter to the monks of Lindisfarne, we might suspect that Charlemagne's ban against women composing poetry may have been instigated by the Anglo-Saxon ecclesiast some time after the emperor had placed him in charge of his palace school.

Despite these hints at women's involvement in vernacular versifying, it is in the Christian-Latin context that women poets are most fully documented, and it is as a part of the religious establishment that women are most often praised for their learning and literary attainments in general. Aldhelm's gushing dedication of the prose *De virginitate* to the nuns of Barking with its praise of the eloquence of their letters and their doctrinal learning is a high testimony to the intellectual calibre of Anglo-Saxon women in religious houses,[14] the only higher testimony being the implication that they could read with understanding Aldhelm's rarefied and grandiloquent prose. Bede's *Super canticum Habacuc prophetiae Allegorica Expositio* is similarly addressed to a nun who had requested the commentary, and the level of explication in it is far from condescending.[15] Whitby's Abbess Hild was, according to Bede, so learned and wise that kings and princes sought her counsel.[16] She had, moreover, a major role in the inauguration of vernacular English poetry treating Christian subjects since it was she who guided the divinely inspired poet Cædmon into her monastery, where he could be taught the scriptural subject matter for his poems. Not only were women described as leaders in learning in the religious houses; they were themselves instrumental in setting up the monastic centers.[17] The close integration of women with the religious establishment placed them in precisely that position which we saw at the opening of this discussion was the one poets would occupy in Anglo-Saxon society. The poets, we saw, were most likely to be clerical, and women were a prominent part of the clerical establishment.

---

[13] J. Knight Bostock, *A Handbook on Old High German Literature*, 2nd edn rev. K.C. King and D.R. McLintock (Oxford, 1976), p.193. Old High German "uuinileod" glosses "plebeios psalmos" and "seculares cantilenas" in three manuscripts of the tenth and eleventh centuries. See Hartwig Mayer, "Althochdeutsche Canonesglossen aus drei Spanischen Handschriften," *Beiträge zur Geschichte der deutschen Sprache und Literatur*, 102 (1980), 315.

[14] *Aldhelmi Opera*, ed. Rudolf Ehwald, *MGH*, Auctores Antiquissimi, XV (Berlin, 1919), pp. 229–30.

[15] *Super canticum Habacuc prophetiae Allegorica Expositio*, Patrologia Latina, ed. J.-P. Migne (Reprint, Turnhout, 1980), vol. 91, col. 1235.

[16] *Venerabilis Baedae Opera Historica*, ed. Charles Plummer (Oxford, 1896), vol. I, p. 254.

[17] M. A. Meyer, "Women and the tenth century English monastic reform," *Revue Bénédictine*, 87 (1977), 34–61.

Women poets among the Anglo-Saxons would not be an isolated phenomenon in the Germanic world. In the one hundred and second chapter of *Njálssaga* the poetess Steinunn challenges Thangbrand Vilbaldsson, the Christian missionary, and chants poems to him about Thor's power. She is obviously a woman well able to improvise verses in the characteristic Icelandic manner. The same is true of Thorhild the Poetess in the thirty-fourth chapter – but with more melancholy results: she addresses such mordant verses to her husband Thrain at a wedding feast that he divorces her on the spot.[18] Regardless of what measure of history or fiction we wish to attribute to *Njálssaga*, such references to women poets in a realistic saga of this kind would be inconceivable if women poets were not a familiar element of Icelandic society either at the time the saga was composed or at the time of the events it narrates. One scholar has even argued that the participation of women in literary production and consumption may be one reason why the vernacular tradition remained so strong in Iceland, since the study of Latin was less accessible to women than was knowledge of Icelandic.[19] The tenth-century nun Hrotsvit of Gandersheim is, of course, one of the most learned and productive poets of the Germanic Middle Ages, but her work seems limited to Latin. This is not the case with her successor Frau Ava, who composed the *Leben Jesu* and other biblical and hagiographical poems in simple, vigorous German verse in the early twelfth century.[20] Berta Lösel-Wieland-Engelmann has made a resourceful and plausible case for the likelihood that the anonymous author of the great medieval German epic *Nibelungenlied* was a nun in the convent of Passau-Niedernburg.[21] And, as we have seen, Charlemagne's decree forbidding Frankish abbesses the composition and circulation of vernacular poetry in his kingdom shows that women verse-writers were at work there.

The vast majority of Old English verse is anonymous and will forever remain so. We shall never know who composed the poem *Judith*, the whimsical riddle-poems of the *Exeter Book*, the Old English poems in which the speaker is a woman, and the various liturgical poems and religious meditations in Old English verse. But we should not pretend to know that women did *not* write them and continue to read these poems with the tacit assumption that they are all the products of male authorship. The evidence surviving from Anglo-Saxon England and from the Germanic cultures in general suggests that there is

---

[18] *Brennu-Njáls Saga*, ed. Einar Sveinsson, Íslenzk Fornrit, vol. 12 (Reykjavik, 1954).

[19] Robert Kellogg, "Sex and the vernacular in medieval narrative," *Proceedings of the First International Saga Conference*, ed. Peter G. Foote, Hermann Pálsson, and Desmond Slay (London, 1973), pp. 244–58.

[20] See, for example, M. O'C. Walshe, *Medieval German Literature: a survey* (Cambridge, MA, 1962), pp. 47–8, references on p. 375.

[21] Lösel-Wieland-Engelmann, "Verdanken wir das *Nibelungenlied* einer Niedernburger Nonne?," *Monatshefte für deutschen Unterricht, deutsche Sprache und Literatur*, 72 (1980), 5–25.

reason to believe that women may have played as much of a role in Anglo-Saxon literary production as they have in the later periods of English literature, and it is perhaps time that our literary histories and our literary interpretations should begin to acknowledge this possibility.[22]

[22] The use of generic "he" to refer to anonymous authors and scribes, a longstanding practice which I have no doubt followed at times in these essays, is perhaps also due for reassessment since some might misapprehend it as identifying all authors and scribes as male.

14
A Metronymic in *The Battle of Maldon*?

Near the end of the Old English poem *The Battle of Maldon*, as the doomed Englishmen make their heroic stand against the Viking invaders, the poet tells of the valor and death of a warrior named Wistan:

> Forð þā ēode Wīstān,
> þurhstānes sunu,   wið þās secgas feaht;
> hē wæs on geþrange   hyra þrēora bana,
> ǣr him Wigelines bearn   on þām wæle læge.[1]
>
> (297–300)

"Then Wistan strode forth, the son of Thurstan, he fought against the [Viking] warriors; he was the slayer of three of them in that tumult before the son of Wigelin took his place among the slain." The manuscript reads *Wigelines* in line 300,[2] as the text quoted here indicates, but often editors emend the proper name to *Wigelmes*, the assumed genitive singular of *Wighelm*, a well-documented man's name in the Anglo-Saxon period. But who is this Wighelm? If Wistan is the son of Thurstan, he cannot also be the son of a man named Wighelm. Attempts to answer this question have been many, but none as yet commands general assent. Dobbie reviews previous efforts at explication, concluding, "There is some difficulty" in the passage "since Wistan ... is described in line 298 as the son of Thurstan."[3] In his edition of 1981, Scragg rather lamely suggests that "Wigelm may be another name for Þurstan ... or

Reprinted from *Essays in Honor of Edward B. King*, ed. Robert G. Benson and Eric W. Naylor (Sewanee, TN, 1991).

[1] Quoted from Bruce Mitchell and Fred C. Robinson, *A Guide to Old English*, 5th edn (Oxford, 1992), p. 252.

[2] The poem survives in an eighteenth-century transcript attributed at the beginning to John Elphinstone but actually made by David Casley, Elphinstone's successor as deputy keeper of the Cottonian Library: see H. L. Rogers, "*The Battle of Maldon*: David Casley's transcript," *NQ*, 230 (1985), 147–55, where Rogers convincingly identifies the hand of the transcriber. The Anglo-Saxon manuscript in which the poem originally survived into modern times (British Library MS. Cotton Otho A.xii, fols. 56^r–62^r) was destroyed by fire in 1731.

[3] *The Anglo-Saxon Minor Poems*, ed. Elliott Van Kirk Dobbie, *ASPR* (New York, 1942), vol. 6, p.146.

bearn may mean 'descendant' rather than 'son'.[4] (*Bearn* means "son" in its other seven occurrences in *Maldon*, as we would expect.) Some have wondered whether a few lines of text have been omitted by the copyist or transcriber between lines 298 and 300, but aside from the problem with the identity of Wigelin, there are no other symptoms of lacuna.

In the edition from which the passage has been quoted above a new explanation is simultaneously proposed and timidly withdrawn: "A metronymic would be very unusual – even in a poem like *Maldon*, which seems to be addressed to an audience which knew the poem's characters and their families."[5] But unusual is not unthinkable. In what follows I should like to investigate the possibility of *Wigelin* being the name of Wistan's mother.

Any impression that a metronymic would be unprecedented in an early Germanic literature may be dispelled by recalling that in Snorri's *Edda*, in the *Lokasenna*, and in the *Thrymskviða* the god Loki is referred to as *Loki Laufeyarson*, the son of his mother Laufey, not of his father Fárbauti. And in the *Nibelungenlied* Siegfried is introduced as the son of Sigmunt *and* Sigelint – that is, of both parents, just as I am suggesting that Wistan may be introduced in *Maldon*:

> Do wuohs in Niderlanden   eins richen küneges kint
> (des vater der hiez Sigmunt,   sin muoter Sigelint)[6]

and subsequently he is repeatedly referred to with the metronymic "der schœnen Siglinden kint" or "daz Sigelinde kint." Bäuml and Fallone's concordance report six occurrences of these metronymics.[7] And in the Anglo-Saxon world, where (as we are becoming increasingly aware)[8] the status of women was generally high, metronymics instead of patronymics are not unusual. In the will of Ætheling Æthelstan reference is twice made to *Eadrice Wynflæde sunu*, and in King Ethelred's confirmation of Ætheric's will *Wulfric Wulfrune suni* is mentioned,[9] a metronymic which also occurs in a charter.[10] In a manumission published by John Earle we encounter the witness *Algares, Leoflæde suna*.[11] Wynflæd, Wulfrun, and Leoflæd are examples of the use of

---

[4] *The Battle of Maldon*, ed. D. G. Scragg (Manchester, 1981), p. 84.
[5] Mitchell and Robinson, *A Guide to Old English*, p. 252.
[6] *Das Nibelungenlied*, ed. Ulrich Pretzel (Stuttgart, 1973), p. 20 (strophe 20, ll. 1–2).
[7] Franz H. Bäuml and Eva-Maria Fallone, *A Concordance to the Nibelungenlied* (Leeds, 1976), pp. 551–2. In the C-manuscript there are seven metronymics for Siegfried: 47.1, 136.3, 180.4, 210.3, 467.3, 471.2, and 494.4. See *Das Nibelungenlied nach der Handschrift C*, ed. Ursula Hennig (Tübingen, 1977). Other metronymics (e.g. using Uote) also occur *passim*.
[8] See Christine Fell, *Women in Anglo-Saxon England and the Impact of 1066* (London, 1984). See also "Old English poetry: the question of authorship," pp. 164–9 above.
[9] *Anglo-Saxon Wills*, ed. Dorothy Whitelock (Cambridge, 1930), pp. 58 and 60, p. 44.
[10] *Anglo-Saxon Charters*, ed. A. J. Robertson, 2nd edn (Cambridge, 1956), no. 38.
[11] Earle, *A Hand-Book to the Land-Charters and Other Saxonic Documents* (Oxford, 1888), p. 264.

metronymics in native Anglo-Saxon contexts.¹² In Christian writings of the period one also finds men being identified as their mothers' sons. In the *Old English Martyrology* the seven sons martyred by Antoninus are introduced as *ðære mæran wudewan suna sancta Felicitan* ("sons of the famous widow St Felicity").¹³ A homily on the passion of St Margaret refers *to ure sceppende Gode ælmihtigne, Sanctae Marian sunu, hælende Criste*,¹⁴ this metronymic possibly being a recollection of Mark 6: 3, where Christ is referred to as "the carpenter, Mary's son" (*se smið Marian sunu* in the *West-Saxon Gospels*).¹⁵ Referring to Constantine as St Helen's son seems to have been conventional: Ælfric speaks of him as *se forma casere þe on Crist gelyfde, sancte Elenan sunu, þære eadigan cwene* ("the first emperor who believed in Christ, St Helen's son, the blessed queen"),¹⁶ while in another homily he is *Constantinus, se mæra casere and se æðela Scē Elena sunu, þære eadigan cwene* ("Constantine, the famous emperor and the noble son of St Helen, the blessed queen").¹⁷ In these metronymics the saint seems almost to overshadow the emperor. These instances of metronymics, along with other instances where men are identified as being the sons of both mother and father,¹⁸ suggest that there is no *prima facie* case against the poet of *The Battle of Maldon* being able to give the name of a character's mother as well as that of his father.

At first consideration, the grammatical ending of the mother's name in the phrase *Wigelines sunu* might seem to present a problem, for women's names in Anglo-Saxon England are normally feminine in gender, the second element of such names typically being a feminine noun. The grammatical ending *-es* of *Wigelines* looks like the masculine/neuter genitive singular inflection. But in fact the ending *-es* appears to have been used with some frequency to form the

---

¹² For other examples, see Maria Boehler, *Die altenglischen Frauennamen*, Germanische Studien, vol. 98 (Berlin, 1930), *passim*.

¹³ *Das altenglische Martyrologium*, ed. Günter Kotzor. Bayerische Akademie der Wissenschaften, phil.-hist. Klasse n.F. Heft 88/2 (Munich, 1981), vol. 2, p. 145.

¹⁴ *Angelsächsische Homilien und Heiligenleben*, ed. Bruno Assmann, rpt with a supplementary introduction by Peter Clemoes (Darmstadt, 1964), p. 171.

¹⁵ *The Gospel according to Saint Mark in Anglo-Saxon and Northumbrian Versions*, ed. Walter W. Skeat (Cambridge, 1871), p. 42.

¹⁶ *Die Hirtenbriefe Ælfrics in altenglischer und lateinischer Fassung*, ed. Bernhard Fehr, rpt with a supplement to the introduction by Peter Clemoes (Darmstadt, 1966), p. 92.

¹⁷ *Wulfstan: Sammlung der ihm zugeschriebenen Homilien nebst Untersuchung über ihre Echtheit*, ed. Arthur Napier, mit einem bibliographischen Anhang von Klaus Ostheeren [rpt] (Dublin and Zurich, 1967), p. 270.

¹⁸ *Liber vitae of New Minster and Hyde Abbey*, ed. Walter de G. Birch (London, 1892), p. 84: "sancta Eormenhild 7 sancta Ercengota wæron Eorcenbyrhtes bearn 7 Sexburge his cwene"; Felix Liebermann, *Die Heiligen Englands* (Hanover, 1889), pp. 1–9: "Eormenburh and sancte ... Æþelbriht þis wæron Eormenrædes bearn and Oslafe his cwene"; T. O. Cockayne, *Leechdoms, Wortcunning and Starcraft of Early England* (London, 1864–66), vol. 3, p. 422: "hi wæron ealle Eadbaldes bearn 7 Imman his cwene."

genitive of feminine names. It seems to have had the status in such instances of a generalized genitive ending. Thus in the *Peterborough Chronicle* entry for the year 656 we read that Wulfhere, King of Mercia (and son of Penda), endowed Medeshamstead with the concurrence of his sisters, Cyneburh and Cyneswith: *be his swustre red Kyneburges 7 Kyneswiðes*.[19] In the entry for the year 1040 in the same chronicle we find this reference to the sons of Ælfgyfu (that is, Emma), daughter of Richard I, Duke of Normandy: *Hi wæron begen Ælfgiues suna seo wæs Ricardes dohtor eorles*.[20] And in a late translation of Genesis we read, *Ðis wæron Racheles suna, Iacobes wiues, Iosep 7 Beniamin*.[21] *Kyneburges, Kyneswiðes, Ælfgiues*, and *Racheles* all show the generalized *-es* genitive singular ending being used with women's names. Boehler adds these documentations of the same ending with women's names in toponyms: *Leoflædes hlæw, Hildes hlæw, Oswiðes mearc, Winwares wic, Tyrwenes sled*.[22]

The etymology of a woman's name *Wigelin(e)* is not entirely apparent. The first element (*Wig-*) is of course common as an element of women's names in the Old English period (*Wigbeorge, Wigburh, Wigflæd, Wigmarc, Wigswith, Wigwen*, etc.),[23] and the element *wig-* followed by *l* often leads to the development of a parasitic vowel *-e-*, as can be seen in the various forms of common nouns like *wigle, wiglere, wiglian*, and *wiglung*, which often occur as *wigele, wigelere*, etc. The second element is less clear. Perhaps *-line* could be the feminine noun *līne* "rope, row, rule," or it might be a diminutive suffix or a reduced form of some word now obscured beyond identification. Whatever their origin, names with this ending do appear in the late period, as Searle's *Onomasticon Anglo-Saxonicum* makes clear:

> The [*Liber vitae Dunelmensis*] contains many peculiar female names of late date, some of which, at least, seem connected with Anglo-Saxon themes; e.g.
>
> | | | |
> |---|---|---|
> | Acelina | Avelina | Lescelina |
> | Adelina | Azelina | Licelina[24] |
> | Amelina | Beuscelina | |
> | Ascelina | Ingolia | |
> | Athelina | Lancelina | |

The claim made here is not for a certainty but for a possibility, a possibility that should discourage continued emendation of *Wigelines*[25] and continued

---

[19] *Two of the Saxon Chronicles Parallel*, ed. Charles Plummer (Oxford, 1892), p. 29.

[20] Ibid., p. 173.

[21] *The Old English Heptateuch*, ed. S. J. Crawford, EETS o.s. 160 (London, 1922), rpt with the text of two additional manuscripts transcribed by N. R. Ker (London, 1969), p. 454.

[22] Boehler, *Die altenglischen Frauennamen*, p. 250.

[23] Ibid., p. 260.

[24] William George Searle, *Onomasticon Anglo-Saxonicum* (Cambridge, 1897), p. xxx.

[25] In the collection of essays *The Battle of Maldon A.D. 991*, ed. Donald Scragg (Oxford, 1991)

speculation based on the prior assumption that the name must refer to a man. Since metronymics are documented elsewhere in Old English, we cannot be sure that we do not have a metronymic in the heroic poem *The Battle of Maldon*. The status of women in Anglo-Saxon times was such that they, along with men, often had places named for them.[26] If places could be known for the women associated with them, is it unreasonable to assume that a son who sheds glory on his family and his nation by upholding the heroic code even unto death might be commemorated by a poet in the name of his mother as well as in that of his father?

Margaret A. L. Locharbie-Cameron (pp. 239, 248) repeatedly gives the name as *Wigelm* without even mentioning that this form is the product of an editorial emendation.

[26] See Doris Mary Stenton, *The English Woman in History* (London, 1957), p. 6, and F. M. Stenton, "The historical bearing of place-name studies: the place of women in Anglo-Saxon society," *Transactions of the Royal Historical Society*, 4th ser. vol. 25 (1943), 1–13.

15
European Clothing Names and the Etymology of *Girl*

George S. Lane's exemplary monograph on clothing names brings into prominence many interesting patterns in the development of the various European vocabularies.[1] In examining his lists, one is impressed, for example, by the frequency with which words denoting an article of clothing subsequently come to denote the *wearer* of the article of clothing. Thus the words he records for "skirt" in Spanish (*falda*), Danish (*skørt*), and English (*skirt*) all come to denote "woman" at one level of usage or other. Spanish *gorra* "cap" has had since the seventeenth century the figurative meaning "persona que tiene por hábito comer, vivir, regalarse, o divertirse a costa ajena."[2] Danish *sok* "sock" in colloquial usage means "spineless person." The word *cassock*, which, as a name for a military coat, may have derived ultimately from the proper noun *Cossack*,[3] comes almost full circle later and, in ecclesiastical context, refers in English to "a wearer of a cassock; *esp.* a clergyman."[4] Numerous clothing terms like Old Icelandic *hǫttr* "hood," *mǫttull* "mantle," and *vǫttr* "glove" come to be used as personal names;[5] the Germanic word which serves for "glove" in Danish,

---

Reprinted from *Studies in Historical Linguistics in Honor of George Sherman Lane* ed. Walter W. Arndt et al. (Chapel Hill, North Carolina, 1967), pp. 233-40.

[1] Lane, *Words for Clothing in the Principal Indo-European Languages*, Language Dissertations, IX (Baltimore, 1931). Subsequently this study was incorporated into Carl Darling Buck's *A Dictionary of Selected Synonyms in the Principal Indo-European Languages* (Chicago, 1949), a monumental compilation to which Lane was a major contributor, especially on questions of Celtic and Germanic etymology.

[2] Martín Alonso, *Enciclopedia del Idioma* (Madrid, 1958), s.v. *gorra*. (Cf. Old Icelandic *motra* "a woman wearing a *motr*," and Danish *hat*, which is used metonymically of persons.) My primary source for Old Icelandic has been the Cleasby-Vigfusson *Icelandic–English Dictionary*, 2nd edn, with a supplement by Sir William A. Craigie (Oxford, 1957); for Danish, Verner Dahlerup's *Ordbog over det Danske Sprog* (Copenhagen, 1919-54); for Swedish, the *Ordbok öfver Svenska Språket* utgifven af Svenska Akademien (Lund, 1898-).

[3] Lane, *Words for Clothing...*, pp. 22-3.

[4] *OED*, s.v. *Cassock*, 4.b., records this metonymical usage for the Renaissance period.

[5] Cleasby-Vigfusson includes in each of these instances the common noun and the proper name under a single entry. I shall not here go into the possibility of one or another of these examples being homonyms of different etymological origin.

Swedish, Old Icelandic, German, etc. occurs in Old English solely as a proper name: *Hondscioh*.

This semantic tendency has not passed wholly unnoticed, of course. Ivan Pauli remarks,

> C'est un phénomène extrêmement fréquent qu'une personne soit désignée par un détail du vêtement. C'est ainsi que le franç. *cotillon*, l'ital. *gonnella*, l'esp. *falda* se disent pour "femme", surtout en parlant des femmes en général. Dans Cotgrave on relève *courtes chausses* au sens de "femmes", mot que nous retrouvons avec la même signification dans le patois rouchi: *courtes cauches*. Dans les patois picards, wallons, et dans le parler messin, on dit *blancbonnet* pour "femme" ou "fille"; et, dans les mêmes contrées, les hommes sont appelés *les chapeaux*. Rappelons que, dans *Werther*, Goethe fait dire à Lotte: "Mein Chapeau walzt schlecht."[6]

It is not difficult to add to these examples. Pauli himself cites as terms for infants or children in various Romance dialects *culottier*, *hannard*, *maronier*, *braiet*, *robichon*, and so on,[7] and there are further instances to be found in other European languages. Spanish *capa negra*, *capa parda*, *capa rota*, all occur as designations for persons,[8] while *chancleta* "little shoe" appears as a playfully pejorative term for a female infant in the Spanish-speaking Caribbean.[9] According to Du Cange, Latin *albati* was used to refer to a newly-baptized child,[10] and nursery terms like *Rotkäppchen* and *Baby Bunting* remind us of the pervasiveness of this type of semantic transference. Further, Old Icelandic *piltr* "boy," Danish, Swedish *pilt* "small boy" and the Breton loanword *paotr* all seem likely to be related to Danish *pjalt*, Swedish *palt* "rag," while Swedish, Norwegian *plagg* "piece of clothing" appears in Swedish dialects with the meaning "rascal, impudent boy."[11] Swedish *flicka* "girl" has been convincingly connected with Old Icelandic *flík* "a piece of cloth, loose end of a garment,"[12] and German *Schlafmütze* "nightcap" has for centuries been used to denote "a sleepyhead, dullard." Clothing terms designating special groups are extremely

---

[6] Pauli, *"Enfant," "Garçon," "Fille" dans les langues romanes* (Lund, 1919), p. 269, n.

[7] Ibid., p. 269.

[8] Alonso, *Enciclopedia del Idioma*, s.v. *capa*.

[9] Communicated to me by Emerson Brown, then of the University of Puerto Rico. Alonso, *Enciclopedia del Idioma*, s.v. *chancleta*, indicates a colloquial figurative use of the word with the meaning "persona inepta."

[10] Charles Du Fresne Du Cange, *Glossarium Mediæ et Infimæ Latinitatis* (Paris, 1840–50), s.v. *alba*, p. 161, col. 2. Cf. Pauli, '*Enfant*', pp. 269–70.

[11] Erik Björkman, "Neuschwed. *gosse* 'Knabe, Junge', eine semasiologisch-methodologische Studie," *Indogermanische Forschungen*, XXX (1912), 272.

[12] George T. Flom, "Semological notes on Old Scand. *Flík* and derived forms in the Modern Scandinavian dialects," *JEGP*, XII (1913), 78–92. On p. 89 Flom cites several other examples of Swedish personal nouns deriving ultimately from clothing terms.

common, as witness *bluestocking, blousons noirs, Braunhemd, redcap, Schwarzrock, starched shirt,* and the like. Even the primary Germanic word for "woman," represented in German *Weib,* English *wife* and *wo(man),* Old Icelandic *víf,* and so on, is thought to be derived ultimately from the name of an article of clothing worn by women.[13]

English is well provided with examples of this semantic pattern. Aside from those already cited, we have *brat* coming from Old English *brætt,* a Celtic loanword meaning "pinafore, cloak." *Clout,* a late Middle English pejorative term for "young man," derives from Old English *clūt* "cloth, patch, piece of clothing." Björkman (p. 272) thought that the puzzling English word *lad* might come from a Scandinavian word meaning "stockings, slipper." A particularly good area for observing this semantic trend in English is American slang. Berry and van den Bark list as either current or passé terms for "girl" or "young woman" many such slang forms as *bobby sox(er), drape, dress goods, fluff, frill, hairpin, muff, piece of calico, petticoat, rag,* and, of course, *skirt.*[14]

Bearing these points in mind, we might profitably turn to that common English word of baffling etymology, *girl.* The *Oxford Dictionary of English Etymology* has the following entry for *girl*:

> *girl* . . . youth or maiden XIII [i.e. thirteenth century]; female child XVI. The ME. vars. *gurle, girle, gerle* suggest an orig. *ü,* and an OE. **gyrela, *gyrele* has been proposed, based on **gur-,* repr. prob. in LG. *göre* boy, girl; but, as with *boy, lad,* and *lass,* certainty is not obtainable on the evidence.[15]

In short, the word first appears in thirteenth-century Middle English, and before that it has no discernible history. The attempts to connect it with Low German *göre* are, as the *Oxford* concedes, problematic; and although the hypothetical Old English etymon **gyrela* (which was authoritatively proposed by Luick[16]) has been generally accepted, no convincing connection between this hypothesized form and any known Old English word has been established. *Webster's New World Dictionary*[17] proposes a connection with southern English dialect *girls* "primrose blossoms," but the presumed semantic relationship is not entirely clear. Holthausen[18] relates the word with Old English *gor* "dung,

---

[13] Friedrich Kluge, *Etymologisches Wörterbuch der deutschen Sprache,* 19. Auflage bearbeitet von Walther Mitzka (Berlin, 1963), s.v. *Weib.* Cf. Ernest Weekley, *An Etymological Dictionary of Modern English* (London, 1921), s.v. *wife*[1].

[14] Lester V. Berry and Melvin van den Bark, *American Thesaurus of Slang,* 2nd edn (New York, 1952).

[15] *The Oxford Dictionary of English Etymology,* ed. C. T. Onions, with the assistance of G. W. S. Friedrichsen and R. W. Burchfield (Oxford, 1966), s.v. *girl.*

[16] Karl Luick, "Die herkunft des ne. *girl," Anglia Beiblatt,* VIII (1897), 235–6.

[17] College Edition (Cleveland and New York, 1964), s.v. *girl.*

[18] Ferdinand Holthausen, *Etymologisches Wörterbuch der englischen Sprache,* 3rd edn (Göttingen, 1949), s.v. *gore*[1].

filth," but again, the semantic (and even phonological) development is not clarified. I believe the *OED* makes a shrewd guess, however, when, after declaring *girl* "of uncertain etymology," it remarks that *girl*, *boy*, and similar etymological enigmas "probably ... arose as jocular transferred uses of words that had originally a different meaning."[19] As has been shown, one type of transference of particularly high probability is the shift from clothing name to personal name. Therefore, in seeking an Old English word similar in form to the conjectured etymon **gyrela*, it would be well to look especially closely among the clothing names.

Doing so, we are led to the documented Old English word *gyrela* (also spelled, although less frequently, *gerela* and *gi(e)rela*), a noun of common occurrence which has the meaning "dress, apparel (worn by either sex)." Apparently this word is presumed by the dictionaries (Bosworth-Toller, *Dictionary* and *Supplement*; Holthausen, *Etymologisches Wörterbuch*; and Clark Hall-Meritt, *Concise Anglo-Saxon Dictionary*) to have died out at the end of the Old English period, leaving no trace in later English. But considering that words for clothing tend to shift their reference to the wearers of the clothing, and remembering that the earliest meaning of *girl* recorded in Middle English is "youth or maiden," one is tempted to conclude that the Middle English word is the direct descendant of the Old English word, though in a previously unrecorded sense. For it is quite conceivable that Old English *gyrela* had already developed the transferred meaning "young person of either sex" in pre-Conquest times, but that the usage was limited to the domestic sphere and never got into literary record, where an ample series of non-colloquial terms such as *bearn, byre, cnafa, cnapa, cnæpling, eafora, fæmne, geonga, geongling, hyse, lytling, mægeþ, meowle, umbor*, and so on, adequately served this expressive need.[20] But after the Conquest, all these native literary words began to fall out of common use, thus depleting the wordstock for this semantic category. Meanwhile, *gyrela* in its primary sense of "dress, apparel" was being displaced by a rush of French loanwords such as *array, attire, cloak, habit, mantle, robe, roket, vestment* (all first recorded in thirteenth-century writings), *apparel, coat, frock, garment, gown, livery, ray, vesture* (all first recorded in early fourteenth-

---

[19] *OED*, s.v. *girl* sb. Buck, *Dictionary*, p. 87, similarly remarks that "a noticeable number of the modern words for 'boy', 'girl', and 'child' were originally colloquial nicknames, derogatory or whimsical, in part endearing, and finally commonplace."

[20] The Old English gloss *gyrlgyden* to Latin *Vesta* is cited in *The American College Dictionary* (New York and Syracuse, 1963), s.v. *girl*, as carrying the meaning "virgin goddess," and if this is so, then we might have here a solitary instance of Old English *gyrela* "girl" preserved in writing. But since the earliest Middle English occurrence of *girl* carries the meaning "young person of either sex" rather than "girl, virgin," the *ACD*'s interpretation of *gyrlgyden* seems dubious. The more likely explanation of the gloss is that it means "clothing goddess," the Old English glossator having associated *Vesta* with *vestis* "garment." See H. D. Meritt, *The Old English Prudentius Glosses at Boulogne-sur-Mer* (Stanford, 1959), p. 69.

century writings). Having been rendered superfluous as a clothing term and being in high demand as a term for "a young person," *gyrela* would seem, then, to have passed, during the centuries when it is absent from written record, into exclusive use in this latter, originally secondary sense.[21] In this respect, *gyrela* may be said to have followed the same pattern of development as *brat*, mentioned above. Old English *brætt* meant "pinafore, cloak" exclusively. Subsequently, however, the word appears to develop the meaning "young person" as well, and now this is the only meaning of the word in standard usage.

Rather than being an etymological puzzle, English *girl* would seem then to have a fairly clear history – once we recognize the semantic trend evidenced in *brat*, *clout*, *flicka*, *falda*, and so on, and reunite Middle English *girle*, which had been thought to have no ancestry, with Old English *gyrela*, which had been thought to have no descendant. For if my explanation is correct, they belong together in a single etymological continuum, and the hypothesized Old English etymon **gyrela* can be disburdened of its asterisk.

---

[21] A possible, remote survival of Old English *gyrela* with its original meaning is the otherwise inexplicable Middle English form *garlement* "clothing, apparel," which is instanced once in the *OED* s.v. *garlement* and twice in the *MED* s.v. *garnement*, all three occurrences being from the fourteenth century. This may be a blend of *girl* "apparel" with *garment*. I should add here that although no previous commentator has hit on the interpretation of *girl* as a descendant of Old English *gyrela*, two have struck close. Rolf Berndt, *Einführung in das Studium des Mittelenglischen* (Halle, 1960), pp. 339–40, suggested as the Old English etymon of *girl* **gyr(w)ela*, which he connected with the verb *gierwan* "dress, clothe, adorn," a word with which the documented *gyrela* "apparel" has also been related. But instead of drawing this connection, Berndt conjectures that his starred form is a unique derivation retaining an original Germanic meaning of the root – "der, die Reifende, Heranwachsende." The *MED*, after offering the traditional etymology for *girl*, adds "? akin to OE *gierela* . . ." but does not go any further. Berndt's derivation of a noun with the form **gyrela* (rather than **gierela*) from the root underlying *gierwan* "dress, clothe," it should be added, is the most satisfactory phonetic form to assume for the documented word *gyrela* "apparel" if this word is to be understood as the antecedent of modern *girl*, for in that case we should expect the Old English word to have precisely the form we find in modern *girl* (with the initial stop) and in the Middle English variant spellings *gerle*, *gurle*, and *goirle*. If the original form were *gierela*, as some have suggested, then the initial stop in modern *girl* would have to be explained as the result of Northern dialect or foreign influence (as is the case with English *giefan*, *giest*, *gietan*, *gilde*, etc.). Although Old English spelling is not to be trusted in this respect, it should be mentioned that of the fifty-nine quotations in Bosworth-Toller, *Dictionary* and *Supplement*, containing the element *gyrela*, thirty are spelled with *y*, fifteen with *i(e)*, and fourteen with *e*. These spellings may well reflect *y* developed from "unstable *i*" in late Old English.

Afterword 1992

I

The distinguished philologist Yoshio Terasawa has kindly pointed out to me that Eduard Müller proposed deriving *girl* from Old English *gyrela*,[1] but was unable to explain the semantic development (which is the subject of my article).

2

In an article which is quite remarkable for its consistent misrepresentation of what this essay says, Bernhard Diensberg rejects my proposed etymology of *girl*, or rather he rejects his distortion of my proposal, and then he restates an old hypothesis of Luick's, for which there is no documentary evidence. In "The etymology of Modern English *girl*,"[2] he begins by saying of my essay, "The author bases his hypothesis on OE *ȝerela, ȝierela, ȝyrela* 'habit, robe' which he takes as typical garments for girls and women, an assumption which is unsupported by evidence. From the supposed designation for female persons Robinson derives the generic term (i.e. *girl*), a procedure which is entirely unfounded." (p. 473)

Anyone who reads my essay, which emphasizes clearly that Old English *gyrela* did *not* refer to "typical garments for girls and women" but rather that it "has the meaning 'dress, apparel (worn by either sex)'," will be as puzzled as I over how Diensberg could have missed so completely what the essay he is criticizing has said. A key part of my argument was precisely the fact that Old English *gyrela* and early Middle English *girle* agree in *not* specifying feminine clothing!

Diensberg continues by saying, "At any rate Robinson's etymology is doomed to failure because of phonological considerations. He cannot explain how OE *ȝierela* 'habit, robe' which has /j-/ should turn up with initial *g* as required by ME *girle*." (p. 474) But as any reader can see, the long paragraph in note 21 of my essay is devoted to explaining precisely this point. There I suggest that if those who propose initial /g-/ rather than /j-/ are wrong (and Old English spelling does not offer firm evidence on the point), then the initial /g-/ in Middle English *girle* must result from "Northern dialect or foreign influence," and I cite the parallel instances of *get, gild, give,* and *guest*. (This list is not exhaustive, of course; cf. *again, begin,*[3] *beget,* etc.) Simply to ignore this explanation and to assert that I "cannot explain" the phonology of the word suggests once again that Diensberg either did not read or could not understand the essay which he claims to be refuting.

Finally, Diensberg says of my argument, "As a parallel he quotes among others Early ModE *brat*, which he wrongly connects with OE *brætt*/ME *brat* 'cloak' (c 1395). The

---

[1] Eduard Müller, *Etymologisches Woerterbuch der Englischen Sprache* (Cöthen, 1878), vol. 1, p. 519.

[2] *Neuphilologische Mitteilungen* 85 (1984), 473–5.

[3] Also at work in the case of *begin* are the forces of analogy, the initial consonant of the preterite and past participial forms reinforcing any dialectal influence on the initial consonant of the present system.

Early ModE word, however, goes back to older *bratchet* 'a little brat' (a [*sic*] 1600, OED), which is of Scottish origin." (p. 473) "... which *he* wrongly connects ..."? Diensberg must know that the derivation I cite is a standard etymology of the word, not an arbitrary and erroneous supposition of my own. It is the only etymology given in all three editions of Webster's unabridged *New International Dictionary*, it is in the more recent *American Heritage Dictionary* and in many others. If Diensberg had said, "Some have recently proposed an alternative etymology, which I prefer," one would have taken him at his word, but "he wrongly connects" is simply dishonest bluster. Diensberg's rudely dismissive assertion about my reference to a standard etymology suggests that in addition to misrepresenting the article he is criticizing he is also capable of misrepresenting the current state of the scholarly question he is discussing when it suits his purpose to do so.

My intention here is not to insist on the rightness of the etymology I suggested in my article; the emergence of further documentations of *girle* in the future may either vindicate or disprove my proposed derivation. My purpose here is simply to call attention to a rather alarming example of misreading and misrepresentation posing as philological scholarship.

Part IV

Names in Old English Literature

16
The Significance of Names in Old English Literature

When a modern reader looks for significant names in literature, he tries generally to find that type of literary onomastics which Kemp Malone has called "meaningful fictive names"[1] – that is, inventions like Shakespeare's *Justice Shallow* and Ben Jonson's *Sir Politic Would-be*. This device affords an author a simple and effective means of expressing judgments about his characters over their heads directly to the reader, and it remains popular among later writers like Dickens, Henry James, and Nabokov. But when we search for literary naming of this kind among Anglo-Saxon texts, the results are meager and disappointing. We find *Widsith* and *Unferth*, the grave-worm named *Gifer* in the Old English *Soul and Body*, and not many more. But before concluding that Old English literary artists took scant interest in the meanings of names, we ought to reformulate the question in terms more historically appropriate. It should be remembered that Anglo-Saxon writers rarely had control over the *selection* of names for their literary characters, for the names were usually received, along with the story, from tradition. The only way they could make use of name-meanings would be to tease from the dictated names some latent etymological senses which could be shown to be appropriate to the characters who bear them. Such a technique appears in Middle English times in Chaucer's *tour de force* on the meanings of St Cecelia's name[2] and before that, of course, in the many name-interpretations in the Bible. This type of literary onomastics, one suspects, would be particularly congenial in an age when etymology was not a minor philological interest, but rather a dominant mode of thought.[3]

It is my purpose in this essay to urge the importance of literary name-etymologizing among the Anglo-Saxons and to suggest that both small textual

Reprinted from *Anglia*, 86 (1968), 14–58.

[1] Malone, "Meaningful fictive names in English literature," *Names*, V (1957), 1–13.

[2] *Prologue to the Second Nun's Tale*, 85–119. The etymologies were not original with Chaucer, of course; see *The Poetical Works of Chaucer*, ed. Fred N. Robinson, 2nd edn (Boston, 1957), pp. 756, 757.

[3] See Ernst Robert Curtius, "Etymology as a category of thought", in his *European Literature and the Latin Middle Ages*, tr. Willard R. Trask (New York, 1953), pp. 495–500.

obscurities and broad features of Old English narrative art can often be related to the writers' lively interest in the etymological significance of names. My evidence is primarily an aggregate of examples – passages from various works in which the authors seem to be making use of the etymological meanings of proper names. Some of the examples are obvious instances which have already been remarked; others are instances which seem to have passed unnoticed – to the confusion, sometimes, of editors and translators. By calling attention to the examples which are obvious, or at least already acknowledged, I hope to establish the prior likelihood of the interpretations which I am offering here for the first time. For the same purpose, I include two brief excursuses into onomastic traditions outside of Old English literature: in the first part of the essay, which deals with Old English uses of biblical names, I advert to the onomastic exercises of the Latin biblical commentators, and in the ensuing section, which discusses vernacular name-etymologizing, I explore the contemporaneous traditions for analogous phenomena. The focus of the discussion, however, remains on specific passages exemplifying the utilization of name-meanings by Old English authors and particularly on those passages where I feel that troublesome obscurities can be clarified by reference to onomastics. By this emphasis I do not intend to suggest that study of Old English onomastics has value solely as a procedure for resolving textual cruces. What the examples suggest, rather, is that further study of Anglo-Saxon literary onomastics may lead us to a better understanding of an important and neglected phase of the Old English literary imagination in general.

I

Since Old English prose draws so pervasively on the form and substance of biblical writings, it is inevitable that scriptural name-etymologies will find their way into the sermons and saints' lives of the Anglo-Saxons. T. M. Pearce has pointed out some instances where Ælfric cites the etymological significance of biblical names in order to drive home doctrinal themes in his sermons,[4] and even a casual perusal of the Ælfric canon and the numerous Ælfrician writings of the period will suffice to verify the impression that onomastic moralizing was an available and popular technique for Anglo-Saxon authors. But the Ælfrician device is only a symptom of a much more complex and pervasive phenomenon in the Old English literary tradition at large – an attention to name-meanings which was so vital and searching that names themselves were sometimes actually displaced in literary usage by the

---

[4] Pearce, "Name patterns in Aelfric's *Catholic Homilies*," *Names*, XIV (1966), 150–6. Previously, Ælfric's use of name-meanings was discussed briefly by Hanspeter Schelp, "Die Deutungstradition in Ælfrics Homiliae Catholicae," *Archiv*, CXCVI (1960), 289–92.

real or fancied onomastic significance of the names. Naturally, such literary effects as this could only be grounded in a long and informed scholarly tradition of name-study.

Many of the Old and New Testament manuscripts from pre-Conquest England are interlined with learned explications of proper names, and very often these take the form of erudite etymologies, although modern editors have not always recognized this.[5] *Barjona*, for example, is accurately rendered by the glossators as *culfran sunu*, *Effraim* as *wæstmbærnes*, *Iacob* as *forscrencend*, *Madian* as *forwyrhte*, *Nazareus* as *se halga*, etc.[6] It is essential to observe that these name-interpretations are not merely extracts from the many name-etymologies scattered throughout the Bible; in large part they are learned interpretations drawn from the long and expert tradition of onomastic analysis in the writings of the Church Fathers and early biblical scholars. This is an important point, still insufficiently appreciated. Pearce, for example, in the article cited above, views with misgiving Ælfric's statement that the name of the Apostle Peter means "acknowledging" (*oncnawende*). "One wonders at Ælfric's reading of the name *Peter* into 'acknowledging'," he says, "for in both Greek and Latin the designation means 'a rock'."[7] That *Peter* means "rock" is entirely true, as a famous passage in Matthew 16 attests, and Ælfric elsewhere alludes to this meaning. But here we must remember that the Bible was not his only source. In the Latin preface to these homilies Ælfric says that in compiling them he has drawn on Jerome, Haymo (of Auxerre), and similar authorities,[8] and when we turn to these writers we find them affirming that, in addition to the meaning "rock," the name *Petrus* also had the meaning *agnoscens* "acknowledging."[9] Rabanus Maurus, moreover, supplies an accumulation of impressive philological data explaining how the name could give rise to plural

---

[5] For a scholarly work that does recognize the importance of name etymologies, see Herbert Dean Meritt, *Fact and Lore about Old English Words* (Stanford, 1954), pp. 207–9, where a section of the book is devoted to Anglo-Saxon glossators' etymologizing interpretations of foreign proper names and the problems which these interpretations have presented to modern lexicographers.

[6] See Meritt, *Fact and Lore*, p. 208, and *Old English Glosses* (New York, 1945), p. 5.

[7] P. 155. Pearce does not indicate where Ælfric's interpretation is to be found, but the "Homily on the Nativity of St Andrew the Apostle" in *The Homilies of the Anglo-Saxon Church*, ed. Benjamin Thorpe (London, 1844), vol. I, p. 586 has *Simon is gereht "gehyrsum" and Petrus "oncnawende"*.

[8] "Hos namque auctores in hac explanatione sumus sequuti, videlicet Augustinum Hipponensem, Hieronimum, Bedam, Gregorium, Smaragdum, et aliquando Haymonem; horum denique auctoritas ab omnibus catholicis libentissime suscipitur" (Thorpe, vol. I, p. 1).

[9] Jerome, *Liber interpretationis hebraicorum nominum*, in Corpus Christianorum, Series Latina, LXXII, Pars I, 1 (Turnholti, 1959): "Petrus agnoscens" (65: 18), "Petrus agnoscens siue dissoluens" (70: 16). (Here and elsewhere I follow the CCL practice of citing pagination and lineation according to the edition of Lagarde.) See also Haymo of Auxerre (Pseudo-Haymo of Halberstadt), *Homiliae de sanctis*, PL, CXVIII, 754, 755; Pseudo-Bede [ca.750–800], *In Matthaei evangelium expositio*, PL, XCII, 22; Pseudo-Isidore [ca.750], *Liber de ortu et obitu patrum*, LXXXIII, 1286.

interpretations.[10] Ælfric was obviously in close touch with these learned writings, and his name-etymologies, like other erudite details of his homilies, reflect the customary diligence and accuracy of his scholarship.[11]

Seeing the importance of scriptural commentaries in assessing the onomastic interpretations of Old English writers, we should perhaps pause before going on to other Old English evidence in order to consider briefly the character and motivation of the Church Fathers' interest in name-meanings; for the English homilists could hardly have embraced this patristic habit to the extent they did without an awareness of the theory as well as the practice of it, and we must share with the Anglo-Saxons that theoretical basis of biblical onomastics if we are to appreciate the seriousness of their interest in the subject. The primary stimulus to patristic name-interpretation was no doubt the precedent of the Bible itself, where etymologies like those of *Eve* (Genesis 3: 20), *Moses* (Exodus 2: 210), and *Jesus* (Matthew 2: 21) abound. Thus the elaborate efforts of Jerome in his *Liber interpretationis hebraicorum nominum* and *Quaestiones hebraicae in Genesim et in libros Regum* ("où tout le Moyen Age puisera ses étymologies hébraïques")[12] can, in a sense, be considered a mere extension of the sporadic name-interpretations in the Bible. Moreover, there is much made over the importance of name-meanings in such scriptural episodes as the dramatic change of names from *Abram* to *Abraham* or from *Saul* to *Paul*. These incidents too excited the interest of the Fathers; St John Chrysostom, for example, devoted four homilies to the subject.[13] Again, the practice can be thought of as growing out of a natural curiosity about etymological origins in general. The ensconcement of many biblical name-interpretations in Isidore of Seville's *Etymologiae* points up this facet of the interest.

But these various stimulants to onomastics are not in themselves sufficient to explain the massive scholarship of Jerome's name-lists or such emphatic imperatives as that which introduces Augustine's interpretation of Psalm 134: 9, "Nomen adtendite ... Audite, audite nomina haec, interpretatione

[10] Rabanus, *Commentarius in Matthaeum*, *PL*, CVII, 888.

[11] At yet another point Pearce finds Ælfric's name-etymologizing unaccountable: "*James* is interpreted 'withering'," he notes (p. 155), but "*James* is an Anglicized diminutive for the Hebrew *Jacob*, yah-ak-obe, meaning 'heel catcher' or supplanter. This does not seem to be related to the idea of withering." The source of difficulty here is an error in Thorpe's translation of Ælfric's Old English. Ælfric wrote "Iacob is gecweden 'forscrencend'" (Thorpe, vol. I, pp. 198 and 586), and Thorpe translates "*James* is interpreted 'withering'," evidently confounding Ælfric's *forscrencend* with the similar Old English word *forscrincend*. *Forscrincend* means "withering," but *forscrencend* means "supplanter." Here as elsewhere, then, Ælfric's onomastic allusions are meticulously faithful to his Latin sources.

[12] C. Spicq, *Esquisse d'une histoire de l'exégèse latine au moyen âge*. Bibliothèque Thomiste, XXVI (Paris, 1944), p. 236.

[13] PG, LI, 113–56. Cf. Philo Judaeus, "On the change of names," in *Philo with an English Translation*, ed. F. H. Colson and G. H. Whitaker (London, 1934), vol. V, pp. 127–281.

typica et sapientia plena."[14] Nor do they account for the faithful copying and elaboration of Jerome's name-etymologies by writers like Alcuin, Bede, and Rabanus,[15] or such remarkable poeticizings of biblical name-etymologies as that in the ninth-century *Versus de nominibus sanctorum*.[16] The high reverence accorded to onomastics grows rather out of the widespread conviction that name-meanings hold the key to the spiritual meaning of scripture. "Non enim nomen propter se nomen est, sed propter id quod significat," declares Augustine in the *Enarrationes in Psalmos*,[17] and in the *De doctrina christiana*, II, xvi, 23, he spells out in detail the vital role of name-etymologies in discovering the true meaning of the *sacra pagina*. Remarking that if we had not known the numinous etymological significance of *Siloa piscina* in John 9: 7, *tam magnus intellectus, lateret*, he proceeds to explain,

> Sic etiam multa, quae ab auctoribus eorundem librorum interpretata non sunt, nomina hebraea non est dubitandum habere non paruam uim atque adiutorium ad soluenda aenigmata scripturarum, si quis ea possit interpretari. Quod nonnulli eiusdem linguae periti uiri non sane paruum beneficium posteris contulerunt, qui separata de scripturis eadem omnia uerba interpretati sunt; et quid sit Adam, quid Eua, quid Abraham, quid Moyses; siue etiam locorum nomina, quid sit Hierusalem uel Sion uel Hiericho uel Sina uel Libanus uel Iordanis et quaecumque alia in illa lingua nobis sunt incognita nomina, quibus apertis et interpretatis multae in scripturis figuratae locutiones manifestantur.[18]

Augustine's impressive affirmation of the importance of name-meanings in biblical exegesis helps us to understand why onomastics is so prominent in the

[14] *Enarrationes in Psalmos*, CCL, XL, 1951.

[15] The frequent recurrence of the names of Rabanus, Alcuin, and Bede in the ensuing footnotes documenting Hebrew etymologies bears witness to their active participation in the tradition of onomastic interpretation. Bede used the Hieronymian explications so extensively that there has grown up a scholars' myth that he was a skilled Hebraist. See E. F. Sutcliffe, "The Venerable Bede's knowledge of Hebrew," *Biblica*, XVI (1935), 300–6.

[16] *MGH*, Poetarum Latinorum medii aevi Tomus IV, fasc. ii, 630–5. Poeticizing of name-meanings is a commonplace in the verses of Theodolfus, Sedulius Scottus, Hucbald of Saint-Amand, and other writers of the period. See *MGH*, Poetarum Latinorum medii aevi Tomus I, p. 478, l. 15 (*Sem*), Tomus III, p. 174, ll. 71–2 (*Bartholomew*), p. 179, ll. 13–17 (*Egypt, Bethlehem*), p. 570, ll. 55–62 (*Andrew, Philip*); Tomus IV, fasc. i, p. 227, ll. 502–4, p. 272, ll. 31–5 (*Egypt*); Tomus VI, fasc. i, p. 123, ll. 33–4 (*Peter*), and *passim*. For an Irish example, see the *Hymnus S. Cuminei longi in laudem apostolorum*, where name-interpretations are incorporated into the poem itself and also are systematically glossed into the margins (mainly from Jerome). The hymn is printed in *The Irish Liber Hymnorum*, ed. J. H. Bernard and R. Atkinson (London, 1898), vol. I, pp. 18–21.

[17] CCL, XXXVIII, 64. Behind such convictions as these lies the long tradition of mystical onomastics including Philo, Origen, and the Clementine writings. For a classic statement, see *Clemens Alexandrinus*, ed. Otto Stahlin (Leipzig, 1909), pp. 146–7. See also n. 13 above.

[18] CCL, XXXII, Pars IV, 1 (Turnholti, 1962), 48–9.

commentaries. It explains why Jerome begins his commentary on Joel (*PL*, XXV, 947–88) with a prologue containing all the proper names which occur in the book, along with their etymological meanings, and why, in fact, so many of the Fathers' scriptural explications begin with an etymologizing of proper names and then move into typological or allegorical interpretation of the passage. It also helps us understand why Bede gives such painstaking attention to his name-etymologies and is careful to correct in his later writings minor inaccuracies which he had discovered in his earlier name-explications.[19]

One result of the commentators' onomastic zeal was that many names came to have multiple etymologies, any or all of which might become starting points for spiritual interpretations. Augustine points out that diverse etymological renderings of a name can be used to advantage in fathoming scriptural meanings,[20] and the Anglo-Saxons were as alive as any to the homiletic possibilities of this phenomenon. The name *Mary*, for example, acquired a host of interpretations among Latin commentators – *stella maris*, *domina*, *dominatrix*, *illuminatrix*[21] – and the anonymous Old English "Homily on the Nativity of the Blessed Virgin" illustrates how one Anglo-Saxon writer could use these meanings for rhetorical amplification in his hagiographic sketch of the Virgin:[22]

Nu is hyre nama gereht hlæfdige oððe cwen oððe sæsteorra. Heo is hlæfdige gecweden, forðan þe heo cende þone hlaford heofonas and eorðan. And heo is cwen gecweden, forðan þe heo com of ðam æðelan cynne and of ðam cynelican sæde Davides cynnes. Sæsteorra heo is gecweden, forðan þe se steorra on niht gecyþeð scypliðendum mannum, hwyder bið east and west, hwyder suð and norð.[23]

---

[19] See Claude Jenkins, "Bede as exegete and theologian" in *Bede, his Life, Times and Writings*, ed. A. Hamilton Thompson (Oxford, 1935), pp. 152–200.

[20] *De doctrina christiana*, II, xii, 17. Jerome, in his commentary on Ezechiel (*PL*, XXV, 258), explains how multiple interpretations of Hebrew names come about.

[21] Jerome, *Liber interpretationis hebraicorum nominum*, 14: 7–8, 62: 16–20, 70: 1, 74: 21; Pseudo-Jerome [Irish: ca.650–700], *Expositio quattuor evangeliorum*, *PL*, XXX, 535; Bede, *In Lucae evangelium expositio*, *PL*, XCII, 316; Rabanus, *Commentarius in Matthaeum*, *PL*, CVII, 744; Isidore, *Etymologiarum sive originum libri XX*, ed. W. M. Lindsay, 2 vols (Oxford, 1911) [hereafter cited as *Etymologiae*], VII, x, 1; Pseudo-Isidore [ca.750], *Liber de ortu et obitu patrum*, *PL*, LXXXIII, 1285; Alcuin, *In genealogiam Christi*, *PL*, C, 725, 728, 732–3; Haymo of Auxerre (Pseudo-Haymo of Halberstadt), *Homiliae de tempore*, CXVIII, 32.

[22] The classical rhetorical backgrounds of the patristic use of name-etymologies are discussed by Spicq, *Esquisse d'une histoire*, pp. 236–41.

[23] *Angelsächsische Homilien und Heiligenleben*, ed. Bruno Assmann. BasPr., III, rpt with supplementary introduction by Peter Clemoes (Darmstadt, 1964), p. 117. The homily proper is an adaptation of the *Pseudo-Matthaei Evangelium* but the etymological *effictio* of Mary was added by the Anglo-Saxon translator, probably from some other Latin source. Such analyses of Mary's name were commonplace, of course; cf. the Irish commentary on Matthew, *PL*, XXX, 552.

Onomastic sermonizing of this kind, so frequent among the Anglo-Saxons (and their Latin sources), bespeaks an interest in name-meanings which goes far beyond mere primitive curiosity;[24] it is a habit of mind fostered by a fully developed tradition encouraging devout readers "in uerbis uerum amare, non uerba."[25]

The Anglo-Saxons' use of name-meanings is not always as explicit as in glosses or in the homiletic use of Mary's name just cited, however; sometimes the prose-writers allude obliquely to the etymology of a character's name, counting on the audience to recognize the onomastic nature of the epithets they use. In his *Epistle to Sigeweard*, for example, Ælfric renders Isaiah 7: 14, "Behold, a maiden shall conceive and bear a son, and his name shall be called, God Himself is with us."[26] Here Ælfric relies on his readers to recognize that "God Himself is with us" is the literal meaning of the Hebrew name *Emmanuel*. Somewhat more complicated is Ælfric's elaborate narration elsewhere of the events set forth in Matthew 16: 15–18.[27] Following Christ's question, "Who do you say I am?" the Vulgate recounts the story in this way: "Simon Peter answered and said, 'Thou art the Christ ...' Then Jesus answered and said, 'Blessed art thou, Simon Barjona ... thou art Peter [that is, "rock"] and upon this rock I will build my church'." Ælfric, however, renders the sequel to the question in this way: "The *obedient* Peter answered him, 'Thou art the Christ ...' The Lord then said to Peter, 'Blessed art thou, *son of the dove*, ... Thou art *of stone* ... And on this stone I shall build my church'."[28] Here in three instances Ælfric has substituted the etymological meaning of a proper name for

---

[24] For example, the etymology of *Jerusalem* discussed below, pp. 211–12, was used not only by Ælfric in his sermons (Thorpe, vol. I, p. 210, and again in vol. II, p. 66, where he also develops a homiletic point by means of the etymology of *Babylon*) but also by the Blickling homilist and in the poem *Christ*, l. 50. Ælfric also explicates the alternate forms of *Abram* and *Abraham*, *Sarai* and *Sarah*, unfolding the significance of each. The etymology of *Israel* was used by Ælfric in his "Memory of the Saints" (EETS o.s. 76, p. 338), to make a homiletic point about faith and also by Byrhtferth in his *Manual*, ed. S. J. Crawford, EETS o.s. 177, p. 136; cf. also pp. 128–30. Ælfric makes similar use of the etymology of *Emmanuel* in Thorpe, vol. I, pp. 192–4; vol. II, p. 14, and he alludes to that etymology in a passage discussed below.

[25] *De doctrina christiana*, IV, xi, 26. It is revealing that Augustine should express this principle through the linguistic word-play concerning the presence of *verum* in *verbum*. For similar examples, see Christine Mohrmann, "Das Wortspiel in den augustinischen Sermones," *Mnemosyne*, 3rd ser., III (1935), 33–61.

[26] *Angelsächsische Homilien und Heiligenleben*, p. 87: *Efne mægden sceal eacnian ond acennen sunu ond his nome bið icwædon god sylf is mid us*. (To facilitate comparison with the Vulgate, I translate the Old English and Latin passages in this paragraph, supplying the original Old English texts in footnotes; manuscript abbreviations preserved in the BasPr. editions are silently expanded throughout this essay.)

[27] In "The Passion of the Apostles Peter and Paul," Thorpe, vol. I, pp. 366–8.

[28] *Him andwyrde se gehyrsuma Petrus, "Ðu eart Crist..." Drihten cwæð to Petre, "Eadig eart ðu, culfran sunu, ... þu eart stænen ... And ic timbrige mine cyrcan uppon ðisum stane."*

the name itself: *Simon* means "obedient";[29] *Barjona* means "son of the dove";[30] and *Peter*, of course, means "stone, rock." Nor is the substitution of meaning for name the only sign of his onomastic alertness. In the passage following "son of the dove" (which I omit in the preceding quotation) Ælfric supplies a moralizing comment about the meekness and grace of the Paraclete, and following the sacral pun on *Petrus* he adds that "on this stone" means further *ofer ðone geleafan ðe ðu andetst* "on the faith which thou dost acknowledge," thus bringing into play the alternative meaning of *Petrus*, "acknowledging." These edifying excursuses from the name-meanings are, of course, in precise keeping with patristic example: by discovering the name-meaning one is led on to spiritual meanings latent in the scriptural text.

Turning from Old English prose to poetic writings, it will be advisable once again to begin with a few obvious and incontrovertible examples of literary onomastics and pass thence to some of the subtler examples which seem to have escaped notice. The poem *Christ* has already been noticed to contain an explicit place-name etymology (n. 24 above), and so it is not surprising to discover in it some equally obvious interpretations of biblical personal names. In lines 130–5, for example, we encounter the same interpretation of *Emmanuel* that Ælfric uses in his *Epistle to Sigeweard*:

>   Eala gæsta god,   hu þu gleawlice
>   mid noman ryhte   nemned wære
>   Emmanuhel,   swa hit engel gecwæð
>   ærest on Ebresc.   þæt is eft gereht,
>   rume bi gerynum: "Nu is rodera weard,
>   god sylfa mid us."[31]

The interesting phrase *rume bi gerynum* in line 134 may reflect the patristic conception of the sacral import of name-meanings.

An equally explicit use of name-etymology is that in *Christ and Satan*, lines 365–7, where the familiar explication of *Lucifer* as "light-bearer" is poeticized:

---

[29] The commonest Latin interpretation of *Simon* is *obediens*: see, for example, Bede, *Expositio Actuum Apostolorum et Retractatio*, ed. M. L. W. Laistner (Cambridge, 1939), p. 48, ll. 25–6 ("ostium Simonis, id est oboedientiae"), and p. 125, l. 28 ("in domo Simonis, id est, oboedientis"); Rabanus, *Commentarius in Matthaeum*, PL, CVII, 789, 888 and *Homiliae in evangelia et epistolas*, PL, CX, 348, and *De universo*, PL, CXI, 86; Pseudo-Isidore [ca.750], *Liber de ortu et obitu patrum*, PL, LXXXIII, 1286; Pseudo-Bede [ca.750–800], *In Matthaei evangelium expositio*, PL, XCII, 22; the anonymous [Pseudo-Jerome] *Commentarius in evangelium secundum Marcum*, PL, XXX, 596. Jerome, *Liber interpretationis hebraicorum nominum*, 73: 7, and Isidore, *Etymologiae*, VII, ix, 6, render *Simon* as *audiens*, which answers equally well to OE *gehyrsuma*. Ælfric himself (Thorpe, vol. I, p. 586) says, *Simon is gereht "gehyrsum"*.

[30] Bede, *Expositio in Actuum Apostolorum*, p. 26, ll. 28–9: "Bariona, id est filius columbae." Similarly, Bede, *Homilia XX in cathedra Sancti Petri*, CCL, CXXII (Turnholti, 1955), pp. 143, 144–5; Jerome, *Liber interpretationis hebraicorum nominum*, 60: 22, and many others.

[31] All quotations from the poetry are taken from *ASPR*.

> Wæs þæt encgelcyn   ær genemned,
> Lucifer haten,   leohtberende,
> on geardagum   in godes rice.[32]

In view of these patent examples of poetic name-etymologizing, it is surprising that only slightly less obvious examples of the same phenomenon have passed unnoticed. Consider, for example, the following passage, which has contributed to the scholarly queries and despairing guesses so familiar in our editions of the Old English *Exodus*. In lines 357-8 the poet says that the race of Israel fathered by Abraham is

> halige þeode,
> Israela cyn,   onriht Godes

that is, "a holy people, the race of Israel, right of God." The last epithet, composed of the adjective *onriht* "right, proper, lawful" and the genitive singular of *God* presents a textual crux which has baffled lexicographers and editors alike. The dictionaries all provide *ad hoc* meanings for this one occurrence of *onriht* ("owned by?" "a right?" "partaking of?"),[33] but none offers evidence to support any of these conjectures. Emendation (for example, to *ānriht* or *on riht*) has proved unavailing. Since the epithet occurs in connection with a proper name, however, and since the *Exodus* poet elsewhere demonstrates his alertness to the etymological significance of names,[34] it should have been suspected that patristic onomastics lay behind the crux. Turning to Jerome's *Liber interpretationis hebraicorum nominum*, we find that the proper name *Israel* means *rectus Domini* "right of God."[35] The *Exodus* poet's *onriht*

---

[32] *Genesis B*, ll. 344-5, contains a reference to Satan's receiving a new name, thus calling to mind subtly this early name *Lucifer*. Elsewhere in *Genesis B*, moreover, there are numerous descriptive details which seem to grow out of the name-meaning. See, for example, ll. 255-6, 257-8, 265-6, 338-9. When the tempter-devil approaches Eve, he presents himself explicitly as a bringer of light (ll. 614-15, 618-20). It is difficult to divorce these allusions from the various Old English discussions of Lucifer's name – e.g. that of Ælfric in *Homilien und Heiligenleben*, p. 81: *Đe hatte lucifer, þæt is lihtberende, for þare mycele beorhtnysse his mæren heowæs*. Indeed, the link between name and characterization may already have been present in the poet's sources. J. Martin Evans, "*Genesis B* and its background," *RES*, XIV (1963), 12, n. 2, suggests that Cyprian, *Heptateuchos*, I, 70, offered the *Genesis B* poet a conception of Satan conditioned by the name-meaning of *Lucifer*. The possibilities of a consciously developed onomastic characterization of the devil in *Genesis B* seem to me worth investigating. Compare my suggestions below concerning the influence of name-meaning on narrative development in the OE poem *Guthlac*.

[33] The suggested definitions are to be found, s.v. *onriht*, respectively in *BTD*, *CHM*, and *A Short Dictionary of Anglo-Saxon Poetry* by J. B. Bessinger (Toronto, 1960).

[34] That the *Exodus* poet had access to Jerome's Hebrew etymologies has been pointed out in the edition of the poem by Edward Burroughs Irving Jr (New Haven, 1953), p. 19, and subsequently (pp. 72, 74, 89) Irving notes two instances of the poet's use of name-meanings – *Etham* in ll. 66ff, and *Abraham* in l. 353b.

[35] *Liber interpretationis hebraicorum nominum*, 63: 22-3: "Israhel uir uidens deum. Sed melius

Godes is simply a translation of the name *Israel*, and all the efforts to torture a different meaning out of the phrase have been misdirected.

After *Israel* the most prominent name in the Old English *Exodus* is probably *Egypte*, and we may fairly inquire whether it, like *Israel*, does not also reflect the poet's familiarity with patristic name-lore. I believe it does. In line 194 the Egyptians are referred to as *eorp werod* "the dark host," and editors have been at pains to account for the reference, for, as Irving has observed, "The Egyptians are not called dark in the Bible, at least not in the book of Exodus" (p. 81). Quite possibly the Old English poet's reference to the darkness of the Egyptians derives, either directly or indirectly, from the commonplace explication of the name *Ægyptus* as *tenebrae*,[36] an etymological meaning which formed the basis of elaborate medieval exegeses of the spiritual significance of Egypt in both Old and New Testaments.[37] The same name-meaning may lie behind the statement *werud wæs wigblac* in line 204 and *flodblac here* in line 498, if *-blac* in these compounds be construed as the Old English adjective *blæc*, *blac* "black" rather than as *blāc* "pale."

But the name-meaning *tenebrae* was not the only medieval interpretation of *Ægyptus*. An equally current derivation assigned to the word the meaning "afflicting, one who afflicts or persecutes" (*affligens, persequens, tribulans*).[38] We might expect the *Exodus* poet to reflect this sister-meaning in his allusions to the Egyptians, for the habit of Anglo-Saxons and of medieval writers at large

---

rectus domini." In his *Hebraicae quaestiones in libro Geneseos*, Corpus Christianorum, Series Latina, LXXII (1959), 51: 29–52, 1–23, Jerome discusses this meaning of *Israel* at length, rendering the meaning as *directus dei*. Jerome's preferred interpretation of the name is reflected in Pseudo-Bede (Pseudo-Remigius of Auxerre), *Interpretatio nominum hebraeorum*, PL, XCIII, 1103. The other interpretation of *Israel* (*vir videns deum*) was also known to the Old English writers; see n. 24 above.

[36] See Alcuin, *Epistola LXXXII*, PL, C, 266–7; Bede, *In Lucae evangelium expositio*, PL, XCII, 564; Jerome, *Liber interpretationis hebraicorum nominum*, 66: 28–9, 72: 14, 77: 25; Augustine, *Enarrationes in Psalmos*, CCL, XXXIX, 1088; Gregory, *In librum primum Regum expositiones*, CCL, CXLIV, 256, 549; Rabanus, *Homiliae in Evangelia et Epistolas*, PL, CX, 171. The extraordinary dissemination of this interpretation is further attested by its occurrence in the writings of Anselm of Laon [Pseudo-Haymo of Halberstadt], PL, CXVI, 420; Remigius of Auxerre [Pseudo-Haymo of Halberstadt], PL, CXVII, 24, 108; Haymo of Auxerre, PL, CXVIII, 77; Rupert of Deutz, PL, CLXVIII, 255; Manegold of Lautenbach [Pseudo-Bede], PL, XCIII, 841, 1041.

[37] That their name means "darkness" was taken by the exegetes to signify that the Egyptians are figures of the angels of Heaven who were cast into darkness, or that they are symbols of the sinful world, or that they represent ignorance, etc. See, for example, the works of Gregory, Alcuin, and Rabanus, cited in n. 36 above, and Remigius of Auxerre, PL, CXVII, 108; cf. Cassiodorus, *Expositio Psalmorum*, CCL, XCVII, 601. Meritt, *Fact and Lore*, p. 26, also gives this etymological interpretation of *eorp werod* in *Exodus*, 194.

[38] Jerome, *Liber interpretationis hebraicorum nominum*, 2: 29–30, 66: 28–9, 73: 14, 77: 25–6, 80: 11; Ambrose, *De Trinitate tractatus*, PL, XVII, 529; Augustine, *Enarrationes in Psalmos*, CCL, XL, 1636; Rabanus, *Enarratio in Ezechielem*, PL, CX, 796, and *De universo*, PL, CXI, 341–2. See also the references in n. 36 above.

was, as is demonstrated above, to exploit the multiple interpretations of names rather than to elect one and exclude others. In tracing the possible reflexes of this meaning in the Old English poem little is to be gained, however, by merely citing the numerous epithets for Egyptians involving the idea of "affliction" (*laðne lastweard*, line 138, *hettend*, line 209, *teonhete*, line 224, etc.). The Egyptians' role being what it is, these epithets could have been used, perhaps, irrespective of any name-meanings (although the curious use of the abstract noun *teonhete* "dire persecution" to refer to the Egyptians does point to a conscious etymological allusion in line 224). It is rather the persistence of the "affliction" motif that argues the presence of the onomastic reference in the poem and, most convincing of all, the fact that the etymology explains at least one locution which has hitherto perplexed students of the poem.

In describing the destruction of the Egyptians, the *Exodus* poet says, according to the unemended text,

> Mægen eall gedreas,
> ðа þe gedrecte,   dugoð Egypta,
> Faraon mid his folcum.
>
> (500–2)

The verse *ðа þe gedrecte* has provoked a medley of emendations, among them *ða he gedrencte* (Grein), *ðа gedrencte wæron* (Krapp), *deaþe gedrencte* (Sedgefield, Irving).[39] Presumably editors have hesitated to accept the odd syntax of the manuscript reading with its absolute use of *gedreccan*, and they have not seen the precise relevance of the literal meaning of the verb – "afflict". But once we observe that the much-emended clause stands parallel with *dugoð Egypta* and recall that the standard meaning of *Ægyptus* in the commentaries was *affligens, tribulans*, or, as Rabanus phrases it, "affligentes, eo quod afflixerunt Dei populum,"[40] we recognize that *ðа þe gedrecte* is a precise, literal rendering of the Fathers' etymological interpretation of the name *Egypt*, and we have no cause to demur at the straightforward meaning of the line as transmitted: "the army, the host of the Egyptians, 'those who afflicted', perished utterly."[41] I suspect that etymological interpretations of this kind may lie at the heart of many of the

---

[39] For a full list of emendations, see Irving, *Exodus*, pp. 63, 95, where he acknowledges that Sedgefield's reading, which he is adopting, "is not wholly satisfactory." Attempts to preserve the manuscript reading were made by von Schaubert (*ðа þege drecte* "those afflicted by drinking") and Blackburn ("when it [i.e. the great sea-wave mentioned just before] overwhelmed the hosts of Egypt"), but later scholars reject these interpretations because of metrical difficulties and overstrained word-meanings.   [40] *De universo, PL,* CXI, 439.

[41] Presumably *ða* in l. 501a is feminine singular, agreeing with *dugoð*, and so a meticulously literal translation would be "that one (host of Egyptians) which afflicted." The grammar agrees in number with the commentators' most usual form of explication, *affligens, tribulans* "the one that afflicts." It is less likely, though possible, that *ða* is plural and *gedrecte*, like *gedreas*, takes its number from the singulars *mægen* and *dugoð*.

textual obscurities in the Old English *Exodus* (including that curious series of epithets for the Egyptians, *ingefolca*, *ingemen*, and *ingeðeode*) which have until now been despairingly branded as manuscript corruptions.

Insufficient attention to Anglo-Saxon onomastics has led to misunderstanding of a different kind in another poem of the Junius MS. In *Genesis*, 1104-13, 1128-45, we are told the story of Seth. He was born to Adam and Eve as a replacement for the slain Abel; he flourished and fathered many children and then

>   eorðe swealh
> sædberendes   Sethes lice.
>
> (1144-5)

It is the epithet *sædberendes* "seed-bearer" which comes into question, for the Bible says nothing about Seth being a seedbearer. In an article published in *Modern Language Review*, Samuel Moore pointed out that if we take this epithet as no more than a generally appropriate description of a son who is carrying on the line of generation, we have no way of explaining why Seth should be singled out for the appellation: Adam begot many progenitive sons after Cain and Abel, and so any of them or their sons would merit the term equally.[42] Moore insists quite logically that there must be some special reason for Seth's being designated by this striking compound, which occurs nowhere else in the corpus of Old English poetry. Moore's suggestion is that the poet is alluding to an Apocryphal medieval legend which describes how Adam, at his death, sent Seth back into the Garden of Eden to fetch the oil of mercy which God had promised him. In some versions of the legend Seth returns, not with oil, but with seeds to plant a tree, and it is this tree which eventually becomes the cross. At first thought attractive, this theory does not stand up under close scrutiny. For one thing, the poet had previously recounted the death of Adam (1125-7) with no intimation that he knew of the extravagant tale about the death-bed injunction to Seth. Again, the "seed-bearing" reference seems peculiarly unmotivated and irrelevant in the passage describing Seth's burial, if the only rationale for it is the Apocryphal legend about carrying seeds from Eden. Finally, there is the serious weakness in Moore's theory that the earliest version of the legend of Seth and the seeds dates from a period several centuries later than the time of the composition of *Genesis*.[43] Krapp, in his edition of *Genesis* in the *Anglo-Saxon Poetic Records*, has wisely rejected Moore's

---

[42] Moore, "The Old English *Genesis*, ll. 1145 and 1446-8," *MLR*, VI (1911), 199-202.

[43] Esther C. Quinn, *The Quest of Seth for the Oil of Life* (Chicago, 1962), p. 10, remarks concerning this legend, "The earliest known form of what we might call the seed versions was interpolated into the *De imagine mundi* of Honorius of Autun between 1154 and 1159."

theory, but all we are then left with is the desperate explanation that the dead Seth is called "seed-bearing" because he had previously been a fertile male.

The reader will have anticipated my solution to the crux. Turning to the standard authorities on the meaning of Seth's name, we discover that Jerome and his followers repeatedly explicate *Seth* as meaning *semen, gramen, resurrectio* – "seed, plant, resurrection."[44] Isidore of Seville spells out the connections among the various significations of Seth's name, explaining that it means *resurrectio* because "in ipso resuscitatum est semen iustum, quod est stirps filiorum dei."[45] Augustine, in the fifteenth book of *De civitate Dei*, chapters 18–20, explains in full how it is "de semine Seth" that the generation of Adam is traced through Noah and Abraham to Christ, and how that generation symbolizes the heavenly city in exile on earth.[46] Since these revered authorities assign such importance to the seed-and-resurrection meaning of Seth's name, it is understandable that the Old English poet would allude to *sædberende* Seth as the earth receives his body. The context in which the onomastic allusion occurs vitalizes poetically the exegetical significance of the name-meaning: as Seth's body descends into the earth, we are reminded that his name assures us that even in death he remains a living plant which bears the seed of resurrection. Bede comments that Seth "juxta mysticos sensus semen aliud appellatur, cum idem Dominus qui occisus est resurrexit, quia nimirum mortalis occisus est, resurrexit immortales."[47] The *Genesis* poet's artful coordination of poetic and religious symbolism would lose its point if we assumed that *sædberende* merely alluded to an irrelevant fable about Seth's journeying to Paradise.

---

[44] Jerome, *Liber interpretationis hebraicorum nominum*, 10: 13 ("gramen aut semen seu resurrectio"), 65: 29–30 ("germen uel resurrectio"). The name-meaning *semen* is suggested, of course, in the Bible itself, Genesis 4: 25 ("vocavitque nomen eius Seth dicens: Posuit mihi Deus semen aliud pro Abel, quem occidit Cain"). The further sense *resurrectio* is cited in Bede, *Hexaemeron*, *PL*, XCI, 76; Pseudo-Bede, *Quaestiones super Genesim*, *PL*, XCIII, 290; Isidore, *Etymologiae*, VII, vi, 9–10. A different name-meaning for *Seth*, growing out of a different etymological association, is *positio, positus* – see Jerome, *Liber interpretationis hebraicorum nominum*, 20: 17 ("Seth positio siue posuit") and Isidore, *Etymologiae*, VII, vi, 10. This second name-meaning is also reflected in the OE *Genesis*, unless l. 1104 (*on Abeles gyld*), l. 1109 (*wæs Abeles gield*), l. 113 (*on leofes stæl*) are to be regarded as meaningless iteration of Genesis 4: 25. Thus the Old English poem seems to reflect the various senses of the name simultaneously: *semen* in l. 1133b (see the discussion below), *semen, gramen, stirps*, etc. in the word *sædberendes* (l. 1145a), and *positio* in the passages just cited. As was demonstrated by the quotation from the Old English sermon on the Blessed Virgin, this is a characteristic way of using the commentators' name-explications.

[45] *MGH*, Auctores antiqissimi, Tomus XI, ed. Theodorus Mommsen (Berlin, 1961), vol. II, p. 426.

[46] For the extraordinary popularity of book XV of the *Civitas Dei* among the Anglo-Saxons, see J. D. A. Ogilvy, *Books Known to Anglo-Latin Writers from Aldhelm to Alcuin (670–804)*, Medieval Academy of America, Studies and Documents, II (Cambridge, MA, 1936), p. 14, n. 26.

[47] *Hexaemeron, PL*, XCI, 77.

Even before the *sædberende* epithet the Old English poet indicates that he is representing Seth in terms of the meaning of his name, but modern editors have unwittingly removed this indication from the text and created thereby an artificial textual problem. In lines 1133-4, just after he has told us the age at which Seth began to propagate sons and daughters, the poet says, according to the manuscript,

>   sedes eafora
> se yldesta wæs   Enos haten

The meaning is clear: "The first offspring of the seed was called Enos."[48] But editors have consistently emended *sedes* to *Sethes*, assuming that a scribal blunder has corrupted the word from the proper noun *Seth* to the common noun *sed* "seed."[49] But when we remember that the name *Seth* means "seed," the editorial suppression of *sedes* seems very ill-advised. Rather this looks like a deliberate substitution of the name-meaning for the name itself, a characteristic device to evoke the name's exegetical significance, which commentators have developed out of the etymological interpretation of the word. We have no more business altering *sedes* to *Sethes*, I suspect, than we would have in altering Ælfric's learned substitution of *gehyrsuma* for *Simon* in the scriptural passage cited above (p. 191). Among learned Anglo-Saxons the meaning of the name was evidently equivalent to the name itself, and if we remove from the text of *Genesis* the rich play on Seth's name in line 1133, we are reducing the poet's statement to something less complex than he intended.

Yet further evidence of the *Genesis* poet's knowledge of patristic name-lore occurs in lines 1303-4, where God instructs Noah to provide an ark for all creatures

---

[48] *Sedes* I assume to be a non-West Saxon form of *sædes*. In Old English MSS. there is much wavering between *æ* and *e* in the spelling of this word; cf., for example, *linsed sawan*, *wadsæd eac* in Felix Liebermann, "Gerefa," *Anglia*, IX (1886), 262, and the citations in *BTD*, s.v. *sædlic*, and *BTS*, s.v. *æcersæd* and *sæd*. I do not believe, therefore, that a non-West Saxon *sedes* in *Genesis*, l. 1133, followed by a West Saxon *sædberendes* in l. 1145 is cause for suspicion. Also, see the ensuing note.

[49] The fortuitous similarity between the Hebrew name *Seth* meaning "seed" and Old English *sēd* "seed" is so apt that one might expect the substitution of *Sēd* for *Seth* to have achieved some currency as a folk-etymologized form of the name. Such may indeed have happened, for in the Parker version of the *Anglo-Saxon Chronicle*, anno 855, *Seth* is spelled *Sed* in the table of generations. (Other versions have *Seth*.) Of course the Parker MS. spelling could also be adopted from some Latin text in which a deviant transliteration of the final consonant of the Hebrew name led to *Seth*'s being spelled *Sed*. Indeed, one might suggest further that this, rather than an intentional translation of the name *Seth*, might lie behind the form *sedes* in *Genesis*, l. 113b, but this seems far less likely. Seth's name occurs in ll. 1106, 1128, 1138, 1145, 1245, and 1257 of the poem, and in every occurrence it is spelled *Seth*. In view of this, it is hard to see how a deviant transliteration would suddenly crop up in l. 1133.

                    on þam þu monegum scealt
reste geryman.

In the biblical account of God's prescriptions for the ark (Genesis 6: 13–21, 7: 1–4), there is no basis for the assertion that Noah shall give "rest" to the creatures in the ark; God simply tells Noah that he shall save specimens for procreation, as the OE *Genesis* elsewhere repeats. But the poet is here once again reflecting onomastic interpretations of the commentaries. The Bible itself suggests in Genesis 5: 29 that Noah's name means "rest," and Isidore, Jerome, Rabanus, and others meticulously explicate the name's meaning as *requies* and proceed from there to the typological equation of Noah with Christ.[50] Ælfric later summarizes the Latin Fathers' argument briefly but accurately in Old English:

> Noe, ðe on ðam arche wæs on ðam miclæn flode, ðe al weorld adrencte buton æhtæ monnum, is iræht *requies*, þæt is "ræst" on englisc, ond he tacnode for ði crist, ðe to us for ði com, þæt he us of ðissere weorlde to ræste brohte ond to blisse mid him.[51]

Ælfric's rendering illustrates the ease with which patristic name-etymologizing could pass into vernacular writings and, specifically, it shows how naturally the Old English word *rest* is educed by the mention of Noah and his story. I believe we must qualify the statement made in the course of one analysis of the Old English *Genesis* poet's adaptation of his source, for it is not quite accurate to say, "The poet drops the puzzling biblical etymology of Noah's name (Genesis 5: 29)."[52] The poet was not puzzled by the name's meaning, nor did he drop it; rather he moved it back to a point in the narrative where its exegetical significance would be more fully apparent.

Before turning from the Anglo-Saxons' adaptation of onomastic detail from scriptural commentary, we should consider a New Testament allusion from the Old English *Christ*, lines 71–3. The poet calls on the Virgin Mary:

[50] See Isidore, *Etymologiae*, VII, vi, 15; Pseudo-Isidore, *Quaestiones de vetere et novo testamento*, *PL*, LXXXIII, 229; Jerome, *Liber interpretationis hebraicorum nominum*, 9: 4, 58: 11, 73: 5, 78: 11; Rabanus, *Commentarius in Genesim*, *PL*, CVII, 510; Pseudo-Bede, *Expositio in primum librum Mosis*, *PL*, XCI, 221, 222.

[51] The preface to the Old Testament translation, *Angelsächsische Homilien und Heiligenleben*, p. 83. Alcuin poeticizes the patristic interpretation in *Carmen* LXVIII, ll. 45ff: "Inde Noe, requies mundi, iam nascitur almus," etc. See *MGH*, Poetae Latini aevi Carolini, I, 289.

[52] Francis Lee Utley, "The Flood narrative in the Junius Manuscript and in Baltic literature," in *Studies in Old English Literature in Honor of Arthur G. Brodeur*, ed. Stanley B. Greenfield (Eugene, OR, 1963), p. 213. Though generally skeptical about extensive influence of exegesis on the Old English *Genesis*, Utley offers acute and judicious identifications of exegetical reflexes in the poem (pp. 211–12).

> Eala wifa wynn geond wuldres þrym,
> fæmme freolicast ofter ealne foldan sceat
> þæs þe æfre sundbuend secgan hyrdon.

The practice in modern editions and translations of *Christ* has been to interpret the word *sundbuend* (73) in the generalized sense "mankind, mortals," as if the literal meaning of the compound "sea-dwellers, seamen" were an embarrassment here. G. Storms has recently objected to the translators' evasions, observing that "*sundbuend* is not just 'men, mortals'; literally it says 'sea-dwellers', i.e. 'voyagers'. The meaning is that nobody, no matter how far he has travelled, can explain the mystery of the virgin birth."[53] Storms's basic point is well taken, but I believe an even stronger case can be made for his interpretation if we turn to the etymological meanings of Mary's name. As we have already seen in an earlier citation of an Anglo-Saxon writer's use of the etymology of Mary's name (pp. 190–1 above), one of the commonest interpretations of *Maria* was *stella maris* "star of the sea." Since the poet of *Christ* elsewhere uses name-etymologies in his invocations,[54] it seems quite likely that the word *sundbuend* in the invocation to Mary is, like the homilist's *scipliðend* (p. 190), motivated by the fact that Mary is the "star of the sea." Indeed, the passage from *Christ*, as I understand it, seems to reflect more than one of the meanings of Mary's name (*illuminatrix, stella maris, domina, felix regina, feminarum regina*),[55] just as the previously quoted etymological essay on Mary had done: "Oh finest of women throughout the splendor of heaven, noblest maid in all the world, as seamen have always heard tell."

II

Thus far the discussion has been limited to Old English poetic uses of biblical names. It would be surprising, however, if there were no concomitant interest

---

[53] Review of *The Advent Lyrics of the Exeter Book*, ed. J. J. Campbell (Princeton, 1959), in *ES*, XLVIII (1967), 164. As Storms's observations rightly imply, we must demonstrate some special appropriateness of the literal sense of *sundbuend* before we can assume such a meaning here, for the few other occurrences of the word in Old English do not afford a context which clearly forces the literal sense. It is this latter consideration which, understandably, led Campbell to gloss and translate the word as he did.

[54] In l. 50, for example, the poet preceded the name *Jerusalem* with the etymological meaning of the word, and in ll. 130–5 he gives a similar explication of the name *Emmanuel*. Storms, Review, p. 165, sees *earendal* in l. 104 as an allusion to the interpretation of *Mary* as "morning star," but I suspect that the reference here is to Christ, as explicated by Rabanus, *De universo*, *PL*, CXI, 274, and Gregory, *Moralia in Iob*, *PL*, LXXVI, 520.

[55] See above, n. 21. The interpretations *feminarum regina* (*PL*, LXXXIII, 1285), *felix regina* (quoted by Rabanus, *PL*, CVII, 744) are extrapolations from the etymologized name-meanings rather than direct etymologizations.

in non-biblical onomastica, for the learned traditions behind and around the Anglo-Saxon poets evince a sustained and vigorous interest in the meanings of vernacular names as well. Isidore explicates the name of the Goths as readily as he does that of the Israelites or the Samaritans,[56] and Bede, it is not always remembered, gave no less attention to the etymological senses of the vernacular names in his *Historia ecclesiastica* (*Æt Twifyrd, Alcluith, Heofonfeld, Dælreuding, Streoneshealh*, etc.)[57] than he did, in his commentaries, to the Hebrew names of the Bible. And Gregory the Great, in an episode from Bede's *Historia ecclesiasetica* which was forever popular among the Anglo-Saxons, prophesied the conversion of the Anglo-Saxons by a series of onomastic inspirations involving the names *Angel, Ælle*, and *Deira*.[58] These "puns," as they are often called, are usually misunderstood by modern readers as ill-timed efforts at wit rather than as serious attempts to discover within a name the ultimate fate and significance of the bearer. Gregory's onomastic ingenuity is not exercised in the spirit of rhetorical display, but rather in the spirit of Augustine's response to another non-Biblical name: "O nomen pulchrum, demonstrans figuram, et indicans rem futuram."[59] Modern readers' failure to perceive the true intent of Gregory's remarks are indicative of a serious misconception about medieval onomastic thinking, and since the Gregorian episode has become a *locus classicus* of Old English name-lore, we may scrutinize the details of the legend a little further before moving on to other onomastic traditions known to the Anglo-Saxons.

It must be remembered that Gregory's allusions to *Angel, Ælle* and *Deira* are not, for him, novel experiments in name-play, but products of the same habit of mind which produced the persistent onomastic interpretations in his commentaries, where he offers solemn explications of the prophetic meanings of *Ægyptus, Abel, Dauid*, and many other names.[60] Also, within its context in

---

[56] *Historia Gothorum, Wandalorum et Sueborum*, ed. Theodor Mommsen, MGH, Auctorum antiquissimorum Tomus XI, vol. II (Berlin, 1961), 268: "Interpretatio autem nominis eorum in lingua nostra tecti quod significatur fortitudo." (In his *Etymologiae*, of course, Isidore etymologizes many vernacular names.) Other fanciful derivations of tribal names (e.g. *Danes* from *Danaus, Ynglings* from the Turkish king *Yngue*) are commonplaces of medieval chroniclers.

[57] See IV, xxviii; I, xii; III, ii; I, i; I, xxvii. Bede was also fond of the type of name-play in which the meaning of a name is substituted for the name itself (as in the *Genesis* poet's substitution of *sed* "seed" for *Seth*, discussed above). See his quotation from Prosper in I, x, where *aequorei* apparently stands for Pelagius's name. [58] *Historia ecclesiastica*, 59.

[59] Augustine, *Sermo XVIII: In natali Quadrati martyris, PL*, XLVI, 883 (referring to the name *Quadratus*). The same concept is suggested by Isidore, who, in speaking of the meanings of various types of names (*Etymologiae*, VII, vi, 1), observes, "Quibus ita prophetice indita sunt vocabula, ut aut futuris aut praecentibus eorum causis conveniant."

[60] *Expositiones in librum primum Regum*, CCL, CXLIV, 104, 256, 271, 605. The long-doubted authenticity of Gregory's commentary on I Kings has now been firmly established by Patrick Verbraken, "Le commentaire de saint Grégoire sur le premier Livre des Rois," *Revue Bénédictine*, LXVI (1956), 159–217.

Bede's *Historia ecclesiastica* the Gregorian name-play stands forth as serious, not frivolous commentary. For Bede indulges in quite similar name-prophecy when he explains the meaning of the OE name *Heofonfeld*, adding that it "certo utique praesagio futurorum antiquitus nomen accepit, significans nimirum quod ibidem caeleste erigendum tropaeum, caelestis inchoanda victoria," etc.[61] That Gregory's interest in the barbaric names was prompted by similar reverential onomancy is made clear, I believe, by his preceding discussion of the English slaves' *gratia frontispicii* and *interna gratia* and by Bede's allusion to the fulfillment of Gregory's *Ælle – Alleluia* prophecy in II, i.[62] But the seriousness of Gregory's comments is made clearest, perhaps, in the version of the legend in the Whitby monk's *Life of St Gregory*, which may antedate Bede's account.[63] There the *Ælle – Alleluia* remark is designated specifically as a "prophecy": "Ælli ... quem sub vaticinatione Alleluiatica ... meminimur."[64] The Whitby author even tries to cap Gregory's prophecy with some original interpretation of the name:

> O quam pulchre quamque hec omnia decenter sibi conveniunt prefata! Ergo nomen Anglorum, si una *e* littera addetur, Angelorum sonat; pro certo vocabulum quorum proprium est semper omnipotentem Deum in celis laudare, et non deficere ... Et Aelli duabus compositum est sillabis,

---

[61] *Historia ecclesiastica*, III, ii.

[62] "Ecce lingua Brittaniae, quae nil aliud noverat quam barbarum frendere, iamdudum in divinis laudibus Hebraeum coepit 'Alleluia' sonare" (quoted from the *Moralia in Iob*). Some may feel that in judging Gregory's name-play so solemnly I am overlooking Bede's phrase "adludens ad nomen," which the Alfredian translator renders literally as *plegode mid his wordum to þæm noman*. But it is doubtful that *adludens* implies "play" or levity, for elsewhere Bede uses the same word in a precisely analogous situation where the intent is profoundly serious. In speaking of Christ's sacral pun on Peter's name, Bede says, "Nam sicut lux uera Christus donauit apostolis ut lux mundi uocentur sic et Simoni qui credebat in petram Christum Petri largitus est nomen cuius alias alludens aethimologiae dixit: Tu es Petrus," etc. (CCL, CXX, II, 133). This is the commentary on Luke; later, in his *In Marci evangelium expositio*, ibid., pp. 470-1, Bede repeats this sentence verbatim, and it is copied subsequently by Rabanus and others. Cassiodorus, it may be noted, uses the noun *allusio* in connection with the figurative as opposed to the literal function of language in the preface to his commentary on Psalms (CCL, XCVII, 14, 25), and R. E. Latham, *Revised Medieval Latin Word-List* (London, 1965), s.v. *allusio*, reports that by the eighth century the word had acquired the meaning "hint, allusion" rather than "play." That we should not press the Old English rendering of the *Historia ecclesiastica* too closely for accurate elucidation of Bede's Latin is suggested by the many failures of the Old English translator to understand the original; the next sentence but one after the *adludens* sentence is grossly misunderstood by the translator. And in any case, OE *plegode* itself does not necessarily imply frivolity or play.

[63] See Bertram Colgrave, "The earliest saint's lives written in England," *Proceedings of the British Academy*, XLIV (1958), pp. 50, 51, for a judicious appraisal of the problems of dating the Whitby *Life*.

[64] *A Life of Pope St Gregory the Great Written by a Monk of the Monastery of Whitby*, ed. Francis Aidan Gasquet (Westminster, 1904), p. 16.

quarum in priori cum *e* littera absumitur; et in sequenti pro *i* ponitur *e*, *Alle* vocatur, quod in nostra lingua *omnes* absolute indicat. Et hoc est, quod ait Dominus noster: *Venite ad me omnes qui laboratis et onerati estis*, et reliqua.⁶⁵

Having reported Gregory's discovery of the predestined grace of the Anglo-Saxons by means of their names, the Whitby writer here confirms the validity of Gregory's onomastic prophecy by further, native English, etymologizing of his own – a clear indication of his reverent sympathy for the mode of thought revealed by the saint's word-play. That modern readers should so often misjudge Gregory's name-prophecies as trivial rhetoric illustrates how far removed we are from the habit of mind which Gregory's comments evince and which Bede and the Whitby writer understood so well.⁶⁶

It is clear, then, that the etymologizing of non-biblical as well as of biblical names enjoyed the sanction of the most revered patristic authorities and that the Anglo-Saxons themselves were quite ready to extend the scriptural commentators' techniques of Hebrew name-exegesis into the realm of vernacular Old English names. But the exegetical procedures of the commentators were by no means the only tradition of secular name-study which the Anglo-Saxons would have observed. The Irish, who indicated so many of the directions which Anglo-Saxon learning was later to take, displayed a lively interest in the names of their legendary and historical figures as well as in the vernacular names of their saints. The ingenious episodes contrived to explain the names of CuChulainn and Finn⁶⁷ are no less famous than Adomnan's hagiographical etymologizing of *Columba*.⁶⁸ Less known, perhaps, is the Irish

---

⁶⁵ Ibid. The reverential attitude toward this type of name-interpretation is further illustrated by the Whitby writer's account of Gregory's divining a sign of the Trinity in King Edwin's name (p. 17) and in his discerning a divine command *Sta in loco* in the name of the insect *locusta*. The fact that these "etymologies" appear in company with standard patristic interpretations of biblical names (e.g. p. 35) is significant.

⁶⁶ *Adomnan's Life of Columba*, ed. Alan Orr Anderson and Marjorie Ogilvie Anderson (London, 1961), pp. 180–2, contains a sentence which sums up precisely the assumption underlying Gregory's responses to the English names as well as the onomastics of Admoan's contemporaries, Bede and the Whitby writer: "Tale tantumque vocabulum homini dei non sine divina inditum providentia creditur." (These are the words with which Adomnan introduces his etymology of St Columba's name.)

⁶⁷ For the name of CuChulainn see *The Book of Leinster*, ed. R. I. Best and M. A. O'Brien (Dublin, 1956), vol. II, pp. 286–7, and *The Stowe Version of Táin Bó Cuailnge*, ed. Cecile O'Rahilly (Dublin, 1961), pp. 31–2. For a convenient summary of the episodes in the Old Irish version, see Rudolf Thurneysen, *Die irische Helden- und Königsage bis zum siebzehnten Jahrhundert* (Halle, 1921), pp. 134–5. For the legend of Finn's name, see *Duanaire Finn*, ed. Eoin MacNeill, Irish Texts Society, VII (1908), 33 (translation, p. 134). Both the CuChulainn and the Finn legends contain many other name-explications as well.

⁶⁸ *Adomnan's Life of Columba*, pp. 180–2. Columba himself was evidently given to analyzing the meaning of his name, for in his epistle to Boniface IV he refers to himself as "rara avis ...

treatise *Coir Anmann* "Fitness of Names," which comprises explanations of the meanings of some three hundred names from early Irish legend and history.⁶⁹ Other Celtic writers were equally attracted to secular onomastics. Gildas's famous allusion to a *superbus tyrannus* has long been suspected to be a literal translation of the British name *Vortigern*, and Nennius in the *Historia Brittonum* offers, among other onomastic feats, a bizarre explication of the name of the *Letewicion* which has many counterparts in later name-lore.⁷⁰

Apart from the Celtic examples, there is ample evidence of literary onomastics in continental Germanic writings to suggest that name-interpretation might well have been a natural propensity for the Anglo-Saxons even before they settled England. The euhemeristic theories of Ari, Snorri, and other Old Icelandic writers, for example, are to a large extent creatures of the Norse penchant for name-etymologizing, as Andreas Heusler has aptly remarked: "Fast alle diese mittelalterlichen Wanderungslegenden besitzen eine – mehr oder weniger phantasievolle – Etymologie oder Namengleichung"; and he observes later, "Schallähnlichkeiten wie Asia : ás-, Scythia : Svíðióð, Tana- : Vana- hatten hypnotisierende Kraft."⁷¹ That writers in other genres should be affected by the same habit of mind is to be expected. The continental West Germanic writers of Latin verse were especially fond of "poeticizing" the etymological senses of vernacular names. In the epic *Waltharius* Ekkehard plays on the meaning of Hagena's name, calling him *Hagano spinosus* in line 1421 and having him addressed in line 1351, *O paliure, vires foliis, ut pungere possis*. It is unfortunate that too little remains of the Old English *Waldhere* for us to determine whether there was similar name-play there. Again, Radbod of Utrecht devotes considerable attention to etymologizing the name of the Anglo-Saxon Leofwine (*carus amicus*) in his *Egloga ... de virtutibus Beati Lebuini et de sancto nomine eius*, lines 57ff, while the same name is etymologized more subtly (*dilectus Wine*) in the prose *Vita Lebuini antiqua*. And of course

---

Palumbus" (*Epistolae sex ad Diversos, PL*, LXXX, 274), and subsequently he etymologizes his name in detail (col. 282). Translating vernacular names into Latin was, of course, common among the Anglo-Saxons too; cf. *Lupus* for *Wulfstan*, *Aquila* for *Arne*, etc.

⁶⁹ The treatise is edited in the third volume of *Irische Texte* (Leipzig, 1897), by Whitley Stokes. For brief discussions of the content and date of the work, see Margaret E. Dobbs, *Sidelights on the Táin age and other studies* (Dundalk, 1917), pp. 57–70, and Thurneysen, *Die irische Helden- und Königsage*, pp. 48–50.

⁷⁰ *MGH*, Auctorum antiquissimorum Tomus XIII, iii (Berlin, 1898), 167, n. 1. Compare the Carolingian explanation that Britain was so named because of the *bruti mores* of its inhabitants (*MGH*, Poetarum Latinorum medii aevi Tomus IV, fasc. i, 246, 467) as well as Geoffrey of Monmouth's later derivation of *Britain* from *Brutus*, along with his discussion of *Cornwall*, for which he offers two alternative etymologies (*The Historia regum Britannie*, ed. Neil Wright (Cambridge and Dover, NH, 1985–8), 2 vols.).

⁷¹ Heusler, *Die gelehrte Urgeschichte im altisländischen Schriftum* (Berlin, 1908), pp. 39–40, 84. On pp. 13–37 Heusler lists the primary sources for the euhemeristic writings.

Hucbald of Saint-Amand made name-etymologizing one of the hallmarks of his style.[72] These habits survive with vigor among the vernacular Middle High German poets. Gottfried's elaborate (and utterly false) derivation of Tristan's name from *triste* and his extraordinary suggestion that the name *England* comes from *Wales* (En*gel*ant : *Gales*!) deserve places alongside some of the more extravagant specimens from Isidore.[73] Similar consciousness of name-meanings is observed in Wolfram's *Parzival*.[74]

Finally, there is the tradition of hagiographical onomastics, which requires a paragraph unto itself. The desire to find some sign of a saint's special powers reflected in his name is evinced even in the modern period. It has been reported that French peasants invoke the Anglo-Saxon St Boni*face* for aid in curing maladies of the *face*, while rural Germans are said to have found him particularly effective in aiding the cultivation of beans (*Bohnen*).[75] Similar are the French superstition crediting St Claire with a power to heal weak eyesight (that is, to make one *voir clair*) and the German folk-belief that St *Augustin* promotes healthy *Augen*.[76] Early medieval onomastics in the British Isles was rarely so artless as this, although there are some instances of Celtic hagiographers yielding to fancy.[77] The onomastics in Anglo-Saxon saints' lives tends on the whole to be learned rather than fanciful, and we find there sober and correct explications such as Cynewulf's interpretation of *Cyriacus* (*Elene*, lines 1058–62) and Ælfric's typical comment, *Gregorius is Grecisc nama, se sweigð*

---

[72] The passages from *Waltharius* and the Leofwine narratives may be found, respectively, in *MGH*, Poetarum Latinorum medii aevi, VI, i, 82, 79; IV, i, 171; Scriptores, XXX, ii, 793; Hucbald's frequent onomastic flourishes are remarked on pp. 264–5 of Poetae Latini aevi Carolini, IV, i.

[73] For further Middle High German examples see Bruno Boesch, "Über die Namengebung mittelhochdeutscher Dichter," *Deutsche Vierteljahrschrift für Literaturwissenschaft und Geistesgeschichte*, XXXII (1958), 241–62. Jakob Grimm, moreover, observed more than a century ago that "unsere volkssage wimmelt von gesuchter und verkehrter namensdeutung." See his *Kleinere Schriften* (Berlin, 1864), vol. I, p. 304. See also p. 215 below.

[74] See Jean Fourquet, "Les noms propres du 'Parzival'," in *Mélanges . . . offerts à Ernest Hoepffner*, Publications de la Faculté des Lettres de l'Université de Strasbourg, Fasc. 113 (Paris, 1949), pp. 245–60, esp. pp. 256–7.

[75] The French superstition is recorded by H. Gaidoz, "L'Etymologie populaire et le folklore," *Mélusine: recueil de mythologie, littérature populaire, traditions, et usages*, IV (1889), 511, the German by E. Kałużniacki, "Über Wesen und Bedeutung der volksetymologischen Attribute christlicher Heiliger," *Zbornik u slavu Vatroslava Jagića* (Berlin, 1908), p. 508. For another discussion of this phenomenon, see Matthias Zender, "Über Heiligennamen," *Der Deutschunterricht*, IX (1957), 72–91.

[76] Gaidoz, *Mélusine*, IV (1889), 506, and V (1890), 152; Kałużniacki, pp. 506 and 508. Such perversions of etymology are doubly ironical in that many of these saints' names had genuine, appropriate senses when they were bestowed. See Joseph Schrijnen, "Die Namengebung im altchristlichen Latein," *Mnemosyne*, ser. 3, II (1935), 271ff.

[77] The twelfth-century Welsh *Vita Sancti Iltuti*, for example, explains that St Illtyd "nominatus est infans Iltutus, uidelicet, ille ab omni crimine tutus." But other name-etymologies in this saint's life (e.g. those of *Rieingulid, Cyflym*, and *Hodnant*) seem more restrained. See *Vitae Sanctorum Britanniae et Genealogiae* by A. W. Wade-Evans (Cardiff, 1944), pp. 194, 203, 219.

on *Ledenum gereorde*, '*Uigilantius*', *þæt is on Englisc*, '*Wacolre*'. *He wæs swiðe wacol on Godes bebodum*, etc.[78] Elsewhere, Ælfric explains accurately the etymology and import not only of saints' names such as *John*, *Stephen*, and *Benedict* but also of the names of other historical figures such as *Augustus* and *Cyrenius*, revealing how they, much like the Hebrew names of the Old Testament, presaged later, Christian events.[79] Yet, though such name-interpretations do have affinities with the exegetical tradition, there is this basic difference: they deal with any vernacular name, not exclusively with the Hebrew names of the Bible.

This survey of name-etymologizing traditions contiguous to the Anglo-Saxon milieu has established, I believe, that the literary use of vernacular name-meanings (as well as of biblical name-meanings) was for the Old English writers an available convention. In the remaining pages of this essay I shall discuss instances in the Old English poems *Guthlac* and *Beowulf* where the etymological senses of proper names seem to be operative. If my examples prove convincing, then it would appear that a deeper inquiry into the possible literary function of name-meanings in Old English poetry at large might be in order.

The Old English *Guthlac* poems are promising texts for the student of name-meanings for two reasons. First, they are saints' lives, and as we have seen, a standard convention in that genre is the elucidation of the prophetic meaning of the saint's name and of other names associated with his story. Second, we are fortunate in having the Latin prose source which lies behind the *Guthlac* poems,[80] and in that source the significance of the saint's name is spelled out prominently at the beginning of the narrative. There can be little doubt, then, that the Old English poet was aware both of the meaning of Guthlac's name

---

[78] Thorpe, vol. II, p. 118. Earlier Anglo-Saxon writers supplied equally correct explications of *Chrysostom*, which they took to be a cognomen of Gregory; see Wæferth's preface to the second of *The Dialogues of Gregory* (BasPr., V [1907], p. 94) and the Whitby *Life*, p. 32. Where the Old English writers fall short of philological accuracy, as when the martyrologist asserts that "Philip" means *leohtfætes muþ* (*An Old English Martyrology*, ed. George Herzfeld, EETS o.s. 116 [London, 1900], pp. 68–9), the error arises not from vagrant fancy but from adherence to erroneous authorities (Isidore and most other medieval scholars explicate *Philip* as *os lampadis*).

[79] Thorpe, vol. I, p. 354 ("John"); vol. I, p. 50 ("Stephen"); vol. II, p. 164 ("Benedict"); vol. I, p. 32.

[80] That *Guthlac A* as well as *Guthlac B* is directly indebted to Felix's *Vita Guthlaci* was argued by Gordon Hall Gerould, "The Old English poems on St Guthlac and their Latin source," *MLN*, XXXII (1917), 77–89, and seems now to be widely accepted: L. K. Shook: "The prologue of the Old-English *Guthlac A*," *Medieval Studies*, XXIII (1961), 302, n. 20, says that "no one now doubts that there is indebtedness," and Charles W. Kennedy, *The Earliest English Poetry* (London, 1943), p. 249, affirms that "it is clear that both poems are in some degree dependent on the Latin *Vita*." But even if the poet of *Guthlac A* did not know Felix's *Vita*, the name-motif (as I demonstrate below) was such an early and popular element of the saint's legend that he would probably have known it anyway when he turned his hand to the story of Guthlac.

and also of the relevance which that meaning had to the saint's legend. Felix, the Latin author, explicates *Guthlac* in characteristic hagiographical fashion:

> ex appellatione illius tribus, quam dicunt Guthlacingas, proprietatis vocabulum velut ex caelesti consilio Guthlac percepit, quia ex qualitatis conpositione adsequentibus meritis conveniebat. Nam ut illius gentis gnari perhibent, Anglorum lingua hoc nomen ex duobus integris constare videtur, hoc est "Guth" et "lac", quod Romani sermonis nitore personat "belli munus", quia ille cum vitiis bellando munera aeternae beatitudinis cum triumphali infula perennis vitae percepisset, secundum apostolum dicentem, etc.[81]

Despite the philological subtlety of Felix's interpretation of Guthlac's name as meaning "reward of battle," it is interesting to note that he does not introduce this detail as an inspiration of his own, but ascribes it to those who are familiar with Guthlac's people. The inference that the meaning of Guthlac's name was a current motif in the legend concerning his life is supported by the frequency with which this motif recurs in the various versions of his biography. The name-explication is carefully preserved in the Old English vernacular prose life adapted from Felix;[82] it is one of the two or three facts about the saint that are mentioned in the brief citation which Guthlac receives in the *Old English Martyrology* (both in the tenth-century and in the eleventh-century redactions);[83] and it survives vigorously in the later Latin accounts of Guthlac's life, such as that of the thirteenth-century chronicle formerly attributed to John of Wallingford.[84] In all probability, the auspicious significance of Guthlac's name was familiar not only to the poet of *Guthlac A*, but also to any Anglo-Saxon who would be likely to attend his poem.

The poet of *Guthlac A* does not reiterate explicitly this traditional comment about the meaning of Guthlac's name, however; rather he reflects his awareness of that name-meaning by several isolated allusions throughout the poem and, if I am not mistaken, he allows the name-meaning to shape the very theme and conception of his narrative to a considerable degree. For it has long been noted that this poet conceives of his saint's trials in curiously warlike terms:

> A militant mind, of a sort, stands behind *Guthlac A* ... A mind that delights in epics of conflict and in the heroic ideal of the fighting

---

[81] *Felix's Life of Saint Guthlac*, ed. Bertram Colgrave (Cambridge, 1956), pp. 76–8.

[82] *Das angelsächsische Prosa-Leben des hl. Guthlac*, ed. Paul Gonser, Anglistische Forschungen, XXVII (Heidelberg, 1909), pp. 106–7.

[83] *An Old English Martyrology*, p. 56.

[84] *The Chronicle Attributed to John of Wallingford*, ed. Richard Vaughan, Camden Miscellany, XXI (London, 1958), pp. 4–5: "Baptizatus autem uocatus est Guthlac, quod nomen sonat belli munis."

champion has converted Guthlac into a mighty man of action, a protagonist ... in the supreme war of the ages ... Guthlac received his reward from his Over-Lord, the Warder of Heaven's realm.[85]

This transformation, it is implied, is what happens when the naive and bellicose Anglo-Saxon mind tries to cope with Christian hagiography.[86] But this martial conception of Guthlac's character is precisely what is suggested by the meaning of the saint's name which keynotes the Latin *Vita* (in the passage quoted above) and which also introduces the saint's life proper in the Old English *Guthlac A*: The events of Guthlac's life are introduced with an allusion to such hermit saints as

> þa gecostan cempan   þa þam cyninge þeowað,
> se næfre þa lean alegeð   þam þe his lufan adreogeð.
>
> (91-2)

This designation of "the proven warrior from whom the king never withholds the reward" is less likely to derive from Germanic bellicosity than from the statement in the *Vita* that Guthlac, as his name suggests, would receive the victor's diadem of eternal life as a reward for fighting against vices.[87] The inspiration for the militant tone of the poem may well be Latin-hagiographical, not Germanic.

References to Guthlac's receiving the reward of eternal life for his struggles against evil recur frequently throughout *Guthlac A*; see, for example, lines 123-4, 171-2, 448-50, 470-1, 778-80, and 784-6, all of which echo the *belli munus* theme. With the promptings of this theme recurring throughout the poem, the connection between the name-meaning "reward of war" and the poet's martial characterization of the saint could hardly have remained obscure to an audience which was already familiar with the saint's legend and its onomastic motif, or indeed to any Anglo-Saxon cognizant of the possible meanings of the name *Guthlac*.[88] The tone and events of the poem validate

---

[85] Benjamin P. Kurtz, "From St Antony to St Guthlac: a study in biography," *University of California Publications in Modern Philology*, XII, 2 (1926), 144-5.

[86] "*Guthlac A* ... is a poetic vision, new and northern, of the saintly anchorite as a greatly performing, never hesitating champion of the Almighty Over-Lord." Anglo-Saxonists in search of the Germanic spirit in early religious poetry often forget the warfaring tone of much early Christian writing. (The frail and pathetic Jesus is generally a late medieval conception which gained currency after the time of St Francis.) Indeed, the Latin *Vita* (for edition, see n. 81 above), is hardly less militant than the Old English poem, if we consider Felix's frequent references to Guthlac as "miles, miles veri Dei, miles Christi, Miles Christi robusta mente," etc. (Colgrave, *Felix's Life*, pp. 74, 90, 96, and *passim*).

[87] "ille cum vitiis bellando munera æternae beatitudinis cum triumphali infula perennis vitae percepisset" (Colgrave, *Felix's Life*, p. 78).

[88] In assuming that Anglo-Saxons were alert to meanings of names *in literature* I am not suggesting that they were equally conscious of the meanings of native Old English names in day-

again and again the hagiographic prophecy latent in the saint's baptismal name. It is well to bear in mind this onomastic theme in the poem when confronting the textual crux in lines 180-4. Removing Krapp and Dobbie's emendation of *Guðlace* to *Guðlaces*, the passage stands,

>   þær se cempa oferwon
> frecnessa fela.   Frome wurdun monge
> godes þrowera;   we þæs Guðlace
> deorwyrðne dæl   dryhtne cennað.
> He him sige sealde.

Modern scholars' perplexity over the word *Guðlace* in line 182 results, I believe, from the fact that they have not recognized that the poet is here indulging in wordplay on the celebrated meaning of Guthlac's name. Actually, one scholar, E. A. Kock, came very close to detecting the onomastic play, but his perception was clouded by his apparent unawareness of the specific name-etymologizing tradition which adhered to the legend of Guthlac. Kock observed,

> The saint, whose very name means "warfare", is in ll. 147-51 [Krapp-Dobbie ll. 176-8] called a *cempa* and an *oretta andwiges heard*, armed with *gæstlicum wæpnum*; he *overwon* [sic] at his *ætstælle* (place of defence) many dangers. The poet, speaking of this warfare, made an intentional or unintentional pun: he even used the word *guðlac*.[89]

It is significant that the context alone was sufficient to alert Kock to the presence of a name-pun here, but if the pun is present, there can be little doubt as to whether it was intentional or not. Considering the meaning of Guthlac's name as it was recorded in the widespread traditions concerning his life, we should probably credit the poet with conscious artistry and see lines 182b-3a as meaning both "we accordingly ascribe his precious lot to *Guthlac* through the Lord" and "we accordingly ascribe his precious lot to *the reward of battle*, to the Lord."[90] The artistic purpose of the pun is not so much its literal meaning (that

---

to-day use. I doubt, for example, that all the name-meanings assigned to Old English names by Rudolf Müller, *Über die Namen des nordhumbrischen Liber Vitae*, Palaestra IX (1901), 138-54, could have been psychologically operative whenever one of the names was used. On the other hand, it should be noted that Gottfried Schramm, *Namenschatsz und Dichtersprache* (Göttingen, 1957), has argued persuasively "daß die zweigliedrigen Personennamen der Germanen aus ihrem engen Zusammenhang mit den formelhaften, traditionellen Mannbezeichnungen der Dichtung heraus verstanden werden müssen" (p. 144).

[89] Kock, "Jubilee jaunts and jottings," *Lunds Universitets Årsskrift*, N. F. Avd. 1. Bd. 14. Nr. 26 (Lund and Leipzig, 1918), p. 41. Kock also suggests here the emendation of *Guthlace* to *Guthlaces* which Krapp and Dobbie adopt in their edition of the poem.

[90] Although the *sige* of l. 184 seems to refer to Felix's *triumphali infula* in the name-etymologizing passage of the Latin *Vita* (see above, n. 87), the Old English poet refers subsequently to divine assistance in this world. This concept of a double reward seems to stem from the Latin passage

the saint's final triumph is the result simultaneously of his own divinely aided efforts and of the explicit "reward of combat" which God had ordained for him), but rather the very name-play itself. The name-play, like the echoing of the "reward of battle" theme throughout the poem, reminds the reader once again that the name *Guthlac* was bestowed as if "ex caelesti consilio" (Felix, chapter X) and that all the marvelous events of this narrative are unfolding just as God in his providence had foreseen and revealed at the saint's baptismal moment.

My suggestion that the name-meaning "reward of battle" functions thematically in *Guthlac A* cannot, of course, be demonstrated by the positivistic kind of evidence that substantiates the operative name-meanings cited earlier in this essay.[91] But the possibility that name-meanings can affect general tone and characterization as well as random epithets in Old English poetry is too important to ignore, and although I have not attempted here a fullblown interpretation of *Guthlac A* (which is ultimately necessary if the thematic energy of the name-meaning in the poem is to be established securely), I believe that my onomastic observations agree in important respects with the interpretation of *Guthlac A* by L. K. Shook. His suggestion that the poem is constructed around the concept of Guthlac's battle for a richly symbolic barrow[92] and his

---

corresponding directly to ll. 174–89 of the poem: "et non solum praesentis saeculi famosa venerantia beavit, sed in gaudio perennis gloriae aeterna beatitudine constituit" (Colgrave, *Felix's Life*, p. 92). I should add that my interpretation of these lines without benefit of emendation agrees, so far as grammar and syntax are concerned, with Father Shook's interpretation in "The burial mound in *Guthlac A*," *MP*, LVIII (1960), 6.

[91] At the same time, it should not be overlooked that saints' legends often undergo radical transformations in response to the etymological meanings of the saints' names. See J. A. Huisman, "Etymologisering van Germaanse heiligennamen als legenden- en cultus-vormende factor," *Mededelingen van de Vereniging voor Naamkunde te Leuven en de Commissie voor Naamkunde te Amsterdam*, XXXIV (1958), 127–37. (Especially interesting to Anglo-Saxonists are Huisman's discussions of South German traditions concerning St Oswald's name [p. 131] and the Dutch cult of St Walburga [pp. 134–5].) Kemp Malone, moreover, has suggested that the characterization of Hygd in *Beowulf* is determined largely by the meaning of her name; see "Hygd," *MLN*, LVI (1941).

[92] Shook, "The burial mound," pp. 2, 10. Father Shook's demonstration of the central importance of the mound or barrow in *Guthlac A* brings to mind another onomastic connection. The name of Guthlac's hermitage, *Crugland* (as Felix renders it), was etymologized by the twelfth-century Odericus Vitalis: "Crulandia enim crudam, id est coenosam terram significat." This attests to an early interest in the etymology of the name, but modern onomastic research suggests that the first element of *Crugland* is cognate with Norwegian *kryl* "a hump" and that the Anglo-Saxon name would therefore have meant "the land of the hump (or mound?)." (See Colgrave, *Felix's Life*, p. 181, for references.) Could this have fostered the poet's inspiration to make the mound a focal image in the structure of his poem? If it is true that the poet's prominent allusions to Guthlac's dwelling as *beorg* reflect his consciousness of the meaning of the name *Crugland*, then it is possible that elsewhere in the poem as well he has subtly translated proper names rather than quoting them directly and that this explains his "somewhat annoying habit of almost never using a personal name" (Shook, "The burial mound," p. 2).

vigorous argument that the prologue is an integral part of the poem[93] accord well with the assumption that the poet is throughout dramatizing Guthlac's fulfillment of the name-prophecy by earning his "reward of battle," and it is striking that the prologue is in large part concerned with the "eternal reward in heaven" (15–16) which awaits the righteous men who "vanquish the cursed spirits and win celestial rest" (25). Indeed, the phrase *ece lean... on heofonum* in lines 15–16 of the prologue could almost be a translation of Felix's explanation of the meaning of Guthlac's name as "munera aeternae beatitudinis" (chapter X).

I shall end this discussion of *Guthlac A* by turning to the closing lines of the poem and pointing to a clear instance of biblical name-etymology there. The presence of this onomastic allusion should add to the probability of the hagiographical onomastics I have been suggesting thus far, and it will also clarify a passage which has not always been rightly understood in the past. *Guthlac A* ends with the assurance that those who have fought against sin and the devil during their lives shall receive their reward when they

> gongað gegnunga   to Hierusalem,
> þær hi to worulde   wynnum motun
> godes onsyne   georne bihealdan,
> sibbe ond gesihðe,   þær heo soð wunað,
> wlitig, wuldorfæst,   ealne widan ferh.
>
> (813–17)

The passage reads straightforwardly except for *sibbe ond gesihðe* "peace and sight" in line 816a, a contextual oddity on which Krapp and Dobbie's notes are silent. The translations bring out the awkwardness of the phrase: R. K. Gordon, following Gollancz, renders lines 814–16 with the slightly ludicrous statement, "They can earnestly look upon God's face in peace with their sight."[94] But the poet is not here explaining that the saints "look ... with their sight." The half-line *sibbe ond gesihðe* stands parallel to, and in apposition with, *Hierusalem* (813), as we should have recognized by the fact that both *Hierusalem* and *sibbe ond gesihðe* are modified by ensuing adverbial clauses introduced by *þær*. *Sibbe ond gesihðe* is an etymologizing interpretation of the name *Hierusalem*, which is explicated in the standard commentaries as a combination of the two words *Jebus et Salem* meaning *visio pacis*.[95] This onomastic commonplace occurs

[93] Shook, "The prologue," pp. 294–304.

[94] *The Exeter Book*, part I, ed. Israel Gollancz, EETS o.s. 104 (1895), p. 155; *Anglo-Saxon Poetry*, selected and translated by R. K. Gordon (London, 1954), p. 269. Charles W. Kennedy, *The Poems of Cynewulf* (London, 1910), p. 287, smooths the translation by rendering the phrase freely as "in peace, in joyful vision."

[95] Jerome, *Epistola XLVI*, *PL*, XXII, 485; *Commentariorum in Ezechielem Liber*, *PL*, XXV, 490; *Commentariorum in Zachariam Liber*, *PL*, XXV, 1513, *Expositio quattuor evangeliorum*, *PL*, XXX, 539; Isidore, *Etymologiae*, XV, i, 5; Cassiodorus, *Expositio in Psalterium*, *PL*, LXX, 473; Gregory, *Homiliarum in Ezechielem*, *PL*, LXXVI, 1048–9, 857, 894, 771; Bede, *Hexaemeron*, *PL*, XCI, 123, 126;

frequently in vernacular Old English texts, both prose and poetry. The Blickling homilist states outright, *þære burge name þe is nemned Gerusalem, is gereht sibbe gesyhþ*, and he even lets the name-meaning stand for the name in the clause *He hie gelædeþ on sibbe gesyhþe*.[96] The poet of *Christ*, line 50, exclaims *Eala sibbe gesihð, sancta Hierusalem!* and Ælfric makes similar use of the etymology.[97] *Guthlac* 816a is clearly a name-etymology, then, and in view of the poet's effortless and subtle use of the device here, we should entertain seriously the prospect of his making conscious use of the name-meaning of *Guthlac* elsewhere in the poem.

Having seen that Anglo-Saxon writers offered studied explications of the vernacular name *Guthlac* and that the Old English poet of *Guthlac A* appears to have utilized onomastic data in his verse history of the saint, we may be encouraged to turn to a more secular poem such as *Beowulf* to inquire whether here too name-etymologizing may not have been among the poet's techniques. In the past a curious attitude toward *Beowulf*ian name-meanings has prevailed. On the one hand, scholars have long suspected that appellations like *Grendel*, *Wealhtheow*, *Herebeald*, and even *Beowulf* itself may have etymological meanings which are relevant to the characters who bear them, but the accumulation of such suspicions has inspired neither confidence nor agreement among *Beowulf* scholars as to what significance, if any, the proper names in the poem are actually intended to have.[98] Usually the question is conceived in terms of mutually exclusive alternatives: either a name is a meaningful fictive name, such as *Unferth* is thought to be, or else it is an inherited element in the story, and hence necessarily meaningless. We can detect the operation of this criterion in past discussions of the character Heremod, who is cited repeatedly in the poem (901–15, 1709–22) as the supreme example of a pugnacious, cruel disposition. Karl Müllenhoff long ago associated the characterization of this figure with the meaning of his name ("kriegerischer Mut"),[99] and it must be conceded that character and name-meaning are remarkably well suited to one

---

Rabanus, *Commentaria in Libros IV Regum*, *PL*, CIX, 82, 141, 142, 299, 327, 423, 424; *De universo*, *PL*, CXI, 90.

[96] *The Blickling Homilies*, ed. R. Morris, EETS o.s. 73 (1880), pp. 79–81.

[97] See n. 24 above.

[98] For etymologies of *Beowulf* and *Grendel* see the convenient summary on pp. xxviii–xxix of *Beowulf and the Fight at Finnsburg*, ed. Fr. Klaeber, 3rd edn with 1st and 2nd supplements (Boston, 1950). For discussions of *Wealhtheow*, see the references in Else von Schaubert's *Glossar*, p. 282, in her edition of *Heyne-Schückings Beowulf* (Paderborn, 1961), and *ES*, XLV (1964), 36–9. Scholars have long noticed that *Hæthcyn* and *Herebeald* contain within them Old English equivalents of the names of the North Germanic gods *Hǫðr* and *Baldr*, whose legendary histories parallel so closely the tragic fate of the Old English princes. On *Beowulf*ian proper names in general, Erik Björkman, *Studien über die Eigennamen im Beowulf* (Halle, 1920), remains standard.

[99] Müllenhoff, *Beovulf: Untersuchungen über das angelsächsische Epos und die älteste Geschichte der germanischen Seevölker* (Berlin, 1889), p. 51.

another. Despite this aptness of the name, however, Klaeber dismisses Müllenhoff's theory with the objection, "But later studies have shown him [Heremod] to be a definite figure in Danish historical-legendary tradition."[100] But is the implied premise valid? Must we exclude the possibility that even unalterable names inherited from tradition can bear pregnant meanings when the poet wishes them to? In view of the foregoing catalogue of instances where Old English writers artfully etymologized both biblical and historical names in their works, I believe we must recognize that in any of their poems Anglo-Saxons may be expected to construct a dramatic situation or shade a character sketch in such a way as to bring alive some poignant etymological meaning in a proper name received from tradition.

Here and there scholars have in the past offered interpretations of Old English names which tend toward the etymologizing spirit which I feel to be so strong in Anglo-Saxon thinking,[101] but by and large such investigation has been conceived in terms of the modern tradition of meaningful fictive names. It is my purpose in the closing pages of this essay to suggest that speculations of the former kind should be considered in the context of the pervasive literary etymologizing which I have already described – that is, that they should be accorded a particularly careful and persuasible audience. I shall not attempt a detailed survey and critique of such speculations. Rather, I shall close with a discussion of one suggestion which I believe deserves a sympathetic hearing, and which, if I am not mistaken, stands to gain even more in persuasiveness by further exploration of the etymologizing aspects of the author's argument.

In an essay entitled "'Hygelac' and 'Hygd'" R. E. Kaske has argued that the name *Hygelac* in *Beowulf* is intended by the poet to carry a name-meaning which functions artistically in the poem, epitomizing the character and role of its bearer.[102] To the modern reader accustomed to fictive naming, nothing could seem more audacious. As every student of *Beowulf* knows, Hygelac is the one firmly documented historical figure in the poem, and his name is historical, not fictional. How, except by outrageous special pleading, could this name be

---

[100] Klaeber, *Beowulf*, pp. 162–3.

[101] Norman E. Eliason's suggestions as to contextual meanings of *Deor* and *Scilling* conform well with the onomastic mode I have described here; see his "Two Old English scop poems," *PMLA*, LXXXI (1966), 189, n. 23, and 191, n. 34. Similarly, Kemp Malone has argued convincingly that Hygd in *Beowulf* "is consistently characterized in terms of her name" and that it was the same habit of mind "which led [the poet] to contrast Hygd with Thryth, whose name means 'strength, might, power, force'." See "Hygd," p. 358. See also his "Royal names in Old English poetry," *Studies in Heroic Legend and in Current Speech*, ed. Stefan Einarsson and Norman E. Eliason (Copenhagen, 1959), pp. 181–8.

[102] Kaske, in *Studies in Old English Literature in Honor of Arthur G. Brodeur*, ed. Stanley B. Greenfield (Eugene, OR, 1963), pp. 200–6. Kaske read the present essay *in toto* and made many helpful comments while it was still in draft. Moreover, when his article appeared in the reprint of the Brodeur Festschrift by Russell and Russell [New York, 1973], he graciously accepted my modification of his argument. See p. 206 of the reprint.

conceived of as an artistically significant one? The answer, of course, is that an Anglo-Saxon would have found it quite natural for a poet to capitalize on the etymological meaning of a historical name. For, if we are to judge by the foregoing accumulation of examples, Kaske has envisaged the onomastic question in just those terms which seem to have been habitual among the Old English writers. The name is dictated by tradition; the poet then searches out a prophetic or ironical significance latent in the etymology of the name and, by means of setting, action, or narrative contrast, draws the readers' attention to the poetically relevant meaning.

At one point, however, I believe Kaske's case can be strengthened by a slight modification of his argument. He notes that the name *Hygelac* is composed of the noun *hyge* "mind, thought" and the second element *lac*, which is generally understood to be the noun *lāc* "play, strife, commotion." He acknowledges (p. 204) that these elements yield a name-meaning "turmoil of mind" which would suit the purposes of his interpretation, but he prefers to analyze the second element differently, assuming it to be an otherwise unattested Old English word *læc meaning "lack." He brings to the defense of this hypothesized form a learned and persuasive argument, and it must be conceded that the resultant name-meaning "lack of thought" is very apposite. But careful weighing of his other alternative -*lāc* persuades me that this is the more probable interpretation.

First, whereas *læc occurs nowhere in our Old English records, the word *lāc* is very common as a second element of Old English compounds and particularly as the second element of compound names – for example, *Cūthlāc*, *Ēalāc*, *Ēadlāc*, *Gūthlāc*, *Hadulāc*, *Ōslāc*.[103] In view of this name-pattern, I suspect that an Anglo-Saxon hearing or reading the name *Hygelac* would inevitably apprehend it as composed of *Hyge* and *lāc*, and the poet would have realized this. Another consideration is the fact that the name of King Hygelac is preserved to us not only in *Beowulf* but also, as Kaske acknowledges, in Frankish, Scandinavian, and other sources where the forms of the name (*Chochilaicus*, *Huiglaucus*, *Hugleikr*, etc.)[104] leave no doubt that the second element of the original name was Germanic *-*laikaz*, Old English -*lāc*. The Scandinavian records, moreover, merit further attention, for they tell us a good deal about Hygelac and his name. (In dealing with vernacular names in secular

[103] *Oslac* occurs in the *Chronicle* poem *The Death of Edgar*, l. 25; *Hadulac* appears in Bede's *Historia ecclesiastica*, V, xxiii; *Guthlac* occurs in the poem so named and elsewhere; the others are cited by Müller (n. 88 above) from the Northumbrian *Liber Vitae*.

[104] For the various sources, see Kemp Malone, "Hygelac," *ES*, XXI (1939), 108–19. R. W. Chambers, *Beowulf: an introduction to the study of the poem*, 3rd edn rev. C. L. Wrenn (Cambridge, 1959), p. 323, is doubtful as to whether the Scandinavian *Hugleikr* is identical with *Hygelac* (although he does not doubt that the two bear the same name); but Malone, in the article just cited, demonstrated convincingly that the two are the same historical figure, and most scholars now accept this view.

heroic narratives the cognate Germanic traditions are, of course, the obvious place to turn for confirming evidence rather than the writings of the commentators and homilists.)

Old Icelandic *Hugleikr* is documented not only as a proper name but also – in a particularly prominent occurrence – as a common word. In the *Völuspá*, stanza 28, *hugleikin* appears with a meaning which has been rendered variously as "sinnverwirrt," "light-hearted," and "a trance."[105] The basic meaning of the word, one would judge, must have been "confused or giddy in thought." The important point here, however, is that any Old Icelandic writer who was intimately familiar with the *Völuspá* would almost certainly have been conscious of the general meaning of the word *hugleikr* when he encountered it as a proper name. And such, indeed, seems to have been the case. Snorri Sturluson, who displays a keen interest in name-meanings throughout the *Ynglingasaga*,[106] appears to maintain his onomastic senstivity when he discusses *Hugleikr* in his twenty-third chapter. The king is depicted as one whose thoughts were ever on play and frivolity instead of on more kingly concerns; and in listing the unworthy objects of Hugleikr's attention, Snorri echoes (in the word *leikara*) the element *-leikr* of his name: "Hann hafði mjǫk í hirð sinni alls konar leikara, harpara ok gígjara ok fiðlara."[107] After this unpromising description of the king, which the implication that his character is little different from his frivolous name, the ensuing account of Hugleikr's defeat and death comes as no surprise, for his adversaries are described as shrewd and powerful champions. In the *Gesta Danorum* Saxo Grammaticus tells the same story. Hugleikr (*Huglecus, Hugletus* in Saxo) is an unserious, hapless leader who "circa mimos ac ioculatores munificencie studiis uti consueuit."[108] When the fateful battle begins, Hugleikr's host is described as "mimorum greges" in whom "instabilitatem

---

[105] Bernhard Kummer, *Die Lieder des Codex Regius (Edda) und verwandte Denkmäler* (Zeven, 1961), vol. I, pp. 1, 84, suggests as the meaning of *hugleikin(n)* "sinnverwirrt, ekstatisch, mit Eifer, mit Leidenschaft." Olive Bray, in her popular edition *The Elder or Poetic Edda* (London, 1908), p. 285, translates it "light-hearted." Sigurður Nordal, *Völuspá* (Reykjavik, 1952), p. 81, suggests that in its application to the witch in *Völuspá*, 28: 3 the word means "*leiðsla* (trance)." *Hugleikin* is not to be found in most dictionaries, for most earlier editions of the *Völuspá* suppressed the word, either by giving precedence to the reading *hon leikinn* or by changing the MS. division of the word to *hug leikin*. But see the arguments of Nordal, p. 81, and Kummer, p. 84. Cf. also the neuter adjective *hugleikit*, which occurs in *Göngu-Hrólfs saga*, chapter XI, as well as in later Icelandic, though with a narrowed meaning.

[106] In the chapters preceding his account of *Hugleikr* Snorri deals explicitly with the meaning or derivation of *Gerseme, Hnoss, Odin, Thor, Æsir*, etc., and he alludes more indirectly to the meanings of *Durnir, Gramer*, and *Skjotan*.

[107] *Heimskringla I*, ed. Bjarni Aðalbjarnarson (Reykjavik, 1941), p. 42. I am not the first to detect that the characterization of Hugleikr both here and in Saxo's account agrees with the meaning of his name. Hermann, Chadwick, Malone, and others have all mentioned it. For references see Malone, "Hygelac," 108–19 *passim*.

[108] *Saxonis Grammatici Gesta Danorum*, ed. Alfred Holder (Straßbourg, 1886), p. 186.

corporum leuitas peperit animorum." In consequence of this *leuitas animorum* – a phrase composed of precise lexical equivalents of the name *Hugleikr* – the host is swiftly defeated. These details and phrases from the accounts of Snorri and Saxo suggest strongly that there was among the Scandinavian writers a conscious awareness of the meaning of Hygelac's name and its appropriateness to the king's unstable or frivolous disposition. And this meaning, as they conceived it, was clearly based upon the two elements' being *hyge* (Old Norse *hugr*) and *lāc* (Old Norse *leikr*). There is good reason to believe, then, that if *Hygelac* is a meaningful name in *Beowulf* its meaning will be roughly that which the name *Hugleikr* bears in Snorri and Saxo.[109]

Since Old English *lāc* had a broad range of meanings, it is not easy to sum up in a single modern English equivalent the precise sense which the word-element had for the *Beowulf* poet, especially when common nouns often underwent a certain amount of idiosyncratic semantic adaptation when they passed into proper names.[110] Nor can we turn to the parallel example *Guthlac*, assuming that the element *-lāc* in *Hygelac* will necessarily carry the same meaning as it does in the saint's name discussed at length above. For it has long been noticed by scholars that the Anglo-Saxons' celebrated interpretation of Guthlac's name imparted to the element *-lāc* a rather unusual meaning, presumably in order to bring out the moralizing point which the hagiographers sought to make.[111] What we can do, however, is observe elsewhere in Old English occurrences of *-lāc* and *hyge* which seem appropriately suggestive and work from these toward an interpretation of *Hygelac*. Two points seem relevant. First, the noun *lāc* frequently appears as the second element of compounds with a pejorative connotation: *hæmedlāc* "fornication," *lyblāc* "sorcery," *scinnlāc* "frenzy," *wīflāc* "fornication," *wrothlāc* "calumny." Second, *hyge* often combines (as first element) with a pejorative second element to form an abstract noun or adjective denoting an unwholesome state of mind: *hygegāl* "loose, wanton," *hygegælsa* "wantoness, pride," *hygelēast* "folly," *hygeðryð* "insolence, pride." (Cf. also the pejorative sense in Old English *lācan* and *gelācan* which, like Old Icelandic *leika*, meant "to delude, trick.") These patterns of word-formation suggest that *lāc* as a second compound-element often had a meaning

---

[109] I do not suggest that the precise nature of Hygelac's inadequacies are identical in *Beowulf* and in the Scandinavian traditions. In the latter he is bent on frivolity and inclined toward niggardliness – serious errors of judgment, to be sure, in a northern prince – while in *Beowulf* we know only that excessive pride misled the king into a disastrous attack on his neighbors. Intellectual unreliability is the fatal flaw in both cases, but the details differ.

[110] Hilmer Ström, *Old English Personal Names in Bede's History*, Lund Studies in English, VIII (1939), p. 44, remarks pertinently, "As will be seen from some of the instances below, it is not self-evident that a word should have the same meaning when it appears in a name as when it appears independently." On the various senses of the name-element *-lāc*, see Ström's data on p. 48.

[111] See the discussion by W. F. Bolton, "The background and meaning of Guthlac," *JEGP*, LXI (1962), 595–603.

which was a fusion of the senses "play" and "strife" (both of which are commonly attested for the simplex *lāc*) and that in combination with *hyge* the word might mean "frivolity" or "perturbation." Considering these possibilities in the light of the meaning which *Hugleikr* seems to have had in Scandinavian tradition, we might venture the interpretation "instability of mind" as the meaning of *Hygelac* in *Beowulf*; and if this rendering is approximately right, we have a name-meaning which is open to all the contextual subtleties which Kaske has so skillfully discerned in his analysis of the contrasting names *Hygelac* and *Hygd*.

But aside from the philological details in the way of interpreting Hygelac's name, the major point here is that the basic notion that the poet may be eliciting an artistically relevant meaning from a historical name is in itself a well-conceived one; despite the paradox it suggests to the modern critical mind, this interpretation accords well with the onomastic thinking of other Old English poets in other Old English poems, and therefore we should perhaps be encouraged to seek similar modes of relevance in the meanings of other *Beowulf*ian names, unperturbed by the possibility that any or all of the proper names in the poem may someday prove to be not creations of the poet but legacies from historical-legendary tradition.

III

In bringing this inquiry into Old English literary names to a close, I should like to emphasize once more the good prospects which further study along these lines offers. There are many other puzzling passages in Old English scriptural and hagiographic poetry which await solution by the literary student who is informed about the ways of medieval onomastics; and in those areas where this essay has worked in a more tentative and exploratory manner, such as in secular, vernacular name-etymologizing and in the poets' amplification of name-meanings through broader devices of characterization and action, I am convinced that much remains to be discovered. Far too much attention was accorded to onomastics by the Anglo-Saxons for the poetic results to be limited to an occasional adventitious subtlety or a random epithet. But in approaching all these questions, it seems above all important that we bear in mind the essential difference between the literary onomastics of the Anglo-Saxons and that of our own writers today. Their precedents then were the sacral etymologies of the Bible, the commentaries of the Fathers, the exuberant interpretations of Isidore and the Irish writings, all of which encouraged a learned searching out of etymological significance in names received from tradition. Our own precedents, by contrast, are the explicit, moralizing names of late medieval drama and the comic sobriquets of Congreve or Dickens. On the whole, their tradition was subtle, learned, and artful, while ours tends to be spontaneous and obvious. We must study to understand and appreciate these distinctions before we can fully reclaim this important aspect of the Anglo-Saxon aesthetic mode.

17
Personal Names in Medieval Narrative and the Name of Unferth in *Beowulf*

Skillful story-tellers have always been sensitive to the potential expressiveness of the names they fashion for the characters they create. From Shakespeare's Mistress Quickly to Nabokov's Hazel Shade, the names which authors devise more often than not reveal something about the people who bear them. This was no less true in the Middle Ages when, in fact, writers gave more attention to the appropriateness of personal names than many do now. Partly this was due to the profound importance during the Middle Ages of the Bible, in which the mystical significance of people's names is repeatedly emphasized (". . . and thou shalt call his name Ishmael ['the Lord hears'] because the Lord has heard thy affliction"), but it was reinforced by the Church Fathers' preoccupation with scriptural names, by the zealous onomastics of polymaths like Isidore of Seville and Rhabanus Maurus, and by a natural interest in names for their own sake – an interest reflected in a host of oft-repeated Latin phrases like *bonum nomen, bonum omen* ("a good name is a good omen"), *sine nomine persona non est* ("without a name the person does not exist"), and Dante's *nomina sunt consequentia rerum* ("names are the consequence of things").

Sometimes the medieval naming practices were direct and simple, as when Wolfram von Eschenbach names the tragically grieved mother of his hero in *Parzival* with the highly apposite Herzeloyde ("heart's sorrow"). Almost as obvious is Chaucer's designation of his mismatched pair of lovers January and May, *January* characterizing the aged husband in his wintry decline and *May* his nubile prize. But Chaucer's appropriateness of name is elsewhere more subtle. The carpenter named Oswald is simply a case of onomastic verisimilitude, the northern English character being aptly provided with a name made famous by two Northumbrian saints of the Anglo-Saxon period.

A special love of medieval writers was tracing the linguistic origins of proper names, and they were not primarily concerned about the scientific accuracy of their speculations so long as the etymologies they conceived were in some way appropriate to the characters who bore the names. Gottfried von Strassburg's explanation of the name of his hero Tristan is typical: "His name came from

Reprinted from *Essays in Honor of Richebourg Gaillard McWilliams*, ed. Howard Creed (Birmingham, AL, 1970), pp. 43–8.

'triste' [the French word for 'sad']. The name was well suited to him and in every way appropriate.... See what a sorrowful life he was given to live.... He was the man that his name said he was, and his name of Tristan said what he was." The exquisite aptness of this fantastic etymology overrode any scruples Gottfried may have had about its manifest implausibility. The same is true of the preposterous etymologizing of the place-name *Eiterhof* in the *Liber de sancto Emmerammo* of Arnoldus. After soberly recording that the name was generally held to mean "courtyard of poison," Arnoldus expresses dissatisfaction with this interpretation, which, though linguistically sound, does not serve his literary purpose. Therefore he proceeds to relate the first half of the name to Latin *aetheris* and the second half to German *Hoffen*, thereby producing the sense "hope of heaven," which, for all its absurdity, provides Arnoldus with the starting point for a brief moral homily. (A similar habit of mind may be seen later in the Renaissance, when writers distorted Machiavelli's name to *Machevill* so as to provide an opportunity for the implicit pun "Make-evil.") The habit of finding significance in names became second nature to medieval writers, as one can detect by giving attention to their ways with proper names in casual moments. The Anglo-Saxon scribe who produced the Cambridge copy of the fifth *Vercelli Homily*, for example, writes *Syrige* for the place-name *Syria*. This is not mere scribal bumbling. Old English *-ige* means "island," and the scribe was here reflecting the fact that medieval scholars explained the place-name *Syria* as meaning "watery," and, indeed, in classical writings Syria is misrepresented sometimes as an island. The scribal *Syrige* is a noteworthy example of how an awareness of medieval name-lore can be of utility even in such an apparently remote discipline as text-editing, for if an editor were ignorant of the medieval conception of the name, he would very likely emend it out of his text or else explain it as a phonological oddity.

It is especially important, however, that the medieval preoccupation with name-meanings be kept in mind when interpreting or criticizing the literary monuments of the period. In the Anglo-Saxon poem *Beowulf*, which is my main concern here, there is ample evidence that significant names are at work. The name *Beowulf* itself seems to be a poetic appellation for a bear, and in battle the hero repeatedly shows bear-like qualities, as when he crushes his foe in a powerful grip. The wise and prudent queen of his people is named Hygd, which means "thought," while her reckless, impulsive husband is called Hygelac, which, it has been suggested, means "frivolity or instability of mind." The two ferocious warriors who kill King Ongentheow are called Wulf and Eofor, which mean, respectively, "wolf" and "boar," while the father from whom they are sprung is named "unreason" (*Wonred*) – all names which typify the brutal violence which encompasses the central action of the poem.

Attention to name-meanings can be of assistance in solving at least one of the problems of interpretation which beset this poem. A particularly vexing puzzle in *Beowulf* is the curious interlude involving the character called Unferth. When young Beowulf is received at the court of King Hrothgar the Dane, whither he has come to offer his services against the monstrous enemy plaguing his hosts, the courtesy of his reception is suddenly jarred by the insulting behavior of Unferth. With no reasonable motivation,[1] this member of Hrothgar's court ridicules Beowulf's past exploits, calls him foolish and overconfident, and predicts a humiliating outcome to his adventures in Denmark. Beowulf answers with corresponding bluntness, the other courtiers laugh, and the reception proceeds as if nothing improper had happened. The curious thing in all this is that no one reprimands Unferth for his gross breach of hospitality, and not even Beowulf seems surprised by it. We are left wondering whether Unferth enjoyed some special status which entitled him to such license of manner.

It is difficult, however, to determine Unferth's status, for we are told little more about him than that he was a *thyle*, and there is uncertainty as to what a *thyle* is. Most commonly, critics have turned to Unferth's name for some hint as to his function in the poem, and they have inferred thereby an answer to the problem, though not a wholly satisfactory one. The first element of the name, they rightly observe, is the negative prefix *un-* meaning, as in modern English, "not" or "non-."[2] The second element of his name, *-ferth* is similar to the word *frith* "peace" and, assuming some distortion in the form of the word each time it is recorded in the poem, this would give us a name meaning "non-peace" or "discord." From this it has been widely assumed that Unferth is an evil schemer in the Danish court, an almost allegorical figure of enmity plotting sedition against lord and kin. But if this is so, then all the more reason for the Danes (and Beowulf) to react with vocal indignation at the plotter's rude hostility. Moreover, Unferth is portrayed in the poem as a cowardly figure, and it is odd that such a person should, in a heroic society, be presented as an outspoken and serious threat to the Danish dynasty.

In the past few years a contrary interpretation of Unferth has begun to

---

[1] The poet's statement that Unferth could not grant that any other man should pay heed to glorious deeds any more than did Unferth himself (503–5) is not so much a motivation as a characterization of the speaker. Since Unferth is portrayed as a craven subsequently, and hence has no liking at all for deeds of valor, the poet's statement in these lines reveals in the garrulous Dane an absurdly unheroic Falstaffian attitude toward heroism. This implication (which is the first evidence for Unferth's being the kind of character I shall subsequently suggest he is) is pointed up by the verb *gehedde* "should pay heed to, should care for" which I have translated as it stands in the manuscript. (Earlier scholars have consistently altered the word to *gehede* "achieve," which obscures the poet's intention, I believe.)

[2] Actually, the manuscript reads Hunferth, the inorganic *h* being a scribal habit borrowed from the Celts, who indicate that a *u* has vocalic rather than consonantal function by prefixing a merely graphic *h*. The alliterative rules of the poem show conclusively that the *h* is to be disregarded in reading the name, and editors have rightly deleted it in modern editions.

emerge, one which promises, it seems to me, a resolution to the problems his character presents. Renewed scrutiny of the word *thyle*, which is the name of his office at the court, has revealed that a prevailing meaning of this word was "scurrilous jester" or "entertainer." (Previously scholars had thought the word must mean "orator," "court spokesman" or "sage.") This suggests a quite different interpretation of Unferth's role in the poem – an essentially comic one.[3] And if Unferth was a humorous figure, an entertainer whom no one took seriously, then it is not surprising that Beowulf would take no offense at his railing or that the Danes would tolerate good-naturedly a jackanapes whose function was to provide a kind of rough comedy in the court.

One obstacle, however, would seem to stand in the way of this humorous interpretation of Unferth. If his name means "non-peace" or "discord," then it is hard to believe that the poet, with his sensitivity to name-meanings, would assign such a designation to a court jester. Rather than implying that Unferth is a quasi-allegorical figure of enmity, the poet would surely have chosen a name which would give some hint of the character's ridiculousness.

It will be recalled that in presenting the traditional interpretation of *Unferth* I mentioned that the name as it stands in the manuscript does not actually mean "discord." In order to arrive at this meaning we must assume that the intended word *Unfrith* "discord" has undergone distortion to *Unferth* each of the four times that it is recorded in the poem. It would seem well to ask, then, just what the name would mean if taken at face value without assuming distortion. The answer is that it would mean "nonsense" or "folly," for *ferth* (also spelled *ferhth*) means "mind," "intellect," and the negative prefix *un-* would alter the meaning to something like "unintelligence" or "folly." One should compare the numerous other instances in Old English where a word for "mind" or "intelligence" is subjoined to the negative *un-* with similar result: *ungemynd* "madness," *ungerad* "folly," *ungewitnes* "folly," *unraed* "folly." Compare Old English *leasferhð* "levity, folly." This straightforward meaning of the recorded form *Unferth* fits precisely the character of Unferth as recent scholarship, working from other evidence, has begun to conceive it. There is, moreover, further evidence in the text of the poem to support this interpretation. In his retort to Unferth, Beowulf makes repeated ironical reference to the intelligence of his bumptious antagonist, first suggesting that he is drunk (531) and then alluding pointedly to his *wit*, *hige*, and *sefa* (590–4), all words for "intelligence." In one passage, line 1166, there seems to be word-play on the element *ferth* in his name.

A character such as I am assuming Unferth to be is not without precedent in the literature of the time. The railing of the all-licensed Loki in the Norse

---

[3] See, for example, Heinz Reinhold's *Humoristische Tendenzen in der englischen Dichtung des Mittelalters* (Tubingen, 1953), p. 48, and the brilliant and provocative study by Norman E. Eliason, "The *thyle* and *scop* in *Beowulf*," *Speculum*, 38 (1963), 267–84.

poem *Lokasenna* comes to mind, and the character Hott in the *Hrolfs Saga Kraka* (a later Norse analogue of *Beowulf*) shares several features with the buffoonish Unferth, just as the hero Boðvar Bjarki does with Beowulf. But most striking, I think, is a parallel from a quite different kind of writing by an Anglo-Saxon contemporary of the *Beowulf* poet. Bede, in his Latin commentary on Acts, alludes to the episode in Acts 20 where St Paul had journeyed to Troas and was addressing a group there. Suddenly, one young man in his audience dozes off and, losing his balance, slips from a third-story window and falls to the ground below, causing a great commotion. Bede pauses to remark that the sleepy fellow who caused this disruption is named *Eutychus* in the Bible, a name, says Bede, which carries the meaning "nonsense" or "folly." I am not suggesting a biblical source for the character Unferth, of course, but it is reassuring to find precedent among Anglo-Saxon writings for a bumptious character bearing a name which means "nonsense."

The assumption of a comic Unferth may not solve every problem in this perplexing episode, and some may feel that the interpretation itself is still not conclusively proven. But it is remarkable that a fresh consideration of the import of Unferth's name should yield results that coincide so precisely with the direction which literary criticism has been taking, and, as the examples listed earlier have suggested, interplay of name and narrative is a typical feature of medieval literature. In this period, as in many others, historical onomastics can on occasion serve the turn of literary criticism, and the possible interdependence of these seemingly remote disciplines are not yet sufficiently appreciated.[4]

[4] This and other studies on this subject should be re-examined in the light of Carol Clover, "The Germanic context of the Unferþ episode," *Speculum*, 55 (1980), 444–68.

18

Anglo-Saxon Onomastics in the Old English *Andreas*

"A characteristically Anglo-Saxon onomastic interpretation" – thus one editor of the *Life of St Ethelwold* describes Wulfstan's etymology of the name of his saint, "Adeluuoldus ... , nomine, mente et opere beniuolus."[1] The annotation is just, and it indicates scholars' growing awareness of a pervasive onomastic strain in much Anglo-Saxon writing,[2] a tradition which frequently combines fact with fanciful speculation about the origin of names. (Old English *æðel-* does mean "noble, excellent" as Wulfstan assumes, but *-wold* has nothing to do with the verb *wolde* "wished.") Yet, despite this increasing attention to the Anglo-Saxons' interest in names,[3] there remains in the literature of the period a number of literary problems which ought to be re-examined in the light of medieval onomastics. One such problem is a textual puzzle in the Old English treatments of the St Andrew legend, which I propose to treat here.

At a dramatic moment in the poem *Andreas* the saint rounds on the Devil, who has arisen to accuse him, addressing him in these words:

Reprinted from *Names*, 21 (1972), 133–6.

[1] *Three Lives of English Saints*, ed. Michael Winterbottom, Toronto Medieval Texts, ed. A. G. Rigg (Toronto, 1972), p. 38.

[2] I try to suggest the range and importance of this habit of mind in "The significance of names in Old English literature," pp. 185–218 above, and "Some uses of name-meanings in Old English poetry," pp. 228–35 below. Before the publication of these two essays, Kemp Malone had published several brilliant studies dealing with individual names such as Hygd, Hrethric, Hrunting, and Unferth; for exact titles see the Malone bibliographies cited and supplemented by Thomas Pyles in *Language*, 48 (1972), 503–5. See also Malone's Presidential Address to the American Name Society, "Meaningful fictive names in English literature," published in *Names*, 5 (March, 1957), 1–13.

[3] John Golden has detected "An onomastic allusion in Cædmon's 'Hymn'," *NM*, 70 (1969), 627–9, and Roberta Frank reveals onomastic effects in the poets' handling of biblical names: see her fine study of "Paronomasia in Old English scriptural verse," *Speculum*, 47 (1972), esp. pp. 216–18. T. D. Hill skillfully integrates onomastics with a typological reading of *Elene* in "Sapiential structure and figural narrative in the Old English 'Elene'," *Traditio*, 27 (1971), 159–777. In *Elene*, however, it is probably *Zachaeus* ("justificatus") which is the relevant name rather than *Zacharias* ("memoria Domini").

                      Hwæt, ðu deofles stræl,
icest þine yrmðo!

(1189–90)[4]

"Lo, thou devil's dart, thou increasest thy misery!" The prose homily on St Andrew reads similarly, *Ana þu heardeste stræl to æghwilcre unrihtnesse*.[5] In the Greek source which ultimately lies behind these early English versions the devil whom the Anglo-Saxon writers call *stræl* "dart, arrow" is named by his name: "Ω Βελία ἐχθρότατε" "Oh Belial most inimical"[6] and then a comment is added concerning the meaning of a byname of Belial: "πρὸς τί οὖν ἐπικέκλησαι Ἀμαήλ; οὐχ ὅτι τυφλὸς εἶ, μὴ βλέπων πάντας τοὺς ἁλίους"; "Why then art thou called Amael [v. l. Samael]? Is it not because thou art blind and dost not see all the saints?"[7] This subsequent comment is absent from the English versions.

There is then a double discrepancy between the Greek version and the Anglo-Saxon versions of this passage: the latter omit the name-interpretation of the source and they substitute the Old English word *stræl* for the name of Belial. Editors of the English texts have passed over the omission without comment but have struggled hard to explain the odd use of *stræl*. Zupitza suggested that there had been an intervening mistranslation of the Greek text in the Latin intermediary presumed to have been used by the Anglo-Saxons, and Brooks adds that "*deofles stræl* here [in the poem], and possible *stræl* alone in the OE prose, may perhaps signify one who serves, armed with darts, in Satan's host."[8] Possibly so, but it should be noted that in the Old English poem the association of Belial with the dart is echoed later in another deviation from the extant sources. Whereas the Greek version and the twelfth-century Latin version printed in Blatt simply say that the demons voice the intention of killing Andreas,[9] the Old English poet adds a speech for the devil in which he says,

                        Lætað gares ord
earh attre gemæl, in gedufan
in fæges ferð ... !

(1330–2)

[4] *Andreas and the Fates of the Apostles*, ed. Kenneth R. Brooks (Oxford, 1961), p. 38.
[5] *The Blickling Homilies of the Tenth Century*, ed. R. Morris, EETS o.s. 58 (London, 1880), p. 241.
[6] Quoted here from Franz Blatt's printing of the text in *Die lateinischen Bearbeitungen der Acta Andreae et Matthiae apud anthropophagos* (Giessen and Copenhagen, 1930), p. 78. This entire section of the narrative is missing from the twelfth-century Latin version, the longer and earlier of the Latin versions published in this volume.
[7] For the variant Σαμαήλ (for *Sammael*) see *Acta Apostolorum apocrypha*, ed. Constantinus Tischendorf (Lipsiae, 1851), p. 157.
[8] Brooks, *Andreas*, p. 104.
[9] Blatt, *Die lateinischen Bearbeitungen*, pp. 80–1.

This specification of *gar*, *earh* as the weapon to be used against the saint may argue for some deliberateness in the earlier allusion to Belial as *stræl*.

Rather than being a mechanically retained translational blunder, this repeated association of darts with Belial is, I believe, a "characteristically Anglo-Saxon onomastic interpretation" which the English poet, along with his prose counterpart, has adopted in lieu of the name interpretation in the source. I suspect that he consciously and deliberately associated the name *Belial* with Greek "βέλος" "dart."[10] This is not a sanctioned etymology of the name, to be sure; there was in fact a bewildering number of meanings for *Belial* in circulation during the Anglo-Saxon period: *pestilens*,[11] *absque jugo*,[12] *filius prævaricationis, apostata, caeca angustia, caecum lumen*.[13] The last two of these would appear to have been the meanings known to the author of the Greek version, who speaks enigmatically of the byname of Belial meaning "blind." The Anglo-Saxon translators discarded this interpretation, possibly because of some uncertainty about the name *Amael*, which in one manuscript appears as *Samael*.[14] Drawing on Greek rather than Hebrew similarities,[15] they substituted the fanciful interpretation *Belial : bélos*, which has an Isidorian plausibility and which, indeed, is no more fanciful than Wulfstan's rendering of *-wold* in

---

[10] I am not the first to cite the obvious similarity between the proper name and Greek *belos*; this similarity was the basis of Zupitza's theory of a mistranslation in turning the Greek text into Latin (see Brooks, *Andreas*, p. 104). The novelty of my own explanation is my assumption that identification of Βελία and βέλος was a deliberate onomastic interpretation contrived by the Old English poet or a predecessor. For an Old English poet this interpretation would have been encouraged, perhaps, by the Anglo-Saxons' conventional association of arrows with devils: see *Die Vercelli-Homilien*, ed. Max Förster (Hamburg, 1932), pp. 103–5, and *Beowulf*, 1742–7.

[11] See *The Harley Latin–Old English Glossary*, ed. Robert T. Oliphant (The Hague, 1964), p. 27: *Belial .i. pestilens*. The same rendering occurs in the Old English Corpus Glossary as well as others. See *Corpus Glossariorum Latinorum*, ed. G. Goetz (Leipzig, 1894), vol. 5, p. 348, l. 11, and p. 402, l. 36. Cf. also Jerome's commentary on Ephesians (*PL*, 26, col. 511), where, following the explication of *Belial*, it is explained how the devil hurls darts before entering a sinner.

[12] Bede, *Com. in I Samuhelem*, CCL, 119, p. 18.

[13] Jerome, *Liber interpretationis Hebraicorum nominum*, CCL, 72, p. 154, and *Com. in Naum Prophetam*, CCL, 76, p. 540; Bede, *Com. in I Samuhelem*, p. 26. Modern Hebraists agree with none of these, seeing the name as meaning "without use, uselessness." A general term of scorn in the Old Testament, *Belial* came to be synonymous with Satan (cf. *Andreas*, 1193) in the intertestamental period and after.

[14] See n. 7 above. Of course, since the exact form, and even the language, of the Anglo-Saxons' source-text is unknown, definite conclusions concerning their deviations from the transmitted narrative cannot be drawn.

[15] It is not uncommon for medieval etymologists to extract multiple meanings based on more than one language when explicating names. I cite one such instance (from Arnoldus' *Liber de sancto Emmerammo*) in "Personal names in medieval narrative and the name of Unferth in *Beowulf*," p. 220 above; for extended discussion of such macaronic interpretations see Roswitha Klinck, *Die lateinische Etymologie des Mittelalters* (Munich, 1970), pp. 62–5.

Ethelwold or Gregory's famous onomancy practiced on the names *Angles, Deira,* and *Aelle*.

Onomastic embellishment of this kind is not uncommon in either Old English prose or poetry. The anonymous Old English prose version of "The Avenging of the Savior," contrary to the account in the surviving Latin source, contains a name-change introduced to celebrate the conversion of a Roman prefect, and the significance of the adopted name is spelled out: *and hyne genemde on þam fulluhte Tytus, þæt ys on ure geðeode arfæst.*[16] T. M. Pearce has called attention to a number of onomastic embellishments in Ælfric, and a further instance is discernible, I believe, in the "Martyrdom of St Vincent,"[17] where the subtle reversal of the roles of Vincent, the triumphant victim, and Datianus, the vanquished persecutor, seems foreshadowed onomastically in the associations *Vincentius : vincere* ("conquer") and *Datianus : datio* ("giving up, surrender").[18] In the poem *Andreas* itself there are, in addition to the passage under discussion here, several hints of onomastic play. I have elsewhere suggested that the poet alludes to the etymologies of *Andrew* and *Israel*,[19] and it seems possible that the phrases *beorhte blican* affixed to *Mambre* (788–9) and *eadig oretta* affixed to *Dauid* (878–9) may reflect the etymological interpretations *Mambre : perspicuus*[20] and *Dauid : fortis manu, utique quia fortissimus in proelis fuit*.[21] Seen within the context of this name-play in the poem and of Anglo-Saxon literary onomastics at large, the *deofles stræl* of line 1189 of *Andreas* ceases to look like a textual blemish and assumes the character of other onomastic effects in the poet-translator's total design.

[16] *Angelsächsische Homilien und Heiligenleben,* ed. Bruno Assmann, BasPr., vol. 3, p. 184. The name-interpretation is drawn, no doubt, from some such source as Isidore, who, in *Etymologiae*, V, xxxix, 28, glosses *Titus* with *Hic facundus et pius* [= Ole English *arfæst*] *fuit*.

[17] *Ælfric's Lives of Saints,* ed. Walter W. Skeat, EETS o.s. 114 (London, 1900), pp. 426–43. For Pearce's essay, see "Name patterns in Ælfric's *Catholic Homilies*," *Names*, 14 (September, 1966), 150–6.

[18] Few will doubt that the meaning of *Vincentius* was apparent to Ælfric. Augustine puns on the name (see *Mnemosyne*, 3 [1935–6], ser. 3, p. 39) and Prudentius's fifth hymn in the *Peristephanon* contains numerous plays on the meaning *vincere*. In the Old English account the verb *oferswiðan* (which regularly renders Latin *vincere* in glosses and translations) occurs ten times, usually in reference to Vincent. The association of *Datianus* with *datio* is more speculative, but I believe it is reasonable in context.

[19] "Some uses of name-meanings," pp. 228–35 below.

[20] Jerome, *Liber interpretationis Hebraicorum nominum*, CCL, 72, p. 69.

[21] Isidore, *Etymologiae*, VII, vi, 64–6; Rabanus, *De universo, PL*, 111, col. 58.

19
Some Uses of Name-Meanings in Old English Poetry

I

It has long been recognized that Anglo-Saxons, like other medieval writers, occasionally embellish their narratives with learned allusions to the etymological meanings of proper names, a literary practice encouraged by the pervasive onomastic strain in the Biblical commentaries which lay behind so much of their religious thought. Ælfric constantly etymologizes names in his *Catholic Homilies*,[1] and Old English poets have been noted in a few instances to versify patristic etymologies. *Christ*, 50, for example, reflects the commonplace interpretation of *Jerusalem* (*visio pacis*) so popular among Old English writers:[2]

> Eala sibbe gesihð,   sancta Hierusalem

And in the same poem, lines 130–5, the biblical explication of *Emmanuel* as *nobiscum Deus* (Matthew 1: 14) is presented rather more elaborately:

> Eala gæsta god,   hu þu gleawlice
> mid noman ryhte   nemned wære
> Emmanuhel,   swa hit engel gecwæð
> ærest on Ebresc!   þæt is eft gereht,
> rume bi gerynum: "Nu is rodera weard,
> god sylfa mid us."

Reprinted from *Neuphilologische Mitteilungen*, 69 (1968), 161–71.

[1] See Hanspeter Schelp, "Die Deutungstradition in Ælfrics Homiliae Catholicae," *Archiv*, CXCVI (1960), 289–92, and T. M. Pearce, "Name patterns in Ælfric's *Catholic Homilies*," *Names*, XIV (1966), 150–6.

[2] For Latin interpretations see, for example, Jerome, *Epistola XLVI*, *PL*, XXII, 485; *Commentarius in Ezechielem Liber*, *PL*, XXV, 490; Bede, *Hexaemeron*, *PL*, XCI, 123, 126. For vernacular Old English allusions to this name-interpretation, see *The Blickling Homilies*, ed. R. Morris, EETS o.s. 73 (London, 1880), pp. 79–81; Ælfric, *Catholic Homilies*, ed. B. Thorpe (London, 1844–6), vol. I, p. 210, vol. II, p. 66, and the poem *Guthlac*, l. 816.

Again, the meaning of *Lucifer*, which Ælfric cites in his *Letter to Sigeward*,³ is poeticized in *Christ and Satan*, 365-6:

> Wæs þæt encgelcyn ær genemned,
> Lucifer haten, leohtberende.

Despite our general awareness of such instances as these,⁴ modern scholars have not, I believe, sufficiently investigated the extent to which the name-etymologizing habit is present in Old English poetry. I have elsewhere sketched out the sources and trends of Anglo-Saxon onomastic thought;⁵ in the present essay I wish to indicate a few difficult passages in Old English writings which require, I believe, for their full understanding a heightened awareness of the force and subtlety of the onomastic mode familiar to the Anglo-Saxons.

II

After St Andrew, in the Old English poem *Andreas*, has visited multiple disasters upon the heathen Mermedonians, they acknowledge at last that they must obey the holy man:

> Is nu þearf mycel
> þæt we gumcystum georne hyran.
> (1605-6)

The striking feature here is that the Mermedonians are said to pledge their obedience not to *Andreas*, but to *gumcystum* "manly virtues." Editors have coped in various ways with this curious use of an abstract noun to designate the saint. Krapp cites favorably the emendation of B. S. Monroe,⁶ who would alter to *gumcystgum* "The excellent (man)."⁷ But in his edition of the poem Krapp retains the form *gumcystum*, translating it as an adverb (whence the dictionaries enter an adverbial function of the word), although he concedes that "no other example of the adverbial use of *gumcystum* is recorded."⁸ Kenneth R. Brooks, in

---

³ *Angelsächsische Homilien und Heiligenleben*, ed. Bruno Assmann, BasPr., III (rpt Darmstadt, 1964), p. 81.
⁴ Others have been pointed out by A. S. Cook, *The Old English Elene, Phoenix, and Physiologus* (New Haven, 1919), p. 95, who notes that *æ hælendes* in *Elene* 1062 is a translation of the foregoing name *Cyriacus*, and Israel Gollancz, in his preface to the facsimile of *The Caedmon Manuscript* (Oxford, 1927), who suggests that the poems in that codex frequently reflect an awareness of patristic name-etymologies; see, for example, pp. xliv, xlv, lxv, lxvi, lxxvii-lxxviii, lxxxiii, and civ.
⁵ In "The significance of names in Old English literature," pp. 185-218 above.
⁶ Monroe, "Notes on the Anglo-Saxon *Andreas*," *MLN*, XXXI (1916), 376.
⁷ Krapp, *ASPR*, vol. II, p. 122.
⁸ Krapp, *Andreas and the Fates of the Apostles* (Boston, 1906), p. 154.

his edition of the poem, retains *gumcystum* with the explanatory note, "*gumcystum*: lit. 'manly virtues', hence (abstract for concrete) 'the virtuous one'."⁹ This judgment is sound, I believe, but one might fairly ask what motivated the peculiar abstract-for-concrete figure at this point in the poem.

If, recalling the Anglo-Saxons' general interest in onomastic lore, we turn to the standard medieval authorities on the meaning of Andrew's name, an answer may be at hand. Jerome, the most revered source of name-explications in the Middle Ages, deals with *Andreas* in his *Liber interpretationis hebraicorum nominum*. Dismissing an improbable etymology formerly current, he explains that *Andreas* is rightly to be interpreted *secundum graecam etymologiam ἀπὸ τοῦ ἀνδρός, hoc est a uiro, uirilis adpelletur*.¹⁰ The Pseudo-Jerome (fifth century) *Commentarius in evangelium Marci* further explains why the quality of *virilitas* expressed by Andrew's name was among the qualities requisite for followers of the Lord: He included *virilitate, ut pugnemus*.¹¹ The Hieronymian interpretation of the name is repeated by Bede, Isidore, Rabanus, and other commentators standard among the Anglo-Saxons,¹² and even the Latin poets of the period pick it up:

> Hinc petit Andreas properando virilis Archaiam
> Ac nomen proprium patrando viriliter implet.¹³

I suspect that this name-lore was in the Old English poet's mind when he referred to Andrew in line 1606 with the Old English word *gumcyst* "manly virtue," for this would be a fairly close rendering of Latin *virilitas*. This seems especially likely when we note that in the Latin sources of the Andrew legend which seem to lie nearest the Old English poet's source,¹⁴ *virilis* is an almost stereotyped epithet of Andrew. In the *Recensio Vaticana*, for example, we find phrases like *Andream virilem apostolum, O tu Andrea virilis robuste, virilis Andrea*; and in the *Recensio Casanatensis* God commands the saint, *surge viriliter, confortare et esto robustus*.¹⁵ (Andrew's companion Matthew, on the other hand, is never so

---

⁹ Brooks, *Andreas and the Fates of the Apostles* (Oxford, 1961), p. 116.

¹⁰ Jerome, CCL, LXXII, i (1959), p. 142, ll. 24–7.

¹¹ PL, XXX, 596.

¹² Bede repeats and elaborates Jerome's interpretation in his commentaries on Luke and Mark, CCL, CXX, ii (1960), pp. 133, 471. Isidore uses Jerome's explanation in his *Etymologiae*, PL, LXXXII, 288. Rabanus, in *De universo*, PL, CXI, 86, and in his commentary on Matthew, PL, CVII, 790, quotes it, as do Druthmar, *Expositio in Matthaeum*, PL, CVI, 1344, and the eighth-century Matthew-commentary once attributed to Bede, PL, XCII, 22, 51.

¹³ *Milonis Carmina*, MGH, Poetae Latini Ævi Carolini Tomus III, 570, ll. 55–6.

¹⁴ *Die lateinischen Bearbeitungen der Acta Andreae et Matthiae apud anthropophagos*, ed. Franz Blatt (Giessen, 1930).

¹⁵ Blatt, *Die lateinischen Bearbeitungen*, pp. 97, l. 17; 104, ll. 10–11; 105, l. 25; 67, ll. 25–6. Elsewhere in the source materials there are suggestions of name-meanings. In the *Recensio Casanatensis* the Israelites are said to be *non cognoscentes neque videntes verbum veritatis dei* (p. 61), alluding, probably, to the standard name-interpretation of *Israel, vir videns Deum vel mens videns Deum* (CCL, LXXII, i

designated.) If such iteration of the epithet lay before the *Andreas* poet's eyes, it would be hard to imagine that he remained oblivious of the commonplace patristic etymology of his hero's name. The fact, moreover, that the Old English poet renders the etymology in the form of an abstract noun, rather than in the adjective form which the Latin versions' *virilis* might seem to suggest, strikes me as a deliberate device for foregrounding the abstract meaning of the name. And thus I would not view the onomastic evidence as furnishing cause to revive Monroe's emendation to *gumcystgum*.

One last datum which may add to our understanding of the patristic onomastics which underlies this passage in the Old English poem is the fact that commentators frequently developed the spiritual significance of the etymology of *Andreas* in close connection with the etymological meaning of his brother Simon's name, which signified *obediens*.[16] The Andrean quality of virility thereby became associated intimately with the companion quality obedience, as we see, for example, in the explanation by the ninth-century Carolingian compiler Paschasius Radbertus (in his *Expositio in evangelium s. Matthaei*) that

> Siquidem Andreas virilis de Graeco interpretatur, ut sit sensus, quod nec obedientia sine virilitate mentis, neque virilitas sine agnitione veri et obedientia coram Domino expletur.[17]

In light of this express connection, it seems not wholly fortuitous that the Old English poet chose to direct attention to the abstract meaning of Andrew's name at the climactic point where the saint had finally won the obedience of the heathen Mermedonians.

III

The poet of the Old English *Exodus* makes repeated use of name-etymologies. E. B. Irving, in his edition of the poem, has pointed out two instances,[18] and there are clearly others.[19] This fondness for name-lore

---

[1959], pp. 41, 75, 139, 152, 155). The Old English *Andreas*, 759–60, retains this onomastic allusion. For a direct reference to the meaning of the name *Amael* in the Greek version, see Blatt, p. 78.

[16] Bede, CCL, CXX, ii, p. 133; *Expositio Actuum Apostolorum et Retractio*, ed. M. L. W. Laistner (Cambridge, 1939), p. 48; Rabanus, *Commentarius in Matthaeum, PL*, CVII, 789, 888, *Homiliae in evangelia et epistolas, PL*, CX, 348, and *De universo, PL*, XCII, 22.

[17] *PL*, CXX, 405.

[18] Irving, *The Old English Exodus*, Yale Studies in English, CXXII (New Haven, 1953), pp. 19, 74, and 89. See also Gollancz, n. 4 above.

[19] For example, the epithet *onriht Godes*, applied to the Israelites in l. 358, is meaningless until we recognize that it is a translation of Jerome's name-interpretation of *Israhel, rectus domini* (CCL, LXXII, i, 139). The poet's introduction of the pursuing Egyptians in l. 136 as *oht inlende* "inland

should be remembered when we weigh the various arguments over the proper reading of *Exodus*, 37–8:

> Hæfde mansceaðan   æt middere niht
> frecne gefylled   frumbearna fela.

The simplest interpretation would appear to be, "He [God] had boldly struck down the persecutors, the many first-born, at midnight." But editors have strained at the seemingly obvious interpretation of *mansceaðan* as direct object of *gefylled* in apposition with *frumbearna fela*. Blackburn would construe *mansceaðan* as dative plural.[20] Irving, following Bouterwek, Mürkens, and Bright, emends to *mansceaða* (or *mānsceaða*), taking the word as subject of *hæfde*, referring to the angel of the Lord.[21] (Psalm 78: 49–51, he notes, "may have suggested the idea of evil angels.") In the face of this eminently reasonable emendation, we might well hesitate to retain the MS. reading unless some further evidence can be cited in support of the attribution of the epithet *mansceaðan* to the Egyptians. Such evidence seems especially needful when we remember that the persons called *mansceaðan* are not Pharaoh's army, the actual persecutors of the Israelites, but rather the Egyptian first-born.

Turning to the commentators, we find that the very name *Egypt* meant "persecutor, oppressor." Jerome says *Ægyptus enim interpretatur persequens, sive tribulans*.[22] Ambrose says *Ægyptus enim, persequens, sive tribulans, atque coarctans interpretatur*.[23] Augustine says *Ægyptus, autem, quoniam interpretatur Afflictio, vel Affligens, vel Comprimens, saepe in imagine ponitur hujus saeculi*.[24] Rabanus says *Ægyptus in tribulantes et affligentes vertitur*[25] and again *Interpretantur autem lingua Hebraica Ægyptii, affligentes, eo quod affixerunt Dei populum*.[26] (Cf. ll. 500–1 of the Old English *Exodus* which, when freed from the encrustation of conjectures and emendations now grown up around it, reads clearly as an onomastic allusion: *Mægen eall gedreas, ða þe gedrecte, dugoð Egypta* "the troop all perished,

---

affliction" is most easily explained, I believe, as an epithet based on the Hieronymian interpretation of *Ægyptus* as *tribulatio coangustans* "enclosing affliction" (CCL, LXXII, i, 61; cf. Rabanus, *PL*, CXI, 341–2, the anonymous *Interpretatio nominum Hebraeorum*, *PL*, XCIII, 1101, and other later commentaries which repeat this explication).

[20] *Exodus and Daniel*, ed. Francis A. Blackburn (Boston, 1907), p. 37.

[21] Irving, *The Old English Exodus*, p. 69. Without the emendation, observes Irving, "the only possible subject would be God in l. 30, a long and awkward carry-over." But similar carry-overs occur elsewhere in *Exodus*, and Blackburn, moreover, observes pertinently (*Exodus and Daniel*, p. 37) that "the intervening sentences would have the same subject if they were not put in the passive form."

[22] Jerome, *Commentariorum in Isaiam prophetam liber*, *PL*, XXIV, 259.

[23] Ambrose, *De trinitate tractatus*, *PL*, XVII, 529.

[24] Augustine, *Enarrationes in Psalmos*, CCL, XL, 1636.

[25] Rabanus, *Enarratio in Ezechielem*, *PL*, CX, 797.

[26] Rabanus, *De universo*, *PL*, CXI, 439.

the host of the Egyptians, *those who had afflicted*.") Since *mānsceaðan* is a fairly exact Old English counterpart for Latin *persequens, affligens, tribulans*, I would conclude that the word in line 37 of *Exodus* is a reflex of the popular patristic explication of *Egyptian* as meaning "persecutor, afflicter" and that we can therefore accept the MS. reading with considerable confidence.

IV

The use of patristic name-etymologies is not foreign to the poet of the Old English *Guthlac A*, for in line 816, at the very conclusion of his poem, he inserts a learned interpretation of the name *Hierusalem* into his closing sentence.[27] Also, the name *Guthlac* itself was consistently etymologized in the Latin and Old English versions of the saint's life, and so the concept of name-interpretation must have been quite familiar to the Old English poet. We should bear this in mind when approaching the curious sentence with which the *Guthlac* poet introduces the first speech of St Bartholomew, Guthlac's patron saint:

> Ofermæcg aspræc,
> dyre dryhtnes þegn,   dæghluttre scan.
>
> (692–3)

We might have expected Bartholomew to be identified more precisely here, for we have not been told his name before, and it is not for another thirty-one lines that we are at last informed, in a strangely inconspicuous way, that the saint who has been speaking is in fact Bartholomew. Instead of naming the saint, however, the poet introduces him with this curious *hapax legomenon ofermæcg* (or *ofermæcga*).[28] The literal meaning of the compound would seem to be "the man above" or "the son from above" (cf. the function of *ofer-* in *ofermearcung, ofersegl*, etc.). But the standard Old English dictionaries translate *ofermæcga* rather freely as "very illustrious being" or "distinguished man." Editors of the poem evince a similar discomfort with the literal sense of the word, for they have emended (e.g. to *ofermettum* or *ofermægne*)[29] or otherwise questioned the transmitted form. Before relinquishing the word preserved in the manuscript, however, we should consider, once again, whether patristic name-lore surrounding Bartholomew may not have a bearing on *ofermæcg*.

The name *Bartholomaeus* is explicated by the commentators constantly and

[27] See n. 2 above.

[28] In l. 692b I have departed from the customary word-division (supported by the scribe's spacing), which is *ofermæcga spræc*, for *mæcg* is a closer equivalent of Latin *filius*, which I shall shortly suggest as the source of the compound element. Even if *ofermæcga* is retained, however, the argument for an onomastic motivation of the Old English epithet seems to me to be strong.

[29] For suggested readings and emendations, see Krapp, *ASPR*, vol. III, pp. 265–6.

consistently as meaning, etymologically, *filius suspendentis aquas*.³⁰ Needless to say, this very peculiar signification prompted the exegetes to strenuous efforts of rationalization. Common expositions are that *filius suspendentis aquas* means loosely *filius suspendentis me* or *filius Dei*. Others, including poetic etymologizings, are more strained.³¹ But the adaptation of the name-meaning which is most relevant to our purposes is the poetic one of Sedulius Scottus:

> Credo: patris nubes tunc suspendentis aquosas
> *Filius* ut *celsus* Bartholomaeus erat.³²

The original etymology is here reduced to *filius* "son" and *celsus* "above"; that is, to almost precise equivalents of the Old English epithet *ofermæcg*. If, as I suspect may be the case, the *Guthlac* poet coined the word *ofermæcg* on the model of the etymology of *Bartholomaeus*, conceiving that etymology in the same way as Sedulius Scottus conceived it in his poem (*filius celsus*), then the epithet is more precise than it at first appears and hence is an appropriate word with which to introduce Bartholomew's speech in lines 692ff; the lexicographers' evasions of the literal meaning of the compound, moreover, would in that case be an unnecessary stratagem.

V

Although my main purpose here has been to call attention to the incidence of name-etymologies in Old English vernacular verse, I should like to emphasize in closing that the onomastic penchant is a common strain through medieval literature in general. Continental vernacular writers share the interest in name-meanings, and many of the Latin poems in the *Monumenta Germaniae historica* swarm with both subtle and explicit name-etymologies, some of which still await detection. By way of illustration, I shall conclude with an instance where a name-etymology in a medieval Latin work has proved too subtle for modern readers. The text in question is the *Vita Lebuini Antiqua* published in *MGH*, Scriptores, XXX, vol. ii, pp. 789–95. This account concerns the Anglo-Saxon saint Leofwine, whose name proved irresistible to the hagiographic etymo-

---

[30] Jerome, *Liber interpretationis Hebraicorum nominum*, CCL, LXXII, 135, 144; Isidore, *Etymologiae*, PL, LXXXII, 288; Bede, *In Marci evangelium expositio*, CCL, CXX, 472, *In Lucae evangelium expositio*, CCL, CXX, 134; Rabanus, *De universo*, PL, CXI, 87; Pseudo-Isidore [ca.750]: *Liber de ortu et obitu patrum*, PL, LXXXIII, 1290; Pseudo-Bede [ca.750–800], *In Matthaei evangelium expositio*, PL, XCII, 22; Druthmar, *Expositio in Matthaeum*, PL, CVI, 1345; etc. Virtually every commentator after Jerome who discusses the Gospels mentions the etymology of Bartholomew's name.

[31] See Bede's comments cited in the preceding footnote and also *The Irish Liber Hymnorum*, ed. J. H. Bernard and R. Atkinson (London, 1898), vol. I, p. 66: *Bartholomei impendamus nutibus / nati pendentis aequora in nubibus*.

[32] *Sedulii Scotti Carmina*, *MGH*, Poetae Latini Ævi Carolini, Tomus III, p. 174, ll. 71–2.

logizers. Radbod of Utrecht, for example, in his poem *De virtutibus Beati Lebuini et de sancto nomine eius*, makes much of the etymological significance of the saint's name, beginning his discussion, quite accurately, with the observation,

> Nam si vertatur, quod *Liafwin* cuna sonabat,
> "Carus amicus" erit.[33]

The writer of the *Vita*, with which we are here concerned, also understands the meaning of the saint's name, but he alludes to it more indirectly than do the verses of Radbod. The *Vita* recounts how a certain Folcbert was given to calling the saint *dilectus-wine* – that is, a half-translation of the name, using the familiar Christian salutation *dilectus* (Old English *leof*) to translate the first element of the saint's name and leaving the second element (*wine*) in its original Old English form. Three times on the same page Folcbert addresses the saint in this playful form, the first time being explicitly remarked by the hagiographer:

> [Folcbertus] dixit inter alia: "Solicitus sum de dilecto meo Wine" – sic enim eum appellare consueverat – "timeo, ne in aliquos incurrat...,"[34]

Despite the writer's emphasis on the name-play here, it seems to have escaped notice in the preparation of Talbot's English translation of this text. In the English rendering the word *dilectus*, which is the crux of the onomastic pun, is left untranslated and the point of the passage is thereby lost entirely:

> [Folcbert] said, among other things, "I feel anxious about Wine" – for this is what he used to call Lebuin – "and I am afraid that if he meets with those...,"[35]

If the onomastic turns of the medieval writers can elude even such distinguished specialists as the translator of the *Vita*, we may reasonably suspect that minds less expert in the ways of medieval thought will miss a great deal more unless we make a conscious effort to watch for this type of name-play in Latin as well as in vernacular texts. A refreshed sensitivity to the onomastic-etymological cast of the early writers' narrative method may well lead to an improved understanding of many passages of literature which otherwise seem obscure or slightly askew to the modern eye.

[33] *MGH*, Poetae Latini Ævi Carolini, Tomus IV, Fasc. i, p. 171, ll. 60–1.
[34] *MGH*, Scriptores, XXX, ii, 793.
[35] C. H. Talbot, *The Anglo-Saxon Missionaries in Germany* (London, 1954), p. 231.

Part V

Old English in the Twentieth Century

20

"The Might of the North": Pound's Anglo-Saxon Studies and *The Seafarer*

> Pound's translation of "The Seafarer" together with *Canto* I, which has been largely influenced by Pound's Old English studies, are, in terms of themes and structures, an anticipation, a nucleus, and a technical synthesis right from the start.... It is Pound's poetics in a nutshell.
>
>   Georg M. Gugelberger, *Ezra Pound's Medievalism*

This emphatic statement of the centrality of *The Seafarer* in Pound's poetic development faithfully represents recent assessments of the poem's importance. But this growing consensus that *The Seafarer* is a key document in the Pound oeuvre carries with it a paradox of literary biography and, ultimately, of literary interpretation, for while there is general agreement that the translation had major consequences for his subsequent career, there is also agreement that this astonishing performance is to a considerable extent the result of schoolboy howlers and naive butchering of the original text by a man who had dabbled only superficially in Anglo-Saxon and who produced no other translations from early English poetry. Preceded apparently by no apprenticeship in such translation and by little serious study of the language, "it is very surprising indeed," says Donald Davie, "coming as it did in *Ripostes* (1912) from the poet who had seemed wedded to the Romance languages of Southern Europe" (*Ezra Pound: Poet as Sculptor*). And others have echoed his surprise. A momentary aberration in Pound's poetic development, we are to understand, is at the same time "an anticipation, a nucleus, and a technical synthesis," and Dr Gugelberger even adds that it is "the thematic link" between all the diverse literary cultures on which Pound drew throughout his career.

    The present essay will argue that this puzzling quality of *The Seafarer* is in fact an illusion resulting from our hitherto incomplete knowledge of Pound's early development and our inattention to the philological methods which he

Reprinted from *The Yale Review*, 71 (1982), 199–224.

applied when he composed his crucial poem. My good fortune in having access to the extraordinary riches of Yale University's Pound Archive and to the equally extraordinary generosity of the curator of the Archive, Mrs Mary de Rachewiltz, enables me to draw attention to earlier poetic translations from Anglo-Saxon by Pound (previously unpublished) and to other materials which document his serious and continuing interest in the subject. It is also possible now to identify the immediate source of the Anglo-Saxon poems which he translated, and this identification requires a new assessment of his methods and intentions in the *Seafarer* translation and of his often derided claim that it is "as nearly literal, I think, as any translation can be."

It is possible that Pound had a taste of Anglo-Saxon as early as his freshman year at the University of Pennsylvania, when he took a course in "English Language and Analysis." A piece of college verse dated 1902 in the Pound Archive registers a hebetic nostalgia for the Germanic world as a whole:

> The Gods of the North are fallen
> Thor's laid his hammer down
> Men fear not the wrath of Odin
> Nor the dark Valkyries frown.

His serious study of the subject, however, began only after he transferred to Hamilton College in Clinton, New York, and became, as a college yearbook tells us, "Bib's pride" – the favorite student, apparently, of Professor Joseph D. Ibbotson, who taught him Anglo-Saxon. Pound took three terms of work with Ibbotson, spanning the academic year 1904–5, and his letters to his parents at this time frequently report on his progress in the subject. To his mother he says that he is translating "Alfred's account of the voyages of Ohthere & Wulfstan" (a prose text usually taken up early in the first term of Anglo-Saxon), and adds that "Anglo-Saxon is for the literature and if you will pay expressage I'll send you a list of a few of the things in Ang.-Sax. worth reading." He mentions Cynewulf, *Beowulf*, and King Alfred among others. "Find Anglo-Saxon very fascinating," says a subsequent letter, and another adds, "The old French & Saxon are the chief matters of interest just now." A terse jotting in one letter to his mother says simply, "Account of Caedmon in Ang. Sax.," from which one would not deduce that he was moved by the old tale of an illiterate neatherd's miraculously acquiring the power of poetic composition and inaugurating the entire tradition of recorded English poetry. But apparently he was moved, for he sketched out a poem on the subject (hitherto unpublished), probably his first experiment with verse based on Anglo-Saxon subject matter:

> Caedmon:
>   Clear eyed draming [sic] above the sun   [1]
>   Child man to father God

>   With heaven for his heart begun
>   While yet earths green ways he trod.
>   Vates and seer stand forth   [5]
>   Singing with all the might of the North
>   behind thee
>   Singing the strong Lord God
>   Thru the seven kingdoms broad
>   Master in visions makeing the cross' high tree   [10]
>   Stand in skys visibly speaking to thee.
>   Maker of that higher state God's kingdom for God's earthly sons
>   Serious tho he ever smiled.

Although an original poem and not a translation like *The Seafarer*, this exercise echoes words and motifs that Pound had been reading in his Anglo-Saxon course with Ibbotson. Line 12, for example, alludes to Cædmon's *Hymn*, in which we are told that the Maker (*Scyppend*), the Lord of the heavenly kingdom (*heofonrices Weard*), created Heaven for earth's sons (*gesceop eorthan bearnum heofon*). (Throughout this essay I have used *th* in place of the two Anglo-Saxon characters for this sound, following Pound's usual practice in his own quotations from Anglo-Saxon.) Lines 10–11 credit Cædmon with authorship of *The Dream of the Rood*, a poem of disputed authorship which has always been included in standard textbooks of Anglo-Saxon. The "seven kingdoms" in line 9 are the Anglo-Saxon Heptarchy, about which Pound would have learned in his background reading or in Ibbotson's lectures.

"We begin Beowulf pretty soon," he says in a letter of February 13, 1905, and a subsequent letter adds that he has "begun Beowulf.... If Dad can find a copy of Beowulf edited by A. J. Wyatt, published by Cambridge Press, please send right away.... No other edition wanted." Pound got his copy of Wyatt's *Beowulf*, and over the ensuing years he came back to it again and again. Since Pound scholars persist in the assumption that the poet knew little about Anglo-Saxon literature outside of *The Seafarer* – even Dr Gugelberger, who is concerned to emphasize Pound's knowledge of Old English, insists that "he probably never read [*Beowulf*] in its entirety" – it will be well to glance ahead at the references he makes to the poem after his school years. Among his papers, three blank cablegram forms which he used for jottings in the late 1920s contain on one sheet the words "Beowulf – Wyatt Cambridge U.P. 1894" followed on the next two sheets by an accurate transcription of lines 1 through 14 of the poem as it appears in Wyatt's edition. On the cover of a pad containing notes toward *Confucius to Cummings* "Wyatt" appears once again; this item dates from the late 1950s. A set of metrical scansions of uncertain date are accompanied by a scribble at the bottom of one page: *Hwaet weh gar dena in gear dagum / eraforth while oft throwade*. This is line 1 of *Beowulf* and line 3 of *The Seafarer*. Both are precisely accurate as to the words, but the spelling deviates several times from the Old English text: evidently Pound was writing the lines out from memory in order to check his scansions against actual Anglo-Saxon verses. Finally, an unpublished, eight-page, typewritten essay called "The Music of Beowulf" which Pound produced around 1920 develops a hypothesis that the music to which Anglo-Saxon epic was chanted survives in the "'heroic chant' of the Gael" as represented by the Aillte Pound heard performed in London. After hearing the concert, he says, he searched through the text of *Beowulf* until he found lines that fit the tune of the Gaelic song.

The evidence of the unpublished letters and papers suggests strongly, then, that Pound knew *Beowulf* and knew it in the original language. Critics who, unaware of this evidence, have insisted that he never read the poem, have made the poet out to be something of a charlatan, for in his published writings he repeatedly implies that he had read the epic and had evaluated it. "We may count the *Seafarer*, the *Beowulf*, and the remaining Anglo-Saxon fragments as indigenous art; at least they dealt with a native subject, and by an art not newly borrowed," he says in one of his *Literary Essays*, and in *The ABC of Reading* he recommends *Beowulf* more than once, although judging it, by implication, to be inferior to *The Seafarer* when considered as a "whole poem": "There are passages of Anglo-Saxon as good as paragraphs of *The Seafarer*, but I have not found any whole poem of the same value." Elsewhere in the *Literary Essays* he recommends "the Anglo-Saxon *Seafarer*, and some more cursory notice of some medieval narrative ... possibly the *Beowulf*," and again, "some knowledge of the Anglo-Saxon fragments – not particularly the *Beowulf* ..." His reaction to the poem is what we might expect: *Beowulf* has grand passages, but judged by the standards of other West European epics it would appear digressive and its architectonics somewhat baffling. But certainly we have no basis whatever for assuming that Pound was passing judgment on a poem he had never read. He quoted the poem from memory, he wrote a small treatise on how it was performed, and years after he had called for Wyatt's edition of the poem during his college days he returned to that edition to refresh his memory of its contents.

Assuming Pound's ignorance of another well-known Anglo-Saxon poem impugns even more directly his integrity as a man of letters. Donald Davie, usually a skillful and sympathetic interpreter of the poet, makes the surprising observation that in translating *The Seafarer* Pound chose to work with a poem generally rated inferior to another Anglo-Saxon elegy, *The Wanderer*, "which one suspects that Pound has never read." If Davie's suspicion is correct, then we must concede that the poet was indeed a humbug, for in one of his *Literary Essays* he ranks "one passage out of *The Wanderer*" along with Dante, *The Seafarer*, and *The Cid* as essential medieval texts, and elsewhere he has praised *The Wanderer* with equal enthusiasm. Was he pretending to knowledge of a poem he had never read? A review of Pound's references to *The Wanderer* in published and unpublished writings shows that he was not. In *Canto* XXVII, line 6, and in LXXVII, line 45, he quotes *sumne fugel othbaer* ("a bird bore one away") from line 81 of *The Wanderer*, and the first of these quotations was inexact in the first edition (*ouitbaer* for *othbaer*), suggesting that he was quoting from memory. He also quotes from memory line 29 of the poem, *Wat se the cunnath* ("He who experiences knows") in *The ABC of Reading*, where he misremembers *cunnath* as *kennath*. In his essay "The Constant Preaching to the Mob," he quotes lines 15–18 so accurately that he must have had the text before him, while in *Mauberley* V, 6 ("There died a myriad, ... / Quick eyes gone under earth's lid") he is recalling in modern English line 23 of *The Wanderer*, which speaks of earth's lid covering a dead comrade. So taken was Pound with *The Wanderer* that he even toyed with making a verse translation of it. Among his unpublished remains are renderings of lines 47–8 and 111:

> seafowl bathing foist [?] forth their feathers
> brawl rime and hail falling with snow mingled
>
> ...
>
> So saith the plausible in mind, sat him apart at { rune / counsel / mystery

The efforts are tentative, and Pound's full *Wanderer* translation never came into being, but there can be no doubt that he knew the poem well and spoke of it with genuine authority. After *The Seafarer* it is probably the Anglo-Saxon poem that he knew best.

But these are not the only poems that haunted his memory. In "The Music of Beowulf" he says, "For twenty years thereabouts I have had in my head a few fragments of Anglo-Saxon:

> Hlude waeron hy la hlude
> Tha hy ofer thon lond rydon
> Waeron anmode, tha hy ofer thon lond rydon

That the verses were indeed "in his head" and not in a text before him is shown by the slight inaccuracies in spelling and phrase. Following are the actual lines from the poem he was remembering – a verse charm of incantation which attempts, through word-magic, to remove from a suffering rheumatic the spearlike pains caused by powerful witches.

> Hlude wæran hy, la hlude,
> tha hy ofer thone hlæw ridan,
> wæran anmode, tha hy ofer land ridan

That he should remember the poem so well is not surprising when we consider his college papers, wherein we find not only a romantic allusion to this poem, or poetry of its kind, in some youthful verses –

> Words of subtle might and terrible
> As some word wizzards woven spell
> That none may grasp –

but also a full-dress translation of the Anglo-Saxon charm in a metrical form imitative of the verse of the original. This is Pound's first sustained effort at "making new" an Anglo-Saxon poem; it is a dress rehearsal for *The Seafarer*. As in his *Seafarer* translation, he deletes parts of the charm poem which he suspects are not genuine, leaving off a brief prose introduction and omitting ten lines at the end which break the rhythm of the previous verses and veer off on a prosier tangent. Scholars and editors of Anglo-Saxon frequently dissected poems in this manner, and Pound was following their lead. In the case of the Anglo-Saxon charms, this seems a reasonable procedure, for many of them seem to have originated as pagan incantations which gradually took on an accretion of Christian elements as Christian scribes copied the texts in monastic scriptoria. The metrical form of Pound's translation differs from that of his *Seafarer*. This is not simply because the charm poem is a verse experiment while *The Seafarer* is authentic poetry. The original verse of the Anglo-Saxon charm is looser than that of the Anglo-Saxon *Seafarer* and the poem as a whole is more plosive and exclamatory – qualities which Pound retains in his translation. The charm translation survives in two typewritten copies, one obviously a revised draft of the other. I reproduce the second draft, with Pound's title, supplying editorially only the second and third commas and a period at the end of line 9.

Fragment

From an ANGLO-SAXON CHARM

> Loud were they, loud as over the hill they rode
> Were resolute, as they rode over the land.
> Shield thee now! that thou escape this malice.
> Out little spear if ye herein be!
> Stood under linden wood under the light shield   [5]
> While all the witch women – mihtigan wif – gathered their power
> Sent spears a-yelling.
> I will send again to them, flying arrows
>   To ward their advances.
> Out little spear if ye herein be!   [10]
> There sate the smith,
> Struck the little sword
> Struck with hammer, mightily.

> Out little spear if ye herein be!
> Six smiths sate wrighting war spears. [15]
> Out spear lie not in spear.
> If herein be any iron at all
> By witch work it to melting shall.

The translation is very close, and yet Pound has managed to render the original in a metrical idiom that establishes its own tone and rhythm while suggesting that of the Anglo-Saxon. By way of preparation for our close look at Pound's translational licenses in his *Seafarer* later in this essay, we might usefully note here the few liberties he takes with the original charm text. First, the refrain "Out little spear if ye herein be" ought to be ". . . if thou herein be" in the first and third occurrences, ". . . if it herein be" in the second. But even an Anglo-Saxon teacher red-pencilling student translations would hesitate to carp at the obviously smoother rendering in Pound's translation. That the women referred to in line 6 are witches is made clear in the latter part of the Anglo-Saxon poem, where they are called *hægtessan* "witches," but in line 6 they are described only as *mihtigan wif* "mighty women." Pound has anticipated the later "witch" in order to provide the alliteration on *w*, which he completes, arrestingly, by preserving the original Anglo-Saxon phrase untranslated in the second half of the line – a presage of his stratagem in *The Seafarer* of retaining some of the Anglo-Saxon words unchanged in order to communicate the flavor of the original poem. (As the poems quoted earlier have shown, "might(y)" was Pound's operative word in describing Anglo-Saxon: "Might of the north," "words of subtle might," and here the "mighty women" are designated in the original language.) Lines 8 and 9 of Pound's poem would be awkward and obscure if they had translated the Anglo-Saxon word for word ("I will send again another flying arrow opposite them"), and he has supplemented the original to bring out the sense more clearly. Similar clarification occurs in line 16 where Pound supplies a verb that is only implied in the Anglo-Saxon, which, if literally rendered, would be "Out spear, not in, spear!" The greatest license is to be found in line 13. The original Anglo-Saxon would yield in modern English "wounded powerfully with iron." Both "struck" and "hammer" have no basis in the Anglo-Saxon text. We shall return to this apparent translational error later when we examine the licenses in *The Seafarer*.

Elsewhere in Pound's early writings we find further experiments with the verse-form that he describes in one youthfully exuberant poem as

> . . . the rumbling line
> That runic letters twine
> In Saxon minstrelsy.

The least impressive of these is "At the Heart of Me: A.D. 751," in which some scholars have perceived a foreshadowing of *The Seafarer*. The poem is spoken by a wayfaring Anglo-Saxon who has attained wealth and security on his voyages but insists that his achievements will be meaningless if he cannot rejoin his beloved across the sea. This subject was probably suggested by the wandering-lover theme in Anglo-Saxon poems like *The Husband's Message*, *The Wife's Lament*, and *Wulf and Eadwacer*. Indeed, Stopford Brooke's *History of Early English Literature*, which Pound appears to have used during his years at Hamilton, summarizes *The Husband's Message* in terms which could almost as well serve as a summary of Pound's poem: "Treasure of gold the Lover has won and a fair land, and many warriors serve him. He has overcome all trouble; but nothing is worth anything unless he have her with him." Brooke dates the poem roughly near the middle of the eighth century, which probably explains Pound's date "A.D. 751" in the title of his poem. But, faithful though it is to the subject matter of the period, in execution Pound's limp, sentimentalized treatment of the theme is more like late Victorian verse than early English. About the only suggestions of Anglo-Saxon diction are a compound word "Whale-ways" and an untranslated Anglo-Saxon word "Middangeard," which Pound footnotes, "Anglo-Saxon, 'Earth.'" For all its youthful pedantry, this gesture is significant: the trick of retaining untranslated words from the original in order to suggest the flavor of Anglo-Saxon is taking hold.

The *Seafarer* theme of the exilic wanderer recurs in many of the schoolboy drafts preserved among the unpublished papers, and sometimes alliterative patterns suggest that Pound was unconsciously associating this theme with Anglo-Saxon verse, even when he was writing in conventional meters. Thus the lines

> There cometh wafting of some witched bazar
> And soundeth calling of an unsailed main

crop up in a sonnet about the sailor who rejects the easy life of landlubbers and embraces the rigors of the sea. Vaguer reminiscences of "Saxon minstrelsy" occur in the first part of the sonnet along with one very distinct one if the curious word *raeds* is to be understood as the Anglo-Saxon noun *ræd* "plan, reading lesson":

> I am sore weary of the raeds they tell
> These loafers mumbling at the wonder door
> The wisdom of the schools it urks me sore
> My tongue is keen for winds and wander lore
> My pulse is hot . . .
> I hear the breakers whining at the oar.

Another on the same theme begins, "There is an unrest in me for the road / And I would be amid the bales of cargo." These groping sketches of poems that never came alive seem repeatedly to strain after the combined persona and perspective which Pound was to discover finally in *The Seafarer*, and the recurrence of alliterative-accentual lines like

> The blaze upon the hearth all baleful strives
> To be but mock'ry of warm merriment.
> Blood is the blaze, the brothers three low bent

amid incongruous pentameters hints that he could not get out of his head the Anglo-Saxon rhythms he would eventually make his own.

Many of the verse exercises among Pound's papers are imitations of the styles of various earlier English poets, and a number are Chaucerian experiments written in a form of Middle English which is linguistically the equal of Chatterton's efforts. But there is a persistent underdrumming of the Anglo-Saxon measure, and at times this ancestral voice becomes dominant and achieves control and assurance of tone even when the subject matter fails to come into focus, as in the following curious lines reminiscent of elegiac passages in *The Wanderer* and *The Seafarer*. (I have silently corrected typographical errors, and where alternative versions of a word or phrase are given, I have printed only the last.)

> Age full of grudges, you hold up the end,
> Sit late in a weary corpse, why, why,
> Let the life out of this dungeon,
> Death is at rest already, life an aching.
> I am not what I was, the great part is perished
> And the relictions full of languor and horror,
> Light heavy in sorrow, grievous amid all glad things.
> Worse than all burials is the desire for death,
> While youths adornment, while mind and senses were left me
> World wide orator a mouth for all worlds' ears,
> Oft amid poets formed I fair feignings,
> Oft having spoken took I the crown of contention,
> Took I my tongues worth, many a treasure,
> What stays undead now, in dying members,
> What is for an old man, out of life's portions, . . .

Here the thumping alliterations of the earliest efforts are overcome and something subtler is emerging, although the firm prosody of *The Seafarer* remains unachieved. But there are suggestions here of both the early poem on Cædmon and of the *nekuia* of *Canto* I. The long experimentation with Old English rhythms has tuned his sense of versification, and the themes and attitudes of the old poets have found a place in Pound's well-stocked mind. At a period in his development when we have heretofore assumed that the poet was becoming imbued exclusively with "the spirit of Romance," he was in fact absorbing with comparable avidity "the might of the North."

"What text Pound used, how it was punctuated, what glosses accompanied it, remains an unsolved problem," observes Hugh Kenner of the *Seafarer* translation. The questions he raises are important, since all the debates over Pound's intentions, his competence in reading Anglo-Saxon, and indeed the very nature of his poem (translation? metaphrase? phanopoeia?) must be inconclusive so long as we are unable to say exactly what text of the Anglo-Saxon poem he was translating. Kenner rules out one possibility, namely that Pound used the text of the poem included in Henry Sweet's *An Anglo-Saxon Reader in Prose and Verse*, a popular and reliable course book then used in many Anglo-Saxon classes. Kenner points out that Pound, in his "Philological Note" to the first printing of the poem in *The New Age*, November 30, 1911, specifically describes and quotes from the concluding section of the Old English poem, which Sweet did not print in his text of *The Seafarer* in his *Reader*. Pound must have used an edition, Kenner reasons, in which the complete text of *The Seafarer* was available. Bernetta Quinn, on the other hand, confidently identifies the source text: "His text was *Bright's Anglo-Saxon Reader*, as familiar to specialists as *Poor Richard's Almanac* is to Americans at large and still in use in some of today's graduate schools." She quotes extensively from Bright and suggests that the reason Pound did not translate all of the Anglo-Saxon poem is that Bright printed only the first part of it. (She apparently ignores Pound's "Philological Note" and the implications Kenner drew from it.) But Bright's *Reader*, though first published in 1891, did not include *The Seafarer* among its readings until the book was revised and enlarged by James R. Hulbert in 1935 – twenty-four years after Pound had published his translation. When Hulbert did print the poem, moreover, he printed only the first sixty-four lines, whereas Pound translated ninety-nine lines. Whatever his source text may have been, it was certainly not *Bright's Anglo-Saxon Reader*. K. K. Ruthven, on the other hand, thinks Pound drew on "various scholars," including the Germans Gustav Ehrismann and Friedrich Kluge and the Dutchman R. C. Boer – dry and dreary reading for a vibrant poet eager to master all the primary sources of Western culture. Surely Pound would have availed himself of one of the many reading editions that synthesized pertinent theories of scholars such as these rather than repeat that task of synthesis himself.

But hypotheses about Pound's source text are now, happily, superfluous, since the book he used for his translation survives and is available for scholars' inspection. Long among the poet's books at Brunenburg, it was for a brief period on deposit in Yale's Beinecke Library and is now at the University of Texas. It is *An Anglo-Saxon Reader in Prose and Verse* by Henry Sweet, seventh edition (Oxford, 1898). This volume is inscribed on both flyleaf and endpaper, and several pages are annotated in Pound's hand. Some of these annotations have direct connection with his remarks on Anglo-Saxon literature in other writings. Lines 15–18 of *The Wanderer*, for example, are carefully bracketed in the left-hand margin for special attention. These are the four lines quoted and translated in his 1916 essay "The Constant Preaching to the Mob" alluded to above. The text of the Anglo-Saxon charm which Pound translated is among the poems printed in this volume, as is Cædmon's *Hymn*, on which he based his poem "Caedmon." *The Seafarer* has several telltale annotations, including a gloss by Pound identifying *byrig* in line 48 as "mulberry" ("cometh beauty of berries" in Pound's translation) rather than as "cities," which scholars have noted to be the correct translation. Most significant, perhaps, is Pound's annotation stating where he thinks the poem should end. In the middle of line 99 he draws heavy vertical lines and in the margin he writes "End" and underscores the word twice, while cancelling the remaining ten lines on the page. This is precisely where Pound's translation of *The Seafarer* ends.

But what of Hugh Kenner's point about Pound's "Philological Note" referring to lines of the poem which are not printed in Sweet's *Reader*? Doesn't this at least prove that Pound must have consulted another text of the poem besides the one in Sweet? It does not, because Sweet in fact prints the full text of the poem, only in two different parts of the *Reader*. In his collection of readings, Sweet prints lines 1 through 108. This is the text that Kenner saw. But if Kenner had turned back to the explanatory notes on the poem on pages 222–4 of the book, he would have seen that there Sweet printed the remaining sixteen lines of the poem, from which Pound quotes in his "Philological Note." Sweet removed this portion of *The Seafarer* from the text proper because he thinks these verses "could not have formed part of the original poem" but must have been tacked on by a latter-day meddlesome scribe. This was a common opinion in Sweet's day, one strongly supported, for example, by Stopford Brooke's *History of Early English Literature*, which is cited by Pound in his copy of Sweet's *Reader* at the beginning of the poem *The Wanderer*. Pound evidently studied Sweet's and Brooke's discussions and accepted the prevailing scholarly rationale for dissecting the poem, but with characteristic independence of mind, he made his own judgment as to where the cut-off should come, indicating this judgment in his emphatic annotation "End."

It is important to note that in cutting off the last part of the Anglo-Saxon poem Pound was simply following through on the assumptions that Sweet and other Anglo-Saxonists of his day made about the genesis of poems like *The Seafarer*. The prevailing view was that these texts were originally pagan poems and that Christianizing scribes had revised them by inserting a Christian reference here and there and then adding a pious homiletic conclusion. The job of the serious student of Anglo-Saxon, they felt, was to disengage the original pre-Christian poem from the monkish adulterations and, by excising the latter, to recover the "real poem." This is what they did in their editions, and this is what Pound sought to do in his translation. It is therefore misleading when Hugh Witemeyer says (with the approval, apparently, of Alexander, Davie, Kenner, Knapp, and virtually every other Pound critic), "The changes he made in the original text subtly modify its spirit and bring it into line with his own preoccupations.... The major change is in Pound's systematic elimination of all Christian elements from the poem.... Pound's translation paganizes the poem." But Pound's changes and his justification for them in his "Philological Note" are simply accurate reflections of the standard scholarly doctrine he read in Sweet's *Reader*. It is Sweet who discards the Christian conclusion of the poem, saying, "It is evident that the majority of these verses could not have formed part of the original poem." Pound is again adhering to the scholarly dictates of his day when he eliminates a reference to the devil in line 76 of the Anglo-Saxon poem and when he translates *Englum* in line 78 as "English" rather than "angels" (a perfectly legitimate translation of the word and not, as some Pound scholars have mistaken it to be, a confusion or a translational error). Anyone who has read E. G. Stanley's *The Search for Anglo-Saxon Paganism*, which details the way in which nineteenth-century scholars and editors revised and dissected their texts in order to recover "the original poem" (that is, the supposed pre-Christian poem), will realize that Pound was rather conservative for his day and respected the integrity of the transmitted text more than many of Sweet's contemporaries. He does not, for example, substitute names of pagan Germanic deities for references to the Christian God, as did some Teutonizing scholars. What is most important, however, is to understand that what little adapting he did do in his *Seafarer* was *not* done to "subtly modify its spirit and bring it into line with his own preoccupations" but rather was done for precisely the opposite reason, to recover the real, original Anglo-Saxon poem, as that process of recovery was understood by scholars in his day. He was probing for "the English national chemical," just as he claimed, and was not overlaying the ancient text with Poundian prejudices and a modern "spirit."

Critics have also suspected that Pound reconceived the essential genre of his Anglo-Saxon text. "In his note he calls the poem a 'lyric,' distinguishing it from some larger narrative which may have contained it," says James F. Knapp, and Michael Alexander seems to agree: "He detected what he calls a 'lyric' behind the more dramatic and meditative poem that has survived... he does not make it clear that he is extensively modernizing his original, perhaps because he did not realize how far he was doing so." But here again what the critics have taken for Pound's revisionary handling of the poem is really an alert adherence to the best scholarly opinion of his day. In the Preface to his *Reader* Sweet introduces *The Seafarer* as "the finest of the Old-English lyrics," and his explanatory note begins by saying "*The Seafarer* ... is by common consent the finest of the Old-

English lyric – or rather half-lyric – poems." And at yet another point, Sweet emphasizes that *The Seafarer*, *The Wanderer*, and a few like poems "show lyric poetry in its earliest stage." It was received opinion recorded in Pound's copy of the poem that proclaimed *The Seafarer* to be a lyric, not some modernizing impulse of Pound's.

The aspect of Pound's *Seafarer* that has received most extensive attention and debate is the "howlers" – those points in his translation where he seems to have misunderstood the Anglo-Saxon words completely and supplied meanings utterly different from the ones intended in the Anglo-Saxon text. Here too some Poundians have argued that he was substituting his own personal feeling and opinions for those of the Anglo-Saxon poet, silently abandoning his stated pledge to render the original literally. "Despite the scholarly rationale," says Witemeyer, dismissing Pound's explanation of his philological method, "the changes mesh too perfectly with Pound's own poetic biases to be motivated by sheerly textual considerations." Yet other critics have tried to excuse the list of translational errors by calling them "deliberate jokes" or by suggesting that Pound was simply imitating the sounds of the original Anglo-Saxon words without regard for their meaning. But most commentators have conceded that the departures from the received text are the result of Pound's ignorance pure and simple, and his admirers no less than his detractors have hooted at his claim to having produced a translation "as nearly literal, I think, as any translation can be." "A great pity," "regrettable," "unfortunate," say his defenders about the mistranslations, and his adversaries respond that the errors are "deplorable marks of the literary fake."

In reassessing the oft-rehearsed list of translational errors we might begin by returning to Pound's earliest poetic translation from Anglo-Saxon, the verse charm printed above. There we noted consistent, faithful adherence to the meanings of words in the original poem, with but one notable exception – the translation of *iserne wund swithe* as "struck with hammer mightily" rather than with the more literal "wounded with iron exceedingly." Before we look too far into Pound's modern biases and linguistic limitations for an explanation of his license here, we should look first at the book from which he was making his translation. On page 215 of Sweet's *Reader*, we find among the explanatory notes to this poem the following annotation to the words in question: "*iserne wund swithe* ... 'wounded with iron'; that is, 'beaten with an iron hammer.'" His apparent departure from his text was in fact the result of his working conscientiously within the terms of the scholarly apparatus at his disposal. What that apparatus teaches in comment after comment is that attaining the true meaning of the Anglo-Saxon texts requires much more than simply reading the literal meanings of the words preserved in the Anglo-Saxon manuscripts. Sometimes, as in this instance, the rather general meanings of the words in a passage must be interpreted and specified in the light of the overall context. At other times, Sweet's annotations suggest that the Anglo-Saxon words have several meanings and that the reader must make a considered choice among alternative meanings. Quite frequently Sweet indicates that the words preserved in the old manuscripts simply do not make sense in the context of the given poem and so must be changed ("emended") by the editor in order to achieve an acceptable sense for the passage as a whole. In not a few cases Sweet suggests several different emendations for a problematic word or passage, implying that none is wholly satisfactory and so the reader will have to judge for himself which is to be preferred.

An example of the latter kind occurs at line 56 of the Anglo-Saxon *Seafarer*. The original manuscript here reads *efteadig secg* "re-blessed man," which makes little sense in context. Sweet's explanatory note points out that some scholars, in an effort to make the two words meaningful (and metrical), have emended the manuscript reading to *sefteadig secg* "man in easy circumstances," while yet others have thought more likely the reading *esteadig secg* "prosperous man." Sweet actually adopts (for metrical reasons) yet another emendation in the text as he has printed it: *secg esteadig* "man prosperous." But his note implies that all these proposals deserve consideration, and Pound in his translation chose from these alternatives the rendering "prosperous man." A thoughtful reader of the texts in Sweet's book would go through this kind of exercise repeatedly every time he read one of the poems or prose selections. That is, he would be forced to review several possible interpretations of the meaning or structure of a word or phrase and then, in the light of the overall meaning of the work or the immediate context, would have to select the most probable meaning for that occurrence. And frequently he would notice that the scholar who edited the book had decided that the range of meanings offered by the word preserved in the ancient manuscript was altogether unsuitable for the context and so had altered the manuscript reading to some more appropriate word. Most students of Anglo-Saxon manage to get through the course without worrying much about these editorial matters. They simply accept whatever the editor prints and follow his glossary for the meanings of the words. They ignore the explanatory notes which discuss the process of philological review and choice by which the editor arrived at the reading he finally commits himself to in his text. Pound could never bring himself to accept passively a text which was the product of another man's decisions as to what the author had intended. As his "Philological Note" to *The Seafarer* clearly shows, he involved himself in the establishment of the text before he translated it. Indeed, he often indulged in philological speculation. A remarkable note at the end of his verse translation of Arnaut Daniel's "Canzon: of the Trades and Love" offers a solution to a philological problem in that text, a solution involving paleography, Latin syntax, Latin accidence, and the possible influence of Vergil's ninth eclogue on Provencal canzon. Moreover, in Pound's copy of Sweet's *Reader* we can see marginalia that show his mind working in this philological vein, as when he marks off part of *The Wanderer* as being "not by original author" and another part as being an addition "of scribe" and not by the author of the poem. At line 44 of *The Seafarer* he appears to question whether *hyge* "thought" might not be a scribe's error for *hyht* "pleasure." We must remember this activist, philological dimension of his reading as we reexamine the list of supposed translational errors critics have long deplored in his *Seafarer*.

The main reason Pound's admirers conceded so meekly that he was a slapdash translator or a willful betrayer of his Anglo-Saxon text is that they were overawed by the intimidating authority of Kenneth Sisam, the eminent Oxford philologist who first pilloried the poet for his translational errors.[1] But upon examination it will become apparent that Sisam was not altogether fair and accurate in his representation of Pound's translational procedure. Consider, for example, the following three "blunders" cited by Sisam. (The first line number given is that of the Anglo-Saxon poem, the second, in parentheses, that of Pound's translation.)

- line 88 (90): Pound confuses the preposition *thurh* "through" with the word *thruh* "coffin, tomb"
- line 48 (49): Pound translates *byrig* "towns" as "berries"
- line 23 (23): Pound translates *stearn* "tern, sea-bird" as "stern (of a ship)"

Sisam asserts that in each of these instances the poet simply blundered, guessing wildly and wrongly at the meanings of words in his text. In the case of the first instance Sisam even reconstructs for us how Pound came to make his embarrassing error: "Here he looked up the preposition *thurh* ('through,' 'in'), came upon *thruh* 'coffin,' 'tomb,' and thought it near enough. The method is very old and uncritical." Indeed, as Sisam has described it, it is the method of dim-witted undergraduates. But let us trace Pound's steps through the procedure described by Sisam. If Pound had looked up *thurh* in Clark Hall's *Concise Anglo-Saxon Dictionary* (as he almost certainly would have done), he would have encountered entries for two different words spelled *thurh*. The first is the preposition. The second entry says simply "*thurh = thruh*": that is, *thurh* occurs as an alternative spelling for the word *thruh*. If Pound then turned to *thruh* to find out what it meant, he would have found the definition "chest, tomb, coffin." The *Dictionary*'s information is precisely right: *thurh* occurs repeatedly in Anglo-Saxon texts as a noun translating Latin *sarcophagus* or in other contexts with the meaning "casket." What Pound found in the dictionary, then, would have placed him in precisely that position he had found himself in so often as he read Sweet's notes. He had to make a choice between two possible meanings of the word before him, basing his choice upon the context and upon his understanding of the poem as a whole. Of the two possible

---

[1] *Times Literary Supplement*, June 25, 1954, p. 409.

meanings of the word, he chose one while Sisam chose the other. I must add that in this particular case I find Sisam's interpretation more attractive than Pound's, because my reading of the meter of the line does not permit *thurh* to have noun stress, because *thurh* "tomb" is statistically rare compared with *thurh* "through," and because the traditional interpretation of *thurh* as the preposition (which is the one Sisam is defending) accords better with my sense of the spirit and meaning of the poem as a whole. But I respect the process by which Pound arrived at his interpretation, and I do not think that process should be misrepresented as a schoolboy blunder by someone so slow-witted as to be incapable of detecting the difference between the forms *thurh* and *thruh*.

Turning to the second example, we might well ask how Pound ever came to translate *byrig* "towns" as "berries." The answer is very much like that in the case of *thurh*, only this time one might well prefer Pound's interpretation to Sisam's. The Anglo-Saxon dictionaries record two separate words spelled *byrig*. One is the plural noun meaning "towns"; the other is a noun meaning "mulberry tree" or, since the singular and plural of this noun have the same form, "mulberry trees." In his copy of Sweet's *Reader* Pound has underlined *byrig* in line 48 and written out in the margin alongside it the meaning "mulberry." In the poem, *byrig* is the subject of a plural verb *fægriath*, which means "become beautiful." If one chooses to read the word as Sisam does, it would mean "the towns become beautiful"; if one prefers Pound's interpretation, it would mean "the mulberry trees become beautiful" or, as Pound has rendered it in his poetic translation, "Cometh beauty of berries." Considering the immediate context of his phrase in the Anglo-Saxon poem, which may be translated literally as "the groves sprout blossoms, the mulberry trees become beautiful, the fields become fair," one might well conclude that there is at least as much to be said for Pound's reading as for Sisam's. In any case, we must acknowledge that the two interpretations of *byrig* – "towns" and "mulberry" – are equally defensible linguistically. There has been no inept blunder of translation.

Pound's reading of *stearn* as "stern" is more complicated. Detractors like Sisam have in the past assumed that Pound came upon the Anglo-Saxon word, fancied that it looked something like modern English "stern" and, without bothering to check further, simply translated the word "stern." But let us assume that he began by looking the word up in the *Concise Anglo-Saxon Dictionary*, as he had looked up *byrig*. This is what he would have found:

STEARN (æ, e) m. sea-swallow? tern? *Gl, Seaf.* ['stern']

What this entry tells us is that *stearn* is a masculine noun, sometimes spelled *stærn* or *stern* rather than *stearn*, that it occurs in Anglo-Saxon glosses and in *The Seafarer*, and that its meaning is doubtful, although scholars have guessed that it might mean either "sea-swallow" or "tern." The bracketed "stern" at the end of the entry means that in modern English the Anglo-Saxon word has taken the form "stern," and such a word does indeed occur in modern English dialects as the name of a variety of bird. Having seen how uncertain the meaning of *stearn* is, Pound might well have returned to his copy of Sweet's *Reader* to examine the word there in context. Doing so, he would find the word printed not as *stearn* but as *stear*[*n*]. The brackets are the editor's device for indicating that the Anglo-Saxon word actually transmitted in the manuscript is *stear* but that he has added the *n* in order to change the scribe's form into a word that he, the editor, finds more suitable. (In fact the word *stearn* is legible in the manuscript and Sweet's *stear*[*n*] is an editorial error, but Pound could not have known this.) All this conjecture about the word would very likely have suggested to Pound that philologically the status of this word was an open question rather than a solved problem, and he would have felt free to do some conjecturing of his own. If he tried to look up *stear* in the Anglo-Saxon dictionaries, he would not have found such a word, but he would have found the very similar *steor*, which means "rudder, helm." Perhaps he decided that since *stearn* is spelled variously *stern* and *stærn*, *stear* could very likely be a variant spelling of *steor*, and this is the source of his rendering (the "stern" of a ship being not too far in meaning from its "helm"). Or conceivably, when he examined the entry for *stearn* his eye fell on "['stern']" and he decided to use this dialect word in his poem, intending the meaning "snow fell on the sea-swallow." Or he may have misunderstood the word as the word for "stern" (part of a ship). My concern here is not to determine with certainty what Pound meant in line 23 of his poem but to point out that if his interpretation of *stearn* (or rather *stear*[*n*]) differs from that which Sisam and other Anglo-Saxon scholars have been accustomed to assume, it is probable, in view of his usual philological bent, that he was deliberately making an independent guess as to the word's meaning rather than just failing to understand received opinion on the passage. Considering the highly conjectural nature of the word as he encountered it in his text and in the dictionary, one can hardly say that his hazarding an original interpretation would be either unlikely or unwarranted. It should be noted that Pound's entire sentence in lines 23–4 is a rather loose rendering, and this may well be because he detected the uncertainty in Sweet's *stear*[*n*] and so chose to improvise verses around the general images of the original without trying to pin down a literal sense that was seemingly no longer accessible.

I do not propose to reconstruct Pound's rationale for each of his departures from the letter of the received text of the Anglo-Saxon *Seafarer*, and I am certainly not suggesting that each of his philological innovations is superior to the traditional readings established by scholars in the field (although I think some of them may be superior). What is important is that we acknowledge that

Pound's version is the product of a serious engagement with the Anglo-Saxon text, not of casual guessing at Anglo-Saxon words and of passing off personal prejudices as Anglo-Saxon poetry. Further examination of the most commonly cited "blunders" may help to establish more clearly his seriousness of purpose.

In line 89 of his poem Pound has translated the Anglo-Saxon *wuniath tha wacran* ("the weaker [ones] remain") as "waneth the watch," confusing the word *wuniath* "remain" with the word *waniath* "wane" and confusing *wacran* "weaker" with heaven knows what – or so the critics have said. But it is helpful once again to return to Pound's copy of Sweet's *Reader*. There, twenty pages before he came to *wuniath tha wacran* in *The Seafarer*, he would have read the word *waniath* "wane" in line 72 of the Old English Poem *The Phoenix*. But there is a footnote attached to *waniath* explaining that the actual word in the original Anglo-Saxon poem is *wuniath*. Assuming that the ancient scribe might easily confuse these two words, the editor has changed *wuniath* to *waniath* in order to give smoother sense. Now when Pound then came upon *wuniath* in *The Seafarer*, he simply repeated the same editorial operation, assuming for himself the scholar's right to emend a word for sense. Professional scholars like Sisam might well regard it as presumptuous for a young poet-translator to thus encroach on the scholar's domain, but they should not dismiss such textual decisions as "careless ignorance or misunderstanding." As for *wacran*, this form could well be interpreted as a nominalized form of the adjective *wacor* "watchful," and Pound evidently chose to read it that way. *Waniath tha wacran* would then mean "waneth the watchful [ones]," and this would be the interpretation that lies behind Pound's "waneth the watch." Although this rendering works very well in Pound's poem, I would not be tempted to incorporate his reading into a scholarly interpretation of the Anglo-Saxon poem. His bold emendation of *wuniath* seems to me unnecessary, and his reading of *wacran* seems trained. But considering his known source (Sweet's *Reader*) and his demonstrated method of translating, one would be reckless to dismiss his rendering as nothing more than a naïf's wild guessing at the meaning of the verse.

In line 81 the Anglo-Saxon poem has *ealle onmedlan eorthan rices*, which is usually taken to mean "all arrogance of the domain of the earth." Pound renders it "all arrogance of earthen riches," and the critics pounce with glee, explaining that he mistook the genitive singular noun *eorthan* "of earth" for a word meaning "earthen" and has misunderstood the noun *rice* "domain, kingdom, power, authority" as meaning "rich." But the genitive singular noun *eorthan* occurs twice elsewhere in *The Seafarer*, and Pound has accurately translated it "earth's" (line 62) and "earthly" (line 91), showing that he understood exactly what *eorthan* means. "Earthen" is a reasonable translation of the attributive genitive in any case. We also know from his poem "Caedmon," printed above, that he knew perfectly well what *rice* meant, for that poem is mainly built around the word *rice* "kingdom, domain" as it occurs in Cædmon's "Hymn" (*heofon-rices Weard* "Lord of the heavenly kingdom"): Cædmon sings throughout the seven kingdoms of the Anglo-Saxon Heptarchy about the kingdom God has prepared for men in Heaven. In the *Seafarer*, however, Pound wants to emphasize wealth rather than just kingdom, apparently because he felt this is a more likely concomitant of "arrogance." His "riches" probably is based upon the entry for the word *rice* in Clark Hall's *Concise Anglo-Saxon Dictionary*, where the adjective "rich" appears along with the nouns "power, authority, kingdom," in the definition of the word.

An interesting example of a Poundian rendering which has been construed as the translator's taking liberties in order to project his personal attitudes onto his text is

>   Nathless there knocketh now
> The heart's thought that I on high streams
> The salt-wavy tumult traverse alone.

This is generally quite faithful to the original Anglo-Saxon, but Georg Gugelberger detects one word here which "emphasizes the solitary nature of that passage over the sea" and emphasizes it, moreover, "even more than does the original text." The word in question is "alone," which translates the Anglo-Saxon *sylf*, usually taken to mean "myself." Anglo-Saxon dictionaries do record a rather rare usage of *sylf* meaning "alone," but apparently Dr Gugelberger (and scholars at large) feel that this rare sense of the word is sufficiently improbable in the *Seafarer* passage that its invocation here can only be the result of Pound's wanting to stress the theme of solitude "more than does the original text." Most people would probably have agreed with this view at the time Pound made his translation and for many years afterward. As it happens, however, one eminent Anglo-Saxon scholar subjected this passage to intensive scrutiny and came to the conclusion that *sylf* here could only mean "alone," and he credited Pound with having anticipated this discovery through "his poet's intuition."[2] In the judgment of one modern scholar, then, Pound's inclination to stress the theme of solitude in this passage is an inclination shared with the Anglo-Saxon poet.

Interesting as such moments of Poundian prescience may be, my concern here is not to argue that Pound's *Seafarer* is a close, scholarly rendering of the Anglo-Saxon text or that he was himself an Anglo-Saxon scholar. He often insisted that he was not a scholar (although he took scholarship seriously and used it himself to open doors to new literary cultures), and his poem *The Seafarer* is often loose and inventive (although inventive within the limits of what he took to be faithful, philological translation). My concern here is to

[2] See John C. Pope, "Second thoughts on the interpretation of 'The Seafarer'," *Anglo-Saxon England*, 3 (1974), 79.

show that Anglo-Saxon literature, the heroic literature of the English, had a larger part in Pound's early development than has been realized. Those who have repeated condescendingly the litany of supposed mistranslations in *The Seafarer* have impeded understanding of Pound's Anglo-Saxon interests by implying that his knowledge of Anglo-Saxon was superficial and trifling. And this, in turn, leads to the improbable paradoxes in the usual interpretations of Pound's poetic development: through his *Seafarer* Pound achieved the only poetic idiom adequate for the *nekuia* in English, but the achievement is the result of "ignorance and misunderstanding." The *Cantos* had their inception in Pound's conversations with his Anglo-Saxon teacher ("the *Cantos* started in a talk with 'Bib,'" said Pound), but the only Anglo-Saxon legacy in his oeuvre is a single slapdash paraphrase. In "The Age Demanded" Pound included "emendation, conservation of 'the better tradition'" among his highest aims as a poet, but in *The Seafarer* he leaves us a crude parody of "emendation, conservation of 'the better tradition.'" Pound judges *The Seafarer* as "fit to compare with Homer," but his translation of the poem is a tissue of hasty guesses and linguistic boners. Considered in the light of the facts, these paradoxes yield to a more probable pattern of poetic development. Scrutiny of Pound's unpublished as well as published writings shows that his engagement with Anglo-Saxon was longer and more serious than our preoccupation with "The Spirit of Romance" has allowed us to see. Examination of the "howlers" in the light of Pound's source text and of the scholarly tradition within which he was operating reveals that his inaccuracies, or seeming inaccuracies, are more often serious applications of the philological techniques which he had learned from his teachers and the books at his disposal. Indeed, his claim to "literalness" and to philological dedication to his text is not an embarrassing pretension but a defensible position, and in his method we can recognize the philological basis of his stated aim in reading all literature – "to see through to the original." Contrary to the misconceptions shared by his admirers and his critics heretofore, Pound's procedures in his *Seafarer* are neither empty pretensions nor jokes and blunders. Empty pretensions would not enable a poet to discover in his Saxon past both "the English national chemical" and the exilic wanderer who, in one guise or another, speaks his sentiments throughout his poetic career. Jokes and blunders would not enable him to gather from the past a live tradition.

21
Ezra Pound and the Old English Translational Tradition

When Ezra Pound produced his verse translations of Anglo-Saxon poems early in this century, he was not doing something unprecedented but rather was following in the path of a long and not very illustrious tradition of modern English verse renderings of Old English poetry. He did not translate much out of Old English – only *The Seafarer*, a seventeen-line verse charm, and some other fragments of verse[1] – but what he did translate stands out for two reasons from all that preceded it: first, it comes to life as modern verse exerting, indeed, a measurable influence on Pound's own subsequent verse and on that of other modern poets;[2] and second, it succeeds in suggesting the quality of Old English verse without seeming quirky or bizarre.

Why did Pound succeed where so many before him had failed? To say that he had genius would be true, but this alone is no explanation. Genius works with the tools at hand and with the available material. For a more informative answer we might survey the tradition of translating Old English poetry into modern English verse prior to Pound's entrance into that tradition with two purposes in mind: first, to gain a sense of just how far Pound advanced the state of the art of rendering Old English verse into modern English, and then to identify those elements in the tradition which he adopted and transformed in creating his own poetry based on Old English texts.

Long before Pound took up the serious study of Old English at Hamilton College in 1904 many scholars and a few poets had labored at turning Old English poems into modern English verse, but the goal of finding an apt medium for such renderings proved elusive. Largely this is because Old English poetry is essentially different from modern English poetry or from any other poetry we know outside the ancient Germanic tradition. Old English

---

[1] These are discussed and the unpublished verses quoted in "The might of the north: Pound's Anglo-Saxon studies and 'The Seafarer'," pp. 239–58 above.

[2] Among many others, Jeannette Lander, *Ezra Pound* (New York, 1971), p. 36, makes the point that "the Anglo-Saxon translations, more than any others up to this point, were the decisive, formative step toward Pound's new language"; cf. Robinson, "The Might of the north," p. 239 above. K. L. Goodwin, *The Influence of Ezra Pound* (London, 1966), pp. 205–8, shows how Robert Lowell, T. S. Eliot, W. H. Auden, W. S. Merwin, and others were influenced by Pound's *The Seafarer* and the Old English diction he advocated.

poetry is elaborate in diction and syntax and uses words and to some extent grammar which are reserved exclusively for poetry. Its rhythm is emphatic and rigorously organized but with superficial variations which to the modern ear seems to obscure the strong underlying patterns or verse types. The narrative movement is halting and resumptive: something is asserted and then restated in different terms which bring out various aspects of the action being described. The first ten lines of *The Seafarer* in Old English followed by a crudely literal translation may suggest some of the qualities of Old English verse:

> Mæg ic be mē *sy*lfum   soðgied*d* wrecan,
> *sī*þas *s*ęcgan,   hū ic ge*s*wincdagum
> *ea*rfoðhwile   *o*ft þrōwade,
> *b*itre *b*rēostceare   ge*b*iden hæbbe,
> gecunnad in *c*ēole   *c*earsęlda fela,
> *a*tol *ȳ*þa gewealc.   þǣr mec *o*ft bigeat
> *n*earo *n*ithwaco [*sic*]   æt *n*acan stęfnan,
> þonne hē be *c*lifum *c*nossað   *c*alde geþrungen.
> Wǣron *f*ēt mīne   *f*orste gebunden,
> *c*aldum cl*o*mmum;[3]

"I can about myself utter a truth-song, tell [my] travels, how I toil-days, travail-time, often suffered, bitter breast-cares have endured, known in [my] ship many a care-house, terrible roll of the waves. Often found me there the anxious night-watch at the ship's stem when it crashed by cliffs. Cramped with cold were my feet, bound by frost, by cold clamps." The early translators of Old English verse were hard pressed to find an adequate medium for rendering this strange poetic idiom. For the most part they searched for a suitable verse analogue among the various conventional meters of modern English.

One of the earliest to be tried was, not surprisingly, that all-purpose workhorse of English poetry, blank verse. John Josias Conybeare, Professor of Poetry at Oxford University at the beginning of the nineteenth century and a forebear of the Conybeare Pound refers to in *Canto* 94, translates *Beowulf*, 198–207 (describing the hero's embarking for Denmark), in loose paraphrase using blank verse:

> And soon that noble soldier bad[e] array
> A goodly ship of strength. The hero spoke
> His brave intent, far o'er the sea-bird's path
> To seek the monarch at his hour of need.

---

[3] I have quoted *The Seafarer* from the text that Pound used, *An Anglo-Saxon Reader in Prose and Verse* with Grammar, Metre, Notes and Glossary by Henry Sweet (Oxford, 1898), p. 171. The volume from which I quote contains Pound's own annotations.

> Full swift address'd them to that enterprise
> His loved associates.[4]

While the verse is not deplorable – one thinks of Wordsworth working at *The Prelude* on an off day – Conybeare's rendering has nothing to suggest the surge and force of Old English verse. The same lines from *Beowulf* were translated at about the same time by Henry Wadsworth Longfellow into a limping line of which the major "poetic" element seems to be awkward grammatical inversions:

> He bade him a sea-ship,
> a goodly one, prepare,
> Quoth he, the war-king,
> over the swan's road,
> seek he would
> the mighty monarch,
> since he wanted men.
> For him that journey
> his prudent fellows
> straight made ready.[5]

At least we can be grateful that Longfellow did not put *Beowulf* into the *Hiawatha* meter.

J. J. Conybeare sought among the standard forms of English verse a vehicle suitable for rendering Old English. In introducing one of his translations he says, "I have ... adopted for my translation the form of the irregular ode: by this means I have been enabled to preserve more faithfully than I could perhaps have done in blank verse the abrupt transitions of the original."[6] His diagnosis of the problem is accurate, but the result is only a rather forced Drydenesque rapture:

> Some the tuneful hand may ply,
> And loud before the list'ning throng
> Wake the glad harp to harmony,
> Or bid the trump of joy its swelling note prolong.[7]

Worse than this is when he turns to tetrameter couplets to render the Old English poem *The Ruin*:

---

[4] *Illustrations of Anglo-Saxon Poetry* by John Josias Conybeare, ed. William Daniel Conybeare (London, 1826), p. 38. For a display of how *Beowulf* could be translated into the styles of various English poets – Pope, Tennyson, etc. – see Henry C. Wyld, "Experiments in translating *Beowulf*," in *Studies in English Philology: a miscellany in honor of Frederick Klaeber*, ed. Kemp Malone and Martin B. Ruud (Minneapolis, 1929), pp. 217-31.

[5] Longfellow, "Anglo-Saxon Literature," *North American Review*, 47 (1838), p. 104.

[6] Conybeare, *Illustrations*, p. 218.

[7] Ibid., p. 222, translating *Christ*, 668-70.

> Rear'd and wrought full workmanly
> By earth's old giant progeny
> The wall-stone proudly stood. It fell
> When bower, and hall, and citadel,
> And lofty roof, and barrier gate,
> And tower and turret bow'd to fate
> And wrapt in flame and drench'd in gore
> The lofty burgh might stand no more.[8]

But there is worse still. John Hookham Frere at the beginning of the nineteenth century translated *The Battle of Brunanburh* into a curious mish-mash in the manner of Chatterton, while at mid-century a man named Wackerbarth translated *Beowulf* into ballad meter:

> But haughty Hunferth, Ecg-laf's Son
> Who sat at royal Hroth-gar's Feet
> To bind up Words of Strife begun
>   And to address the noble Geat.[9]

The fourteeners selected for the same purpose by Lieut.-Colonel Lumsden have much the same effect:

> To none on earth would he allow a greater fame 'mong men
> Beneath the heavens than his: "Art thou the same Beowulf then,
> Who swam a match with Breca once upon the waters wide,
> When ye vainglorious searched the waves, and risked your lives for pride
> Upon the deep?"[10]

In the early twentieth century the poet-scholar William Ellery Leonard translated *Beowulf* into something he called "the Nibelungen couplet." Supposedly this was an English adaptation of the verse form used in the Middle High German *Nibelungenlied*, but it came out sounding very much like jaded ballad measure:

> When with my troop of tribesmen, I mounted on the sea,
> And sate me in my sailor-boat, I had this thought in me.[11]

Such jigging veins of rhyming mother wits suggest that the problem of finding a way of translating Old English poetry would never be solved, but both poets and scholars continued to seek a solution. In 1880 Alfred Lord Tennyson

---

[8] Conybeare, pp. 251–2.
[9] *Beowulf, An Epic Poem*, tr. A. Diedrich Wackerbarth (London, 1849).
[10] *Beowulf: an Old English poem*, tr. Henry W. Lumsden (London, 1881).
[11] *Beowulf: a new verse translation for fireside and classroom*, tr. William Ellery Leonard (New York, 1923).

produced a verse translation of *The Battle of Brunanburh* which at the beginning seems promising – almost an attempt at an imitative measure like Pound's, although a timid one:

> Athelstan King,
> Lord among Earls,
> Bracelet-bestower and
> Baron of Barons,
> He with his brother,
> Edmund Atheling,
> Gaining a lifelong
> Glory in battle,
> Slew with the sword-edge
> There by Brunanburh...[12]

But then it wilts into a kind of revenant of "Merlin and the Gleam."

Apparently the first attempt to make a verse translation of *The Seafarer* into modern English was G. R. Merry's partial version published in the magazine called *The Academy* in 1890. Unfortunately Merry adopted a rollicking anapestic measure and for dignity turned, one suspects, to the contemporary hymnal:

> The thought that was pent in my heart
>   Is roaming the roaring sea;
> It hath sped to the home of the whale,
>   Where my soul ever yearned to be.
> It hath flown to the ends of the earth,
>   It hath traversed the trackless main,
> And back with a ravening swoop
>   It hath rushed on my heart again.[13]

If Pound ever knew this, it would only have reinforced those influences which led to early, sentimental poems like Pound's

> The Gods of the North are fallen
> Thor's laid his hammer down
> Men fear not the wrath of Odin
> Nor the dark Valkyries frown[14]

or "At the Heart of Me," which is seen by some as a highly romantic dry run for *The Seafarer*. At first thought one might doubt that Pound ever saw Merry's

---

[11] Tennyson, *Ballads and Other Poems* (London, 1880).
[13] George R. Merry, "The Seafarer: translation from Old English," *The Academy*, 37 (1890), 99–100.
[14] Robinson, "The might of the North," p. 240 above.

translation of *The Seafarer*, tucked away as it was in this journal addressed to academicians. But it is interesting to note that when Pound ended his translation at line 99 of the 124-line Old English poem he was ending at exactly the same point where Merry's poem ends.[15] Also, in 1915 Pound tried to take over *The Academy* and make it an outlet for his own ideas and his friends' work,[16] and so it is conceivable that he had been familiar with its contents in earlier years. But Pound's own *Seafarer* translation owes nothing whatever to the style of Merry's precursory version; indeed, it could be said that his rugged, energetic poem is rather a reaction against that tradition of translating Old English which we have been reviewing here and which Merry exemplifies.

But if Merry is an exemplar of the flaccid style of verse-translation of Old English that Pound rejects, what resources was he drawing on when he developed the supple, vigorous idiom of his own *Seafarer*, with its carefully restrained imitation of Old English alliterative-accentual meter and its richly suggestive use of archaisms? The answer to this question which I am going to propose here is twofold. First, the strenuous apprenticeship for poetry which Pound devised for himself while he was at Hamilton College and the University of Pennsylvania included some exercises in composing poems in early English language and meter – exercises which prepared him particularly well for his successful translation of *The Seafarer*. Second, running contemporaneously with the tradition of verse-translation that we have been examining thus far, there was another, rather eccentric, tradition of translating Old English which Pound seized on and brought to poetic life.

First, Pound's autodidactic apprenticeship: As one leafs through the early papers of the poet in Yale's Beinecke Library – the papers from his days in college and university – one sees amid the various verse experiments scansions of various kinds. Some are clearly classical, while others are medieval English. For example, on one page he has experimental scansions – patterns of breves and macrons with occasional acute accents – and scribbled alongside them are two Old English longlines, one from *The Seafarer* and one from *Beowulf*. It seems as if he is calling before his eyes the actual lines of poetry from which he is trying to abstract the rhythmic principle. (The spelling of the verses makes clear that he is quoting them from memory and not copying them from any printed text.) The results of his verse experiments may be seen in many of his

---

[15] Sweet's *Reader*, from which Pound translated the poem, ends *The Seafarer* at l. 108. Recently an Anglo-Saxon scholar independently arrived at the conclusion that l. 102 is where the original poem may break off. Jackson J. Campbell, "Ends and meanings: modes of closure in Old English poetry," *Medievalia et Humanistica*, no. 16 (1988), 21–2, argues that there is a major shift in style and voice at the end of l. 102. He adds that "at line 102 . . . , a folio and a gathering end. The material beginning at the top of folio 82 could well be from a totally different poem." So codicology as well as style may confirm Pound's (and Merry's) intuition in sensing a break just before l. 102.

[16] Humphrey Carpenter, *A Serious Character: the life of Ezra Pound* (Boston, 1988), p. 276.

early verse exercises, such as those where he tries combining alliterative-accentual features with conventional forms like the iambic pentameter:

> ... my tongue is keen for winds and wander lore
> my pulse is hot, my feet no longer dwell
> at peace with ways that all have known so well
> that none may find a thing unfound before ...

In many of these early efforts Pound seems to be laboring to open his mind and ear to new harmonies of tone and accent, to break through the exhausted rhythms of his immediate predecessors to something literally radical – formed from the root of his English literary heritage.

Another, quite different exercise which the young Pound favored was composing verse in the language and style of earlier periods of English. He composes sonnets in the manner of the Elizabethan sonneteers. He has an amusing Tennysonian imitation called "The Lord of Shallott." A poem called "A Strained Conceit" is written in the manner of the worst imitators of Donne. A long poem on a drunken sailor tries to be funny and fails but is impressive in that it is written in sustained dialect, somewhat in the manner of Kipling. Especially prominent among these exercises are several poems which Pound wrote entirely in Middle English. These make no claim to being serious poems, but neither are they idle jests. They are serious experiments performed to help tune the poet's ear for later poems which Pound will write in earnest. An incomplete poem on Chaucer's *Troilus* may serve to illustrate his exercises in this vein:

> Ne wight in all the world there nis
> Ne knight ne man ne maid
> But woll love well this tale I tell
> > of Troilus and Cresseyde
> As Dom Chauser the tale Y-told
> In cointë rhymëd measure
> It sall be said as I have read
> > take ye of it your pleasure

> How in the mount of Troy citee
> Whan Greekës layed it bare
> Ne man there nas like Troilus
> Ne mayd like Cressyd fair
>
> How she him tooke for lovës playe
> > And made him cockwold
> Dom Diomed brocht hir to bed
> > Soon sall my tale be told.

I have added diereses above the unaccented vowels which must be sounded in the Middle English manner to maintain the iambic pattern. These show that Pound was not merely archaizing in a superficial way but rather was really trying to make verse in Middle English. Another exercise strains to control a complex verse form:

> Wherefor tho I ne know ye not
> I sendë you thys scryveninge
> of the prayse I woldë say
> Of yourë sotyl limeninge
> For mayster Chauceres roundelay
> It hath moch plaisir to myn eyn y-brot.

I have read better imitations of Chaucer's Middle English by academic versifiers, but these have usually been more in the nature of cautious *centos* – an arrangement of lines and phrases drawn from various poems of Chaucer's with a name or a noun substituted here and there to make the fragments appropriate to the subject or occasion at hand. Pound's youthful verses are actually saying something of his own in Middle English, making the words and the meter speak his own thoughts. He is, as it were, testing the sinews of the language at various stages in its history, and one can hardly imagine a better calisthenic prior to undertaking the creation of an appropriate modern medium for translating Old English.

It seems then that Pound's self-directed apprenticeship was an almost ideal preparation for his crucial success in the *Seafarer* translation. But even the most original genius usually finds a triggering suggestion in the inherited tradition on which he is building. Such a suggestion for Pound lay in a minor and rather unsuccessful approach to rendering Old English verse which would have appealed instantly to Pound's special enthusiasm for recovering the essence of ancient masterpieces. This approach to translation seeks to find, wherever possible, modern English descendents of Old English words to render the poetry and to adapt a measure that is imitative of the Old English meter rather than a selection from the conventional iambic, trochaic, and other meters of modern English. Hugh Kenner once characterized the practitioners of this method as those who "teutonize from word to word without quite knowing what was happening."[17] The method begins, it seems, with an eccentric scholar named Samuel Henshall, who, in the late eighteenth century, published a book with the self-important title *The Saxon and English Languages reciprocally illustrative of each other, the Impracticality of Acquiring an Accurate Knowledge of Saxon Literature through the Medium of Latin Phraseology Exemplified in the Errors of Hickes, Wilkins, Gibson, and other Scholars and a New Mode suggested of Radically Studying the Saxon and English Languages* (London, 1798). Henshall's knowledge of Old

[17] *Ezra Pound: translations* with an introduction by Hugh Kenner (Norfolk, CT, 1954), p. 9.

English and of its relation to later English was actually rather limited and he tended to guess at the connections between vocabulary items, often incorrectly. Thus the first line of Cædmon's *Hymn* (*Nu we sculon herigean heofonrices weard*), which means "Now we must praise the ward [that is, guardian] of the heavenly kingdom," Henshall renders, "Now we shall hearen heaven's Reach word." This is gibberish, but it is gibberish resulting from a principle which we can understand.

The principle appealed to a later scholar named George Stephens, an Englishman who spent all his adult life in Sweden studying runes and other Germanic antiquities. In 1844 he published a translation of the Old English poem *The Phoenix*, in which he adopted the "resolution to admit into our lines *nothing foreign*. Greek, and Latin, and Italian, and French, &c., &c. words and phrases dove-tailed into a composition of this chaste and antique national character are, we imagine, perfectly preposterous and absurd."[18] Henshall would have been pleased, but it is unfortunate that Stephens suggested to our minds the words "preposterous and absurd" just before presenting us with passages like

> O wong ever winsome!
> How its wolds stretch greenly
> Summer-skies under!
> Snow nor eke rain there,
> Not frost's fell snort-bite,
> Fire's ruddy glare-light,
> Hail's hard rush-fall,
> Hoar-rime's drear-pall,
> Sun-stroke blasting.[19]

The comical effect of Stephens's resolute Teutonizing should not prevent us from sensing that there is *in posse* a verbal mode of some power in strong Germanic compounds like *rush-fall* and *glare-light*. Here and there in Stephens' strange composition there are hints of phrasing that would quicken with life when Pound made deft incursions into the Teutonizers' wordhoard:

> Storm-ghost none stalketh
> The soul-bowing dread,
> No frost howleth Havoc
> Chill hung with sharp ice.
>   Rime there earth robes not,
> There rusheth no hail-sleet,
> No wind-cloud round wanders ...

---

[18] Stephens, "The King of Birds; or, the Lay of the Phoenix: an Anglo-Saxon Song of the Tenth or Eleventh century," *Archaeologia*, 30 (1844), p. 258.

[19] Ibid., p. 260.

> Nor hero-song gaysome
> Not any on earth heard,
> Nor organ-sigh mildest,
> Nor swan-dirge faint falling,
> More silv'ry on-sweep them –
> Nor of heart-joys the happiest ...
>
> He Winters abideth
> A thousand, as told in the
> Times of this earth.[20]

Stephens is not an isolated crank but part of a tradition. The Rev. Oswald Cockayne in 1863 published a translation along with a text "in Old English now first edited from the skin books"[21] which has passages like this: "Lord, do thou ward me wit ever to thee: nor thole thou ever the unwight that he worry my wit, nor make-to-wane my wisdom."[22] Stephens and Cockayne had many contemporaries who shared their preference for the ancient Germanic words,[23] and indeed, elements of this attitude are traceable in some earlier poets of English – in Spenser, in Richard Stanyhurst, and in Gavin Douglas, whose translation of the *Aeneid* Pound once declared "better than the original."[24]

The culmination of this tradition of Teutonizing translation of Old English verse was William Morris's curious translation of *Beowulf*.[25] This is important for our purposes because Pound was an enthusiastic reader of Morris's poetry in his early years (when he made his translation of *The Seafarer*). Nagy shows how extensively Pound drew on Morris's works for both matter and style in his early poems,[26] and Witemeyer confirms that Morris was among the writers who "most concerned Pound in the poems he wrote before 1912."[27] Hilda Doolittle reports that he read Morris to her with such enthusiasm that he shouted the

---

[20] Ibid., p. 263, 268, 269.

[21] Cockayne, ed. *Seinte Marherete* (London, 1862). "Skin book," Cockayne's Germanic term for "(vellum) manuscript," appears on the title-page.

[22] Ibid., p. 53. Realizing that his translation itself requires translation, Cockayne occasionally glosses some of his more bizarre Germanicisms. I have not reproduced these glosses.

[23] See Dennis E. Baron, *Going Native: the regeneration of Saxon English*, publication of the American Dialect Society, no. 69 (University of Alabama, 1981).

[24] *Literary Essays of Ezra Pound*, ed. T. S. Eliot (London, 1954), p. 35.

[25] *The Tale of Beowulf, Sometime King of the Folk of the Weder Geats*, tr. William Morris and A. J. Wyatt (London, 1898). Wyatt was an Anglo-Saxon scholar who provided Morris with a literal translation which Morris then turned into alliterative verse, no doubt studying the original Old English carefully as he did.

[26] N. Christoph de Nagy, *The Poetry of Ezra Pound: the pre-imagist stage*, the Cooper Monographs, no. 4, 2nd edn (Bern, 1968), pp. 54–68.

[27] Hugh Witemeyer, *The Poetry of Ezra Pound: forms and renewal, 1908–1920* (Berkeley, CA, 1969), p. 44.

verses, and apparently he wrote poems imitating Morris for her.[28] Morris's *Beowulf* translation must have provided a strong nudge toward the Henshall-Stephens-Cockayne school of translating Old English. It is easy to cite passages which are unintentionally comical:

> I therefore to Hrothgar
> Through my mind fashion'd roomsome the rede may now learn him
> How he, old-wise and good, may get the fiend under,
> If once more from him awayward may turn
> The business of bales, and the boot come again.
>
> (277–81)

Obsoletisms like *rede* and *awayward* and words like *business*, *bales*, and *boot*, whose most obvious modern meanings have little to do with the Old English meanings, make this passage barely intelligible. Similarly the following passage, which is trying to say that the hero Sigemund enjoyed fame after slaying the dragon, will leave some readers puzzled at more than one point:

> And to Sigemund up-sprang
> After his death-day fair doom unlittle
> Sithence that the war-hard the Worm there had quelled,
> The herd of the hoard; he under the hoar stone,
> The bairn of the Atheling, all alone dar'd it . . .
>   and the drake died the murder.
>
> (884–92)

For this to make sense one must know that in Old English *doom* meant "fame," *Worm* meant "dragon," *quell* meant "kill," *herd* meant "guardian," and *murder* meant "death." One must also understand archaisms like *Sithence*, *upsprang*, *bairn*, and *Atheling*. Morris's contemporaries found his diction so inscrutable that they persuaded him to provide his translation with a glossary of the terms he uses; that is, to provide a translation for his translation. But in slightly less quirky sections of Morris's poem one can see why Pound would have found it stimulating. The account of Beowulf's sea-journey back home from Denmark is fairly clear:

>   thunder'd the sound-wood.
> Not there the wave-floater did the wind o'er the billows
> Waft off from its ways; the sea-wender fared,
> Floated the foamy-neck'd forth o'er the waves,
> The bounden-stemm'd over the streams of the sea;

---

[28] See Carpenter, *A Serious Character*, p. 62, and H. D., *End to Torment* (New York, 1979), pp. x, 45–6. Michael Alexander, *The Poetic Achievement of Ezra Pound* (Berkeley, CA, 1979), p. 53, names Morris among Pound's "enthusiasms."

> Till the cliffs of the Geats there they gat them to wit,
> The nesses well kenned. Throng'd up the keel then
> Driven hard by the lift, and stood on the land.
>
> (1906–13)

The most prominent feature of this is the compounds used to refer to the ship. They have been simply modernized from the original Old English forms: *bounden-stemm'd* (referring to the curved prow or stem), *wave-floater*, *sea-wender*, *foamy-neck'd*, and *sound-wood* (with *sound* as in "Long Island Sound") give one a good sense of how Old English poetic diction actually sounds. Pound also modernizes Old English compounds or forms new ones on the model of Old English: *flood-ways*, *hail-scur*, *doom-gripped*, and *mood-lofty*. Pound also adopts Morris's trick of using strong words like *kenned* and *throng'd* which are in the original – even though the meanings have shifted slightly in modern English. Pound does this much more sparingly than Morris did, however, and thereby manages to catch the flavor of Old English without lapsing into unintelligibility.

An important feature of Morris's translation, seen as a forerunner of Pound's poem, is the meter. Both poets were wise enough not to observe all the rules and sub-rules of the original metrical form, most of which would not be perceived by the modern English ear, so greatly have the language and our principles of versification changed over time. Instead both employ a rhythm which is loosely imitative and suggestive. Morris's, however, tends to fall into a rather sing-song anapestic measure too often, while Pound's taut rhythm is a careful selection of just those features of the original which the modern ear can detect and an avoidance of those features which would suggest randomness to our ears. Stephens too adopted an alliterative-accentual measure, but it is undisciplined, and he makes his system less obvious to the eye by breaking up the Old English longlines into short halflines arranged one over the other. Pound's metrical form grew directly out of the Henshall-Stephens-Morris tradition, then, but Pound's superb ear for verbal rhythms gave the style dignity and force.

There were other translators who worked in this tradition. A few years before Pound published his *Seafarer*, F. B. Gummere published a verse translation of *Beowulf* "in the original metres" using the same kind of diction and syntax.[29] A few randomly chosen lines will show both the similarity to Morris and the fatal tendency to fall into anapestics:

> Now Beowulf bode in the burg of the Scyldings
> for he waxed under welkin, in wealth he throve
> most baneful of burdens and bales of the night

---

[29] Gummere, *The Oldest English Epic* (New York, 1909). "in the original metres" appears on the title page.

Pound may well have known Gummere's version, but by the time it appeared he had already produced his translation of the verse charm "Loud were they, loud,"[30] in which his own metrical principles for rendering Old English are clearly taking shape.

The syntactical features which Pound apparently drew from Morris and his precursors will be sufficiently obvious to anyone who compares *The Seafarer* with these earlier translations, but we might pause to note one or two examples. Inversion of subject and verb is especially striking. Pound has "Waneth the watch," "cometh beauty of berries," and "cometh oft to me ... the crying lone-flyer." Morris has "came a many to flood then," "went his ways the hard one," "shone the world's candle," and "offer'd him Hygd then the kingdom." Stephens had "glittereth the sun-grove, gladdeth her wood-holt," and "bolden'd his breast-thought." Placing the adjective after its noun is another notable feature: Pound has "man eager of mood," "days little durable," "heart ... eager and ready." Morris says Beowulf "trod the mould grassy" and speaks of "steeds apple-fallow." Predicate adjectives, past participles, and direct objects which normally follow the verb are also moved to the head of the sentence: Pound says "chill its chains are" and "bitter breast-cares have I abided" while Morris has "upreared is the fame-blast" and "wrath Thrytho bore." Evidently the Teutonizing tradition identified in such inversions apt signals that the language they were translating was different, archaic; and Pound agreed, although he used the devices with more restraint than his predecessors.

Before leaving Morris we should perhaps acknowledge that while most have regarded his performance as impossibly quirky and inscrutable, not everyone has found it so. Some like the uncompromising Germanics of it and find the verbal power an adequate justification for the obscurity of the diction. The composer Howard Hanson was inspired by Morris's rendering to write *The Lament for Beowulf*, a work scored for orchestra and chorus. Hanson says of Morris's version:

> If the story of the death and burial of the warrior king of the Vikings moved me deeply, so did this particular translation with its reliance upon words of Anglo-Saxon derivation. No Gallicisms here, no capitulation to Rome or Athens![31]

Pound's essay "The Music of *Beowulf*" was never published in his lifetime and so cannot have been a factor in Hanson's decision to interpret the poem through music, but the two men evidently agreed in finding more worth in Morris's experiment than others have.

---

[30] Robinson, "The might of the North," pp. 244–5 above.

[31] Hanson, "*The Lament for Beowulf*," in *The Composer's Point of View: essays on twentieth-century music by those who wrote it*, ed. Robert Stephan Hines (Norman, OK, 1963), p. 16.

Morris was certainly a major influence on Pound, but there is one source which is probably more immediate and may be more important than Morris: Stopford A. Brooke's *The History of Early English Literature*, published by Macmillan in 1892 and cited by Pound in a note scribbled in his copy of his Old English textbook, Sweet's *Reader*, which he was using at Hamilton College.[32] I have suggested elsewhere that Brooke is the immediate source of Pound's early poem "At the Heart of Me,"[33] and I believe that Pound's famous remark about his translation from Old English having isolated "the English national chemical" is a sharpened recasting of Brooke's comment, "In this Anglo-Saxon poetry of which I write we grasp most clearly the dominant English essence."[34] Brooke's *History* is centered on a series of verse translations of selections of Old English poetry, which Brooke then explicates with enthusiasm and learning. His manner of translating is distinctly in the Henshall-Stephens-Morris tradition:

> Then our hearers many,   haughty of their heart,
> They that couth it well,   clearly said in words
> That a better lay   listed had they never.[35]

The imitation of Old English alliterative-accentual meter, the inversions, and archaisms like *couth* and *listed* leave no doubt where the roots of his translational style are to be found.[36] In his preface Brooke makes a vigorous defense of his imitative form of translating, and some of his phrases remind one of Pound's own defense of his *Seafarer* translation:

> Translations of poetry are never much good, but at least they should always endeavour to have the musical movement of poetry, and to obey the laws of the verse they translate.
>
> A translation made in any one of our existing rhyming metres seemed to me as much out of the question as a prose translation. None of these metres resemble those of Anglo-Saxon poetry; and, moreover, their associations would modernise the old English thought.... I felt myself then driven to invent a rhythmical movement which would enable me, while translating literally, to follow the changes, and to express, with

---

[32] Pound's penciled citation of the book is slightly inexact. He refers to it as "Brooke, *History of Old English Literature*."

[33] Robinson, "The might of the North," pp. 245–6 above.

[34] Brooke, *History of Early English Literature*, p. vi.

[35] Ibid., p. 3.

[36] Although the book as a whole is a stout defense of the Henshall-Stephens-Morris style of translation, in an appendix Brooke curiously straddles the traditions of Morris and Conybeare, supplying translations of *The Wanderer* and *The Seafarer* in blank verse (ibid., pp. 478–82). This is odd, for on p. viii he rejects the use of blank verse for translating Old English poetry, supplying several compelling reasons for doing so.

some approach to truth, the proper ebb and flow of Anglo-Saxon verse. ... I think the method used is on the whole the right method, but I am by no means satisfied with what I have done. I submit it with much deference to those who understand the difficulties of such a translation.[37]

I suspect that the young Ezra Pound took this as a personal challenge to "invent a rhythmical movement ... to express ... the proper ebb and flow of Anglo-Saxon verse" which *was* satisfactory, and that Stopford Brooke's preface may well have been the stimulus which set Pound planning his own translation of *The Seafarer* and of other Old English verse.

To see just how closely Pound was working to Brooke's precept and example, one should read Brooke's preface in detail and compare Pound's *Seafarer* with Brooke's translation of the poem on pages 362–4 of his *History of Early English Literature*. Here I present only a comparison of select phrases in Pound's poem with the corresponding phrases in Stopford Brooke's version. Not all the verbal correspondences imply that Pound was drawing from Brooke, of course; the two men were after all rendering the same text using a similar method of translation. But in some cases it does seem likely that Pound was remembering Brooke's precursory version. In line 45, for example, *ring-having* seems likely to be a recollection of Brooke's *having of the rings* since this is a slightly odd rendering of the Old English word *hringðegu*, one not suggested by any of the dictionaries or glossaries. Elsewhere the two translators choose with remarkable frequency the same word for rendering an Old English term, while the dictionaries give a broad range of modern meanings.

Line	Pound	Brooke
4	bitter breast-cares have I abided	bitter breast-care I have been abiding
7	narrow night-watch	narrow watch at night
10	chill its chains	chains of cold
14	how I, care-wretched on ice-cold sea	how I, carked with care in the ice-cold sea
19	at whiles the swan cries	'whiles the crying of the swan
28	this he little believes	little then does he believe
33	frost froze the land, hail fell on the earth then	frost the field enchained, fell the hail on earth
34	corn of the coldest	coldest of all corns
38	fare forth that I afar hence	set afaring; so that far from hence
45	he hath not heart for harping, nor in ring-having	for the harp he has no heart, nor for having of the rings
46	nor world's delight	in the world he's no delight
63	the crying lone-flyer	that lonely flyer
64	whets for the whale-path the heart irresistibly	whets upon the whale-way irresistibly my heart

[37] Brooke, pp. viii–x.

In others of his translations Brooke repeatedly uses a selection of archaisms which Pound also favors, such as *nathless*, *'neath*, *garths*, *scours of hail* (Pound respells it *scurs*), and *burgs*. A systematic comparison of Pound's translation of the Old English charm against a sudden stitch with Brooke's version on pages 160–1 of his *History of Early English Literature* will reveal similar echoes of phrasing.

Recognizing that a particular translational tradition, and especially Stopford A. Brooke's manifestation of that tradition in a book which Pound used, provided a starting point for Pound's uniquely successful rendering of Old English verse in no way diminishes the magnitude of his achievement. Indeed, Hugh Kenner's assessment of that achievement stands unchallenged: "Pound . . . had both the boldness and resource to make a new form, similar in effect to that of the original, which permanently extends the bounds of English verse."[38]

"The very great is never new," observed Goethe. Genius discerns possibilities in material which others had found unpromising and by renovating it lends it greatness. One thinks how passages from North's Plutarch assume freshness and life when used by Shakespeare (even when North's phrasing remains unchanged) or of Gauguin's paintings which had their origins in Tahitian postcards. Or one thinks of the dramatic orchestral effects and dynamic contrasts which make Beethoven sound so startling and sublime but which musicologists tell us are merely a genius's recasting of standard features of the old Mannheim school with its sudden pianissimos, its explosions of sound, and the arpeggio effects known as "Mannheim rockets." Pound was in good company when he adopted the quirky and sometimes comical style of the old Teutonizing school of translators and gave it gravity and power.[39]

---

[38] Kenner, *Ezra Pound: translations*, p. 9.

[39] For a recent survey of translations of Old English poetry see Eric Gerald Stanley, "Translation from Old English: 'the garbaging war-hawk,' or, the literal materials from which the reader can re-create the poem," in Stanley's *A Collection of papers with emphasis on Old English literature* (Toronto, 1987), pp. 83–114. It may be appropriate to add here something that will be obvious to most readers but perhaps not to Stanley: my observation in the final paragraph of this essay that Pound shares with other artists the technique of renovating existing materials does not say or imply that Pound is an artist equal to or better than or worse than Shakespeare, Gauguin and Beethoven. See *NQ* 237 [n.s. 39] (1992), 78.

22

The Afterlife of Old English: A Brief History of Composition in Old English after the Close of the Anglo-Saxon Period

In the archives of the Dictionary of Old English at the University of Toronto, included amid an exhaustive repository of Old English texts, there is a 41-line verse fragment of a translation of Vergil's *Aeneid*, book II, into classical Old English alliterative verse. The fragment recounts the first part of Aeneas's narration to Dido of the fall of Troy, and it is a remarkable example of how the content and diction of one heroic tradition can come alive in the formulas and epithets of another, as the Old English alliterative verses encompass and reshape the meanings of the Latin hexameters, transforming them into something new and Germanic. Reading this translation one gets a vivid sense of what elements of the heroic poetry of these two cultures are shared in common and what elements are unique and resist translation.

This manuscript survives in a late hand, and its author and provenance are known. It was composed and written down by Alistair Campbell, late Rawlinson and Bosworth Professor of Anglo-Saxon in the University of Oxford. The papers containing the Old English verses came to Toronto several years ago when the Dictionary of Old English acquired Professor Campbell's library. In addition to the *Aeneid* translation there is an Old English prose summary of *Beowulf* (much briefer than the prose version published by Henry Sweet in the nineteenth century)[1] and several lines of an Old English verse translation of *The Song of Roland*, another experiment in testing the ability of Old English verse to replicate the heroic poetry of a foreign culture. Here are a portion of the *Aeneid* translation (rendering verses 1–9 of book II) and all of the *Roland* (rendering verses 1–7). Both are quite free, especially the *Roland*.[2]

---

[1] Sweet, *First Steps in Anglo-Saxon* (Oxford, 1897), pp. 39–67. Sweet's version covers only the first two episodes in the poem. He entitles this portion *Beowulfes Sīþ* and composes titles for the subsections, such as *Be Hrōþgāre, Dena cyninge* and *Hū Hrōþgār getimbrede Heorot*.

[2] Anyone inclined to find fault with Campbell's rendering of the *Aeneid* passage (e.g. with *scolde* in l. 2, *wolde* in l. 6, or *mīn* in l. 10) should remember that Campbell never intended that this *jeu*

Aeneid ii

þær wæron swigran hæleþ   samod ætgædere,
þa ærgewin   eahtian scolde
sæmanna helm   sorgum gedrefed
mænan modceare   meodobence on.
    "Hwæt þu bealoniþas,   beaghroden cwen,   [5]
on healærne   hyran wolde,
hu we earfoðhwile   oft þrowedon,
eagum onsawon   ealuburge hryre,
æþelinga ellorsiþ: ic þæt eall geman.
    "Huru ic ne hycge   hygeþoncum min,   [10]
þætte ænig eorl   ofer eorþan sie,
heortceald heaþorinc   se þe hildespell,
sorgfulle siþas,   secgan cuþe,
swa him tearas ne hruron   tornþoliendum,
weollon wægdropan.   Nu we witon georne,   [15]
hwær on uprodor   æþeltungla heap,
fus heofonbeacnu   fyre onæled,
sigaþ to setlum,   slæp on geþrang,
rest on recede   reordberendum...."

Roland

    Oft Carl cyning   casera mæst
mære ofer moldan   mægðe geeode,
swa brimu bebugeð   bradum yðum
heabyrh hæleða   hreðgotum on,
oðþæt ymbe seofon gear   sigefæst dryhten   [5]
dyre dædfruma   dreamleasra byrh
billa ecgum   tobrocen hæfde,
let him behindan   hettend swefan
garum forgrunden;   ðæt wæs god cyning.
    þæm orlege wearð   æfter boden   [10]
atol ecghete,   siððan anum weol
wælgifre geþoht;   werod samnode
on þære sidan byrg   Saraguce.
    Wæs se mæra   Marsilie haten,
hæleþ heorogrim   se ðe on heortan wæg   [15]
wælniþ frecne   wið weroda Frean
Dryhtne urum, . . .

---

d'esprit should be published, and that we do not know at what age he composed it. *Scolde* in l. 2 could be correct if we translate, "The warriors all together there became more silent as the protector of seamen, stirred by sorrows, had to address the ancient strife, to lament the sorrows of his heart on the mead-bench."

These experiments in testing the sinews of a language whose speakers are long extinct are representative of a considerable body of Old English composed since the end of the Anglo-Saxon period. This corpus of post-Conquest Old English is analogous to the respected literary tradition that we call "Neo-Latin," and one of my purposes here is to suggest that we should begin to treat the Old English material with something like the same seriousness that has long characterized the study of Neo-Latin.[3] Some might even think it appropriate to prepare in the future an anthology of post-Conquest Old English along the lines of Fred Nichols's very successful anthology of Neo-Latin poetry.[4]

The particular aim of this essay, however, is to review the history of composition in Old English since the end of the Anglo-Saxon period and to observe the variety of motives for composing in Old English from one period to the other and the variety of results to appear in these compositions. There are, I believe, interesting things to be learned from a study of this hitherto neglected subject.[5]

The earliest post-Conquest composition in Old English probably arises from intent to defraud. A number of charters and writs produced long after the end of the Anglo-Saxon period are written in the best Old English which Middle English or Anglo-Norman scribes could muster to give the documents an air of antique authenticity.[6] But the grammar of texts like the supposed charter of Æthelred, King of Mercia (dated 682), which begins *In seo nama of ure Hælend Cryst wurthmynt of God* betrays its spuriousness,[7] as does the spelling of a supposed writ of Edward the Confessor containing the phrase *it formest hauchten*

---

[3] To make the analogy precise, I should say that post-Conquest Old English corresponds to late medieval Latin and Neo-Latin, for the beginning of Neo-Latin is usually thought to be in the Renaissance.

[4] *An Anthology of Neo-Latin Poetry*, ed. and tr. Fred J. Nichols (New Haven, 1979).

[5] Post-Conquest Old English has been studied piecemeal in articles cited below and in Michael Murphy's "Scholars at play: a short history of composing in Old English," *Old English Newsletter*, 15, no. 2 (1982), 26–36, but the present essay attempts to address the tradition as a whole.

[6] P. H. Sawyer, *Anglo-Saxon Charters: an annotated list and bibliography* (London, 1968) speaks of "spurious texts that were obviously confected long after the Norman Conquest" (p. vii), and in his listings he flags several vernacular charters as "forged," "spurious," "suspicious," and "probably concocted in the early 14th century," while Florence E. Harmer, *Anglo-Saxon Writs* (Manchester, 1952), p. 118, lists eight English writs which are "fabrications of various kinds." John Earle thought there was a renaissance of writing in Old English at the close of the twelfth century (p. 348), when charters were composed by scribes who showed "a real taste for the royal style of the old language and a sincere passion to master the charm of it"; see *A Hand-Book to the Land-Charters and Other Saxonic Documents* (Oxford, 1888), p. cviii, and cf. A. S. Cook in *Scottish Historical Review*, 12 (1915), 213–15. See further Derek Pearsall's comments on Rochester, Canterbury, Peterborough, and Worcester in *Old and Middle English Poetry* (London, 1977), p. 75.

[7] See H. P. R. Finberg, *The Early Charters of Wessex* (Leicester, 1964), p. 281. Sawyer, *Anglo-Saxon Charters*, p. 90, dates this manuscript "s. xvi."

7 þider inne beqwað. on allen þingen.⁸ The crudity of such efforts provides a measure of the extent to which people living in the Middle English period had lost touch with the language as it had been spoken and written in earlier years.

A careful study of the manuscript descriptions in Ker's *Catalogue*⁹ enabled Angus Cameron to demonstrate long ago that Old English manuscripts were being read and understood by readers from the beginning of the thirteenth century well into the early sixteenth century.¹⁰ Further scrutiny of Ker's entries shows that some Middle English speakers were also capable of *writing* Old English. In the copy of the *West Saxon Gospels* in BM MS. Royal 1 A.xiv, as in all other copies, the first part of John 7: 23 is missing, but in the Royal manuscript a thirteenth-century hand has supplied *gyf ymbsnyðenesse tache man on restdaige* to fill the lacuna.¹¹ A late Old English homily on the Festival of St Mary included in a manuscript collection of sermons mostly by Ælfric is, Ker notes, a translation of a Latin sermon by Ralph d'Escures, archbishop of Canterbury from 1114 to 1122.¹² The Middle English glossator of a homiliary in the Bodleian Library who normally writes Middle English equivalents over Old English words in the text occasionally introduces an Old English synonym and writes it over the lemma, as when he writes *reordede* over "ett."¹³ In another manuscript a hand dated about 1500 supplies missing English glosses, imitating as he does the letter-forms of the Old English script.¹⁴ And a mid-twelfth-century hand supplies an Old English comment in the margin of a homiliary in Corpus Christi College Library, Cambridge.¹⁵ If, as Linda Ehrsam Voigts and Jane Hetherington Brown cautiously suggest, the thirteenth-century inscription on the last folio of a Glasgow manuscript is a somewhat garbled Old English charm, then here we have another Middle English scribe writing Old English.¹⁶

A distinct but related activity which demonstrates a continuing interest in Old English by Middle English readers is the occasional effort to copy, adapt, or preserve Old English words or texts in the post-Conquest era. The Middle English rhyming narrative on the life of the ninth-century Anglo-Saxon St

---

⁸ Harmer, *Anglo-Saxon Writs*, p. 341. She dates the manuscript early fourteenth century (p. 494).

⁹ N. R. Ker, *Catalogue of Manuscripts Containing Anglo-Saxon* (London, 1957).

¹⁰ A. F. Cameron, "Middle English in Old English manuscripts," *Chaucer and Middle English Studies in Honor of Rossell Hope Robbins*, ed. Beryl Rowland (London, 1974), pp. 218–29.

¹¹ Ker, *Catalogue*, p. 316.

¹² Ker, *Catalogue*, p. 275. The homily, which was published in *Early English Homilies from the Twelfth Century MS. Vesp. D.xiv*, ed. Rubie D.-N. Warner, EETS o.s. 152 (London, 1917), pp. 134–9, begins *Se godspellere Lucas sæigð on þyssen godspelle þæt se Hælend com* ...

¹³ Ker, *Catalogue*, p. 368.

¹⁴ Ibid., p. 342.

¹⁵ Ibid., p. 113.

¹⁶ Voigts and Brown, "University of Glasgow, Hunter MS. U.3.2, f. 210ᵛ," *Old English Newsletter*, 14, no. 1 (1980), 12–13.

Cynhelm tells of the pope saying mass in Rome when a dove descends with a message from God written in two English alliterative longlines specifying the location of the martyred saint's body. The Italian pope does not understand God's English, and so he must find an Anglo-Saxon to translate it for him. Since the two verses, which are preserved elsewhere in an earlier manuscript, are in late Old English metrical form, this is apparently an example of a Middle English poet trying to preserve verses from the preceding period.[17] Something similar may be going on in the late Old English poem *The Grave*, which, it has been thought, was continued for three verses by an early Middle English poet.[18] And it is common knowledge that Ælfric's *Grammar* and some of his Old English homilies continued to be copied by scribes well into the Middle English period.[19] The inclination of some post-Conquest Englishmen to perpetuate and even expand the Old English legacy is illustrated again by the claim that *The Proverbs of Alfred* were the work of the Anglo-Saxon king and by the use of Old English epithets like *Engle derling* (cf. Layamon's similarly archaizing *Englelondes deorling*) to lend the claim linguistic plausibility.[20]

In Renaissance England composition in Old English was well underway as early as the sixteenth century, and the practice sometimes created problems for later scholars. A notable case is that of two Old English texts printed in William Lambarde's *Archaionomia*[21] of 1568 but witnessed in no surviving Anglo-Saxon manuscript. Athelstan's *Ordinance* and a version of the law code *I Athelstan* in the *Archaionomia* must have been based upon original manuscripts now lost, according to Felix Liebermann, the editor of the standard edition of the laws.[22] But Kenneth Sisam argued resourcefully that these texts are in fact examples of

---

[17] See *Early Middle English Verse and Prose*, ed. J. A. W. Bennett and G. V. Smithers (Oxford, 1966), p. 104 for the text and pp. 96–7 for discussion.

[18] See *A Manual of the Writings in Middle English*, ed. Albert E. Hartung (Hamden, CT, 1972), p. 846, where it is described as a twelfth-century poem continued in the thirteenth century. In *Old English Verse Texts from Many Sources*, ed. Fred C. Robinson and E. G. Stanley, Early English Manuscripts in Facsimile 23 (Copenhagen, 1991), p. 27, an alternative explanation of the text is proposed.

[19] For a classic example of a Middle English scribe faithfully (though not slavishly) copying an Old English text, see the version of the Old English *Herbarium* in BL MS. Harley 6258 B, which was copied by a thirteenth-century scribe (according to Ker, who therefore excludes the manuscript from his *Catalogue* – see p. xix) but which remains in Old English: see *The Old English Herbarium and Medicina de Quadrupedibus*, ed. Hubert Jan de Vriend, EETS o.s. 286 (London, 1984), p. lxxv.

[20] For a good account of Layamon's response to his Anglo-Saxon heritage see J. A. W. Bennett, *Middle English Literature*, ed. and completed Douglas Gray (Oxford, 1986), pp. 68–89. See also the account in the same volume of how Middle English scribes of the *Peterborough Chronicle* connect with their Anglo-Saxon precursors (pp. 260–1).

[21] Lambarde, *Archaionomia, sive De priscis Anglorum legibus libri, sermone anglico, vetustate antiquissimo* (London, 1568).

[22] Liebermann, *Die Gesetze der Angelsachsen* (Halle, 1903–16), vol. 1, p. xxxiii, and vol. 3, pp. 96–8.

"Elizabethan Anglo-Saxon,"²³ that the odd diction and syntax of such passages as *án sconc spices oþþe án rám weorþe .IIII. peningas* could only have been composed by an Elizabethan antiquarian who had "a good knowledge of Old English vocabulary and a special familiarity with the phrasing of the Laws" but whose grammar and *Sprachgefühl* were not those of a native speaker of the language.²⁴ Sisam suggests that Laurence Nowell probably translated Anglo-Saxon laws surviving only in Latin versions into Old English, perhaps simply to complete his collection of vernacular laws, and that Lambarde printed Nowell's translations, mistakenly assuming that they were transcripts Nowell had made of original Old English documents.²⁵ In response to Sisam's exposé Liebermann stoutly defended the authenticity of the texts he had edited,²⁶ but the subsequent discovery that Nowell elsewhere translated Latin versions of Old English texts into "Elizabethan Anglo-Saxon" and inserted them into his transcriptions of genuine vernacular documents virtually clinched Sisam's case.²⁷ Or so it seemed until Roland Torkar, in a thorough scrutiny of all the evidence, presented reasons for believing that there may actually have been more Anglo-Saxon manuscripts available to Nowell for the *Archaionomia* texts than Sisam's work had assumed.²⁸ That Nowell did at times exercise his considerable control of Old English to concoct vernacular texts remains beyond question, but Torkar's argument that Nowell might have had access to manuscripts of the laws which no longer exist reopens the question of the status of the two *Archaionomia* texts and in doing so reminds us of the unwitting mischief that Nowell's composition of post-Conquest Old English can cause.

Another antiquary who freely exercised his facility at recreating Old English texts was William L'Isle (1579?–1637). When he made his transcript (now Bodleian MS. Laud Misc. 201) of the *Eadwine Psalter* and of some prayers from the *Ancrene Riwle*, he archaized the language of the latter texts, transforming the early Middle English of the *Ancrene Riwle* back into a form of Old English. Thus "For þe seoue ʒiftes of þe hali gast" is copied as *For þa seofen gyftes þæs*

---

²³ Sisam, "The authenticity of certain texts in Lambard's *Archaionomia* 1568," in his *Studies in the History of Old English Literature* (Oxford, 1953), p. 234. This essay is a conflation of papers previously published in 1923 and 1925.

²⁴ Ibid., p. 242.

²⁵ Ibid., p. 236.

²⁶ Felix Liebermann, "Ist Lambarde's Text der Gesetze Æthelstans neuzeitliche Fälschung?," *Anglia Beiblatt*, 35 (1924), 214–18. See further his "Angelsächsischer Gesetztext gefälscht?," *Anglia Beiblatt*, 36 (1925), 345–7.

²⁷ Robin Flower, "Laurence Nowell and the discovery of England in Tudor times," *Proceedings of the British Academy*, 21 (1935), p. 73, n. 6. See also Raymond J. S. Grant, "Laurence Nowell's transcript of B.M. Cotton Otho B.xi," *Anglo-Saxon England*, 3 (1974), 111–24, esp. p. 114. For clear evidence of Lambarde himself composing Old English see Carl T. Berkhout, "William Lambarde's Old English Ex Libris," *NQ*, 31 (1984), 297–8.

²⁸ Torkar, *Eine altenglische Übersetzung von Alcuins De virtute et vitiis, Kap. 20*, Texte und Untersuchungen zur Englischen Philologie, 7 (Munich, 1981).

halgan gastes and "þe fowr goddspelles þe haldeð al cristendom up" is copied as *þa feower godspelles þe healdaþ eall cristendom up*.[29] The restoration of older forms is imperfectly executed, but L'Isle's intention is clear: he wanted to construct an Old English text of the *Ancrene Riwle*. To complete the antique appearance of his prayers he adds Old English titles to them, titles which have no basis whatever in the manuscript he was copying: *To þam hælende criste*, *To þam* [!] *halgan þrynnesse*, etc. Nothing sinister seems to have motivated L'Isle's performance but only the exuberance of the scholar-pioneer. His lust for recovering ever more Old English texts was so strong that, as in other circumstances, desire has led to propagation. But for later Anglo-Saxon scholars the consequences could be unfortunate. A scholar in Göttingen came to the conclusion that L'Isle's transcript of the *Ancrene Riwle* must have been taken from an older manuscript now lost and that it indicates that the *Ancrene Riwle* was originally composed in Old English.[30] His thesis was promptly exploded,[31] but, as in the case of Lambarde and Nowell, one is left a little uneasy. There is reason to think that more transcripts of Old English texts by sixteenth- or seventeenth-century antiquaries may turn up in the future; if they do, they must be treated with caution.

A less troublesome kind of composition in Old English by seventeenth-century scholars was probably suggested to them by the analogous Neo-Latin tradition. On festive or solemn occasions it was the custom to prepare eulogies or laments in the classical languages or even in Hebrew. When English royalty was the subject, Old English was sometimes included among the dead languages considered a fit medium for ceremonial expression. Such is the case in a volume of poems by various hands published in 1641 to celebrate the return of Charles I from Scotland, where he had gone to negotiate (unsuccessfully) with the Scots several months before the outbreak of the Civil War.[32] Among the tributes in Greek and Latin by various Cambridge men, *Irenodia Cantabrigiensis* includes two poems in Old English, one by Abraham Wheelock (1593–1653), Professor of Arabic (who provides a Hebrew version of his poem as well), and another by William Retchford, presumed to be a student of Wheelock's. Of all the poems composed in Old English in the seventeenth and eighteenth centuries these are the ones that modern scholars are most likely to

---

[29] Arthur S. Napier, "The 'Ancren Riwle'," *MLR*, 4 (1909), 433–6, provides in parallel columns (pp. 434–5) the text of L'Isle's transcript and the corresponding text from Cambridge MS. Corpus Christi College 402 (fol. 6ᵛ), whence he copied it.

[30] W. Heuser, "Die Ancren Riwle – ein aus angelsächsischer Zeit überliefertes Denkmal," *Anglia*, 30 (1907), 103–22.

[31] Napier, "The 'Ancren Riwle'," explains the nature of L'Isle's transcript. Th. Mühe, "Über die Ancren Riwle," *Anglia*, 31 (1908), 399–404, is less to the point.

[32] *Irenodia Cantabrigiensis: Ob paciferum Serenissimi Regis Caroli è Scotia reditum Mense Novembri 1641* (Cambridge, 1641). In transcribing these and other poems I have routinely substituted modern typefaces for the Anglo-Saxon characters of the early printers.

know, for they have been published repeatedly. Wülcker published Wheelock's Old English poem in 1885,[33] and in 1942 Francis Lee Utley published both Wheelock's and Retchford's poems along with translations and an elaborate commentary.[34] Both poems are written in jigging modern meters with rhyme, Wheelock preferring trimeter, Retchford tetrameter lines. The quality of their prosody and grammar can be assessed from a sampling of each. Wheelock poses a rhetorical question:

> Eala Huntingdon hwære
> Is þine dryman ðæt ðære
> From Norþ dæl ure freondas
> Woldon don ure feondas
> Ond Breoton gehergian
> Ðurh wordum to flitan.[35]

"Oh Huntingdon, where is thy sorcerer [glossed 'pseudopropheta' in the margin] that wanted to make our friends from the north our enemies and to harry Britain, to quarrel with words?" Retchford, in answer to his own question as to why England is in pain, says,

> Forþam þin Ceorl Cyninga betst
> Na ofer Breoton lond's gemær
> Ac to ðam Orcadas gan ðær;
> þæt ðeos Iglond seo iu wæs an
> Fram þis annysse ne gewan.[36]

"Because your Ceorl, the best of kings, goes not beyond Britain's border, but to the Orkneys; so that this island that was one of yore has not struggled [away] from this unity." Retchford seems more enthusiastic about than learned in Old English.[37] But in both pieces number and gender are almost systematically ignored (*woldon* is used as a singular, *Iglond* is made feminine and *annysse* neuter, etc.), the infinitive *gan* is used as a finite verb, and the infinitive form *to flitan* is as anachronistically modern as is the syntax in general. To make *ðær* rhyme with *hwære* Wheelock simply adds an *-e* which has no linguistic justification, while Retchford, to make *gemære* rhyme with *ðær*, simply removes

---

[33] Richard Wülker, *Grundriss zur Geschichte der angelsächsischen Litteratur* (Leipzig, 1885), p. 15.

[34] Utley, "Two seventeenth-century Anglo-Saxon poems," *Modern Language Quarterly*, 3 (1942), 243–61. In 1982 Murphy, "Scholars at play," reprinted them yet again (in part) on p. 28.

[35] *Irenodia*, sig. A4a, ll. 5–10.

[36] *Irenodia*, n.p. A marginal note specifies that *Ceorl* means "maritus, sponsus," presumably in order to make clear that the pejorative sense "churl, peasant" is not intended. *Ceorl* was selected, no doubt, for the sake of a tasteless pun on *Charles*.

[37] In a letter of February 12, 1978, J. D. Pickles kindly calls my attention to Retchford's appearance as a subscriber in the list of names at the end of Somner's *Dictionarium Saxonico-Latino-Anglicum* (Oxford, 1659), Ttt2ᵛ col. 1.

the *-e*, which is required linguistically. From these poems we can see that scholars at Cambridge in this period were just beginning to understand Old English.

An Old English poem by Joseph Williamson (1633–1710) in a volume celebrating the Treaty of Westminster (April 1654) ending Cromwell's Dutch war (*Anne theod ætforan wæron we, / Anes modores sunu, oth thæt sæ / (Swa men secgeath) us todælod*) shows that at Oxford the understanding of Old English verse was as rudimentary as it was at Cambridge.[38] Alberta Turner, in her edition of the poem, credits Williamson with "advancing slightly over Wheelock and Retchford by using alliteration,"[39] but such alliteration as there is seems fortuitous and hardly more noticeable than that in Wheelock's and Retchford's verses; rhyming tetrameters remain the verse form, although the rhymes (*we : sæ, todæloth : beoth*) reveal a poor understanding of Old English pronunciation.

A vast improvement over the verses of Retchford, Wheelock, and Williamson can be seen in a poem by Humfrey Wanley (1672–1726) which J. D. Pickles has brought to light.[40] In a volume published at Oxford in 1700, poems by Wanley and others lament the death (at the age of eleven) of William, Duke of Gloucester (July 24, 1689–July 29, 1700), the only surviving son of Princess (later Queen) Anne. Wanley's verses are more than a ceremonial exercise; they express with formal eloquence, good grammar, and appropriate historical allusions the poignancy of the occasion.[41] Most remarkable is the prosody of these verses. Abandoning the rhymes, trimeters and tetrameters of earlier versifiers, Wanley produces verses much more like the original Old English halflines, about three-fourths of his 49 lines being scannable according to Sievers's five types, especially if we permit liberal use of anacrusis. At times Wanley seems even to have sensed the alliterative principle –

> Þæt geara feallon   fela Æðelingas
> Cinewulf ond Oswald,   Cynric ond Eadmund –

---

[38] The poem appears in *Musarum Oxoniensium* (Oxford, 1654) and bears the title *On thære sibbe betweox Breotone & Holland*. For the view in this period that England and the Lowlands (especially Frisia) were once "one people," see Rolf H. Bremmer, Jr, "Late medieval and early modern opinions on the affinity between English and Frisian: the growth of a commonplace," *Folia Linguistica Historica*, 9 (1991), 167–91.

[39] Turner, "Another seventeenth-century Anglo-Saxon poem," *Modern Language Quarterly*, 9 (1948), 32.

[40] *Exequiæ Desideratissimo Principi Gulielmo Glocestriæ ab Oxoniensi Academia Solutæ* (Oxford, 1700). Wanley's poem appears sig Ii2 verso. I am deeply grateful to Mr Pickles for sending me a copy of these verses and permitting me to include them here.

[41] Minor slips of grammar are *syllen* for *seald* (l. 8), *Ealla* for *Ealle* (l. 33), *wæs* for *wæron* (l. 35), *winsum* for *winsumum* (l. 43), and *Heretoges* for *Heretogan* (l. 48). More puzzling is the grammatically odd *Be deað unripene* (l. 20). Wanley drew this phrase from the glossary known as "Archbishop Alfric's Vocabulary" (Thomas Wright, *Anglo-Saxon and Old English Vocabularies*, 2nd edn by Richard Paul Wülcker [London, 1884], vol. 1, col. 149), but he failed to integrate it into the grammar of his sentence in the poem.

but alliteration occurs only sporadically. To some degree the metricality of these lines results from the fact that Wanley was simply lifting halflines from extant poetry. Lines 1 through 5 are a *cento* of the fourth *Meter of Boethius*, lines 1–2, 33, and 53–4; lines 11–14 and 17 draw on *The Death of Edgar*, lines 3, 11, 24, 26, and 27. But elsewhere Wanley seems to be expressing his own thoughts in his own words, and although the syntax and idiom do not always ring quite true, the quality of the verses bears witness to the familiarity with Old English that he had attained in the preceding two years while engaged by George Hickes to search throughout England for Anglo-Saxon manuscripts.

Gulielmi Glocestriæ Ducis Exequiæ
Carmen Anglo-Saxonicum

Eala ðu Scippend.	[1]	Cynric 7 Eadmund.
Heofones 7 eorðan.		Ær þam þe hi mohton
Ðu þe ealle ofer-sihst		Ðone Rice onfengan.
Worulde gesceafta		Ðone Cyne-helm weran. [30]
Hwi wolde þu ece God [5]		Ðone Cyne-gerd wealdan.
Ðas þry leodas		
Mid yrre on-locian:·		Soðlice se Willhelm
Hwi wæs us syllen		Ealla Æðelingas
Willem se Æðeling		Ðe to Engla ðeode
Gleawceastres Ealdorman. [10]		Ær wæs geboren. [35]
Hwy wæs he wlitig.		Mægðum ofer-scinode:·
Deormod 7 winsum.		And eala ðu Drihten.
Wis 7 word-snotor.		Ðe Scopas on-bryrdast.
Gamol feax Hæleð.		Mid godcundum Geddum.
Mid Scanc-bende Hæg-steald. [15]		Aræra ðu sona [40]
Eallum gelufod.		Sumne Cedmon swete.
Cild unweaxen.		Ægðer sumne Ælfred
On feawum gearum.		Se mid winsum gliwnissum
Fram us afangen.		Dreamlice of us miht
Be deað unripene:· [20]		Gnornunge ut-adrifan. [45]
		Be hwylcum we synd gedrefed
Swa eac we findon		Ðurh þone woplice forð-fare
On Writ-bec writene		Ðæs æðeles Heretoges
Istorias gehaten.		Ðæs we synd bereafod:·
Ðæt geara feallon		
Fela Æðelingas. [25]		*Humfredus Wanley*
Cinewulf 7 Oswald.		è Coll. Univ. J. V. S.

"Oh thou Creator of heaven and earth, thou who overseest all creatures of the world, why, eternal God, didst thou wish to look with anger on these three nations? Why was he given to us, William the Prince, Duke of Gloucester? Why was he taken from us by a premature death – handsome, brave, and delightful, wise and eloquent, a flowing-haired hero, a bachelor with the Garter, beloved by all, a child not grown, of few years. Likewise we find written down in books called histories that long ago many princes fell before they were able to ascend the throne, wear the crown, and wield the scepter – Cynewulf and Oswald, Cynric and Eadmund. Truly that William outshone all the princes who were ever born among nations to the people of the English. And oh thou Lord who inspirest poets with divine songs, raise thou quickly some sweet Cædmon or some Alfred who with winsome melodies might drive out of us through music the grief that afflicts us through the lamentable death of him of whom we are bereaved."

The reference to Duke William as *Gamol feax Hæleð / Mid Scanc-bende Hægsteald* (14–15) requires comment. In 1695, when the Duke was six years old, William III made him a member of the Order of the Garter – hence line 15 "a bachelor with the Garter." More puzzling at first is the question why Wanley would call the little boy *Gamol feax Hæleð* ("hoary-headed hero") in line 14. Here we must recall that Wanley's primary source of information about the meaning of individual Old English words would have been William Somner's *Dictionarium* published in 1659.[42] Somner, s.v. *gamol*, defines the word as "a Camel," adding that *Gamol-ferhð* means "fortasse, aut quod, cum Camelo, ad onera ferende (i. ærumnas vitæ) idoneus." *Gomol-feax*, he says, means "bush-haired" (presumably, "hair bushy as a camel's"). In deference to this curious misapprehension I have rendered the word "flowing-haired." (One can only marvel at the ingenuity of seventeenth- and eighteenth-century readers of Old English who could contrive to account for the presence of a camel in each context where the word *gamol* "old" occurred.) It is worth noting further that some of the words Wanley uses are not in Somner's dictionary. *Scanc-bende* does not occur there; Wanley apparently found it in one of the manuscripts of the glossary long ascribed to "Archbishop Ælfric."[43] *Writ-bec* (22) and *gliwnissum* (43) are presumably coinages by Wanley since they occur neither in Somner nor in subsequent dictionaries of Old English. Perhaps they attest to a certain easy confidence on the part of Wanley in handling (and even expanding) the vocabulary of the Anglo-Saxons.

Following (although not immediately) Wanley's poem in the Oxford volume are contributions by William Elstob (1673–1715), older brother of Elizabeth Elstob, who outlived him by over forty years and published the earliest Old English grammar written in modern English. William Elstob's two compositions are part of a single memorial exercise entitled "Gulielmi Glocestriæ Ducis Exequiæ."[44] The first composition, subtitled "Epitaphium Runicum," is printed in runic letters and imitates the conventions of Old Norse memorial

---

[42] See n. 37 above.   [43] See n. 41 above.   [44] *Exequiæ*, sig P.

stones. It begins *GullialmR hilmR Einglans einualösgogR rist stin ŏene eft Gullialm sin frenþa Georgs sun og Annu* ("King William, England's absolute monarch, carves this stone in memory of his kinsman, William, son of George and Anne") and concludes *Riit þisn runeR i Ohsnaforþi skalþskapR* ("Poetry writes these runes in Oxford"). The 21-line *tour de force* is not merely ostentatious but is in fact quite appropriate since the deceased duke's parents (George and Anne) were still prince and princess of Denmark at the time of his death. Immediately following the epitaph is an Old English poem subtitled "Carmen Anglo-Saxonicum":

Ealle leorning cnihtas.
Ælc snotor gewritere.
Ælc bocera. 7 scop.
Đe Oxnaforda onbugað.
Ealle þ on þam scole. [5]
Đe Ælfred mæra cyning.
Hæfde geo getimbred.
And ær gestaþelode.
Synd gelæred 7 afed:·
Nu magon ge to somne. [10]
Singan lioða fela.
Forþon þe Engla leofast.
Bearn hæfð nu lif forlet:·
Nu sceal ic geomriende.
Geornfull lioðwyrhta. [15]
Mid siofigende
Wope secgan sarcwidas:·
   Gleawceastres æþel Beorn.

Se mæra Heretoga.
Hæfð eorðandreamas. [20]
Nu sona geendode.
And ceas him oðer leoht:·
Eala cyld unweaxen.
To swiðe forðgewiten.
Eorla tyrfest ealdor. [25]
Đam Willhelm wæs nama:·
   Nu is us micel gnornung.
Wide 7 wel hwær.
Soðum Cristenmannum.
Swa micel on þam lande. [30]
Swa ic ne secgan mæg.
Đurh gedrefednysse:·

Wilhelmus Elstob A.M.
   & Collegii Universitatis Socius

"All students, each wise author, each scholar and poet who dwells in Oxford, all who are nourished and instructed in the school which the illustrious King Alfred founded and built in time past, now you can sing together many odes, because the most beloved son of the English has now taken leave of this life. Now I, an eager, mourning poet, must with sighing lamentation speak sorrowful sentences. The noble man of Gloucester, the renowned Duke, has now ended his earthly joys and chosen another place for himself. Oh child ungrown too quickly departed, glorious leader of noblemen whose name was William, now there is in this land among true Christian men far and wide much lamentation, so much that I cannot put it in words because of my distress."

Elstob's syntax does not mesh with the verse units as well as Wanley's does, but he handles Old English with fewer solecisms than do the contributors to *Irenodia*. He follows Wanley's lead in looking to the *Meters of Boethius*[45] and *The*

---

[45] Compare ll. 14–17 with *Meter* 2, ll. 2–4.

Death of Edgar[46] for some of his diction. In my translation I have sometimes shaded the sense of an Old English word in the light of Somner's definitions, since these are what Elstob would have consulted.

William Elstob's next known effort is a poem written two years later to celebrate the ascension to the throne of Queen Anne.[47] The volume in which it appears is very much an Oxford production, and the queen shares the limelight with Oxford notables like Thwaites and Lhuyd, whom Elstob also celebrates in his poem:

Pietas & Gratulatio Univ. Oxon.
Carmen Anglo-Saxonicum

Eala Engla Lond		Eowera gode cwen
Hwi eart ðu nu		Æt samne gebeorgað:·
Æfre on mode		Ealle cyric hadas
Swa geomriende.		Ealle lewed men:· [30]
Secgað sum lof sang [5]		Ælc lioðwyrhta of Seaxum.
Singað lioða fela		Ælc Brittena Bard.
Be ANNAN seo rixað		Oððe THWAITES gleawast
Ofer eallum ðam lande		Oððe snotor LHWYD.
Seo godcunda cwen		Ælc scop ðe mid his cræfte [35]
Seo Cristenesta:· [10]		Mæg on hwilcum dæle
Heo beoð Engla leode		Be cyninga dædum
Eowera ealra heafod.		Lioða geweorcan.
Ac nu sæligost		And ða micellice cyningas
Swa ic secgan mæg.		Ðe ær hæfdon anwealde [40]
Eowera ealra hæl:· [15]		Ofer Engla ðeode
Eowera ealra modor		Mid lofsange gemunian:·
Seo eow hire bearnas		Willað eower gehwilc
Frefriað eornostlice		Nu on his agenre
Mid miltsiende heorte		Ðære Engliscan gereorde [45]
Ac swa HEO cwæð [20]		Ðe nu mon Seaxena gehaten
Ðæt us sweotolost		ANNAN ÐA CWEN
And us leofost beð		Lofbærende ðenian.
Æfre. mid ENGLISCAN:·		ANNAN ÐA SELESTAN
Eala Engla waru		And þa Eþelestan [50]
Mid heorte 7 mid hande [25]		Ðe æfre feng to rice
Mid feoh 7 sworde		Siððan mæra Ælfred

---

[46] Ll. 20–8 are largely drawn from *The Death of Edgar*.

[47] *Pietas Universitatis Oxoniensis in Obitum Augustissimi Regis Gulielmi III et Gratulatio in exoptatissimam Serenissimæ Annæ Reginæ inaugurationem* (Oxford, 1702), Sig K2. Once more I am grateful to J. D. Pickles for supplying information about this poem and for giving me permission to use this information in the present essay.

And se Eadig
Hæfde his lif forlet:·
   Nu sceal Ic giornfullice [55]
Mid agenre stefne
Lioðwyrhta clypian.
Ðe ær eom upbecom
Of ðam Norðmestan dæle.
Ðær Arfæsta eadig Cuðbercht [60]
And breoma bocera Beda
In in ðem mynstre
Eardiað æt ðem eadige:·
   Ac nu in þam Scole
Ða se Arwurða Ælfred [65]
Hæfde geo to Gode
And to leornunge gesette.
Eom be lytlum
On boc-cræfte gelæred:·
La hu mæg Ic nu [70]
Secgan oððe singan
Sona giornfullice
On Engla gereorde
Fela soðcwida:·

Ðonne seo mærlica Cwen [75]
Urne ealdne gespræc
To lofian 7 to frefrian
Nu wille uparæran
Æt Oxnaforda
Oððe sumne SPELMAN godne [80]
Oððe SYDENHAM.
Ða to heora lofe
And to Seaxena lare
Sillað heora feoh.
Lioðwyrhtas to afedanne [85]
On æfter dagum
And to gebeorganne.
ÐONNE ANNA CWEN
Seo eðelesta.
ÐONNE SYDENHAM [90]
Sceal on monna geðancum
Mid wuldor gewunian
And mid Lufe rixian:·

Gulielmus Elstob A.M.

"Oh land of the English, why are you always so mournful in spirit now? Utter a hymn of praise, sing many songs about Anne, the heaven-sent, the most Christian queen, who rules over all the land. She is the head of all of you, oh people of England, and, as I can now say, the most blessed salvation of you all. The mother of all of you, she comforts you her children earnestly with a compassionate heart, and thus she has said that it [that is, her heart] will be among the English most devoted and most open to us forever. Oh citizens of the English, all ecclesiastical orders and all lay people, together protect your good queen with heart and with hand, with treasure and with sword. Each poet of the Saxons, each bard of the Britons, either Thwaites the most learned or the wise Lhuyd, each scop who with his talent can in every region make poems about the deeds of the kings and commemorate with songs of praise those magnificent kings who previously held power over the nation of the English: which of you will in his own English tongue (which one now has called Saxon) serve Anne the queen giving praise, Anne the finest and noblest who has ever ascended the throne since the renowned and blessed Alfred departed his life? Now I, a poet who erstwhile came up from the northernmost region where the blessed, pious Cuthbert and the famous scholar Bede abide in the blessed minster, must speak in my own voice with eagerness. And now that I am somewhat learned in letters in the school which the pious Alfred in time past founded for God and for learning, lo! how many true words I can eagerly speak or sing forthwith now in the English language. Then the illustrious Queen will wish now to raise up our ancient language at Oxford (or some good Spelman or Sydenham) to praise or to console. Then they will give their treasure to the teaching of the Saxons, to support and protect poets in after days. Then the most noble Queen Anne, then Sydenham, shall dwell with glory in the thoughts of men and rule with love."

This poem is more ambitious than Elstob's effort of 1700, and it exposes more fully the weaknesses in his command of Old English. Tense, number, and case are occasionally askew, and grammatical oddities like *Ðe nu mon Seaxena gehaten* (46) and *eom upbecom* (58) crop up. (The form *hæl* in line 15 is legitimized by Somner as an alternate form of *hælu*.) Some of Elstob's allusions require explication. Thwaites in line 33 is of course Edward Thwaites (1677–1711), the leader among the Oxford Saxonists, who published an edition of Ælfric's *Heptateuch* among other works. "Lhwyd" in the next line is Edward Lhuyd (1660–1709), a Celtic scholar at Oxford who supplied materials for Hickes's *Thesaurus* and composed his own Cornish lament on the death of William III, "Carmen Britannicum Dialecto Cornubiensi," an achievement that may have prompted Elstob to invoke him as a *Brittena Bard* in the present poem. Spelman in line 80 could conceivably be Sir John Spelman (1594–1643), the author of a biography of Alfred the Great, but is more likely his better-known father, Sir Henry Spelman (?1564–1641), who wrote extensively on Anglo-Saxon history and endowed an Anglo-Saxon lectureship at Cambridge. The physician Thomas Sydenham (1624–89) studied at Oxford and became an eminent medical authority called "the English Hippocrates" in the eighteenth century; it may be he to whom Elstob alludes in lines 81 and 90. Lines 16–23 seem to allude to Anne's first speech to Parliament after her accession. On this occasion she declared her "heart to be entirely English," a statement much discussed at the time, since some thought it reflected unfavorably on her predecessor, William III, who was felt by the English to be a foreigner. The autobiographical remarks in lines 55–69 refer to the facts that Elstob was born in Newcastle-upon-Tyne (his family had long been settled in the diocese of Durham) and attended Queen's College, Oxford, receiving the BA in 1694 and the MA in 1697. The closing prediction that the queen will wish to call forth a (deceased) Spelman or Sydenham (lines 80–1) seems to be a motif borrowed from Wanley's poem (lines 40–9), although Elstob's meaning is not as clear as Wanley's. What is clear, however, is that the close of the poem makes an appeal for financial support. Elstob followed up his poem with a sermon on the anniversary of the queen's accession to power in 1704,[48] and some years later he

[48] *Dictionary of National Biography*, ed. Sir Leslie Stephen and Sir Sidney Lee (London, 1908–9), vol. 11, pp. 1096–8. Several items in this paragraph have been verified in this source.

wrote another Old English poem to celebrate George I's arrival in England from Germany to take the English throne.[49]

Elstob's imagined runic epitaph may have suggested a later eighteenth-century composition in Old English with a frankly malevolent motive. George Steevens (1736–1800), man of letters, Shakespeare scholar, and friend of Dr Johnson, held a grudge against the Director of the Society of Antiquaries, Mr Gough, whom he decided to entrap and expose by concocting a supposed Anglo-Saxon memorial stone on the death of Harthacnut and then seeing to it that this forgery would come to the attention of his intended victim, who, he hoped, would be duped. Steevens very nearly succeeded, and the hoax was much discussed in *The Gentlemen's Magazine* for March 1790 (pp. 217–18, 429–31, and *passim*).[50] The content of the inscription is so crude that one who accepted it as genuine would indeed be proven a novice: *Har akŏnut cyning gedronge winhyrn to drigen 7 ymbstarud 7 swelt*, that is, presumably, "King Harthacnut drank a wine-horn dry, stared around, and died."

The eighteenth and early nineteenth centuries saw the emergence and popularity of a minor subspecies of composition in Old English that merits attention because its effects are still present in editions and reference works – that is, the composition in Old English of titles for Old English texts. We noticed above that William L'Isle provided his archaized prayers with Old English titles, and Lambarde has done the same in his presentation of legal texts from Corpus Christi College, Cambridge, MS. 383, a practice which Liebermann continued in his edition of the laws, which frequently have Old English titles with no manuscript authority.[51] In the nineteenth century Ludvig Ettmüller not only gave his book the Old English title *Engla and Seaxna Scôpas and Bôceras*, but in this book he also provided Old English titles for all the prose and poetic texts that he prints: *Fäder lârcvidas* ["Precepts"], *Be monna môde* ["Vainglory," lines 13–73], *Be manna wyrdum* ["Fortunes of Men"], *Hû Deór hine silfne* [!] *frêfrôde, Heodeninga scôp* ["Deor"], *Beóðgifole!* ["Almsgiving"], *Byrhtnôðes deáð ealdormannes* ["The Battle of Maldon"], *Hvy Äðelstan cyning and Eadmund his broðor læddon fyrde to Brunanbyrig and þær gefuhton við Anlaf and sige häfdon* ["The Battle of Brunanburh," with *hwy* used, as it is elsewhere, with the sense of *hu*], *Se guðræs ät Finnsbyrig* ["The Fight at Finnsburg"], and many more.[52] When he presents the *Meters of Boethius* (which he entitles *Boëties leóðcvidas, of Lêdene on Englisc gevended be Älfrede Vestseaxna cyninge*), he gives each meter a title in Old

---

[49] Murphy, "Scholars at play," pp. 31–3, prints this with a translation.

[50] Also in *The Gentlemen's Magazine* for April, 1790, pp. 290–2. There is a discussion of the incident in John Nichols, *Illustrations of the Literary History of the Eighteenth Century* (London, 1817–58), vol. 5, pp. 429–31. I am grateful to Peter S. Baker for calling my attention to these sources.

[51] See Ker, *Catalogue*, p. 111. Liebermann continued this tradition in *Die Gesetze der Angelsachsen* and also in his own book-titles, as in *Die Heiligen Englands, angelsächsisch und lateinisch: þa halgan on Angelcynne* (Hanover, 1889).

[52] Ettmüller, *Engla and Seaxna Scôpas and Bôceras* (Quedlinburg and Leipzig, 1850).

English: *Be þam êcum gôde, tô þam æghwylc man fundjan sceal* [Meter 21], *Hvŷ Aulixes þegnas vurdon forsceapene tô vildeôrum* [Meter 26], and *þät se vîsdôm nâ ne mæge gemenged beón við ofermêtta*, for example. He divides *Beowulf* and *Genesis* into sections, and gives these sections titles, such as *Hvŷ* [= *hu*] *Grendles môdor hire suna deáð gevräc, and Beóvulf hî ofslôh* and *Hvŷ se engel ofermôdes gode viðsôc, and hvŷ he siððan his vräcsîð giddôde*. Some of the Old English words that Ettmüller used as titles, such as *Ealdcvidas* [*Gnomes*] and *Heófsang* [*The Riming Poem*], were his own coinages. Altogether, Ettmüller's original Old English in his titles and headings amounts to 367 words in *Engla and Seaxna Scôpas and Bôceras*, and he continues the practice of composition in Old English in subsequent works, such as his Old English lexicon, which he closes with the words *Hvät ic väs bliþeheort bec ät ende* ("Lo, I was happy at the end of the book").[53]

Ettmüller was by no means the only scholar to give Old English titles to poems and prose works. Thorpe had done the same before him,[54] as have others after him. Felix Grendon fashioned names for the charms, sometimes coining otherwise unattested words for the purpose, such as *Æcerbot, Galdorstæf, Horswreccung*, and *Siðgaldor*.[55] Our bibliographies and dictionaries continue to refer to titles like *Bi Monna Cræftum, Bi Manna Lease, Calendcwide*, and *Be Dômes Dæge*. And as recently as 1975 Jackson J. Campbell suggested *þrymma Sum* as an apt title for the three "Storm Riddles."[56]

A related practice is that of providing modern scholarly books about the Anglo-Saxons with Old English titles. In the eighteenth century Joseph Strutt produced his two-volume *Horda Angel-cynnan* (London, 1775), which was followed by his book with the equally ungrammatical title *Glig-gamena angel-þeod* (London, 1801), which was revised by J. C. Cox (London, 1903). Book titles of the same order are: J. Ingram, *Anglo-Saxon Stæf-cræfte* (London, 1823); Ebenezer Thomson, *Stæf-Cræft, or an Anglo-Saxon Grammar* (Ayr, 1823), and *Godcunde Lār and Theōwdōm* (London, 1875); Walter Ramsay, *Godes Wyrhtan: or the Labourers in the Vineyard* (London, 1878); William Barnes, *Se gefylsta* (London, 1849); Benjamin Thorpe, *Ða Halgan Godspel on Englisc: the Anglo-Saxon Version of the Holy Gospels* (London, 1842), and many others. Some have favored subtitles in Old English: Henry W. Norman, *The Anglo-Saxon Version of the Hexameron of St. Basil, or, Be Godes six daga weorcum* (London, 1848), and Samuel Henshall, *The First Number of the Etymological Organic Reasoner: Or Yldestan Radchenistres Gewitnessa, Oldest Reason's Witness* (London, 1807). As the dates of

[53] Ettmüller, *Vorda Vealhstôd Engla and Seaxna* (Quedlinburg and Leipzig, 1851).

[54] E.g. Benjamin Thorpe, *Analecta Anglo-Saxonica* (London, 1834), p. 49, where Thorpe provides *Be life and forðfore Hilde þære Abbudissan* as title for a section of Bede's *History* in Old English. Richard Morris similarly provides titles like *Sauwle þearf, Seo Gebyrd S. Johannes þæs Fulwihteres*, and *þisses Middangeardes Ende Neah Is* for homilies in his edition of *The Blickling Homilies of the Tenth Century*, EETS o.s. 58, 63, 73 (London, 1874–80).

[55] Grendon, *The Anglo-Saxon Charms* (New York, 1909).

[56] Campbell, "A certain power," *Neophilologus*, 59 (1975), 129.

these volumes suggest, this practice died out for the most part in the nineteenth century.

Another subspecies of composition in Old English is the scholarly habit of composing bits of Old English to fill (conjecturally) the lacunae in defective texts. To many this will seem no more than an editor's duty, and so it may be. But taken in aggregate, the sum total of these efforts at reconstruction constitutes a considerable Old English *oeuvre*. Also these efforts at times extend beyond mere textual criticism to something more substantial. It may be his editor's prerogative for Klaeber to compose opening verses for the two parts of the scop's song of praise to *Beowulf* in lines 867–97: *Ic Sigemundes secgan hȳrde / ellendǣda* and *hwæt, wē Heremōdes hilde gefrūnon*,[57] or when, "indulging in a guess," he completes the defective opening of the *Battle of Maldon*: [*ǣr sē burhstede ā]brocen wurde*.[58] O. D. Macrae-Gibson goes a step further when he supplies us with a conclusion for the poem:

> He, Oddan bearn, earglice fleah;
> He and his geferan fuhton oð swulton.[59]

Far more bemusing is Tilman Westphalen's reconstruction of *Beowulf*, 3151a (which he concedes to be "unwiederbringlich verloren" in the manuscript), as *Biowulfes cwen* followed by a 58-page essay exploring the literary implications of Beowulf having married (something for which there is no evidence whatsoever in the remaining portion of the text) and of his widow's mourning him at his funeral.[60] Similarly when Friedrich Wild composes the Old English passage which he obviously wishes he could have found in extant texts to support his argument that dragon-standards were commonly known in writings of the Anglo-Saxons –

> Æðelhun forð bær, ealdormon cene,
> dracan gyldenne, dryhtlicne segn,
> cyninges cumbol.[61] –

this would seem to come dangerously close to manufacturing evidence.

---

[57] *Beowulf and the Fight at Finnsburg*, ed. Fr. Klaeber, 3rd edn with 1st and 2nd supplements (Boston, 1950), p. 158.

[58] Fr. Klaeber, "Jottings on Old English poems," *Anglia*, 53 (1929), 228. On the whole, Klaeber is one of the more cautious textual scholars; it is the proclivity of scholars like Holthausen, Sievers, and Trautmann for emending and reconstructing texts that has produced the bulk of this kind of post-Conquest Old English in this century.

[59] Macrae-Gibson, "*Maldon*: the literary structure of the later part," *NM*, 71 (1970), 196.

[60] Westphalen, *Beowulf 3150–55: textkritik und editionsgeschichte*, Bochumer Arbeiten zur Sprach- und Literaturwissenschaft, vol. 2 (München, 1967), pp. 287–345. He calls the verse "unwiederbringlich verloren" on p. 284.

[61] Wild, "Das Drachenfeldzeichen als 'Königsstandarte' in England," *Moderne Sprachen*, Organ des Verbandes der Österreichischen Neuphilologen, 7 (1963), 143.

But the dubious palm for this kind of composition surely goes to the nineteenth-century scholar Armin Kroder, who composed a 148-line episode which he proposed inserting into *Beowulf* after line 607.[62] Because of its length, and because it was published in a learned journal still available to readers in libraries, I quote only the opening and closing verses of Kroder's composition but supply a prose translation of the entire text.

Neuaufgefundene Fitte zum Bêowulf
umfassend 148 Langzeilen, einzulegen nach Vers 607.
Gedichtet und übersetzt von Armin Kroder

... Swîgode Bêowulf;	benc-swêg âstâh,	[608]
drêam in healle	duguðe ond geogoðe;	
þone heaðo-mæran æghwylc	herian wolde	[610]
þâra þe æt symle	sinc-bunan hêold.	
butan Unferðe,	Ecglâfes bearne:	
fulla fêowertig	forð-gerîmed	
druncen hæfde,	syððan dôgor wanode.	
hlûde âhlôh	(heal-wudu dynede),	
bêor-fæge gan	gylp-word wrecan:	

bêor-egesa micel	Bêowulf him wearð.	[742]
benc-swêg âstâh,	ellen-drêam in recede,	
duguðe ond geogoðe;	drync-cræftigne þêoden	
hlûde heredon,	hælo him âbudon;	
ne him Bêowulf gearwe,	ac Bêor-wulf clypodon.	
þâ eft gewât	Wealhþêow fram stapole	
hyre sin-frêan sêcan,	sittan on gif-stôle.	
Ecgþeowes swîðmôd sunu,	sige-rôf rinc semninga	
be earme his geþegen hæfde,	þêawum lædde tô þêodne.	[750]
hâdre þâ searo-gimmas sungon,	in þære sele-cwêne earum swungon	
þær hêo sigore wlanc gewât,	wîf mid þæm bêor-cræftigan wine-dryhtne.	
wynsumu wæs reord; be reste	þæm rince hyre hond ræhte.	
Bêowulf cwên þâ grêtte,	cynna gemyndig bêah,	
swancre hond gecyste;	þanon bê his heal-gesîðum hwearf.	[755]

"Beowulf fell silent. The mirthful sounds of old and young warriors rose along the benches in the hall. All of those who lifted treasure-cups at the banquet wanted to praise the battle-famed one – except Unferth, Ecglaf's son. Since daylight had faded he had drunk all told forty cupfuls. The beer-fated man

[62] Kroder, "Neuaufgefundene Fitte zum Beowulf," *Neuphilologische Blätter*, Organ des Cartell-Verbandes Neuphilologischer Vereine Deutscher Hochschulen, 6 (1898/99), 138–45. He provides his Old English verses with a translation into modern Greman.

laughed loudly (the hall-wood resounded) and began to utter words of boasting: 'Famous as you are, don't recount wave-struggles that you performed who knows when? I have not heard a thing about your deeds of strength either in the land of the Finns or in the world at large. It is easy (not a work of valor) to fight marvelously under the waves where your own dear companions cannot see their prince perform the hidden sea-fight. But I have performed battle-work with my sword among the sons of men in full view of everyone while the candle of the world, the bright pacer of the skies, was shining brightly.' Beowulf the son of Ecgtheow leapt up and drew his iron sword to avenge the insult. The prince of the Storm-Geats, swollen with anger, let words pass from his bosom; the stout-hearted one raged. His voice bright with a battle-cry came resounding through the walls of the hall: 'It is indeed a weird song you have sung, Unferth! Guard against pride, most grim of warriors; you don't know Nægling, who slew many nickers at the bottom of the sea, vanquished sea-beasts. It could easily pierce the heart of a drunken warrior and deprive him of the joys of life.'

"Hrothgar, the hoary-headed lord of the Scyldings, arose; the bear-hall brawl was a heart-sorrow to him, the greatest of troubles. He covered with his hands the one [assuming *þone* was intended, not *þonne*] who sat at his feet, the þyle, the best of thanes. 'Dear Beowulf, you little remember that you are [assuming *bist* for *bis*] sitting among the Scylding folk in Denmark far from your kinsmen. Indeed, there is no need at all for a sword [assuming *billes* for *bille*] at the beer-drinking, young man, a weapon which, in the hands of warriors, might stir up war-bale when, after the beer-drinking, the alien creature, the battle-grim invader, is coming to this hall with cunning snares to accomplish the death of my warriors. Remember that we are enjoying abundantly the beer in this hall with cups along the tables; and with us is Wealhtheow, my strong-bosomed, winsome bride and bed-companion.'

"Beowulf quickly returned the best of iron swords to its sheath and refrained from sword-hatred. Mindful of etiquette, he saluted the queen together with Hrothgar, the dispenser of gold treasure. Then he took up the ale-flagon while staring at Unferth and with dark thoughts spoke strong words: 'Now since you would start up bench-strife at the beer-drinking with the weapon of ale, with the tankard-full (for little cups are not proper for princes), let it be clear and seen by all which of us two is the better warrior. Hear me well, unhappy man: you are a boy at beer-drinking – answer me if you dare!' Then was the heart of the strong one [assuming *heardan* for *heartan* and *heorte* for *heorde*] ready to seek a fight. The rash man swung up his tankard toward Beowulf and spoke boastful words: 'Fear not, clever man! I say it with words: Your "boy at beer-drinking" is standing fast, Beowulf. Oh boastful stranger who are interrupting our mirth, I am ready – if our queen, the bride of Hrothgar, can graciously judge this contest before the shield-warriors.'

"Wealhtheow, the winsome bride dazzling with her gems, arose (all fell silent); her eyes burned and her breast heaved. Thus did the ring-adorned queen speak before the spectators on the benches: 'I am the judge of this little beer-contest between the two best warriors sitting in the hall. Beer-server, quickly fill and bring two ale-tankards adorned by hands; this drinking contest will be a famous interchange.' The servants hastened. None of the words that the queen spoke were strange to them. They quickly filled two ale-tankards with the best of beer. Thus must a cup-bearer do. The two angry men stood up. Shoulder to shoulder they stood erect before their judge. The bellicose men held in their hands the ornamented drinking vessel. Their breasts heaved with breathing. In each of the hostile ones was fear of the other. The hall thanes, the seated warriors, put aside their pastimes and fell silent.

"Wealhtheow, the lady with a powerful bosom, arose. Gemstones shone on her ears. The renowned peace-weaver strode majestically and stood on the threshold with a cup in her hands. She gazed around the hall and unlocked her wordhoard: 'Properly chosen to decide this little contest of the two bold noblemen, I now say, as all can see, that the battle-weapons (these tankards) are filled with ale fully and equally, so, if he wishes, each of the men can exchange one for the other. The battle-cry will be "hall-beer-drinking-contest-thane-drink." My command is at hand: One, two, three.'

"That was a great encounter, as I have been told, when those two warriors contended with such bizarre weapons in hostile competition. Nor was that the least of angry meetings where the two drank. There was no crash of battle or bloody sword blades; they sought revenge for injury with ale-tankards. They did not desist from imbibing but drank like lords. Lip-wide mouth gulped waves of mead. Then the warriors saw beer-floods gush from Unferth's cheeks. Painfully he had drunk; he was in difficulty. Competitive drinking was his undoing. His breath, hot battle-vapor, left the warrior. The thane could not achieve manliness, could not carry out his boast. The nobleman's throat failed him at his need; the þyle's fame diminished. He fell to the floor, the wretched warrior plopped to the ground beside the hall-benches.

"Beowulf, Ecgtheow's son, drank; mead-waves surged down his throat quickly indeed. The victorious one's huge beer-tankard was empty to the bottom. The prince did not leave a drop within it. His glory, the beer-fame of Beowulf, was achieved; the happy man roared out the wonderful battle-cry that Wealhtheow had fashioned: 'hall-beer-drinking-contest-thane-drink!' It was not concealed from any of the retainers to which of the heroes victory would be assigned. Beowulf became a great beer-awe to them all. Bench-rejoicing, delight in valor among young warriors and old, arose in the hall. They praised the prince with great drinking power loudly, wished him luck. They did not call him Beowulf now, but Beer-wulf. Then Wealhtheow left the threshold to seek out her husband, to sit on her throne. Ecgtheow's high-spirited, victorious son forthwith took her courteously by the arm and led her to the king. The fine gems on the queen's ears swayed and sang brightly when the woman proceeded with the beer-strong prince, proud of his victory. Pleasant was her speech; she extended her hand to the warrior by the couch. Beowulf saluted the queen, bowed gallantly and kissed her slender hand. Then he turned thence to his hall-companions."

In assessing this elephantime humor we do well to recall how crudely condescending some nineteenth-century attitudes toward Anglo-Saxon society were. "When we consider the uncultivated age which produced these poems," observes Samuel Fox, then we realize that "they were composed, not to please the refined eye of the fastidious critic, but the rude ears of the barbarian chieftain and his equally barbarian vassals."[63] And Robert Spence Watson explains to his readers that the Anglo-Saxons were "child-like" and "not sensitive nor much troubled with thought."[64] In their mead-halls, he says, "the guests sat around stone tables upon rude forms, eat with their fingers, and slept where they fell senseless from their deep carouse."[65] It is such a setting as this that Armin Kroder imagines for his *Beowulf* episode. The form of his verses as well as the content is coarsened. Kroder's alliterations repeatedly depart from the rules observed by the *Beowulf* poet, and at times (as in his line 743) alliteration is missing altogether. His meter is undisciplined, and occasionally the grammar shows lapses. But by and large his control of Old English is competent, and he has written his pastiche with care, however pointless some may think it to be.

There have been other more or less light-hearted compositions in Old English. A late nineteenth-century specimen is *Se Gleoman* by J. Bolland, student of the Dutch scholar Pieter J. Cosijn, consisting of about eighty verses. It is accompanied by a Dutch translation, "De minstreel."[66] Other poems are donnish attempts to celebrate a fellow scholar on some special occasion. Such is the 33-line poem with a ponderously arch title and apparatus provided by Edward Schröder, which begins

>   Hwæt, wē Gyddinga   in geardagum
>   mōdfæstra monna   mǣrða gefrūnon,
>   hū þā bōcera   blǣd wīde sprang.[67]

---

[63] *Menologium seu calendarium poeticum*, ed. Samuel Fox (London, 1830), p. vi.

[64] Watson, *Cædmon: the first English poet* (London, 1875), pp. 14–15.

[65] Ibid., p. 18.

[66] Rolf H. Bremmer, Jr, of the University of Leiden will publish these two texts in the near future.

[67] Schröder, "*Incerti auctoris poematium anglosaxonicum in honorem Laurentii Morsbacchi octogenarii primum edidit amicus haud incertus,*" *Anglia*, 64 (1940), 1–2. More modest are the uses of quotation and adaptation in the dedication to *Philologica: the Malone anniversary studies*, ed. Thomas A. Kirby and Henry Bosley Woolf (Baltimore, 1949), pp. vii–viii. Hans Ferdinand Massmann long ago went his

A more functional kind of exercise is when scholars compose Old English in order to illustrate a point about the English language or early English meter. Thus Hickes in the eighteenth century translated a longline from *Piers Plowman* into Old English verse in order to show the similarity between Old and Middle English alliterative poetry:

And I hote the, quod hunger, as thou thy hele wilneste.
And ic ðe hate, cueþ hungor, swa ðine hæle ðu wilnest:·[68]

With similar purpose John Josias Conybeare translates the Old High German *Wessobrunner Gebet* into Old English verse, printing the two texts in parallel to facilitate comparison.[69] Much later Moritz Trautmann "reconstructs" the Old English "original" of the *Hildebrandslied* in support of his argument that the poem was originally composed in Old English.[70] And in an admirably lucid exposition of the oral-formulaic theory R. P. Creed recomposes a passage from *Beowulf*, showing us how the poem might have looked had a different performer produced it using the techniques of an oral poet.[71] More recently J. B. Bessinger, Jr, and Marijane Osborn have composed (using Cædmon's *Hymn* as a model) a pagan hymn to Hrothgar, thus providing us with examples of the kind of poetry that was probably precursory to Cædmon's *Hymn*.[72] Finally, André Crépin has improvised two dynastic histories in verse to show us what Bede's sources may have looked like when he drew on "ancient tradition."[73] In addition to the individual points that these scholars have made with their improvisations, in aggregate these compositions demonstrate (since they are all *centones*, more or less, drawn from the extant poetic corpus) that lettered men and women lacking any experience in oral-formulaic performance can compose quite creditable formulaic poetry, pen in hand.

Crépin has modestly referred to composition in Old English as a "parlour

---

colleagues one better when he composed a graceful dedication to Jacob Grimm in Gothic: see his book *Die deutschen Abschwörungs-, Glaubens-, Beicht- und Betformeln vom achten bis zum zwölften Jahrhundert* (Quedlinburg and Leipzig, 1839), pp. [v]–[vi].

[68] George Hickes, *Linguarum veterum Septentrionalium Thesaurus Grammatico-criticus et Archaeologicus*, vol. 1, pt. 1 (Oxford, 1705), p. 107.

[69] Conybeare, *Illustrations of Anglo-Saxon Poetry*, ed. William Daniel Conybeare (London, 1826), pp. li–liii. On pp. xlii–xlvi he does the same thing with selected stanzas from the *Guðrunarkviða*.

[70] Trautmann, "Das altenglische *Hildebrandslied*," *Bonner Beiträge zur Anglistik*, 7 (1903), 121–3.

[71] Creed, "The making of an Anglo-Saxon poem," reprinted in *Essential Articles for the Study of Old English Poetry*, ed. Jess B. Bessinger, Jr, and Stanley J. Kahrl (Hamden, CT, 1968), p. 370.

[72] Bessinger, "Homage to Cædmon and others: a Beowulfian praise song," in *Old English Studies in Honour of John C. Pope*, ed. Robert B. Burlin and Edward B. Irving, Jr (Toronto, 1974), p. 91, and Osborn, "Translation, translocation, and the native context of *Cædmon's Hymn*," *New Comparison: A Journal of Comparative and General Literary Studies*, 8 (1989), 12–23.

[73] Crépin, "Bede and the vernacular," in *Famulus Christi: essays in commemoration of the thirteenth centenary of the birth of the Venerable Bede*, ed. Gerald Bonner (London, 1976), pp. 174–5.

game" (p. 175). If this be true, it is a parlour game with some serious hazards, for the person who has the courage to compose and publish Old English texts is exposing his knowledge of Old English to easy scrutiny. This was demonstrated with painful clarity in 1807 when James Ingram, in his inaugural lecture, revealed for all the world to see just how abysmal a Rawlinsonian Professor of Anglo-Saxon's knowledge of Old English could be.[74] In order to demonstrate the prominence of the native English element in John Milton's supposedly Latinate diction, Ingram translated the first sixteen lines of *Paradise Lost* into Old English. This is the result:

> Of mannes fyrst unhyrsumnesse and þæs wæstmes
> of þat forbiddene treowe, hwa's tæst
> broht deaþ in to þe world, and eall ure wa,
> wiþ lose of Eden, til an greater man
> an-steor us, and an-g'ahne þe blisful sæt,   [5]
> sing, heofenlic Muse, þe on þam diglod top
> Of Oreb, oþþe of Sinai, onbeblew'st
> ðone sceaphyrd, hwa fyrst tæ'hte the ceosen sæd,
> on þe beginning hu þe heofen and eorþ
> ras ut of Chaos; oþþe, gif Sion hill   [10]
> ðe lystath mare, and Siloa's broc þat flow'd
> faste bi þe stefne of God; þanon ic nu
> call on þine aide to min gedyrstig song,
> ðat wiþ na middel fliht upgangan wolde
> begeond þe Aonisc munt, hwile hit ehte thing   [15]
> unwriten get on forth-rihte oþþe on rime[75]

Ingram's feeble effort gives an altogether unintended meaning to *wiþ na middel fliht upgangan wolde*, and the ludicrous *call on þine aide* shows how limited his knowledge of Old English was at this time. There could be no better illustration of how the study of Old English at Oxford had decayed since the days of Wanley and the Elstobs.

Omitted from this survey are compositions in Old English for festive occasions or simply for fun by late and living colleagues whose seriousness of purpose is not always easy to assess. Manfred Görlach's *Maccus and Mauris*,[76] the publications of þa Engliscan Gesiðas,[77] J. R. R. Tolkien's various *jeux*

[74] Ingram, *Inaugural Lecture on the Utility of Anglo-Saxon Literature* (Oxford, 1807).
[75] I have taken this text from Wülker's printing of it in his *Grundriss*, p. 41.
[76] Görlach, *Maccus and Mauris, Largiedd on Seofon Fyttum* (Heidelberg [privately printed], 1977). The book celebrates the seventieth birthday of Rudolf Sühnel and has the charming dedication Hroðulfe Synele   Seaxna holdoste / lareowa liðoste   þas lytlan boc / giefð se gieddwyrhta   Garlac gehaten.
[77] E.g. the collection of previously printed essays by members of the Gesiðas, *Seo Freolsungboc ðæs Teoþan Gemynddæges ðara Engliscra Gesiþa*, ed. Malcolm Dunstall (Folkstone, Kent, 1977).

d'esprit in Old English, Peter Glassgold's renderings of modernist American poems into Old English,[78] and *Dægboc anes Nathwæs*[79] are familiar to most Anglo-Saxonists and are for the most part amply available. These works and others like them require no introduction here.

The last post-Conquest Old English text to be considered here is perhaps the most seriously interesting of all. It is the poem which Nikolai Frederik Severin Grundtvig (1783–1872) composed (in parallel Old English and modern Danish versions) as an introduction to his edition of *Beowulf*, which he entitled *Beowulfes Beorh*, "the tomb of Beowulf."[80] This poem is the result of a lifelong meditation on the Old English poem by a world-renowned poet, theologian, educational reformer, and scholar. As early as his book on Scandinavian mythology,[81] published when he was twenty-five years old, Grundtvig's imagination had been fired by Old English literature, and his interest in it grew as he published his translation of *Beowulf* (with a fifty-page introduction)[82] in his thirty-seventh year, his long essay on the poem when he was fifty-eight,[83] and, finally, the poem we are to examine now, which was published together with Grundtvig's impressive edition of *Beowulf* when the poet was seventy-eight years old.

Although Grundtvig's Old English poem and his Danish poem are printed in parallel columns and have the same theme – the prospect of the poem *Beowulf*'s enabling the English to recover their northern heritage and their ancient kinship with the Danes – they are two independent poems. The closely rhymed Danish poem is in a form reminiscent of other poems by Grundtvig, and it draws on northern mythology and Danish history and topography more extensively than does the Old English poem. The latter takes its moving force from the *cento* technique, which calls to mind powerful moments in the poem *Beowulf* even as it comments on the poem.[84] Both poems anticipate Tolkien's famous analogy between *Beowulf* and a tower, one built out of old stones with hidden inscriptions and looking out over the sea.[85] But in Grundtvig's poem

---

[78] Glassgold, *Hwæt! A Little Old English Anthology of American Modernist Poetry* (Washington, DC, 1985).

[79] *Dægboc anes Nathwæs and The Werkes of Umffrey*, ed. Walter Nash ([Nottingham], 1985).

[80] *Beowulfes Beorh eller Bjovulfs-Drapen, det Old-Angelske Heltedigt*, ed. Nik. Fred. Sev. Grundtvig (Copenhagen and London, 1861).

[81] Grundtvig, *Nordens Mythologi, eller Udsigt over Eddalaeren* (Copenhagen, 1808).

[82] Grundtvig, *Bjowulfs Drape. Et Gothisk Helte-Digt fra forrige Aar-Tusinde af Angel-Saxisk paa Danske Riim* (Copenhagen, 1820).

[83] Grundtvig, "Bjovulfs Drape eller det Oldnordiske Heltedigt," *Brage og Idun*, 4 (1841), 481–538.

[84] Of the 122 halflines in Grundtvig's poem seventy are drawn from *Beowulf* and twenty-five from *The Phoenix*. A handful of other verses may be found (sometimes more than once) in *Judith*, *Elene*, *Judgment Day II*, *Daniel*, *The Fight at Finnsburg*, and *The Meters of Boethius*. There are fewer than twenty verses for which I could find no corresponding formula in the extant corpus.

[85] Kemp Malone, "Grundtvig as *Beowulf* critic," *RES*, 17 (1941), 129–38, points out passages in other writings of Grundtvig's which anticipate Tolkien's British Academy Lecture.

the tower is Beowulf's tomb. The tomb of Beowulf, like the poem about the hero, is a memorial which links the present to the Germanic past, and hence Grundtvig names the poem *Beowulfes Beorh*.

The poem regrets England's alienation from its northern origins and expresses the hope that through poetic monuments the English may rediscover their Germanic brotherhood with the Danes, just as Shakespeare's works helped them to turn their minds from domination by the Pope. He calls for a Phoenix-like rebirth of their ancient selves and a return to the second Germanic Golden Age promised in the *Völuspá*. The poem is an expression of that conviction which was central to Grundtvig's thought as poet, theologian, and philologist, the conviction that language, and especially poetic language, is a sacred medium which can harmonize ancient Germanic and modern Christian worlds in a way that strengthens the identity and clarifies the world view of all those who are inheritors of a culture of north-European origin. Grundtvig's use of the Phoenix legend, and his appropriation of many verses from the Old English poem on that legend, are especially effective and remind us that after his work on *Beowulf* the Dane's single most important contribution to Old English studies is his edition (the first) of the Old English *Phoenix* together with a Danish translation.[86]

Since Grundtvig's edition of *Beowulf* is still available on library shelves and is still consulted by scholars of the poem, I shall not reproduce entire his two poems on *Beowulf* but will only quote the first eighteen to twenty lines of Grundtvig's Old English and Danish poems and then provide a literal translation of the complete text of each.

Beowulf maðelode,	Det var Stærkhjorts Banemand,
bona Stearcheortes:	Bjovulf, Drot i Gotheland
for leoda þearfe	Saa tog han til Orde:
ne mæg ic her leng wesan;	I, som skifte skal min Arv,
hatað heaðomære	Sørger vel for Folkets Tarv,
hlæw gewyrcean	Giører, som jeg gjorde!
beorhtne æfter bæle	Brat har Aske jeg for Been,
æt brimes nosan!	Da, I Venner gæve!
Se sceal to ge-myndum	Kæmpe-Høi med Bauta-Steen
minum leodum	Over den sig hæve!
heah hlifian	Staae den skal paa Roneklint,
on Hronesnæsse,	Hvor mod Klippen Bølger trindt
þæt hit sæliðend	Bruse ind fra Dybet;
syððan haten	Kneise skal min Høi ved Hav,
Beowulfes Beorh,	Falde flux i Øie,

[86] *Phenix-Fuglen: et Angelsachsisk Kvad*, ed. Nicolai Frederik Severin Grundtvig (Copenhagen, 1840).

þa, þe byrðingas	Under Navn af Bjovulfs Grav,
ofer floda genipu	Dem, som Bølgen pløie,
feorran drifað!	Staae for dem til Seile-Tegn,
	For mit Folk til Mindes-Hegn,
	Synlig i det Fjerne!

Translation of the Old English Version

"Beowulf, the slayer of Starkheart,[87] spoke: 'I cannot be here longer to serve the needs of the people. Command the battle-famed ones to build a bright barrow at a promontory of the sea after the funeral fire. It shall tower aloft on Whale-cliff as a remembrance to my people so that seafarers who drive their ships from afar over the darkness of the waters may call it *Beowulfes Beorh*.' For the aged man that was the last word from his heart's thoughts before he chose the funeral pyre, the hot, fierce flames. His soul passed from his bosom to seek the judgment of those firm in truth.

"The poet of *Beowulf*, a man of the Scefings, remembered all that best, so far as I have heard, he who remembered a great many ancient sagas, a leader of men. He made a barrow high and famous in memory of his friend's deeds, on the place of the funeral pyre, that high tumulus, since he was the most glorious warrior of all men throughout the world while he was able to enjoy his city's treasure. *Beowulfes Beorh* is seen from afar by seafarers, the most shining of structures, designed as a memorial in the mightiest of words. There on those panels of bright gold it was righly written in runic letters 'that now peace must be enjoyed between the Geatas and the Danes, and strife must slumber, hostilities which they formerly experienced. The ring-prowed ship must bring over the waves gifts and tokens of affection. I know the people to be firmly disposed toward both friend and foe, altogether blameless in the ancient way.'

"To such performers of good it will be granted that the English people, a troop good of old, who, though bound by works of art to the *wiccung-dome*,[88] forget and neglect this portion of honor that God, the Lord of glory, gave to them in their native land on one occasion, will, urged by the spirit (most like a bird), think of the winsome, delightful forests in Scandinavia, poets and thinkers, the joy of heroes, of Danes and of Geatas. When He who has power over times and seasons (that is the true God) releases the bonds and fetters of frost, unwinds the water-ropes, then birds will sing and the sun will bestow

---

[87] Grundtvig thought that the adjective *stearcheort*, which occurs twice in *Beowulf* (ll. 2288 and 2552) and nowhere else in Old English, was the name of the dragon. He capitalizes it in both of its occurrences, and at l. 2275 he emends it into the text, reconstructing 2274-5 *hyne fold-búend / Stearcheort nemnað, / steápe bi wealle* (p. 171).

[88] Grundtvig evidently thought that *wiccung-dome* meant "the Viking realm, Scandinavia." It actually means "witchcraft," but this makes no sense in his poem.

gloriously bright weather, when winter is past and the bosom of the earth beautifully adorned! Then the golden gambling-pieces are easy to find on the meadow of Ida-plain,[89] as in days of yore Woden and Frea had the glorious heirloom of Weland. Then the golden year will have come to the world, the light will shine over many a land; all is renewed, his life and his feather-raiment, as it was at the beginning when God first placed him on the noble plain, triumphant against the sky!"

Translation of the Danish Version

"It was the slayer of Stærkhjort, King Beowulf of Geatland, who spoke: 'You who will distribute my legacy provide as I did for the good of the people! For bones, doughty friends, I shall soon have ashes. Raise over them a barrow with a dolmen! It shall stand on Whale-bluff where the waves all round will roll in toward the cliff from the deep. My barrow shall tower up by the sea in immediate view of all – with the name of *Beowulfes Beorh*. For those who plow the waves it shall stand as a ship's beacon visible from afar, a memorial mound for my people!' That was the last word of the old man ere he was consigned to the fire. His heart burst and the Geatish hero sank cold to the ground, his body in the shelter of the cliff. The flames were calm, his soul sought honor's steadfast dwelling place above the clouds!

"No one remembers the swan-song of the hero better than you, skald of *Beowulf's Drapa*! You, rich in legend and sharp in sight, royal in mind, have studded with lightning the memory of the hero's glory by the swan's road! You were matchless, like him, while you enjoyed the skald's life in the Angle's liberally granted alodial land! Like Bragi in Valhalla you sat on the hero's grave, your lay without equal between the seas.[90] It is most like a royal hall, built of a dolmen, where thousands of runes artfully entwine, to be seen across the strand clearly there in Denmark a hundred miles away where Hrothgar sank to his rest – to be written in the still chambers with episodes like a glorious picture-script from the high hammers![91]

"On the Danish side the best carved rune is the one which betokens a folk festival in northern lands where the common source will reconcile all quarrels between the kinsmen's feasts in the folklife of the far north. The ship will

---

[89] I.e. *Iðavöllr*, the meeting place of the Norse gods (*Völuspá*, 7: 2 and 60: 2).

[90] Bragi, the Norse god of poetry, is described at the beginning of Snorri Sturluson's *Skáldskaparmál* as sitting at mead in the hall of the Æsir, telling stories of the gods to a man named Ægir.

[91] Grundtvig imagines Beowulf's tomb standing in Skåne, the erstwhile home of the Geatas, and facing across the Øresund (mentioned below) to Zealand, where Heorot had stood. (He uses the word *rune* in the sense both of a written character and of a poem or narrative.) On the "high hammers" see Jacob Grimm, *Teutonic Mythology*, tr. from the 4th edn James Steven Stallybrass (London, 1880–4), p. 1345.

always bring over Øresund a message about the green heart's grove and its golden rings, without sorrow or distrust, as in Fredegode's time.[92]

"God grant that the clan of the Angles, now alienated from the north, might remember old Denmark, might remember the Vanir-home and tear off that Grendel-hand which drove out in gibberish the heart's own word for 'love' along with the English spirit! Yes, may we soon hear the song of the swan of Avon, in which the spirit goes its way without fear of the pope! Then the Phoenix with feather-raiment will once again sing praises and swing itself with speed into the sky over wind and wave, with its father's burned bones in a basket of flowers and sing loudly on a beech-branch about a Fimbul-summer. Yes, three summers in a row granted to the northern lands, like a triple beech-leaf, the day's golden year! The old snow will melt, even on Glacier-mountain, meeting like three golden rivers its final destination in the evening, stirring old brotherhood to acknowledge itself. Dane and Angle will shake hands like brothers in the middle of the sea, while the nine sisters of Heimdal, the mermaids of Øresund, dance and sing over lily hills. They chant about the white god who has defended the green god-home on Heaven-mount through the passing of many an hourglass! Then like golden playing pieces in the north which the giant hid, old, golden words are found suddenly on Ida-plain and a game of chance is played under the green lindens, as the Norns have desired. All is at risk in the game of chance in which all may win!"[93]

---

[92] See the references in *Ordbog over det Danske Sprog*, ed. Verner Dahlerup, vol. 5 (Copenhagen, 1923), s.v. *Frede-*.

[93] The close of the poem is a loose paraphrase of stanza 60 of the *Völuspá* describing the rebirth of the world after Ragnarok. I am indebted to Carl Berkhout for reading this essay in typescript and offering valuable suggestions for its improvement.

23
Medieval, the *Middle Ages*

As the italicization of the words in my title indicates, my concern in this essay is with the terms *medieval* and *Middle Ages*, not with the period itself. Members of the Medieval Academy of America, whether historians, philologists, iconographers, Byzantinists, or specialists in any of the other disciplines that enrich our Academy, will all presumably have a common interest in the terms by which our subject matter is known to the world at large. I propose to begin by offering some observations on the pronunciation and spelling of our terms and then turn to the matter of the origin of *medieval* and *Middle Ages* and the puzzling question as to why English has a plural noun *Middle Ages* whereas other major European languages seem to have a *singular* – *moyen âge, edad media, Mittelalter, medioevo,* and so on. Finally, I shall give some attention to the meaning and popular usage of terms like *medieval* and *Middle Ages* in the various languages of Europe and shall try to draw some conclusions from this as to the status our subject has in the world community.

I begin with pronunciation. I see no problem in the case of the term *Middle Ages*. For *medieval*, however, dictionaries and manuals of elocution record several pronunciations, the two most prominent of which are [ˌmiːdɪˈiːvəl] and [ˌmɛdɪˈiːvəl], the former being recommended by American authorities, the latter by British. Which is correct? In the Latin word from which *medieval* is derived, the first vowel is short (*med-*), a fact which may seem to justify the Englishman's way with the word. But this is false logic, for both English and American speakers pay little attention generally to the pronunciation guidance offered by Latin etymons. Certainly few Englishmen are persuaded to give up their pronunciation of *vitamin* ([ˈvɪtəmən]) merely because the Latin long *i* in *vita* supports the American pronunciation. And the pronunciation [mɛd-] in the Englishman's *medieval* is itself inconsistent with his own usual pronunciation of the same root in other words: one does not hear in England of "mass [ˈmɛdɪə]," nor do Englishmen pronounce the *e* short in *mediocre* or *immediately*.[1]

Reprinted from *Speculum*, 59 (1984), 745–56. This essay was originally delivered as the presidential address at the annual meeting of the Medieval Academy of America at Emory University on March 24, 1984.

[1] Although I have not heard it myself, my authority on British pronunciation indicates that a

The pronunciation of *Medieval* is simply one more of those instances where Englishmen and Americans agree to pronounce the same word differently without either nation trying to impose its pronunciation on the other.

I hesitate to draw attention to the other recorded pronunciations of *medieval* for fear that someone may be induced to imitate them. Most egregious, perhaps, is the pronunciation of the word as if it were spelled *medievial*. This has been recorded and condemned in usage manuals,[2] but colleagues inform me that they still hear it today. Other pronunciations, which modern dictionaries regard as acceptable variant pronunciations, seem nonetheless to be somehow unpleasant to me. I refer to the pronunciations which reduce *medieval* to a trisyllable: [ˌmɪdˈiːvəl], [ˌmɛdˈiːvəl], [məˈdiːvəl]. I am not sure why these pronunciations strike my ear so gratingly. Perhaps they remind me of that curious coinage introduced into English in 1840 to refer to our period, *mideval*, which was formed, apparently, by analogy with *primeval* and *coeval*. I am grateful that this strange hybrid did not last, and I think we should avoid inadvertently reviving it with a trisyllabic pronunciation of *medieval*.

Whim plays a role in pronunciation preferences, as my own confessed prejudices have just illustrated. In matters of spelling, however, we seek an authority who will make binding decisions, even if those decisions are purely arbitrary. Should we spell *medieval* with the digraph *æ* or simply with *e*? Fowler recommends the form with *e*, as do many authorities in America as well as England.[3] And yet university presses on both sides of the Atlantic continue here and there to affect the digraph, and we must face the fact that in our profession today there exists a state of orthographic anomy verging on an identity crisis in respect to this question. Are we medievalists or mediævalists? In the fair city of Toronto alone the Pontifical Institute of Mediæval Studies stands firmly in the ranks of the digraph, while the University of Toronto's Centre for Medieval Studies, which is only a short walk from the Institute, rallies behind the spelling with *e*. Even when the names of the two institutions appear together (as they sometimes do) on the title page of one and the same book, each clings tenaciously to its own spelling of *medieval*.

It is odd that this onomastic schism should exist, for the question as to which spelling is correct was settled once and for all in 1980 when, in its revision of its

---

short *e* is occasionally heard in the first syllable of *mediocre* in England: see Daniel Jones, *Everyman's English Pronouncing Dictionary*, 11th edn (New York, 1956), p. 302.

[2] See for example George Philip Krapp, *A Comprehensive Guide to Good English* (Chicago and New York, 1927), p. 384.

[3] As long ago as 1923 The Society for Pure English urged that the spelling *medieval* be preferred to *mediæval* (SPE Tract 13, p. 35), and modern American dictionaries regularly follow this practice. H. W. Fowler, *A Dictionary of Modern English Usage*, 2nd edn rev. Sir Ernest Gowers (Oxford, 1965), p. 356, also recommends *medieval*. It has been observed that if we adopt the spellings *primeval* and *coeval* we would be inconsistent to write *mediæval*.

By-Laws, the Medieval Academy of America announced that henceforth it would adhere exclusively to the spelling with *e*. To this authoritative decree nothing need be added. And yet I will add just one approving observation on the Academy's resolution of the question. Since the reduction of the classical Latin digraph *æ* to *e* is usually cited in handbooks as one of the symptoms of medieval Latin (as opposed to classical Latin), it seems only logical that we should preserve this bit of medievalia in the name we assign to our field of study. The force of this argument is for me undiminished by the fact that the Latin word *medievalis* is neither classical *nor* medieval in origin, but Neo-Latin.

I turn now to the grammatical number of English *Middle Ages*, a problem which will require that we investigate the Latin source for European words referring to the medieval period. In a study which has long been cited as authoritative, George Gordon assembles a number of facts about the English and Latin words for the Middle Ages, and in the course of his study he twice observes that the plural form is an English peculiarity, all other languages using a singular form.[4] Now it is true that many of the languages that will spring to mind do have a singular noun meaning "Middle Ages." German *Mittelalter*, Italian *medioevo*, French *moyen âge*, Spanish *edad media*, Greek μεσαίων (or, the now more usual demotic form, μεσαιωνας), Danish and Norwegian *middelalderen* are all singular. But Gordon was in error when he said that English is the *only* language that has a plural form. Dutch *Middeleeuwen* is plural, as are Russian средние века[5] and Modern Icelandic *miðaldir*. (Modern Hebrew and Modern Arabic use plural forms as well, but I believe we can safely disregard terms in these languages since they would almost certainly be recent coinages modeled on European nomenclature; that is, they are simply translations of the English, or possibly the Russian, plural forms.)

The Dutch plural *Middeleeuwen* is explained by Kluge in his etymological dictionary as resulting from the fact that in Dutch *eeuw* can mean "century" as well as "age" or "era," and therefore the Dutch must use the plural lest someone think there was but a single medieval century.[6] One could advance the same rationale for Russian средние века since век too can serve to mean "century" (if one chooses not to use the more normal стодétиe). But this explanation will not do for English or Icelandic, and I suspect it is also somewhat doubtful as an explanation for the Russian form – especially when we see that in Polish the same compound, *średniowiecze*, is invariably singular, as is the Czech *stredovek*. In Slovene, moreover, where *vek* is the normal term for "century," the word for Middle Ages is the singular *srednjeveski*. If there is

[4] George Gordon, "*Medium Aevum* and the Middle Age," SPE Tract 19 (Oxford, 1925), p. 9, n. 2, and p. 14.

[5] Russian also has a singular form, средневековье, but the plural seems to be more common, as is the case in English.

[6] Friedrich Kluge, *Etymologisches Wörterbuch der deutschen Sprache*, 21st edn (Berlin, 1975), s.v. *Mittelalter*. For the relevant sentence see below, n. 7.

no problem with the dual meanings of *vek* and *wiecze* in these closely related languages, why should срéдние векá require a plural in Russian?

Here it is necessary to investigate where each of the European words for "Middle Ages" originated. If one consults the standard reference works on the subject, they will usually explain that all the European words are simply calques or loan translations of the Latin phrase *medium ævum*, an explanation that leaves one all the more puzzled as to why some of the European vernaculars should have wound up with a singular and others with a plural form.[7] The earliest English attestation recorded in the *Oxford English Dictionary* is dated 1722 and has the surprising plural form – *Middle Ages*. The *Supplement* to the *Oxford English Dictionary*, however, volume *H–N* (published in 1976), has supplied earlier documentations of both singular and plural forms from the writings of John Donne, Thomas James, Henry Spelman, and others, the earliest of these antedating the word to 1616.[8] The *Supplement* records the adjectival form *middle-aged*, moreover, as early as 1611.[9] This presses the date of the introduction of the English term almost as far back as the date of the earliest documentation of Latin *medium ævum*, which was used by Melchior Goldast in 1604.[10]

The assumption that all the modern vernaculars derived their terms for "Middle Ages" by translating *medium ævum* is, however, erroneous. As Gordon has shown, Neo-Latin writings (wherein the term as well as the idea certainly originated) display a variety of ways of expressing the idea "Middle Age(s)," including *media ætas*, *media antiquitas*, *medium sæculum*, and *media tempestas* as well as the plural forms *media sæcula* and *media tempora*. The earliest of these is documented in 1469 (*media tempestas*). The earliest documentations for the plurals *media tempora* and *media sæcula* are 1531 and 1625 respectively, and it is interesting to note that Englishmen were among the earliest users of the Latin plural terms: Henry Spelman was the first person to use *media sæcula*, and although *media tempora* appeared first in a book published in Switzerland, Francis Bacon used the term sometime before 1620 in the *Novum Organum*.[11] So, before Neo-Latin writers settled down with the term *medium ævum*, which became more or less standard in Latin usage, there was this plethora of terms for "Middle Ages," and the various vernaculars were modeling their terms on the whole range of Neo-Latin terms, both singular and plural. It is no surprise,

---

[7] See for example Kluge, *Etymologisches Wörterbuch*, s.v. *Mittelalter*: "Lat. *medium aevum* hat Lehnübersetzung zu frz. *moyen âge*, engl. *middle age(s)*, nnl. *middeleeuwen* (Mz. weil *eeuw* 'Jahrhundert' bedeutet), dän. *middelalder* usw. erfahren."

[8] Most of the *Supplement*'s antedatings seem to be derived from Gordon, "*Medium Aevum*."

[9] The full context supplied by *Supplement* s.v. *middle-aged* 2 is as follows: "The open or secret wrongs done vnto Fathers, aunctient, middle-aged, or moderne writers, by the Papists." The quotation is from the advertisement to a religious polemic by T. James.

[10] In *Paraeneticorum veterum pars I*, p. 380.

[11] See Gordon, "*Medium Aevum*," p. 12, n. 1.

then, that some of the modern languages should have a singular term today (for example, French, German, Italian, Danish, Greek, Polish) while others (English, Dutch, Russian, Icelandic, and their imitators) have plural forms.

When one examines the emergence of terms for "Middle Ages" in the various vernaculars, one finds, not surprisingly, that a number of different terms, some singular and some plural, were often tried out before the standard modern term became standard. As the *Oxford English Dictionary* entry shows, English had at different times both *Middle Age* and *Middle Ages*, to say nothing of a host of also-rans like *Barbarous Age(s)*, *Dark Age(s)*, *Obscure Age(s)*, *Leaden Age(s)*, *Monkish Ages*, *Muddy Ages*, and of course the eighteenth-century favorite, *Gothic Period*. Similarly German *Mittelalter* had to compete with the plural *die mittleren Zeiten* as well as with *das mittlere Zeitalter* and *die Mittelzeit*.[12] The Dutch plural *Middeleeuwen* had to compete with the singular *Middeltijd*. Why a language ends up choosing a singular or a plural form is probably a question which cannot be answered definitively. Chance very likely plays a major role. But whatever the reason, the result is not in doubt. Surely speakers of those languages which use a plural form will be more likely to think of the medieval period as a succession of subperiods rather than as an unbroken continuum of years.

Before leaving the matter of the origin of the terms for the Middle Ages, it may be well to mention that from time to time scholars have thought that the idea of a "Middle Age" actually existed in the Middle Ages themselves. Thus St Augustine speaks of things happening "in hoc interim sæculo," and Julian of Toledo in the seventh century speaks of his time as a "tempus medium." But the context of these phrases shows that this is not our concept at all. These medieval Christians are referring to the "middle" period between the Incarnation and Judgment Day. In this sense we are still living in the Middle Ages.[13] It is only with the Renaissance that writers begin to identify a Middle Age between Antiquity and the modern period.[14]

I turn now to the question of the meaning and status of the words *medieval* and *Middle Ages*. As for setting the precise dates at which the Middle Ages begin and end, you may expect only crafty evasions from me. Scholars have advocated many different termini for our period, and there seems to be little agreement and indeed little basis for reasoned argument on these points. The Middle Ages begin, we are told, with the death of Theodosius in 395, or with the settlement of Germanic tribes in the Roman Empire, or with the sack of Rome in 410, or with the fall of the Western Roman Empire (usually dated

---

[12] See Kluge, *Etymologisches Wörterbuch*, s.v. *Mittelalter*.

[13] See Jaroslav Pelikan, *The Christian Tradition: a history of the development of doctrine*, 3: *The Growth of Medieval Theology (600–1300)* (Chicago, 1978), p. 2.

[14] On this matter Theodor E. Mommsen has written eloquently in "Petrarch's conception of the 'Dark Ages,'" *Speculum*, 17 (1942), 226–42.

AD 476), or even as late as the Moslem occupation of the Mediterranean. It ends, according to Oscar Halecki, with the fall of Constantinople, or with the invention of printing, or with the discovery of America, or with the beginning of the Italian wars (1494), or with the Lutheran Reformation (1517), or with the election of Charles V (1519).[15] Several reference works I have consulted simply assert that the Middle Ages ended in 1500, presumably on New Year's Eve. Yet another terminus often given for the Middle Ages is the so-called "Revival of Learning," that marvelous era when Humanist scholars "discovered" classical texts and restored them to mankind after the long Gothic night. Medievalists must always smile a little over these "discoveries," for we know where the Humanists discovered those classical texts – namely, in medieval manuscripts, where medieval scribes had been carefully preserving them for mankind over the centuries.

There is an added difficulty for periodization in that the Middle Ages last longer in some countries than others. Italy seems somehow well into the Renaissance at a time when much of the rest of Europe is still happily medieval. I have been shown medieval churches in Finland which date from the seventeenth century. And in Russia the Middle Ages seem to last almost as long as the winter. The dictionary of the Russian language published by the Academy of Sciences of the USSR defines the limits of the Middle Ages as follows: "Embracing the period from the collapse of the Roman slave-holding empire (end of the fifth century) to the beginning of capitalism (end of the seventeenth century)."[16] The Marxist tinge of this definition is enhanced by quotations from Maxim Gorki which reflect a conception of the Middle Ages which could only have been derived from an Eisenstein film. In view of all this disagreement over the duration of the Middle Ages, perhaps we should content ourselves with saying that our period extends from the close of the classical period to the beginning of the Renaissance. If classicists and Renaissance scholars don't know when their periods begin and end, then that is their problem.

One topic which deserves mention here is the term *Dark Ages*, a concept which Lucie Varga examines in a monograph which was published in 1932 and is still definitive.[17] In popular encyclopedias and in many of the older dictionaries *Dark Ages* is defined as simply a synonym of *Middle Ages*. In 1904, however, W. P. Ker in his book *The Dark Ages* said that the two terms "have

---

[15] Halecki, *The Limits and Divisions of European History* (Notre Dame, 1962), pp. 149–50 and p. 224, n. 7.

[16] Akademiia nauk SSSR, СЛОВАРЬ СОВРЕМЕННОГО РУССКОГО ЛИТЕРА-ТУРНОГО ЯЗЫКА, 14 (Moscow, 1963), s.v. Средневековье, я, *ср.* Иьторическая эпоха, охватывающая время от крушения Римской рабовладельческой империи (конец V в.) до начала нчкапитализма (конец XVII в.).

[17] Varga, *Das Schlagwort vom "Finsteren Mittelalter"* (Baden, 1932).

come to be distinguished, and the Dark Ages are now no more than the first part of the Middle Age, while the term medieval is often restricted to the later centuries, about 1100 to 1500."[18] This is a distinction which was for a time carefully observed by some historians, such as Sir Frank Stenton in his book *Anglo-Saxon England*.[19] Here *Dark Ages* consistently refers to pre-Conquest England and *Middle Ages* and *medieval* to post-Conquest. The reason the term *Dark Ages* has fallen into disrepute may be inferred from such entries as the following in *Webster's Unabridged Dictionary*, second edition, which says s.v. *Middle Ages*, "The term *Dark Ages* is applied to the whole, or, more often, to the earlier part of the period because of its intellectual stagnation."[20] If we could rehabilitate this term by interpreting *dark* as referring not to the qualities of the period but to our dim perception of the period (owing to limited documentary evidence about it), then the *Dark Age–Middle Age* distinction might be worth reviving or retaining. A similar segmentation of the period seems to serve scholars well in Swedish, where *medeltiden*, when used in the context of Swedish history, is said to begin with the conversion to Christianity around AD 1000, the period before that being designated by the nonpejorative term *Vikingertiden* "the Viking era."[21] Similarly, the Finns sometimes restrict the meaning of *keskiaika* "Middle Ages" to the late Middle Ages, the earlier period (or "Dark Ages") being called "the Age of the *Kalevala*," although this usage seems now to be on the wane. But periodization being the vexed question it is, some will be reluctant to complicate our subject with elaborate subdivisions of time periods. We all know how eminent historians in this Academy and elsewhere began discovering Renaissances in the twelfth century, and then the tenth century, and then the Carolingian period, much to the confusion of simple souls. And then the French introduce *haut moyen âge* and *bas moyen âge* (with their resulting English counterparts), while the Germans have given us *Früh-*, *Hoch-*, and *Spätmittelalter*, and there are many other such subdivisions. In view of all this, it seems almost providential that the English language wound up with a plural noun to designate the period.

We turn now to the last question I have posed about the words for *medieval* and *Middle Ages* in the various European languages, namely, the status they have in the world and what we can gather from this status about the popular standing of our subject. We may begin by asking how much the public at large thinks about things medieval at all. To get a reading on this issue I turned to the word-frequency study published at Brown University by Henry Kučera and the erstwhile medievalist W. Nelson Francis.[22] These scholars made a statis-

---

[18] Ker, *The Dark Ages* (Edinburgh, 1904), p. 11.
[19] Stenton, *Anglo-Saxon England*, 3rd edn (Oxford, 1971).
[20] *Webster's New International Dictionary*, 2nd edn, unabridged (Springfield, MA, 1934).
[21] Svenska Akademien, *Ordbok över Svenska Språket*, 17 (Lund, 1945), s.v. *medeltiden*.
[22] Kučera and Francis, *Computational Analysis of Present-Day English* (Providence, 1967).

tical analysis of words in a corpus consisting of a carefully selected cross-section of contemporary American English, including newspaper articles, learned journals, fiction, humor, and other specimens of present-day writing in our country. Their corpus included 1,014,232 words all told. How many times does the word *medieval* occur in that corpus? Exactly eighteen – the same number of occurrences logged for the words *aluminium*, *angel*, *Arkansas*, *Tokyo*, the date *1945*, and the numeral *400*. But then *Renaissance* appeared only twenty times, and *classical* only thirty-three times. *Modern*, not surprisingly, occurred 198 times. What is depressing about these statistics, however, is that most of the eighteen times that *medieval* occurred it probably had nothing to do with the historical period we study, for *medieval* is most often used in Modern English simply as a vague pejorative term meaning "outmoded," "hopelessly antiquated," or even simply "bad." *Renaissance* and *classical*, although they too refer to long-ago periods of history, are never used in this pejorative way. It is this troubling phenomenon which will occupy the remainder of my discussion.

When we look at the words for *medieval* in other European vernaculars, we find that they too are often used in simple pejorative senses. A German calls his government's attitude toward illegal narcotics *mittelalterlich*, while a young Greek would refer to the same attitude as μεσαιωνικός. An antiquated, inefficient bureaucratic procedure is dismissed by a Polish student as *średniowieczny*. A Finnish newspaper condemns the toilets in modern Finnish prisons as *keskiaikainen*. This is something medievalists should ponder. It gives us a realistic picture of the preconceptions about the Middle Ages which students all over the world are likely to bring to our subject.

Recently I spent some time looking through the citations for *medieval* and *Middle Ages* in the hospitable offices of the Merriam-Webster Company in Springfield, Massachusetts. Adding what I learned there to my own private log of popular uses of these terms, I concluded that we medievalists have an image problem on our hands. And the problem is apparently growing, for the first and second editions of *Webster's New International Dictionary* (published in 1909 and 1934) record no pejorative sense for the adjective *medieval*, while the third edition, published in 1961, adds the sense "antiquated, outmoded," presumably because occurrences of the word in this sense have been increasingly common in Merriam-Webster's files on current usage. The day I spent inspecting Merriam-Webster's files I saw citations from books, newspapers, and magazines in which the most astonishing array of modern phenomena were stigmatized as "medieval" when the writer disapproved of them: the British coal industry, General Electric Company, labor laws, the Carnegie Commission, streetcars, certain methods of photocopying documents, peep shows, the method of trash disposal in Los Angeles, and the weather in Northern Europe. The entire state of Tennessee is dismissed as "medieval," and the steel mills of Pittsburgh are "medievalesque." Venereal disease in San

Antonio is said to be related to that city's "medieval political structure," while *Rolling Stone Magazine* (May 11, 1972, p. 16) complains that Rock and Roll was destroyed by "the medievalism of union officials." David Halberstam in 1971 says that Ford Motor Company is "sick" because of the "medieval quality" of its production practices (*Harper's Magazine* for February, p. 45), and a character in a novel complains that his car has "a medieval carburetor." Even the future is called "medieval" if one thinks it will be bad: *The New Yorker* for July 12, 1982, says the dystopian movie *Blade Runner* depicts "a medieval future" (p. 82). Most dismaying of all, the most widely known medievalist of our time, J. R. R. Tolkien, was reported in the *London Review of Books* (5/13 [1983], 16) to have habitually used the adjective *medieval* as a term of abuse when he was denouncing the way things were managed in his Oxford college.

I am especially annoyed by the way ultramodern techniques for administering torture and waging war are frequently described as "medieval." In *Time* magazine, December 3, 1968, p. 38, I saw reference to the "medieval tortures" which had been inflicted on political prisoners in Greece. The "medieval tortures" consisted of beating people with plaited steel wire and applying electric shocks to sensitive parts of their bodies. An uncomfortable writing desk is described in one Merriam-Webster citation as "a medieval instrument of torture." Last November 30 my attention was arrested when Tom Brokaw on NBC Nightly News announced that the Dutch beer magnate Freddie Heineken had been kidnapped and held in "medieval conditions." Mr Brokaw went on to explain that Mr Heineken was held captive in a concrete block room and fed takeout dinners from a local Chinese fast-food restaurant.

The New York Times Magazine, February 2, 1975, describes the Molotov cocktails and random bombings in Northern Ireland as – what else? – "medieval warfare in the twentieth century." Jacobo Timmerman in a book published in 1982 describes Israel's electronically guided bombing, rocketing, and shelling of civilian populations in Beirut as "a descent into the darkness of a disguised Middle Ages."[23] In usages such as these *medieval* and *Middle Ages* seem to mean simply "evil," and I have sometimes wondered whether there may not be a folk-etymological misconception that the syllable *-eval* in *medieval* has something to do with *evil*. A 1972 article in *Commentary* (April issue, p. 90) overtly associates the two words: "Céline was of a medieval turn of mind: he needed a principle of evil so as to be able to justify his ferocious indignation." Another bizarre verbal association may be reflected in a *New York Times Magazine* article (January 27, 1918) wherein *medieval* in the pejorative sense is spelled *madiaeval*; but I nurse the hope that this may be a printer's error.

A remarkable subcategory of pejorative *medieval* is the frequent use of it to refer to a government or ruler which the writer means to describe as tyrannical or totalitarian. Around 1980 writers for most newspapers and magazines seem

---

[23] Timmerman, *The Longest War* (New York, 1982), p. 157.

to have reached the conclusion that *medieval* was an official title of the Ayatollah Khomeini, so rarely does his name appear in print without *medieval* prefixed to it. And this despite the fact that Persia never really had a Middle Ages, being outside the orbit of western Europe. Similarly, during the First World War the Kaiser, according to Merriam-Webster's files, was with monotonous regularity called a "medieval" ruler, and his allies were similarly described. *The Yale Review* in 1917, for example, speaks of people living "under the mediæval yoke of Austria-Hungary, without the most fundamental rights" (p. 99). The dual monarchy of Austria-Hungary only came into being with the *Ausgleich* of 1867, but never mind. *The New York Times* on July 7, 1918, solemnly observes that "one outcome of the present war may be that the masses will themselves join in a movement to liberate their land from the mediæval Bastille of the boche." The Bastille prison was completed in 1557 and is usually associated more with the French than with the "Boche." But the real *bêtise* underlying all these absurdities is the notion that political absolutism, which was institutionalized only in the Renaissance and eighteenth century, is somehow synonymous with the Middle Ages, a period when, in fact, the power of monarchs was usually limited by the counterbalancing power of the church, of consultative bodies like the Anglo-Saxon *witena gemot*, of feudal lords, and of medieval customs generally. Still the misconception gains strength year by year. In the October 1975 issue of *Esprit*, for example, occurs the sentence, "In amateur athletics, officialdom has an almost medieval power over athletes" (p. 42).

Even the word *medievalist*, the term by which we proudly identify ourselves in the academic community, has become contaminated in the process of this sinister semantic trend. When Senator Hubert Humphrey in 1964 rudely attacked one of his Senate colleagues, the *Saturday Evening Post* (October 10, 1964, pp. 83–4) reported that "the medievalists froze him out of the Senate's inner councils." The optimists among us who assume from this sentence that we medievalists are at last moving into the centers of power where we so richly deserve to be are destined for disappointment. For this reporter, *medievalist* simply means anyone whose political views strike him as offensively retrograde.

Against all this antimedieval mischief recorded in my files and in those of Merriam-Webster, I can set only three lonely examples of *medieval* used in a purely positive sense. A Princeton University Press book on the Pennsylvania Dutch speaks of "serene ... countrysides over which the peace-loving Pennsylvania Germans have woven their medieval spell."[24] *The New Yorker* for November 29, 1952, describes a man as having "a gentle, handsome, medieval face" (p. 39). And an Australian novelist remarks, with seeming approval, that a teacher "was medievally fond of students," although even here might lurk a leering allusion to Abelard and Eloise.[25]

[24] G. Paul Musselman, *The Pennsylvania Germans* (Princeton, 1942), p. 81.
[25] Eve Langley, *White Topee* (Sydney, 1954), p. 19.

I should perhaps repeat that the use of *medieval* in a purely disparaging sense is not limited to English. The same usage is common in most European languages, although there are subtle and interesting differences among them. The French, in their elegant way, preserve the integrity of their adjective *médiéval*, using it exclusively as a historical term. But as a term of disparagement they use *moyenâgeux*. Perhaps the most outspokenly disparaging definition of our term is the pejorative sense recorded in Ushakov's explanatory dictionary of the Russian language, where the adjective средневековый is said to mean "not in accord with the ideas of modern civilization, barbarian, inhuman, typical of the Middle Ages."[26] My first thought on reading this was that Marxist ideology was inciting the lexicographer to a frenzy of disparagement. But on reflection, and after querying some native speakers, I came to suspect that the explanation lies elsewhere. The Middle Ages (средние века) are for the Russian a foreign phenomenon, something that happened far away in western Europe, not "Russian-medieval" (древнерусский). This feeling that the term refers to something not merely primitive but also alien might intensify the pejorative meaning of the word. This curious situation may also serve to remind us of the importance of considering the national perspective from which speakers of each language view the Middle Ages and to adjust accordingly for any assessment expressed from that perspective.

One happy note: from a study of the Swedish dictionaries and from conversations with native speakers of Swedish, I gather that that enlightened nation does not normally use *medeltida* as a simple pejorative. I think this was confirmed when Swedish Finns who had been asked to translate for me some Finnish sentences containing the word for "medieval" (*keskiaikainen*) in a disparaging sense refused to use the Swedish equivalent *medeltida* for *keskiaikainen*. They insisted that in Swedish the only proper rendering would be *ålderdomligt* "antiquated," *hemskt* "horrible," or *grymma* "grim."[27]

In conclusion, I confess that I have no sure remedy to offer for the sorry semantic state of *medieval* and *Middle Ages* in popular thought today. We could perhaps counterattack by complaining loudly about the depraved Renaissance absolutism of the Ayatollah Khomeini or about the classical Greek carburetor in our lemon of a car, but I don't think we would have much success. Probably our best course is simply to correct wherever we can such misconceptions as come to our notice, and especially misconceptions among students, who are

---

[26] Dmitri N. Ushakov, Толковый словарь русского языка (Moscow, 1940), s.v. СРЕДНЕВЕКОВО́Й: Не соответствующий понятиям современной цивилизации, варварский, негуманный, характерный для средневековья (книжн.).

[27] The three sentences referred to a rural method of hiring mailmen (*Ajan suunte*, 1937, 271, s. 4, p. 2), to prison conditions in Finland (*Vapaa Sana*, 1944, no. 7B, p. 2), and to the Franco government (*Suomen Kuvalehti*, 1975–6). In the case of another sentence, however, the Swedish speakers considered the use of *medeltida* acceptable: "Using phosphorous bombs on innocent civilians was an example of truly medieval cruelty" (". . . var ett exempel på verklig medeltida grymhet").

the ones who concern me most. I might cite in closing an experience of my own a few years ago. When I was chairman of Medieval Studies at Yale, I received once a letter from a high-school student who informed me he was writing for his history class an essay on torture, and he wanted to know whether the chairman of Medieval Studies wouldn't be willing to give him some expert advice on the subject. In response I told him that contrary to his expectation, torture was no more a parameter of medieval life than it was of life in other periods, and I suggested that the Middle Ages were perhaps less given to torture than were earlier and later periods. In ancient Greece it appears that the testimony of slaves was admissible evidence only when given under torture, I observed, and we know from the accounts of pagan Rome's persecution of Christians that torture was not unknown in the later classical period. The Renaissance, moreover, could lay juster claim to Torquemada than could the Middle Ages.[28] I apologized to my young correspondent for the relative poverty of torture in the medieval era, and in an effort to be helpful I referred him sadly to the experts who are in a position to know more about torture than any medievalist would know. I referred him to the chairman of Yale's interdisciplinary program in Modern Studies.[29]

[28] Malise Ruthven, *Torture: the grand conspiracy* (London, 1978), p. 24 and pp. 23–42. The periodic reports by Amnesty International give little hope that matters are improving in our own day. See *Report on Torture* (London, 1973), esp. p. 28, and *Torture in the Eighties* (London, 1984), *passim*.

[29] For help on various points of language I am grateful to Dmitri Gutas, Merja Kytö, Andrei Navrozov, and George Schoolfield, and above all to Frederick C. Mish, Editorial Director of the Merriam-Webster Company in Springfield, Massachusetts.

List of Essays and Notes by Fred C. Robinson Not Included in this Volume

"Notes on the Old English *Exodus*," *Anglia*, 80 (1962), 363–78.

"Is Wealhþeow a prince's daughter?," *ES*, 45 (1964), 36–9.

"Verb tense in Blake's 'The Tyger,'" *PMLA*, 79 (1964), 666–9.

"Old English lexicographical notes," *Philologica Pragensia*, 8 (1965), 303–7.

"Beowulf's retreat from Frisia: some textual problems in ll. 2361–2362," *SP*, 62 (1965), 1–16.

"Old English research in progress," *NM*, 66 (1965), 235–50; 67 (1966), 191–204; 68 (1967), 193–208; 69 (1968), 472–87; 70 (1969), 518–34; 71 (1970), 489–501; 72 (1971), 504–12.

"Notes and emendations to Old English poetic texts," *NM*, 67 (1966), 356–64.

"Two non-cruces in *Beowulf*," in *Tennessee Studies in Literature*, vol. 11, ed. Richard Beale Davis and Kenneth L. Knickerbocker (Knoxville, 1966), pp. 151–60.

"The OE *Genesis*, ll. 1136–1137," *Archiv für das Studium der neueren Sprachen und Literaturen*, 204 (1967), 267–8.

(with J. B. Bessinger, Jr) "A survey of Old English teaching in America in 1966," *Old English Newsletter*, vol. I, no. 1 (1967), 1–13.

"A bibliography of writings on Old English literature," *Old English Newsletter*, vol. 1, no. 2 (1967), 1–3.

"The royal epithet *Engle leo* in the Old English *Durham* poem," *MÆ*, 37 (1968), 249–51.

"The American element in *Beowulf*," *ES*, 49 (1968), 508–16.

"Coleridge, personification, and the personal genitive," *Die neueren Sprachen*, n.f. 11 (1968), 564–6.

"Linguistics and literature," *Encyclopedia of World Literature in the Twentieth Century*, vol. 2 (New York, 1969), 270–5.

"Early writers and modern readers," *American Benedictine Review*, 20 (1969), 198–207.

"'Strength stoops unto the grave': Nash's *Adieu, Farewell Earth's Bliss*, l. 22," *Papers on Language and Literature*, 6 (1970), 89–92.

[Planning for a Dictionary of Old English], *Computers and Old English Concordances*, ed. Angus Cameron, Roberta Frank, and John Leyerle (Toronto, 1970), pp. 103–7.

"Old English bibliography" [annual], *Old English Newsletter*, vol. 3, no. 2 (1970), 12–38; vol. 4, no. 2 (1971), 10–30.

"The devil's account of the next world," *NM*, 73 (1972), 362–71.

"Appropriate naming in English literature," *Names*, 20 (1972), 131–37.

"Syntactical glosses in Latin manuscripts of Anglo-Saxon provenance," *Speculum*, 48 (1973), 443–75.

"Old English *awindan*, *of*, and *sinhere*," in *Festschrift Prof. Dr. Herbert Koziol zum siebzigsten Geburstag*, vol. 75, *Wiener Beiträge zur englischen Philologie* (Vienna, 1973), pp. 266–71.

"Preface," in *Word-Indices to Old English Non-Poetic Texts: a collection of three previously published glossaries with a preface by Fred C. Robinson* (Hamden, CT, 1974), pp. v–vii.

"Foreword," in *The Translations of "Beowulf": a critical bibliography*, by Chauncey B. Tinker with an updated bibliography by Marijane Osborn (Hamden, CT, 1974), pp. v–vii.

"Anglo-Saxon studies: present state and future prospects," *Medievalia*, 1 (1975), 62–77.

"The Complaynt off sanct Cipriane, the Greet Nigromancer: a poem by Anthony Ascham," *RES*, 27 (1976), 257–65.

"Old English literature in its most immediate context," in *Old English Literature in Context: ten essays*, ed. John D. Niles (Woodbridge, Suffolk, 1980), pp. 11–29, 157–61.

"Tradition and innovation in the Middle Ages: a summation," *Chronica*, 26 (1980), 1–5.

"Introduction," in *Beowulf: a likeness*, by Randolph Swearer, Raymond Oliver, and Marijane Osborn (New Haven, CT, 1990), pp. 1–7.

"Morton Wilfred Bloomfield (19 May 1913–14 April 1987)," *The American Philosophical Society Year Book 1987* (Philadelphia, 1988), pp. 116–21.

"'Bede's' envoi to the Old English *History*: an experiment in editing," *SP*, 78 (1981), 4–19.

"Print culture and the birth of the text," *Sewanee Review*, 89 (1981), 423–30.

"Latin for Old English in Anglo-Saxon manuscripts," in *Language Form and Linguistic Variation: papers dedicated to Angus McIntosh*, ed. John Anderson (Amsterdam, 1982), pp. 395–400.

"Metathesis in the dictionaries: a problem for lexicographers," in *Problems of Old English lexicography*, ed. Alfred Bammesberger, Eichstätter Beiträge, vol. 15, *Abteilung Sprache und Literatur* (Regensburg, 1985), pp. 245–65.

"Consider the source: medieval texts and medieval manuscripts," *Medieval Perspectives*, 2 (1987), ed. Merritt Blakeslee, William Provost, and Katharina Wilson, 7–16.

"*The Rewards of Piety*: 'two' Old English poems in their manuscript context," in *Hermeneutics and Medieval Culture*, ed. Patrick J. Gallacher and Helen Damico (Albany, NY, 1989), pp. 193–200.

"Medieval English studies at Yale University," in *Medieval English Studies Past and Present*, ed. Akio Oizumi and Toshiyuki Takamiya (Tokyo, 1990), pp. 166–70.

"*Beowulf*," in *The Cambridge Companion to Old English Literature*, ed. Malcolm Godden and Michael Lapidge (Cambridge, 1991), pp. 142–59.

"Why is Grendel's not greeting the *gifstol* a *wræc micel?*," in *Words, texts and manuscripts: Studies in Anglo-Saxon culture presented to Helmut Gneuss on the occasion of his sixty-fifth birthday*, ed. Michael Korhammer, Karl Reichl, and Hans Sauer (Cambridge, 1992), pp. 257–62.

"Introduction," in *Old English Anthology*, ed. Antonio Bravo, Fernando Garcia, and Santiago Gonzales (Oviedo, 1992), pp. 7–13.

"The Accentuation of *nu* in *Cædmon's Hymn*," in *Heroic Poetry in the Anglo-Saxon Period: Studies in honor of Jess B. Bessinger, Jr.*, ed. Helen Damico and John Leyerle (Kalamazoo, MI, 1993), pp. 115–20.

"A Further Note on *dollicra* in *Beowulf* 2646," *ANQ* 6 (1993), pp. 11–12.

"Philological criticism," to be published in a collection of essays edited by John Hollander et al. for Yale University Press.

Memoirs of Old English scholars published in *Medieval English Studies Newsletter* (Tokyo): Stanley B. Greenfield (no. 17 [1987], 4–5), Herbert Dean Meritt (no. 22 [1990], 24–6), Robert E. Kaske (no. 22 [1990], 33–5); (all reprinted in *Medieval English Studies Past and Present*, ed. Akio Oizumi and Toshiyuki Takamiya [Tokyo, 1990], pp. 234–6, 258–62, and 239–43), and Norman E. Eliason, *Medieval English Studies Newsletter* no. 24 (1991), 6–8.

Memoirs of medievalists published in *Speculum*: Robert W. Ackerman (56 [1981], 692–3), Dorothy Whitelock (58 [1983], 875–6), Cora Lutz (61 [1986], 763–4), Morton W. Bloomfield (63 [1988], 756–8, Robert E. Kaske (65 [1990], 818–20), Kenneth Hurlstone Jackson (67 [1992] 796–7).

Memoir of Robert E. Kaske published in *The Yearbook of Langland Studies*, 5 (1991), 1–5.

Index

This index is comprehensive but does not include references to persons, places, things, or texts cited merely for passing comparison. Names of scholars are not included when they appear only as "see also" in footnotes. Entries are ordered as follows: literary works (1) textual commentary (with line numbers of poems and page numbers of prose works in **bold**, the pages where they are discussed being in roman), (2) general references, (3) sub-listings; authors (1) general, (2) sub-listings, (3) works.

For purposes of alphabetization, æ comes after a and þ/ð after t; the prefix ge- is disregarded in alphabetical ordering, as are diereses and umlauts. Old English and Scandinavian names are entered as they appear in the text; thus, Thryth, not þryð, but Þorgerðr, not Thorgerthr.

Abraham, 46
Academy, The, 263–4
Adam, 159
Adam of Bremen, 8
adludens ad nomen, 202 n.62
Adomnan, 203
Adrastus of Sicyon, 7
ad sepulchrum, 9
Aeneas, 7
Aeneid, 7, 47, 77, 148 n.20, 268, 275–6
"afflicting" *see* Egypt, epithets for
Aillte, 242
Alcuin, 44; letter of, to monks of Lindisfarne, 45–6, 64, 167; onomastics in, 189, 199 n.51; puns in, 149 n.24; *De virtutibus et vitiis*, 96
Aldhelm, 79, 101, 161, 164, 167; puns in, 149 n.24
Alexander the Great, 7, 12
Alexander, Michael, 250
Alfred the Great, King, 144, 240, 289; *Pastoral Care*, 90; *Proverbs of*, 279; *see also De consolatione philosophiae*, OE translation of; *Meters of Boethius*, OE translation of; *Orosius*, OE translation of
Alfred (Prince), 113
alliteration, 104 n.25, 245, 283–4
allusion *see Beowulf*: allusion in
Almsgiving, 290
Amali, 8
ambiguity, verbal *see* onomastics; puns; variation, poetic: clarifying
Ambrose, 232
Amos, Ashley Crandell, 37
Ancient Laws and Institutes of England, 100
Ancrene Riwle, transcript of, 280–1
Andersson, Theodore, 47
Andreas, **759–60**: 231 n.15; **1189**: 224–7; **1330–1**: 225–6; **1606**: 229–31; 83; *see also* onomastics: *Andreas*
Andrew, St *see Andreas*; *Blickling Homilies*: 19
Andrew, S. O., 24, 25 n.13
Anglo-Saxon Chronicle, 17, 109, 113–14, 119, 127–8, 198 n.49
Anne, Queen, 286, 287–9
ansis, 8

Index

Apocrypha, OE translations of, 109
apotheosis *see Beowulf*: apotheosis of;
 herotheism
apposition, 72–3; *see also Beowulf*: juxtaposition, syntactic; *Beowulf*: narrative method in; variation, poetic
Aragon, Louis, 93 n.25
Archaionomia, 279–80
Ashdown, Margaret, 116, 136
Asser, 12
Athelstan, ordinance and law code of, 279–80
Atlakviða, 148
Attila, 160–1
attitudes towards Anglo-Saxons, 19th century, 296
audience of OE poetry, 159–63 *passim*, 208; *see also Beowulf*: audience of; *Beowulf*: Christian attitudes towards paganism in; *Maldon, Battle of*: audience of
Augustine, 42, 94, 205, 308; onomastics in 188–90 *passim*, 197, 201, 232
authorship of OE poetry, 164–9
Ava, Frau, 168
Avenging of the Savior, 227
Azarias, 24, 99

Æduwen, 165
Ælffled, 157
Ælfgyfu (Emma), 173
Ælfric *Epistle to Sigeweard*, **87.204–5**: 191; *Martyrdom of St Vincent*, **426–43**: 227; *Passion of the Apostles Peter and Paul*, **366–8**: 191–2; 95, 144, 145 n.13, 279; euhemerism in, 10–11, 12, 18; metronymics in, 172; onomastics in, 186, 187–8, 191–2, 193 n.32, 198, 199, 205–6, 212, 227, 229; wise women in works of, 160 n.25, 162; *De falsis Diis*, 10–11, 12, 18; *De initio creaturae*, 12, 145 n.13; *Grammar*, 279; *Heptateuch*, 289; *Passion of St Sebastian*, 12
Ælfric, Archbishop, glossary of, 285
Ælfwine, 117, 132–4
ærdæg, 25 n.12

Æsir, 8
Æscferth, 118
Æthelred (Ethelred the Unready), 116, 118–19, 125, 127–9, 171
Æthelred, King of Mercia, charter of, 277
Æthelstan, Ætheling, will of, 171
Æthelweard, 13
Ætheric, will of, 171

Bacon, Francis, 49, 307
Bartholomew, St, 233–4
Bartlett, Adeline C., 84
Barðr, 8
Battle of Brunanburh see Brunanburh, Battle of
Battle of Maldon see Maldon, Battle of
Baum, Paull F., 165 n.5
Beaty, John O., 84
Beaw, 13
becn, 17–18
Bede, 44, 144, 149 n.24, 167; *Death Song*, 110, 164; *De die iudicii*, 111; *see also Historia ecclesiastica gentis Anglorum*
Beethoven (Ludwig van), 274
Belial, 225–6
Benedictine Rule, Old English, 90, 100, 101 n.14
Benson, Larry D., 42–3, 46
beorh, 5, 17
beorhtian, 147–8
beornes, þæs, 131
Beowulf: as aged warrior, 136; apotheosis of, 6, 11, 14–16, 18–19; appositional characterization of, 57–60, 85; "historical" dates of, 37, 39; as human/superhuman, 20–35 *passim*; as *lofgeornost*, 142–3; name of 220; as narrator of Breca episode, 28–9; retort of, to Unferth, 31–3, 85, 222; second burial of, 5–6, 16–18; speeches of, to Hrothgar, 59–60, 65, 77–9; virtues/Christ-like qualities of, 65
Beowulf, **505**: 31, 35; **539**: 28–9; **542**: 28; **560–1**: 150 n.26; **581**: 28–9; **588**: 31–3; **743**: 143–6; **817**: 143 n.7; **1122–3**: 75; **1143–4**: 74–6; **1161**: 147–9; **1177–87**:

Beowulf (*cont.*)
157–8; **1226–31**: 157–8; **1495**: 22–6; **1523**: 75; **1829–35**: 77–8; **1901–2**: 146–7; **2283–4**: 80–4; **2359–68**: 26–7; **2369–72**: 158; **2499–500**: 151; **2663–8**: 21 n.4; **2765–7**: 96; **2917**: 78; **2936**: 143 n.7; **3150–5**: 40, 158; **3172**: 14; **3177**: 16 n.50; **3182**: 142–3

Beowulf, allusion in, 55–6, 143–6; audience of, 7 n.9, 13–14, 18, 41–51 *passim*, 55, 58, 63, 66 (*see also* audience of OE poetry; [*Beowulf*]: Christian attitudes towards paganism in); Breca episode in, 28–35, 221; Celtic influence in, 47; Christian attitudes towards paganism in, 3, 13–14, 18–19, 41–2, 45–7, 49, 63–7 (*see also* paganism: Christian attitudes towards); Christianity in, 15, 45–6; description of artifacts in, 50–1, 62 (*see also* [*Beowulf*]: purpose of ritual in); effect *vs.* appearance in, 56–7; evil in, 60–1, 65–6; fame in, 41–2, 48–9, 56–7 (*see also* [*Beowulf*]: "shame culture" in); Finnsburg episode in, 5, 42, 53–4, 61, 75 (*see also Fight at Finnsburg*); fire imagery in, 74–6; friendship and loyalty in, 48, 65 (*see also Maldon, Battle of*: loyalty in); Frisian episode in, 26–7; funeral rites in, 4–7, 11, 14–18, 39, 40, 42, 65, 85, 158 (*see also* funerary practices, Germanic; herotheism; women: as prophets); gift-giving in, 49–50, 146–7; Grendel's mere episode in, 22–6; heroic code in, 59–60, 63 (*see also* [*Beowulf*]: fame in; *Maldon, Battle of*: heroic quality of); historical background of, 36–40; juxtaposition, narrative, in *see* narrative method in; juxtaposition, syntactic, in, 53–4 (*see also* variation, poetic); language of, 52–5 (*see also Beowulf* poet: dictional skill of); maxim in, 96; moral judgment in, 63; narrative method in, 37, 55–61 (*see also* variation, poetic); nature in, 50–1, 62–3; OE prose summary of 275; oral composition of, 44, 47, 297 (*see also* formulas); performance of, 242; personification in, 151; proposed additions to, 292–6; purpose of ritual in, 50, 62–3 (*see also* [*Beowulf*]: description of artifacts in); sectional titles for, 291; "shame culture" in, 48–9 (*see also* [*Beowulf*]: fame in); structure of, 57–61 (*see also* [*Beowulf*]: narrative method in; variation, poetic: structural); synaesthesia in, 147–8; themes in, 54, 58, 62; "thought-world" of, 36–7, 41–4, 47–51, 61–6, 157–8, 162–3 (*see also* [*Beowulf*]: Christian attitudes towards paganism in); translations of, 260–1, 262, 268–71 (*see also* Pound, Ezra: *Beowulf*); understatement in, 151; women in, 48, 157–8, 162 (*see also* Hygd; Thryth; Wealhtheow; women); youth *vs.* age in, 57–8, 85, 136; *see also* onomastics: *Beowulf*

Beowulf: poet, 3, 7 n.9, 28, 40, 55–61 *passim*; dictional skill of, 74–6; "thought-world" of, 36–7, 41–51 *passim*, 61–7; *see also Beowulf*: Christian attitudes towards paganism in; *Beowulf*: "thought-world" of

"Beowulfes Beorh," 5, 299–303
Berhtgyð, 166
Berndt, Rolf, 179 n.21
Bessinger, J. B., 126 n.11, 297
best(e) (ME), 151–2 n.29
Bethurum, Dorothy, 18, 149 n.24
bitan, 75
-blac, 194
Blackburn, Francis A., 232
Blake, N. F., 117
blæd, 149
Blickling Homilies, 6 **79–81**: 212; *19* **241**: 225; *15* **187**: 88–9; OE titles for, 291 n.54
Blomfield, Joan, 86 n.52
blood, identified with soul, 145
blood-drinking, 143–6
Bloomfield, Morton, 30 n.32, 37–8, 88, 108
Boberg, Inger M., 156
Böckenhoff, Karl, 144 n.8

body as house, 53–4
Boehler (Maria), 173
Boethius *see De consolatione philosophiae*, OE translation of; *Meters of Boethius*, OE translation of
Bolland, J., 296
Bolton, W. F., 44, 216 n.111
Boniface, 46, 111, 166, 205; correspondence of, 9, 11, 12
Bonjour, Adrien, 16 n.48, 31
"Book-Moth Riddle" *see Riddle*, 47
Borges, Jorge Luis, 141 n.3
Boðvarr Bjarki, 34, 223
brat, etymology of, 177, 179, 180–1
Britton, G. C., 142 n.5
Brodeur, A. G., 33 n.40
Brooke, Stopford, 246, 249, 272–4
Brooks, Kenneth R., 225, 229–30
Brown, Jane Hetherington, 278
Bruder, Reinhold, 155, 156
Brunanburh, Battle of, 71–2, 128, 141, 148, 262–3, 290
Brut, **14992**: 113 n.33; **18090–3**: 150 n.26; **28357ff**: 148–9; 279
Bülach brooch, 165
Byrhtferth's Manual, 108, 149 n.24, 191 n.24
Byrhtnoth: and abbot of Ramsey, 134 n.34; as aged warrior, 136; death of, 107–12 *passim*; and defense of island, 129–30; error in judgment of, 118–19, 129–30; mutilation of, 134–6; in non-*Maldon* sources, 111, 114, 127, 135; Wanley on, 105
Byrhtwold, 105, 121, 136–7
byrig, 249, 253, 254

Cain, 65, 66
Calder, Daniel, 161 n.28
Cameron, Angus, 278
Campbell, Alistair, 13, 29 n.26, 128, 275–6
Campbell, Jackson J., 291
Campoamor, Ramón de, 93
Casley, David, 138–9
Cassidy, Frederick G., 89, 100 n.7
Cædmon, 164, 167; *Hymn*, 267, 297; *see also* Pound, Ezra: *Cædmon's Hymn*

Cecelia, St, 185
Chadwick, H. Munro, 41, 44, 164
Chambers, R. W., 6, 23, 31–2, 38, 214 n.104
Chance, Jane, 157 n.11, 159 n.22
Charlemagne, 42, 167, 168
Charles I, 281–2
Charms, 9.**14–15**: 82, 83–4; *4 see* Pound, Ezra: *Anglo-Saxon Charm*; titles for, 291
charters, OE *see* legal documents
Chaucer, Geoffrey, 150, 185, 219, 265–6
Chaunticleer, 150
Cheruscians, prophetic women of the, 158
Chickering, Howell D., 18 n.57
Christ, **50**: 191 n.24, 212, 228; **71–3**: 199–200; **134–5**: 192; **668–70**: 261
Christ and Satan, **132**: 142; **365–7**: 192–3, 229; *see also* onomastics: *Christ and Satan*
Cid, El, 17 n.51
Circhieri, Tommasino dei, 92–3
Claire, St, 205
Clement of Alexandria, 17 n.51, 146
clothing names, 175–81
Clotild, Queen, 10
Clovis, 10
Cockayne, T. Oswald, 172 n.18, 268
Coir Anmann, 203–4
Columba, 203
comitatus, 106, 124 n.8
composition, in OE, post-Conquest: antiquarian/scholarly, 275–7, 279–303; eighteenth-century, 283–90, 291, 297; eulogistic, 281–90, 296; to fill ms. lacunae, 278, 292–6; functionally illustrative, 297; of inscriptions, 290; of legal documents, 277–8, 279–80, 290; Middle English, 277–9; nineteenth century, 290–303 *passim*; playful, 298–9; poetic, 275–6, 278–9, 280–90, 292–303; in prose, 277–8, 279–80; Renaissance, 279–81; seventeenth century, 281–3; of titles, 290–2; twentieth century, 291, 292, 296–9

compounds: root meanings of, 74–9, 101, 102, 130, 143, 145, 233; translators' use of, 53–4, 267, 270; *see also* onomastics
Constantine, 172
Conybeare, John Josias, 72 n.4, 197, 260–2
Cook, A. S., 229 n.4
Corpus Christi College, Oxford, MS, 90, 197
Cotton Otho A. xii, foliation of, 131–2
Cotton Tiberius B. i, spelling in, 90
Creed, R. P., 15 n.48, 297
Crépin, André, 297–8
Cromwell, Oliver, 283
Cross, J. E., 142 n.5
Crugland (Croyland), 210 n.92
CuChulainn, 203
cwide, 100–1
Cynewulf, 161, 164, 205, 240; *see also Elene*
Cynhelm, St, life of, 278–9
Cyprian, St, 65, 193 n.32

dadsisas, 9, 14
Daniel, bishop of Winchester, 12
Daniel, Samuel, 58
Daniel, **33–4**: 81–4; **36–7**: 81–4; **321–2**: 82–4
Dante, Alighieri, 219
Dardanus, 7
Daria, St, 162
Dark Ages, 309–10
Dating of Beowulf, 37, 43
Davie, Donald, 239, 242
Dawson, R. MacGregor, 94
Dægboc anes Nathwæs, 299
De consolatione philosophiae, OE translation of, 11–12, 51, 146 n.17, 161–2
De virtutibus Beati Lebuini et de sancto nomine eius, **57ff**: 204, 235
Death of Edgar, 284, 286–7
Delasanta, Rodney, 21–2
deman, 15
dennade see dynian
Deor, 290
d'Escures, Ralph, archbishop of Canterbury, 278
destiny *see* fate

dialect *see Maldon, Battle of*: dialect, literary use of, in
diction, poetic, 259–60; *see also Beowulf*: language of; *Beowulf* poet: dictional skill of; compounds; formulas; Pound, Ezra: and OE poetic diction
Dicts of Cato, OE translation of, 11, 95
Diensberg, Bernhard, 180–1
Dio Cassius, 158
Diogenes Laertius, 92
Dobbie, E. V. K., 24, 125
Dodds, E. R., 48–9
Domitian, 8, 12
Donahue, Charles, 4 n.3, 32, 43, 46
Donaldson, E. Talbot, 40
Doolittle, Hilda, 268–9
Douglas, Gavin, 268
Dream of the Rood, **21**: 151; 119, 241
gedreccan, 195, 232
Dryhthelm, 109
Dunnere, 117–18
Durham, **7–8**: 82–4
Durham Proverbs, 88, 91
dynian, 148

Eadburg, 166
Eadgils, 39
Eadwig, King, 109
Eadwine Psalter, transcript of, 280
eald geneat, 136–7
ealle onmedlan eorthan rices, 256–7
earendal, 200 n.54
Earl, James, 35
Earle, John, 277 n.6
"echo-words," 84
Edith, Queen, 166
editorial interpretation, problems of: *Andreas* 225; *Beowulf* 22, 23, 26, 27, 78, 213; *Genesis*, 196; *Guthlac A.*, 211; *see also* emendation, problems of; lexicography
Edward the Confessor, writ of, 277–8
efteadig secg, 252
Egypt, epithets for, 194–6, 231–3
Eiterhof, 220
Ekkehard *see Waltharius*
elaboration of sources, OE poets; 103–4, 159–62 *passim*, 191–2, 227

Elene, **64**: 78; **214–17**: 80–4; **313–15**: 81–4; **1058–62**: 205, 229 n.4; 161; onomastics in, 205, 224 n.3, 229 n.4; *see also* Helen, St
Eliason, Norman E., 29 n.28; 213 n.101
Elliott, R. W. V., 117
ellipsis, 134
Elphinston(e) (John), 133, 138
Elstob, Elizabeth, 285
Elstob, William, 285–90
Ely, History of see Liber Eliensis
emendation, problems of: *Andreas*, 229–30, 231; *Beowulf*, 26, 27 n.20, 28 n.25, 31, 79, 80–4, 292–6; *Charm*, 9, 80–4; *Daniel*, 80–4; *Durham*, 80–4; *Elene*, 80–4; *Exodus*, 80–4, 193–4, 195, 232; *Genesis*, 198; *Guthlac A*, 209, 233; *Maldon, Battle of*, 123, 132–4, 138–9, 170; *Maxims ii*, 87–97; *Riddle*, 60, 80–4; *Seafarer*, 252, 256, 258; *Vercelli Homilies*, 5, 220; *see also* editorial interpretation, problems of; lexicography
Emmanuel, 191, 192, 200 n.54, 228
Englan, 250
England, derivation of, 205
Engliscan Gesiðas, þa, 298
Enoch, Apocryphal Book of, 145
"envelope patterns," 84
Eofor, 220
Eomær, 13
eorp werod, 194
eow friþes healdan, 124
Eric, King, 8
Ethelred the Unready *see* Æthelred
Ettmüller, Ludwig, 290–1
etymology *see* compounds, root meanings of; onomastics
Eufrasia, St, 162
euhemerism, 9–13, 204; *see also* herotheism
Euhemerus, 9
eulogies in OE, post-Conquest, 281–90
Eutychus, 223
-eval, 312
Evans, J. Martin, 159, 193 n.32
Eve, 159

Exeter Book, inflection in, 101 n.12
Exodus, Book of, 194
Exodus, **37**: 231–3; **42**: 151; **91–2**: 80, 82–4; **136**: 231–2 n.19; **157**: 78, 79; **204**: 194; **224**: 195; **358**: 193–4; **462–3**: 148; **498**: 194; **501**: 195; variation in 76–9 *passim*, 84; *see also* onomastics: *Exodus*

fate: in *Beowulf*, 37, 51, 57, 66–7; in *Genesis*, 159; in *Maldon*, 106; name as, 201; in *Riddle*, 47, 102–3
fatum, 103; *see also* fate; *wyrd*
Faulkes, Anthony, 13
feasceaft, 151
Felicity, St, 172
Felix (*Vita Guthlaci*), 206–7, 208 n.86
Fell, Christine, 157 n.12, 166
feng, 76
feorhlast, 145
Festival of St Mary, OE homily on, 278
Fight at Finnsburg, 290; *see also Beowulf*: Finnsburg episode in
Finn, 203
Fitness of Names, 203–4
Flateyarbók, 8
fleotan, 28
Florence of Worcester, 127
forheawan, 135
formulas: OE poetic, 28 n.25, 75, 85, 103, 133, 149–50; in reconstruction of orally composed *Beowulf*, 297; *see also Beowulf*: oral composition of
forscrencan, 188 n.11
Fortunes of Men, 290
forþringan, 143 n.6
Fox, Samuel, 296
Francis, W. Nelson, 310–11
Frank, Roberta, 35, 43, 83
Freawaru, 38
Freondlic Mynegung, 108
Frere, John Hookham, 262
Frey, 10
friþ, 124
frod feores, 136
funerary practices, Germanic, 8–11, 17, 42; *see also Beowulf*: funeral rites in; herotheism; women: as prophets

Furseus, 109
fus, 151
fyrbendum fæst, 76
fyres feng, 76

gafol see gofol
gamol feax, 285
garholt, 77–8
garræs, 123
Gauguin, Paul, 274
Geat(a), 12, 13
Geats, 4, 39–41
geirstaðaálfr, 8
Genesis, Book of, 159, 173
Genesis, **113**: 197 n.44; **370**: 132; **1104**: 197 n.44; **1109**: 197 n.44; **1133–4**: 198; **1145**: 196–8; **1303–4**: 198–9; **1518–20**: 144, 145; 15, 119–20, 158–9, 291; *see also* onomastics: *Genesis*
Gentlemen's Magazine, The, 290
George I, 289–90
Gesta Danorum see Saxo Grammaticus
gied, 99 n.4; *see also wordgyd*
gierwan, 179 n.21
gif ge spedaþ to þam, 124
Gifer, 185
Gildas, 204
girl, etymology of, 177–81
Gíslasaga, 109
Glassgold, Peter, 299
gleaw, 101
glosses/glossaries, 25 n.12, 30, 79, 103, 135, 161 n.30, 167 n.13, 178 n.20, 187, 227 n.18, 254, 278, 285
Gneuss, Helmut, 118, 129
Gnomes, 291
Godric, 120
Godwin, 113
Goethe (Johann Wolfgang von), 274
gofol, 126 n.12
Goldast, Melchior, 307
Gollancz, Israel, 229 n.4
Göngu-Hrólfs saga, 146
Goodwin, K. L., 259 n.2
Gordon, E. V., 126–7, 132 n.31, 136
Gordon, George, 306, 307
Gordon, R. K., 26, 99

Gorki, Maxim, 309
Gottfried von Strassburg, 205, 219–20
Grammar, Ælfric's, 279
Grave, The, 279
Greenfield, Stanley B., 35, 73
Gregory I, Pope, the Great, 102 n.18, 109, 201–3, 205–6, 227
Gregory III, Pope, 9
Gregory of Tours, 9, 10, 158 n.19
Grendel, 50, 60, 62–3, 65–6; as blood-drinker, 143–6
Grendel's mere, 50, 56, 58–9, 74
Grendon, Felix, 291
Grimm, Jacob, 109–10, 156, 158
Grimr, 9
Grímr, 146
grið, 123
Grundtvig, N. S. V., 5–6, 299–303
Gugelberger, Georg M., 239, 241, 257
gumcyst, 229–31
Gummere, Francis B., 36–7, 270–1
Guthlac, St, 206–7, 216; *see also* Felix; *Guthlac A*
Guthlac A, **91–2**: 208; **182**: 209–10; **692**: 233–4; **816**: 211–12; *see also* Guthlac, St; onomastics: *Guthlac A*
Guðmundr, King, 8
*gyrela, 177–81

h, inorganic, 221 n.2
Hagena, 204
Halm, Karl von, 72
Hanson, Howard, 271
hapax legomena, examples of, 14, 90, 96, 101, 102, 142, 143, 229, 233
Harmer, Florence, 277 n.6
Harthacnut, 290
Hathagat, 136–7
Hávamál, 91–2
Haymo of Auxerre, 187
hæft(e), 149
healdan, 124, 150
healdend, 150
Healfdane, 38
heall see hell
Hearne, Thomas, 131, 132, 133

Heathobards, 38
Hector, 7
gehedan, 31, 35, 221 n.1
Heinzel, Richard, 72
Helen, St, 172; *see also Elene*
Helgi, 8–9
Heliand, 135
hell, 31–3
Hengest, 56, 61
Henry of Huntingdon, 114
Henry, James, 72
Henry, P. L., 94
Henshall, Samuel, 266–7
Heorot, 38, 51, 56, 60–1, 76
Heremod, 13, 50, 56, 62–3, 66, 212
herian, 15
heroic culture *see Beowulf*: fame in; *Beowulf*: friendship and loyalty in; *Beowulf*: heroic code in; *Maldon, Battle of*: heroic quality of; *Maldon, Battle of*: loyalty in
heroön, 7, 8, 9, 17, 18, 65
herotheism, 7–11; *see also* Beowulf: apotheosis of; *Beowulf*: funeral rites in; euhemerism; funerary practices, Germanic
Herzfeld, Georg, 104
Heuser, W., 281
Heusler, Andreas, 204
Hickes, George, 284, 289, 297
Hild, 157, 167
hilde dælan, 123, 138
Hildebrandslied, 297
Hildeburh, 61
hildeleoma, 74
Hill, Thomas D., 46–7, 161 n.28
Historia ecclesiastica gentis Anglorum, II, i: 201–2, 203; III, iii: 202; 109, 157, 291 n.54, 297; onomastics in, 189, 190, 197, 201–2, 203, 223; *see also* Bede
Historia Francorum see Gregory of Tours
Historia Norvegiae, 10
hlæw, 17
Hnæf, 56
-holt, 77–9
Holthausen, Ferdinand, 177–8, 292 n.58

Homer, 7, 56, 76, 112, 146, 258
homilies, OE, 41, 42, 108–9, 172, 225, 278, 279; *see also* Ælfric; *Blickling Homilies*; onomastics: in OE homilies; saints' lives, OE; Vercelli Homilies; Wulfstan
Hopkins, Gerard Manley, 54, 55
Hott(r), 34, 223
Hrethel, 49, 79
Hrethric, 38
hring, 150
Hrolfs saga kraka, 34, 223
Hrothgar, 38, 48, 49, 51, 297; as foil to Beowulf, 57–8, 85; speeches of 58–9, 74, 76
Hrothulf, 38, 40
Hrotsvitha of Gandersheim, 162 n.32, 168
Hucbald of Saint-Amand, 204–5
Hugh Candidus, 114
Hugleikr, 215–17
Hulbert, James R., 248
Husband's Message, 246
hwil dægas, 23–6
Hygd, 56, 158; name of, 162, 210 n.91, 213 n.101, 220; *see also* onomastics: as characterization; onomastics: *Beowulf*
hyge, 253
Hygeburg, 166
Hygelac, 37, 39, 48; name of 213–17, 220; *see also* onomastics: as characterization; onomastics: *Beowulf*

Ibbotson, Joseph D., 240–1, 258
Iliad see Homer
Illtyd, St, 205 n.77
in þystro see þystru
Indiculus superstitionum et Paganiarum, 9, 14
Ine, 12
Ingeld, 12, 38, 46, 64
Ingram, James, 298
Irenodia Cantabrigiensis, 281–3, 286
irony, 89, 125, 127–9, 222
Irving, Edward B., 15 n.48, 59, 80 n.28, 84, 193 n.34, 194, 231, 232
iserne wund swiðe, 251–2
Isidore of Seville, 10, 103, 188, 197, 201
Íslendingabók, 10
Israel, etymology of, 191 n.24, 193–4

James, St, 188 n.11
Jerome, 187–90 *passim*, 193, 197, 230, 231 n.19, 232
Jerusalem, etymology of, 191 n.24, 200 n.54, 211–12, 228
Joel, Book of the Prophet, 190
John of Wallingford, chronicle formerly attributed to, 207
Jordanes, 8
Judex, 96
Judith, Book of, 159–60, 162; *see also Judith*
Judith, 23–6: 113 n.33; 159–60, 162
Julian of Toledo, 308
Juliana, 161
Julius Caesar, 155

Karlmann, 9
Kaske, R. E., 160 n.25, 162 n.33, 213–14
Kenner, Hugh, 248, 249, 266, 274
kennings, 78
Kentigern, St, life of, 12
Ker, Neil R., 127
Ker, W. P., 22, 107, 309–10
Kiernan, Kevin, 37, 41
Kintgen, Eugene R., 84 n.48
Klaeber, Friedrich, 6, 14–15, 21, 23, 26, 31, 77, 213, 292
Kluge, Friedrich, 306
Knapp, James F., 250
Knipp, Christopher, 79
Kock, E. A., 209
Kögel, Rudolf, 72
Krapp, George, 196–7, 229
Kroder, Armin, 293–6
Kučera, Henry, 310–11
Kuhn, Hans, 124 n.8
Kurtz, Benjamin P., 208

-lac, 216–17
Lambarde, William, 279–80, 290
Lament for Beowulf, 271
Lander, Jeannette, 259 n.2
landes to fela, 118, 129
Landnámabók, 9
Lane, George S., 175

Laufey, 171
Laxdæla Saga, 157
Layamon *see Brut*
lædan, 16 n.50
legal documents, OE, 17, 100, 144, 171, 290; falsification of, 277–80 *passim*
LeGentil, Pierre, 47
Leire (Denmark), 38
Leisi, Ernst, 146
Leoba, 157, 166
Leofsunu, 117
Leofwine, 204, 234–5
Leonard, William Ellery, 262
Leslie, Roy F., 71 n.2
Lewis, C. S., 48
lexicography: *ad hoc* function created by, 229; allusional errors in, 143–6; denotational errors in, 141–3, 146–7, 233–4; flattening of figurative language in, 147–9; inadequate treatment of punning in, 149–50; inadequate treatment of understatement in, 151; and literary interpretation, 140–52 *passim*; *see also* editorial interpretation, problems of; emendation, problems of
Llhuyd, Edward, 287, 289
Liber de sancto Emmerammo, 220
Liber Eliensis, 111, 123, 126, 134
Liber Historiae Francorum, 157 n.11
Liber Monstrorum, 39
Liber Scintillarum, OE translation of, 104
Liber vitae of New Minster and Hyde Abbey, 172 n.18
Liebermann, Felix, 96, 126 n.11, 136, 172 n.18, 279–80, 290
Life of St Gregory, 202–3
Lioba *see* Leoba
L'Isle, William, 280–1, 290
Locharbie-Cameron, Margaret A. L., 173–4 n.25
lofgeornost, 142–3
Loikala, Paula, 6
Loka-senna, 171, 223
Loki, 171, 222–3
Longfellow, Henry Wadsworth, 261
Lösel-Wieland-Engelmann, Berta, 168

loyalty *see Beowulf*: friendship and loyalty in; *Maldon, Battle of*: loyalty in
Lucan, 77
Lucifer, 192–3, 229
Luick, Karl, 177
Lumsden, Henry W., 262
lyt, 151
lytegian, 118

Machiavelli, 220
Mackie, W. S., 96
McKinnell, John, 129 n.20
Macrae-Gibson, O. D., 117, 292
Maldon, Battle of, **29–41**: 115–16; **45–61**: 116; **86–90**: 118; **89–90**: 129–30; **94–5**: 112–13; **94–6**: 130; **130–1**: 131–2; **146–8**: 113; **173–80**: 107–12; **181**: 134–6, 141–2; **181–2**: 134–6; **190**: 132; **212**: 132–4; **223**: 135; **262–4**: 113; **300**: 170–4; **310**: 136–7; **314**: 134–6
Maldon, Battle of, anacoluthon in, 132; artistry of, 122–39, 141–2; audience of, 126 n.11 (*see also* audience of OE poetry); beasts of battle in, 130; Christian context of, 105–15 *passim*; date of composition of, 125–9; death in, 107–12; depiction of Vikings in, 121, 124, 130, 135–6, 141–2; dialect, literary use of, in, 115–16, 122–4, 138–9; ellipsis of pronoun subject in 134; epithets for Vikings in, 141–2; and Ethelred's payment of tribute, 125, 127–8; God in, 112–15; heroic quality of, 105, 107, 114–15, 121, 124, 128–9 (*see also Beowulf*: heroic code in); historical background of, 125–9; ironic juxtaposition in chronicle accounts of, 125, 127–8; irony in, 125, 128–9; justifications for flight from battle in, 118–19; juxtaposition, narrative, in, 112–13, 130 (*see also* variation, poetic: structural); Klaeber's opening for, 292; language of, 126; loyalty in, 115–21, 136 (*see also Beowulf*: friendship and loyalty in); manuscript of, 126–7, 131–2; meter of, 126, 133; moral tension in, 121, 130, 135–6, 141;

narrative lapses in, 131–2, 135, 136; place of composition of, 126, 128; scribal inattention in transcription of, 131–2, 138–9; sequence of speakers in close of, 117–18; shieldwall in, 120–1; singular and plural in, 116, 133–4; struggle for soul in, 108–12; title of, 290; Viking messenger's challenge in, 115–16, 122–4
Malone, Kemp, 16 n.50, 32, 71 n.99, 100 n.7, 165, 185, 210 n.91, 213 n.101, 214 n.104, 224 n.2, 299 n.85
manna mildust, 15, 16
Manneswert, 146
manweorðung, 11, 14
Margaret, St, homily on, 172
Mary, Blessed Virgin, 190, 199–200, 278
Maxims i, 157
Maxims ii, **10**: 87–97 *passim*; **57–62**: 112–13
mæl, 133–4 n.34
medieval: pejorative use of, in English, 311–13, 314–15; pejorative use of, in other European languages, 314; positive use of, 313; pronunciation of, 304–5; spelling of, 305–6; statistical frequency of, 310–11; torture, 312, 315; *see also* Middle Ages
medievalist, 313
medium ævum, 307
meiosis, 151
Merritt, Herbert Dean, 140, 152, 187 n.5
Merry, G. R., 263–4
meter of OE poetry, 126, 133, 260, 283–4; approximation of, in translation, 242, 245, 247, 264–5, 270, 272–3
Meters of Boethius, OE translation of, 284, 286–7, 290–1
metronymics, 170–4; *see also* onomastics
Meyer, Richard, 9
middle-aged, 307
Middle Ages: dates of, 308–9; grammatical number of, 306–8; origin of term for, 307–8; pejorative use of, in English, 311–13, 314–15; pejorative use of, in other European languages, 314;

Middle Ages (cont.)
  subdivisions of, 309–10; variety of terms for, 308; see also medieval
mideval, 305
Mildred, St, life of, 17
Milton, John, 71–2, 298
Mitchell, Bruce, 7 n.9, 25 n.13
Mod, 161
Mogk, E., 156
Monroe, B. S., 229
Moore, Samuel, 196
Morris, John, 12 n.38
Morris, Richard, 291 n.54
Morris, William, 54, 268–70
motan, 123
Motif-Index of Early Icelandic Literature, 156
moððe, 101
Müllenhoff, Karl, 34, 212–13
Müller, Eduard, 180
gemunan, 133–4
Muspilli, 109

Nagy, N. Christoph de, 268
names, genitive ending of feminine, 172–3; see also metronymics; onomastics
narrative method in OE poetry, 207–8, 260; see also Beowulf: narrative method in; Maldon, Battle of: juxtaposition, narrative, in; variation, poetic: structural
Nativity of the Blessed Virgin, OE Homily on, 190
Nennius, 12, 204
Neo-Latin, 277, 281, 306, 307
Nibelungenlied, 56, 158, 168, 171, 262
Niles, John D., 35
Njalssaga, 156, 168
Noah, 198–9
Nowell, Laurence, 280

Odin, 10; see also Woden
Odyssey see Homer
Oedipus, 7
ofer-, 78–9
oferholt, 78–9
ofermæcg(a), 233–4

ofermod, 118, 129
ofersprecola, 90
ofersweocola, 90
oferswimman, 27
Offa (*Beowulf*), 13, 56
Offa (*Maldon*), 105, 117, 120, 135 n.39
oft, 151
Ohthere, 39
Ohthere and Wulfstan, 240
Olaf, King, 8
Olaf, Tryggvason, 125, 128
Old English Martyrology, 172, 207
Old English poetry, 58, 164; character of, 259–60; see also audience of OE poetry; authorship of OE poetry; diction, poetic; formulas; meter of OE poetry; narrative method in OE poetry; performance of OE poetry; variation, poetic
Olsen, Alexandra, 96
Onela, 39, 136
onomastics: in apocryphal works, 224–7; Biblical, 185, 187, 188, 191, 199, 211, 219, 228; Biblical/patristic, in OE works, 186–200 *passim*, 211, 228, 230–4 *passim*; as characterization, 30, 162, 185, 193 n.32, 208–10, 212–17, 219–23; macaronic, 226 n.15; as mode of thought, 185–6, 191, 198, 201, 203, 204, 213, 214, 217–18, 228–9, 234–5; and multiple etymologies, 190–2, 194–5, 226 n.15; as narrative device, 207–8, 213, 231; in OE homilies, 186–8, 190–2, 205–6, 212, 220, 225, 227, 228; patristic, 187–90, 193–5 *passim*, 197, 199, 201, 211, 219, 230–4 *passim*; of place-names, 17, 173, 174, 191 n.24, 200 n.54, 202, 205, 210 n.92, 211–12, 228; of saints' names, 185, 186, 203, 205–11, 224, 229–31, 233–4, 234–5; as thematic device, 207–11, 231; vernacular, 200–5; see also metronymics
onomastics: *Andreas*, 224–7, 229–31; *Beowulf*, 30, 33 n.41, 162, 185, 210 n.91, 212–17, 220–3; *Christ*, 191 n.24, 192, 199–200, 212, 228; *Christ and Satan*,

192–3, 229; *Exodus*, 193–6, 231–3; *Genesis*, 193 n.32, 196–9; *Guthlac A*, 206–12, 233–4
onriht Godes, 193–4, 231 n.19
Origen, 145
oral composition *see Beowulf*: oral composition of; formulas
Orosius, OE translation of, 8, 12, 16, 39–40, 148 n.21, 161 n.30
os, 8
Osborn, Marijane, 52–5, 297
Osperin, 160–1
Otten, Kurt, 161

Pachaly, Paul, 72
Paetzel, Walther, 73
paganism: Christian attitudes towards, 3, 10–12, 13–14, 18–19, 41–3, 45–6, 63, 64–5; mythology of, 65–6; *see also Beowulf*: Christian attitudes towards paganism in; *Beowulf*: funeral rites in; euhemerism; funerary practices, Germanic; herotheism; *Maldon, Battle of*: Christian context of
Page, R. I., 43
Palinurus, 7
Panzer, Friedrich, 26, 27, 34
Parker Chronicle, 127–8, 198 n.49
paronomasia *see* puns
Parzival, 205, 219
Pascal, Blaise, 92
Paschasius Radbertus, 231
Paul, St, 88–9, 223
Pauli, Ivan, 176
Pearce, T. M., 186, 187, 188 n.11, 227
penitentials, A-S, 11, 42, 78, 109, 112, 144
performance of OE poetry, 166, 242
personification, 101–2, 147, 149–50, 151
Peter, St, 88–9, 109, 135, 187, 191–2, 231
Peterborough Chronicle, 114, 173
Phillpotts, Bertha, 123, 124 n.8
philosophia, 161 n.30
Philosophy, Lady, 161
Phoenix, 256, 267–8, 300
Pickles, J. D., 283
Piers Plowman, 297

Pliny, 7
Pope, John C., 18, 20, 35, 131, 133, 257
Pound, Ezra: alterations of OE texts in, 244, 245, 249–50, 251–8; centrality of OE in, 239, 247–8, 258, 259; and contemporary A-S scholarship, 244, 249–58; and conventionalizing school of OE translation, 263–4; and "English national chemical," 272; experiments of, in ME style, 247, 265–6; experiments of, in OE style, 240–1, 245–7, 264–5; influence of OE translations of, 259; and "might," 245; metrical approximation of OE poetry in, 245, 270; and OE poetic diction, 244–5, 246, 270, 274; philological methods of, 239–40, 251–8; study of OE of, 239, 240–1; syntactic approximation of OE in, 271; and teutonizing school of OE translation, 268–74; and theme of exile, 246, 257, 258; translations of, from OE, 239–40, 243–5, 251–8, 264, 270–1, 273–4; unpublished papers of, 240–7 *passim*, 264–6
Pound, Ezra: works of: *ABC of Reading*, 242, 243; "At the Heart of Me: AD 751," 245–6, 263, 272; *Cantos*, 243, 247, 260; "Canzon: of the Trades and Love," 252; "Constant Preaching to the Mob," 243, 249; "The Gods of the North," 240, 263; *Literary Essays*, 242; *Mauberley*, 243; "Music of Beowulf," 242, 243, 271; "Philological Note," to *The Seafarer*, 248–50 *passim*, 252
Pound, Ezra: *Anglo-Saxon Charm, 4*, 243–5, 249, 274; *Beowulf*, 240, 241–2, 264; *Cædmon's Hymn*, 240–1, 247, 249, 256–7; *Husband's Message*, 246; *Phoenix*, 256; *Wanderer*, 242–3, 247, 249, 251; *Wife's Lament*, 246; *Wulf and Eadwacer*, 246
Pound, Ezra: *Seafarer*: echo of, in other works, 245–6, 247; genre of, 250–1; "howlers" in, 251–8; references to, in other works, 241, 242, 264; source text for, 248–9; translation of, 239–40, 244–7 *passim*, 248–58, 264, 268, 271,

Pound, Ezra: *Seafarer (cont.)* 273–4; truncation of, 248–50, 264; use of Sweet's *Reader* for, 248–56 *passim*, 258
Precepts, 290
Procopius, 39
prosopopoeia, 149–50; *see also* personification
Proverbs, Book of, 92
Proverbs of Alfred, 279
Psalm 21, OE translation of, 101
Pseudo-Clementine, 145
Pseudo-Jerome, 230
Ptolemy, 39
puns, 83, 98–104, 116, 147, 149–50, 201; *see also* onomastics

Quinn, Bernetta, 248
Quinn, Esther C., 196 n.43

Rabanus Maurus, 10, 187–8, 189, 195, 232
Radbod of Utrecht, 204, 235
Renoir, Alain, 44
Resignation, 110, 112
Retchford, William, 281–3
revenge *see* vengeance
Rhyming Poem, 37: 96; 291
Riddles, 20 **23**: 149–50; *31* **14**: 149; *37* **7**: 149; *47*: 98–104; *60* **12-13**: 80, 82–4; *73* **22**: 149; *3* 151
Rimbert, 8
Ringler, Richard N., 89, 100 n.7
Robertson, D. W., Jr, 44
Rogers, H. L., 138–9
Roland, Song of, 47, 56; OE translation of, 275–6
Rosier, James L., 30 n.30, 84, 150 n.26
Rousseau, Jean-Jacques, 50, 62
rowan, 28, 29 n.26
royal genealogies, A-S, 12–13
Ruin, The, 261–2
Ruiz, Juan, 97
rune bi gerynum, 192
runes, 42, 285–6
Russom, Geoffrey R., 85 n.48
Ruthven, K. K., 248

sagas, 26, 27, 34, 112, 168, 222–3; *see also* Sturlusson, Snorri
saints' lives, OE, 12, 17, 111, 161, 162; *see also* Ælfric; homilies, OE; onomastics; Wulfstan
Sarrazin (Gregor), 34
Saussaye, Chantepie de la, 91
sawldreor, 145
Sawyer, P. H., 277 n.6
Saxo Grammaticus, 10, 38, 92, 135, 136, 215–16
sædberende, 196–7
Gesceadwisnes, 161
scealc, 141–2
Schrader, Richard J., 157 n.10, 161 n.28, 165 n.5
Schröder, Edward, 296
Scragg, D. G., 138–9
Scyld Scefing, 13, 38, 57, 85
Seafarer, **35**: 257; **48**: 254; 263–4, 273; *see also* Pound, Ezra: *Seafarer*
Searle, William George, 173
Sedulius Scottus, 234
semideos, 8
sermons, OE *see* homilies, OE
Seth, 196–8
Shakespeare, William, 27 n.19, 51, 274
Shook, L. K., 210–11
sibbe ond gesihðe, 211–12
Siegfried, 171
Sievers, Eduard, 292 n.58
Sigelint, 171
Sigemund, 55–6, 269
Simon *see* Peter, St
sin- compounds, 143 n.7
Sisam, Kenneth, 38, 40–1, 253–6, 279–80
Skáldskaparmál, 8
Slevin, James, 21–2
Solomon and Saturn (poetic), 100 n.6
Solomon and Saturn (prose), 145 n.13
Somner, William, 285, 287
soð bið (...) (*swicolost*): emendation of, 87, 89–90; meaning of, 87, 89, 90–7; proverbs expressive of, 91–4; (*switolost/swutolost*): meaning of, 87; proverbs expressive of, 88–9

Soul and Body, 147–8, 185
Southern, R. W., 106
Spelman, Sir Henry, 289, 307
Spelman, Sir John, 289
Spenser, Edmund, 268
Spinoza (Baruch), 93
Stanley, E. G., 75, 250
Stanyhurst, Richard, 268
Starcatherus, 136
staþol, 100
stælgiest, 101–2
stearcheort, 301 n.87
stearn, 253, 254–5
Steevens, George, 290
Steinunn, 168
Stenton, F. M., 157, 310
Stephens, George, 267–8, 270
Stjerna, Knut, 6
Storms, G., 200
strangan, þæs, 100
stræl, 225–6
Ström, Hilmer, 216 n.110
Sturlusson, Snorri, 8, 10, 17 n.51; *Edda*, 171, 204; *Ynglingasaga*, 4, 215–16
sundbuend, 200
sundnytt, 27 n.18
Sweet, Henry, 72, 89, 248–56, 275
swelgan, 99–100
swicolost see soð bið (. . .)
Swinburne (Algernon Charles), 148
switolost see soð bið (. . .)
swutolost see soð bið (. . .)
Sydenham, Thomas, 289
sylf, 257
syllan . . . sylfra dōm, 124
Symphosius, 104
synaesthesia, 147–9
synsnæd, 143–7
Syrige (Syria), 220

Tacitus, 40, 155–8 *passim*
Tennyson, Alfred, Lord, 262–3
Tertullian, 64, 145
Theseus, 7
Thorhild the Poetess, 168
Thorkelin, G. J., 28 n.25

Thorkelin transcripts, errors in, 32–3
Thorpe, Benjamin, 100, 291
Thryms-kviða, 171
Thryth, 56, 213 n.101
Thwaites, Edward, 287, 289
Timmer, B. J., 160
titles in OE, 281, 290–2
Tolkien, J. R. R., 65, 105, 298–9, 312
Torkar, Roland, 96, 280
translation of OE poetry, 52–5; *see also* compounds: translators' use of; Pound, Ezra
Trautmann, Moritz, 292 n.58, 297
Treaty of Westminster, 283
Tristan, 205
truth: money and, 95–7; proverbial attitudes towards, 88–9, 91–4
Tupper (Frederick J.), 149 n.25
Turner, Alberta, 283
Turner, Sharon, 72 n.4

þa ("as"), 25
þe, 132
þon, 123, 138–9
þorgerðr Hölgabrúðr, 8–9
þrymfæstne cwide see cwide
þurh, 253–4
þyle, 30, 221–2
þystru, 101

Unamuno, Miguel de, 66–7
understatement, 151
Unferth, 85; character of, 29–31, 33, 220–3 *passim*; name of, 30, 33 n.41, 185, 212, 220–3 *passim*; as narrator of Breca episode, 28–9; rehabilitation of, 33–4; spelling of, 221–2; *see also* onomastics: as characterization; onomastics: *Beowulf*
Utley, Francis Lee, 199 n.52, 282
uuinileudos, 167

Vainglory, 290
Valkyries, 156
Varga, Lucie, 309

variation, poetic: clarifying, 73–9; definition of, 73; "echo-words" as, 84; "envelope patterns" as, 84; historical development of, as a critical term, 71–3; repetitive, 79–85; structural, 79, 85; stylistic functions of, 73–86; *see also Beowulf*: juxtaposition, syntactic, in; *Beowulf*: narrative method in; *Maldon, Battle of*: juxtaposition, narrative, in
Veleda, 158
vengeance, 42, 49, 136
Vercelli Homilies, *5* 220; *19* 27
Vespasian Psalter, 133–4
Vita Anskarii, 8
Vita Lebuini antiqua, 793: 204, 234–5
Vita Oswaldi, 111, 135
Voigts, Linda Ehrsam, 278
völur, 156
Völuspa, 156, 158, 215, 299, 303 n.93
völva, 156

Wackerbarth, Diedrich, 262
w[a]du weallendu, 28 n.25
Waldhere, 204; *see also Waltharius*
Waltharius, 77, 160–1, 204
Wander, Karl Friedrich Wilhelm, 92
Wanderer see Pound, Ezra: *Wanderer*
Wanley, Humphrey, 105, 127, 283–5, 286, 289
Watson, Robert Spence, 296
wælstow, 130
wælwulf, 130
Wealhtheow, 38, 40, 49–50, 61, 157–8
Wentersdorf, Karl P., 26–7, 35
geweorðian, 146–7
Wermund, 13
Wessobrun Prayer, 15, 297
Westphalen, Tilman, 292
West-Saxon Gospels, 172, 278
Wheelock, Abraham, 72 n.3, 281–2
Whitehead, Alfred North, 50
Whitelock, Dorothy, 42, 43, 100 n.7, 126 n.11, 128
Whitman, Cedric, 76
wiccung-dom, 301 n.88
Widsith, 135, 185

Widukind of Corvey, 136–7
Wife's Lament, 246
Wigelin: etymology of, 173; genitive ending of, 172–3; identity of, 170–1, 173–4; *see also* metronymics
wiges heard, 131
Wighelm, 170
Wiglaf, 21 n.4, 39, 58, 85, 120
Wild, Friedrich, 292
William, Duke of Gloucester, 283–7
William of Malmesbury, 77–8
William of Newburgh, 114
Williams, Blanche Colton, 89, 91
Williamson, Joseph, 283
wills, OE *see* legal documents, OE
Winterbottom, Michael, 224
Wisdom, 161
wisdom literature, character of, 88; *see also Maxims i*; *Maxims ii*; *soð bið* (. . .); truth
Wistan, 170–1
Witemeyer, Hugh, 250, 251, 268
Woden, 12, 13, 18; *see also* Odin
Wolfram von Eschenbach, 205, 219
women: as authors of OE literature, 165–9; as prophets, 4, 5, 39, 40, 155–63; status of, in A-S society, 157, 171, 174; *see also* Hygd; metronymics; Thryth; Wealhtheow
wong(e), 149
Wonred, 220
wordgyd, 14
wordum wrixlan, 71 n.1
Wormald, Patrick, 43–4
wrætlicu wyrd see wyrd
wrætlicum wordum, 103
Wrenn, C. L., 28 n.23, 100 n.7
Wülcker, Richard, 282
Wulf, 220
Wulf and Eadwacer, 246
Wulfhere, 173
Wulfmær, 135 n.39
Wulfstan, 93, 114, 144; onomastics in, 224, 226–7; puns in, 149 n.24; *Canons of Edgar*, 11, 144 n.10; *De falsis Deis*, 10, 12,

18; *Life of St. Ethelwold*, 224, 226–7;
  Sermo Lupi ad Anglos, 119
wuniað þa wacran, 256
Wyatt, A. J., 136, 241, 242
Wynfrith, letter of, to Eadburga, 108
wyrd, 51, 102–3; *see also fate*

wyrm, 101

Zachaeus, 224 n.3
Zacharius, Pope, 11
Zupitza, J., 28 n.25, 32, 225, 226 n.10